Anonymous

Fort Wayne, Indiana, City Directory

Anonymous

Fort Wayne, Indiana, City Directory

ISBN/EAN: 9783337307882

Printed in Europe, USA, Canada, Australia, Japan

Cover: Foto ©ninafisch / pixelio.de

More available books at **www.hansebooks.com**

CARIER & CAMPBELL'S

FORT WAYNE

CITY DIRECTORY

FOR 1873-4.

CONTAINING

MUCH VALUABLE INFORMATION,

AMONG WHICH ARE

A LIST OF EXPRESS STATIONS IN MOST PARTS OF THE UNITED STATES; THE NAMES OF ALL STATIONS, WITH DISTANCES, ON ALL RAILROAD LINES LEADING TO AND FROM FORT WAYNE; DISTANCES AND RATES OF FARE BY RAILROAD FROM FORT WAYNE TO MANY CITIES OF THE UNITED STATES; INTEREST TABLE, ETC., ETC.

PRICE, $2.50.

FORT WAYNE, IND.:
SENTINEL PRINTING HOUSE, COR. CALHOUN AND WAYNE STS.
1873.

1873. **CALENDAR.** 1874.

1873.	Sunday.	Monday	Tuesday	Wednes	Thurs.	Friday.	Satur.
Jan.	...	...	...	1	2	3	4
	5	6	7	8	9	10	11
	12	13	14	15	16	17	18
	19	20	21	22	23	24	25
	26	27	28	29	30	31	...
Feb.	...	...	...	...	...	...	1
	2	3	4	5	6	7	8
	9	10	11	12	13	14	15
	16	17	18	19	20	21	22
	23	24	25	26	27	28	...
Mar.	...	...	...	...	...	...	1
	2	3	4	5	6	7	8
	9	10	11	12	13	14	15
	16	17	18	19	20	21	22
	23	24	25	26	27	28	29
	30	31	...	...	...	...	...
Apr.	...	...	1	2	3	4	5
	6	7	8	9	10	11	12
	13	14	15	16	17	18	19
	20	21	22	23	24	25	26
	27	28	29	30	...	...	...
	...	...	...	...	...	...	...

1873.	Sunday.	Monday	Tuesday	Wednes	Thurs.	Friday.	Satur.
May.	...	...	...	...	1	2	3
	4	5	6	7	8	9	10
	11	12	13	14	15	16	17
	18	19	20	21	22	23	24
	25	26	27	28	29	30	31
June.	...	...	...	...	...	...	...
	1	2	3	4	5	6	7
	8	9	10	11	12	13	14
	15	16	17	18	19	20	21
	22	23	24	25	26	27	28
	29	30	...	...	...	...	...
July.	...	...	1	2	3	4	5
	6	7	8	9	10	11	12
	13	14	15	16	17	18	19
	20	21	22	23	24	25	26
	27	28	29	30	31	...	...
Aug.	...	...	...	...	...	1	2
	3	4	5	6	7	8	9
	10	11	12	13	14	15	16
	17	18	19	20	21	22	23
	24	25	26	27	28	29	30
	31	...	...	...	...	...	...

1873.	Sunday.	Monday	Tuesday	Wednes	Thurs.	Friday.	Satur.
Sept.	...	1	2	3	4	5	6
	7	8	9	10	11	12	13
	14	15	16	17	18	19	20
	21	22	23	24	25	26	27
	28	29	30	...	...	...	...
Oct.	...	...	...	1	2	3	4
	5	6	7	8	9	10	11
	12	13	14	15	16	17	18
	19	20	21	22	23	24	25
	26	27	28	29	30	31	...
Nov.	...	...	...	...	...	...	1
	2	3	4	5	6	7	8
	9	10	11	12	13	14	15
	16	17	18	19	20	21	22
	23	24	25	26	27	28	29
	30	...	...	...	...	...	...
Dec.	...	1	2	3	4	5	6
	7	8	9	10	12	13	14
	14	15	16	17	18	19	20
	21	22	23	24	25	26	27
	28	29	30	31	...	...	...
	...	...	...	...	...	...	...

1874.	Sunday.	Monday	Tuesday	Wednes	Thurs.	Friday.	Satur.
Jan.	...	...	...	...	1	2	3
	4	5	6	7	8	9	10
	11	12	13	14	15	16	17
	18	19	20	21	22	23	24
	25	26	27	28	29	30	31
	...	...	...	...	...	...	...
Feb.	1	2	3	4	5	6	7
	8	9	10	11	12	13	14
	15	16	17	18	19	20	21
	22	23	24	25	26	27	28
	...	...	...	...	...	...	...
Mar.	1	2	3	4	5	6	7
	8	9	10	11	12	13	14
	15	16	17	18	19	20	21
	22	23	24	25	26	27	28
	29	30	31	...	...	...	...
Apr.	...	...	...	1	2	3	4
	5	6	7	8	9	10	11
	12	13	14	15	16	17	18
	19	20	21	22	23	24	25
	26	27	28	29	30	...	...
	...	...	...	...	...	...	...

1874.	Sunday.	Monday	Tuesday	Wednes	Thurs.	Friday.	Satur.
May.	...	...	...	...	...	1	2
	3	4	5	6	7	8	9
	10	11	12	13	14	15	16
	17	18	19	20	21	22	23
	24	25	26	27	28	29	30
	31	...	...	...	...	...	...
June.	...	1	2	3	4	5	6
	7	8	9	10	11	12	13
	14	15	16	17	18	19	20
	21	22	23	24	25	26	27
	28	29	30	...	...	...	...
July.	...	...	...	1	2	3	4
	5	6	7	8	9	10	11
	12	13	14	15	16	17	18
	19	20	21	22	23	24	25
	26	27	28	29	30	31	...
Aug.	...	...	...	...	...	...	1
	2	3	4	5	6	7	8
	9	10	11	12	13	14	15
	16	17	18	19	20	21	22
	23	24	25	26	27	28	29
	30	...	...	...	...	...	...

1874.	Sunday.	Monday	Tuesday	Wednes	Thurs.	Friday.	Satur.
Sept.	...	1	2	3	4	5	6
	7	8	9	10	11	12	13
	14	15	16	17	18	19	20
	21	22	23	24	25	26	27
	28	29	30	31	...	...	...
Oct.	...	...	...	...	1	2	3
	4	5	6	7	8	9	10
	11	12	13	14	15	16	17
	18	19	20	21	22	23	24
	25	26	27	28	29	30	...
Nov.	...	...	...	...	...	..	1
	2	3	4	5	6	7	8
	9	10	11	12	13	14	15
	16	17	18	19	20	21	22
	23	24	25	26	27	28	29
	30	31	...	...	...	...	...
Dec.	...	...	1	2	3	4	5
	6	7	8	9	10	11	12
	13	14	15	16	17	18	19
	20	21	22	23	24	25	26
	27	28	29	30	...	...	...
	...	...	...	...	...	...	...

JAMES M. KANE & BRO.,

Wholesale and Retail Dealers in

NOTIONS, TOYS

Fancy Goods, Children's Carriages,

BIRD CAGES, FISHING TACKLE, TRAVELING BASKETS, HOSIERY, JEWELRY, ROCKING HORSES,

POCKET KNIVES, RAZORS, SCISSORS,

REVOLVERS AND PISTOLS OF ALL KINDS,

Albums, Pocket Books of all styles, Buttons, Threads, Traveling Satchels, Boys' Carts and Wagons, Dolls and all kinds of Toys,

FANCY CHINA GOODS,

Combs, Brushes and Beads.

We invite the attention of buyers to our immense stock of JEWELRY. Children's Carriages and all kinds of Notions, Toys and Fancy Goods direct from importers and manufacturers. Call and see the largest assortment of Notions to be found in the State, and be convinced that our's is the place to buy goods CHEAP.

JAMES M. KANE & BRO.

19 CALHOUN STREET.

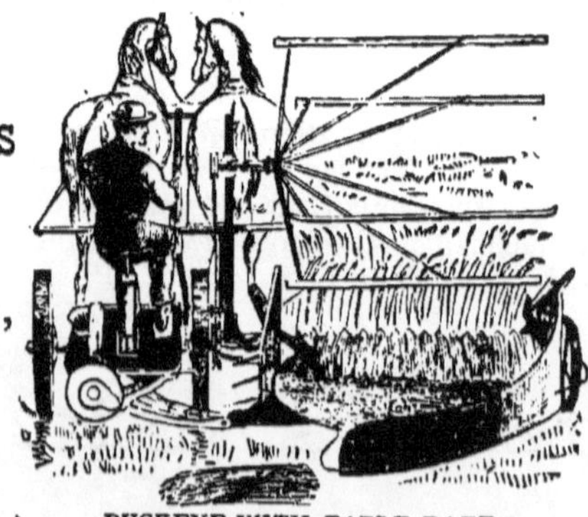

BUCKEYE WITH TABLE RAKE.

INTEREST TABLE.

Showing the Interest on any Sum from $10.00 to $10,000.00.

AT SIX PER CENT.

	1 Day.	15 Days	1 Month.	1 Year.
$10......	0	3	5	50
20......	0	5	10	$1 20
30......	1	8	15	1 18
40......	1	10	20	2 40
50......	1	13	25	3 00
60......	1	15	30	3 60
70......	1	18	35	4 20
80......	1	20	40	4 80
90......	2	23	45	5 40
100......	2	25	50	6 00
200......	3	50	$1 00	12 00
300......	5	75	1 50	18 00
400......	7	$1 00	2 00	24 00
500......	8	1 25	2 50	30 00
600......	10	1 50	3 00	36 00
700......	12	1 75	3 50	42 00
800......	13	2 00	4 00	48 00
900......	15	2 25	4 50	54 00
1,000......	17	2 50	5 00	60 00
2,000......	34	4 99	10 00	120 00
3,000......	52	7 49	15 01	180 00
4,000......	69	9 99	20 01	240 00
5,000......	86	12 48	25 02	300 00
6,000......	$1 03	14 98	30 02	360 00
7,000......	1 20	17 48	35 02	420 00
8,000......	1 36	19 97	40 03	480 00
9,000......	1 55	22 47	45 03	540 00
10,000......	1 72	24 97	50 03	600 66

AT SEVEN PER CENT.

	1 Day.	15 Days.	1 Month.	1 Year.
$10......	0	3	6	70
20......	0	6	12	$1 40
30......	1	9	18	2 10
40......	1	12	23	2 80
50......	1	14	29	3 50
60......	1	17	35	4 20
70......	1	20	41	4 90
80......	2	23	47	5 60
90......	2	26	53	6 30
100......	2	29	58	7 00
200......	4	58	$1 17	14 00
300......	6	86	1 75	21 00
400......	8	$1 15	2 33	28 00
500......	10	1 44	2 92	35 00
600......	12	1 73	3 50	42 00
700......	13	2 01	4 08	49 00
800......	15	2 30	4 67	58 00
900......	17	2 59	5 25	63 00
1,000......	19	2 88	5 83	70 00
2,000......	38	5 75	11 67	140 00
3,000......	58	8 63	17 50	210 00
4,000......	77	11 51	23 33	280 00
5,000......	93	14 38	29 17	350 00
6,000......	$1 15	17 26	35 00	420 00
7,000......	1 34	20 14	40 83	490 00
8,000......	1 53	23 01	46 67	560 00
9,000......	1 73	25 59	52 50	630 00
10,000......	1 92	28 77	58 33	700 00

C. D. BOND, Pres't. J. D. BOND, Cashier.
PLINY HOAGLAND, Vice Pres't. J. C. WOODWORTH, Ass't Cash.

FORT WAYNE

NATIONAL BANK

OF FORT WAYNE, INDIANA.

CAPITAL, $350.000. — SURPLUS, $70,000.

Successors to Branch at Fort Wayne of Bank State of Indiana, organized 1836, and Bank State of Indiana, organized 1856.

DIRECTORS:

PLINY HOAGLAND. JESSE L. WILLIAMS. O. P. MORGAN. B. W. OAKLEY. CHAS. D. BOND

FORT WAYNE HAT FACTORY

JAS. HARPER & CO.,

Manuf'rs and Wholesale & Retail Dealers in

Silk AND Cassimere Hats

HATS, CAPS,

FURS,

STRAW GOODS, ETC.,

JAMES HARPER.
CHAS. A. ZOLLINGER
DENNIS MONAHAN.

No. 3 Phœnix Block and 11 Columbia St., Fort Wayne, Ind.

A. HATTERSLEY,

Manufacturer of all kinds of

Brass Cocks, Valves, &c

FOR GAS, STEAM AND WATER.

—DEALER IN—

WROUGHT IRON PIPE,

STEAM AND GAS FITTINGS FOR SAME.

Sheet Lead, Lead Pipe, Rubber Hose, Hydraulic Rams, Bath Tubs, Pumps, Copper Boilers and Plumbing Material of every description.

No. 48 East Main Street, - FORT WAYNE, IND.

Reciprocal Distances of the Principal Cities of the United States.

	Natchez.	Portland.	Portsmouth.	Montpelier.	Boston.	Providence.	Hartford.	New York.	Trenton.	Philadelphia.	Wilmington.	Baltimore.	Richmond.	Raleigh.	Charleston.	Savannah.	Cahawba.	Monticello.	New Orleans.	Murfreesborough.	Frankfort.	Columbus.	Indianapolis.	Vandalia.	St. Louis.	PLACES.
	1208	554	492	524	436	410	336	227	167	137	110	38	123	288	544	657	915	1230	1260	708	565	418	964	808	879	Washington, D.C.
	1751	—	54	150	118	158	218	341	401	431	459	559	719	842	1098	1211	1469	1784	1814	1269	1119	852	1002	1242	1331	Portland, Maine.
	—	—	446	145	56	96	156	279	340	369	397	469	629	780	1039	1149	1407	1722	1752	1200	1059	790	1034	1180	1269	Portsmouth, N. H.
Erie, Pa.			—	—	160	190	183	211	357	387	415	487	647	812	1068	1141	1439	1754	1784	1232	1089	288	1946	1212	1301	Montpelier, Vermont.
St. Johns, N. B.				230	—	40	109	223	283	313	341	413	573	748	994	1107	1351	1666	1696	1144	1001	734	946	1124	1213	Boston, Massachusetts.
Iowa City, Iowa				1360	1332	—	74	197	257	287	316	387	547	721	969	1081	1331	1646	1676	1124	981	715	927	1105	1193	Providence, R. I.
Montgomery, Ala.				1550	1424	1383	—	110	183	213	241	313	473	638	894	1007	1253	1568	1598	1046	903	636	848	1026	1115	Hartford, Conn.
Tallahasse, Fla.				1570	1434	1393	1335	—	60	90	118	190	350	515	771	884	1145	1457	1487	935	792	525	737	910	994	New York, N. Y.
San Francisco, Cal.				1836	3711	3670	3611	3497	—	30	58	130	290	455	711	824	1082	1399	1427	875	932	465	677	855	944	Trenton, N. J.
Independence, Mo.				3682	1557	1516	1457	1343	1284	—	28	110	260	426	681	794	1052	1367	1397	845	702	435	647	825	914	Philadelphia, Pa.
Jackson, Mo.				1672	1546	1505	1431	1333	1274	1245	—	72	232	397	653	766	1024	1339	1369	817	674	415	627	805	894	Wilmington, Delaware.
Little Rock, Ark.				1707	1581	1540	1482	1360	1308	1280	1153	—	160	325	581	694	953	1268	1298	746	703	433	645	805	890	Baltimore, Md.
Milwaukee, Wis.				1222	1128	1227	1150	1033	974	945	918	958	—	165	421	534	792	1107	1137	652	541	472	704	821	855	Richmond, Va.
Burlington, Vt.				40	230	271	282	299	358	387	414	484	642	—	256	369	627	942	972	548	533	532	742	813	847	Raleigh, N. C.
Memphis, Tenn.				1549	1423	1382	1324	1210	1151	1122	1095	1025	844	786	—	113	436	758	768	530	635	703	844	894	921	Charleston, S. C.
Halifax, N. Sc.				401	211	252	335	524	583	612	639	709	867	1037	1276	—	378	693	713	571	630	761	875	887	998	Savannah, Ga.
Nashville, Tenn.				1287	1161	1120	1062	948	889	860	833	763	614	556	589	571	—	315	345	373	669	865	820	809	746	Cahawba, Ala.
Apalachicola, Fl.				1630	1504	1463	1405	1291	1232	1203	1276	1106	948	710	563	491	438	—	147	422	719	915	870	767	699	Monticello, Miss.
Galveston, Tex.				2334	2258	2217	2159	2045	1986	1957	1930	1860	1702	1429	1361	1206	763	745	—	486	783	965	834	847	813	New Orleans, Louisiana.
Mobile, Ala.				1759	1633	1592	1534	1420	1361	1332	1305	1235	1077	815	547	592	149	290	164	—	297	485	448	468	430	Murfreesboro' Tenn.
Norfolk, Va.				722	597	556	497	400	324	300	268	200	120	178	402	512	921	1089	1245	670	—	196	209	280	314	Frankfort, Kentucky.
Louisville, Ky.				1120	1006	955	906	792	733	704	677	723	585	590	772	754	568	652	829	216	94	—	232	430	510	Columbus, Ohio.
Detroit, Mich.				846	852	851	780	657	598	569	542	582	660	836	1174	1156	974	1040	1233	620	402	185	—	198	269	Indianapolis, Ind.
Cincinnati, O.				983	869	828	769	655	596	567	540	586	448	596	880	990	619	755	939	326	83	27	105	—	94	Vandalia, Mo.
Chicago, Ill.				1125	1131	1130	1083	936	919	848	821	861	755	1029	1137	1116	926	1000	1196	583	341	464	202	240	342	
Buffalo, N. Y.				519	525	524	453	470	470	441	468	538	612	782	1021	1131	1250	1415	1410	796	554	337	526	700	763	
Albany, N. Y.				194	200	199	128	150	204	233	260	330	488	658	897	1007	1416	1540	1767	1122	879	662	851	1013	1088	
Montreal, C. E.				139	329	370	371	400	457	486	513	563	741	911	1150	1260	1669	1816	1993	1266	1022	706	995	1162	1232	

The greatest distance is from Fort Kent, Me., to San Francisco, Cal., 4,180 miles.

GRAHAM & GOTSHALL,

Attorneys at Law,

Collecting, Real Estate and Insurance Agents

NO. 7 EAST MAIN STREET.

☞ Collections made in all parts of the United States. ☜

SHOAFF'S GALLERY,

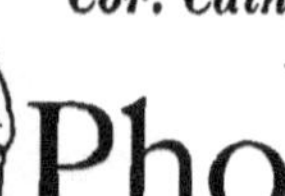

Cor. Calhoun & Columbia Sts.

Photographs

OF EVERY DESCRIPTION.

Old Pictures ENLARGED and Framed. Satisfaction Guaranteed.

ROBERT S. TAYLOR,

ATTORNEY AT LAW,

No. 34 East Berry Street,

P. O. Box 1648. **FORT WAYNE, IND.**

TRENTMAN, MONNING & SON,

Manufacturers and Wholesale Dealers in

SPICES, MUSTARDS

Cream Tartar, White Fawn Baking Powder, Roasted Coffee, &c.

59 E. Main St., Fort Wayne, Ind.

Officers of the City Goverment

OF THE

CITY OF FORT WAYNE, INDIANA,

FROM 1840 TO 1873.

NOTE.—The Original City Charter was writen by Hon. F. P. Randall, and passed by Act of the General Assembly of the State of Indiana, incorporating the city of Fort Wayne, approved February 22, 1840, provided for the election, by the people, of a President, (or Mayor,) and six members of the Board of Trustees (or Common Council,) and the election of General Officers by said Board, or Council.

1840.

Mayor—Geo. W. Wood.
Recorder—F. P. Randall.
Attorney—F. P. Randall.
Treasurer—Geo. F. Wright.
High Constable Samuel S. Morss.
Collector—Samuel S. Morss. *a*
Assessor—Robert F. Fleming.
Market Master—James Post.
Street Commissior—Joseph H. McMaken.
Chief Engineer—Samuel Edsall.
Lumber Measurer—John B. Cocanour.

ALDERMEN.

Wm. Rockhill. Samuel Edsall.
Thomas Hamilton, *b* William S. Edsall.
Madison Sweetser, *b* William L. Moon.

a Appointment resigned January 15, 1841, and Joseph Berkes appointed to fill vacancy same day.
b Resigned May 6, 1840, and Jon. E. Hill and Joseph Morgan elected June 5, 1840, to fill their vacancies

1841.

Mayor—Geo. W. Wood. *a*
Recorder—F. P. Randall.
Attorney—F. P. Randall.
Treasurer—George F. Wright.
Collector—Bradford B. Stevens.
High Constable—Richard McMullen. *b*
Assessor—S. M. Black.
Lumber Measurer—John B. Cocanour.
Flour Inspector—Daniel Maginnis.
Market Master—Robert Hood.

ALDERMEN.

H. T. Dewey, Henry Sharp, Chas. G. French, Philo Rumsey. A. S. Johns. William L. Moon

---

1842.

Mayor—Joseph Morgan.
Recorder—Wm. Lytle.
High Constable—Bradford B. Stevens. *c*
Treasurer—Geo. F. Wright. *d*
Street Commisisoner—Henry Lotz.
Assessor—Robert E. Fleming.
Collector—Edward Stapleford.
Flour Inspector—Daniel Maginnis. *e*
Lumber Measurer—John. B Cocanour.
Attorney—Henry Cooper.
Chief Engineer—Wm. L. Moon. *f*
Surveyor—O. Bird.
Market Master—Peter Kiser.

ALDERMEN.

Hiram T. Dewey, Henry Cooper, Joseph Scott, Philo Rumsey. Henry Sharp, Wm. L. Moon. *g*

BOARD OF HEALTH.

Dr. John Evens, Dr. Wm. H. Brooks, Dr. Brenard Seveniek.

a Resigned July 5, 1841. and vacancy filled August 2, 1841, by election of Joseph Morgan.
b Superseded August 2, 1841, by Bradford B. Stevens.
c Resigned August 3, 1842, and James Crumley elected same day to fill vacancy.
d Resigned September 10, 1842, and Edward Stapleford elected same day to fill vacancy, which he resigned September 15, 1842, and was succeeded by O. W. Jeffords.
e Resigned August 26, 1842, and Daniel E Garnsey appointed September 5, 1842, to fill vacancy.
f Resigned August 26, 1842, vacancy continued.
g Resigned August, 26, 1842, and S. C. Freeman elected September 26, 1840, to fill vacancy.

1843.

Mayor—Henry Lotz.
Recorder—William Lytle.
Attorney—Lucian P. Ferry.
Treasurer—Oliver W. Jeffords.
Collector—James Crumley
High Constable—James Crumsley.
Street Commissioner—Wm. Stewert.
Assessor—Wm Rockhill.
Chief Engineer—John Cochrane.
Surveyor—O. Bird.

ALDERMEN.

Franklin P. Randall, John B. Cocanour.
Hugh McCulloch, Philo H. Taylor.
Lysander Williams, Melancthon W. Hubbell.

BOARD OF HEALTH.

Dr. Chas. Schmitz, Dr. Lewis Beecher, Dr. H. P. Ayers.

1844.

Mayor—Henry Lotz. *a*
Recorder—Wm. Lytle. *b*
Attorney—Samuel Bigger. *c*
Chief Engineer—Thomas Pritchard.
Assessor—S. M. Black.
High Constable—Wm. Stewart.
Collector—Wm. Stewart.
Street Commissioner—Wm. Stewart.
Treasurer—O. W. Jeffords.
Market Master—Peter Kiser.

ALDERMEN.

Morgan Lewis, *d* Cleves S. Silver.
Samuel H. Shoaff, Jno. Cochrane.
Henry Williams, Jno. B. Dubois.

BOARD OF HEALTH.

Dr. Lewis Beecher, Dr. Lewis Thompson, Dr. Chas. Schmitz

a Discharged July 1, 1844, and succeeded by Jno. M. Wallace.
b Resigned May 5, 1844, and Robert Lowry elected same day to fill vacancy.
c Superseded by Jno. W. Dawson, December 9, 1844.
d Resigned August 6, 1844, and S. M. Black elected August 26, 1844, to fill vacancy.

1845.

Mayor—Jno. M. Wallace. *a*
Recorder—O. P. Morgan.
Treasurer—O. W. Jefl'ords.
High Constable—W. B. Wilkinson.
Attorney—Jno. W. Dawson.
Collector—Wm. B. Wilkinson.
Assessor—Wm. H. Prince.

ALDERMEN.

S. M. Black, James Humphrey.
Philo Rumsey, *b* Charles Paige.
Henry W. Jones. Jno. B. Dubois.

BOARD OF HEALTH.

Dr. Lewis Beecher, Dr. Lewis Thompson, Dr. Chas. Schmitz.

1846.

Mayor—M. W. Huzford.
Recorder—Wm. Lytle. *c*
Attorney—Jno. W. Dawson.
Assessor—Joseph Morgan.
Market Master—Robert Hood.
Treasurer—O. W. Jeffords.
High Constable—Cleves S. Silver.
Street Commissioner—S. M. Black.
Surveyor—S. M. Black.
Flour Inspector—I. D. G. Nelson.

ALDERMEN.

James B. Hanna, *d* Richard McMullen. *e*
Henry Sharp, Samuel S. Morss. *f*
James Humphrey, Charles Fink.

BOARD OF HEALTH.

Dr. Lewis Beecher, Dr. Lewis Thompsgn, Dr. Chas. Schmitz.

a Resigned May 8, 1846, M. W. Huxford elected May 26, 1846, to fill the unexpired term.
b Resigned May 26, 1846, and Chas. Fink elected to fill vacancy.
c Resigned June 12, 1846, and Jno. B. Dubois elected same day to fill vacancy.
d Resigned October 5, 1846, vacancy continued.
e Resigned May 4, 1846, and J. P. Munson elected June 1, 1846, to fill vacancy.
f Resigned September 8, 1846, and Samuel Stophlet elected October 5, 1846, to fill vacancy.

1847.

Mayor—M. W. Huxford.
Recorder—Jno. B. Dubois.
High Constable—Cleves S. Silver. [a]
Assessor—Samuel Stophlet.
Treasurer—Oliver P. Morgan.
Collecton—Cleves S. Silver. [b]

ALDERMEN.

Jacob Lewis,	James P. Munson. [c]
Henry Sharp,	Jno. Cocanour.
Jno. Cochrane,	Charles Fink.

BOARD OF HEALTH.

Dr. Lewis Beecher, Dr. Lewis Thompson, Dr. Chas. Schmitz.

1848.

Mayor—M. W. Huxford.
Recorder—O. P. Morgan.
High Constable—T. J. Price. [d]
Treasurer—N. P. Stockbridge.
Assessor—Chas G. French.
Collector—Jacob Hull.

ALDERMEN.

Chas. Muhler,	Henry Sharp.
John Cochrane,	John B. Cocanour.
John Conger,	Alexander McJunkin.

BOARD OF HEALTH.

Dr. Henry Wehmer, Dr. P. H. Ayers, Dr. C. E. Sturgis.

a Resigned June 10, 1847, and vacancy filled same day by election of Jacob Hull.
b " " " " " " " "
c Resigned May, 1847, vacancy continued.
d Office declared vacant August 7, 1848, and Daniel Gaylord elected to fill vacancy 7, 1848.

1849.

Mayor—Wm. Stewart.
Recorder—O. P. Morgan.
High Constable—Samuel C. Freeman. a
Collector—Samuel C. Freeman. a
Street Commissioner—Samuel C. Freeman, a
Assessor—Chas. G. French.
Treasurer—N. P. Stockbridge.
Chief Engineer—John B. Cocanour.

ALDERMEN.

A. M. McJunkin, Peter P. Bailey, James Humphrey, Michael Hedekin. B. W. Oakley. Charles Muhler.

BOARD OF HEALTH.

Dr. Henry Wehmer, Dr. H. P. Ayers. Dr. C. E. Sturgis.

1850.

Mayor—Wm. Stewart.
Recorder—O. P. Morgan.
Attorney—W. W. Carson.
Assessor—Henry R. Colerick.

ALDERMEN.

A. M. McJunkin, Henry Sharp, W. H. Briant, C. Anderson, James Humphrey, B. W. Oakley.

BOARD OF HEALTH.

I. D. G. Nelson, John Cochrane, D. W. Burroughs.

a Appointed January 6, 1851, to fill vacancy caused by John B. Cocanour's departure for California.
a Resigned all three offices April 6, 1849, and succeeded by John B. Griffith, April 7, 1845, who resigned September 14, 1849, and was succeeded same day by John Spencer.

1851. *a*

Mayor—Wm. Stewart.
Recorder—Duties performed by Mayor.
Treasurer—Thomas D. Dekay, County Treasurer.
Attorney—Wm. W. Carson.
High Constable—Morris Cody.
Street Commissioner—Morris Cody.
Chief Engineer—Benjamin H. Tower.
Collector—No appointment.
Assessor— ——— ———

ALDERMEN.

O. W. Jeffords, O. Bird,
James Howe, Peter Kiser,
D. P. Hartman, Robert Armstrong.

BOARD OF HEALTH.

I. D. G. Nelson, John Cochrane, D. W. Burroughs.

1852.

Mayor—P. G. Jones.
Recorder—Duties performed by Mayor.
Treasurer—T. D. Dekay, County Treasurer.
High Constable—Wm. Fleming.
Chief Engineer—Samuel C. Freeman.
Street Commissioner—Edward Smith.
Collector—office abolished.
Assessor—office abolished.

ALDERMEN.

R. McMullen, O. Bird,
H. R. Colerick, R. Armstrong,
James Humphrey, Jonas W. Townley.

BOARD OF HEALTH.

I. D. G. Nelson, John Cochrane, D. W. Burroughs.

a Charter amended by the General Assembly in 1851, Act approved February 8, abolishing the offices of Treasurer, Assessor, Collector and Recorder, making it the duty of the Mayor to perform the duties of Recorder. The duties of the Treasurer, Assessor and Collector were transferred to the proper officers of the County.

Section 7 of said Amended Act also provides for the annual election of Mayor and High Constable.

1853

Mayor—Charles Whitmore.
Recorder—Duties performed by Mayor.
Treasurer—Thomas D. Dekay, County Treasurer.
High Constable—Samuel C. Freemann.
Attorney—F. P. Randall.
Street Commissioner—Wm. Lannin.
Chief Engineer—S. C. Freeman.
Wood Measurer—Washington Dekay.
Assessor—No appointment.

ALDERMEN.

John J. Trentman, James Vandegriff,
Milton Henry, Fred. Nirdlinger,
John Drake, *a* Henry Drover.

BOARD OF HEALTH.

I. D. G. Nelson, John Cochrane, D. W. Burroughs.

1854. *b*

Mayor—Charles Whitmore.
Clerk—W. E. Ellis. *c*
Treasurer—Charles Muhler.
High Constable—F. J. Frank.
Street Commissioner—Bernard Hutker.
Attorney—Charles Case. *d*
Chief Engineer— Lewis Wolke.
Assessor—S. S. Morss. *e*
Sealer Weights and Measures—D. W. Burroughs.

ALDERMEN.

Wm. Boerger, John M. Miller,
John Orff, Moses Drake,
John Arnold, Platt J. Wise,
H. Wehmer, Isaac Lauferty,
Francis Aveline, W. H. Link,
John M. Snively, A. M. Webb.

BOARD OF HEALTH.

Dr. Wm. H. Brooks, Dr. P. M. Leonard, Dr. James Ormiston. *f*

a Resigned May 10, 1853, and succeeded by Richard Chute, who resigned June 17, 1853.

b The Act of the General Assembly of the State of Indiana, amending the Charter of the City of Fort Wayne, approved ———, 1854, provided for the election, on the second Tuesday in March of each year, by the qualified voters, of a Mayor, [who shall be the presiding officer of the Common Council,] two Councilmen from each Ward, [by the voters thereof respectively,] a Clerk, Assessor, Treasurer, Street Commissioner and Marshall, who shall severally hold their offices for one year.

c Defaulter and absconded, office declared vacant July 29, 1854, and A. J. Emerick elected August 23, 1854, to fill vacancy.

d Resigned October 18, 1854, and Isaac Jenkinson elected same day to fill vacancy.

e Resigned January 13, 1855, and William D. Henderson elected January 24, 1855, to fill vacancy.

f Resigned June 1, 1854, and succeeded by Dr. Francis Leiber.

1855.

Mayor—Wm. Stewart.
Clerk—R. N. Godfrey.
Treasurer—C. A. Rekers.
Attorney—W. W. Carson.
High Constable—Pat. McGee.
Street Commissioner—John Greer.
Chief Engineer—James B. Teller. *a*
Civil Engineer—E. McElfatrick.
Market Master—John Fairfield. *b*
Sealer Weights and Measures—Benjamin Saunders.

ALDERMEN.

P. Hoagland,	F. P. Randall,
E. Bostick,	John M. Miller,
Henry Baker,	Andrew Gamble,
John Arnold,	C. W. Allen,
Charles Fink,	A. M. Webb.

BOARD OF HEALTH.

Dr, Bricker, J. D. Worden, F. J, Frank.

a Succeeded by Henry Baker, October 16, 1855.
b Resigned August 28, 1855, and A. M. Webb elected September 4, 1855, to fill vacancy, and succeeded by Henry Monning, September 18, 1855.
c Deceased March 17, 1856, vacancy continued.

1856.

Mayor—Wm. Stewart.
Clerk—A. C. Probasco.
Treasurer—C. A. Rekers.
Assessor—Henry Crist.
Street Commissioner—John Hardendorf.
Marshal—Pat. McGee.
Civil Engineer—Charles Forbes.
Chief Engineer—S. C. Freeman.
Sealer Weights and Measures—S. C. Freeman.
Attorney— ———————— b

ALDERMEN.

James Ormiston,	Thomas Stevens,
Michael Hedeken,	Henry Baker,
H. Nierman,	J. D. Worden,
Wm. McKinley,	Wm. T. Pratt,
A. M. Webb,	Conrad Baker.

BOARD OF HEALTH.

Dr. H. Wehmer, John Cochrane, Thomas Tigar.

1857.

Mayor—S. S. Morss.
Clerk—Christian Tresselt.
Treasurer—Conrad Nill.
Marshal—Pat. McGee.
Street Commissioner—Christian Cook.
Chief Engineer—George Humprey.
Assessor—James Howe.
Market Master—Wm. Stewart.
Sealer Weights and Measures—Benjamin Saunders.

BOARD OF HEALTH.

D. H. Wehmer, John Cochrane, O. W. Jeffords.

a Resigned May 27, 1856, and Thomas Meegan elected to fill vacancy June 3, 1856.
b On motion of Councilman Webb, the office of City Attorney was abolished.
c Wards reduced from 6 to 5, with two Aldermen from each.

1858.

Mayor—S. S. Morss.
Clerk—J. C. Davis.
Treasurer—W. H. Link. *a*
Assessor—Joseph Price.
Marshal—Pat. McGee.
Civil Engineer—Samuel McElfatrick.
Chief Engineer—L. T. Bourie.
Street Commissioner—Charles Baker.
Market Master—Wm. Stewart.
Attorney--John J. Glenn.

ALDERMEN.

H. N. Putnam,	John M. Miller,
E. Vordermark,	John S. Irwin,
Charles D. Bond,	Jacob Foellinger,
Wm. T. Pratt,	O. D. Hurd,
A. M. Webb,	Christian Becker.

1859.

Mayor--F. P. Randall.
Clerk—Moses Drake, Jr.
Treasurer--Wm. Stewart.
Marshal—Joseph Price.
Street Commissioner--Henry Tons.
Market Master--Wm. Miller.
Chief Engineer--George Humphrey.
Sealer Weights and Measures--Pat. McGee.
Assessor—H. H. Bossler.

ALDERMEN.

John Trentman, *b*	B. D. Miner, *a*
John Burt, *a*	Daniel Nestle, *a*
Benjamin H. Tower, *a*	A. C. Beaver, *b*
Morris Cody, *b*	O. D. Hurd, *b*
H. Nierman, *b*	James Humphrey. *a*

BOARD OF HEALTH.

Dr. B. S. Woodworth, Dr. L. Meinderman, James H. Robinson

a Resigned April 21, 1859, vacancy continued.
b Aldermen marked with an *a* drew the long term, and those marked with a *b* drew the short term.

1861. *a*

Mayor—F. P. Randall.
Clerk—L. T. Bourie.
Treasurer—H. N. Putnam.
Marshal—Pat. McGee.
Street Commissioner—Henry Tons. *b*
Attorney—Wm. S. Smith.
Chief Engineer—O. D. Hurd. *c*
Civil Engineer—O. Bird.
Barr Street Market Master—W. D. Henderson.
Broadway Market Master—J. S. Leach. *d*
Sealer Weights and Measures—Joseph Price.

ALDERMEN.

John Burt,	Morris Cody,
Edward Slocum,	B. H. Tower,
Daniel Nestle,	C. D. Piepenbrink,
B. H. Kimball,	B. D. Miner, *e*
James Humphrey,	John S. Harrington.

BOARD OF HEALTH.

Dr. E. Sturgis, M. Hedekin, W. H. Bryant.

The above Board of Health, appointed May 17, 1861, failing to qualify, Drs. B. S. Woodworth, C. Schmitz, and Henry Baker appointed July 9, 1861, as such Board.

a An Act to repeal all general laws now in force for the incorporation of cities, prescribing their rights and powers, and the manner in which they all exercise the same, approved March 9, 1857, among other things, prescribes that after the first general election, the officers of said city shall respectively hold their offices two years each. The Councilmen shall be chosen by the legal voters of their respective wards, and one Councilman from each ward, to be determined by lot at the first regular meeting after the election shall hold his office two years, and the other, to be determined in like manner, shall hold his office for four years, and biennially thereafter, one Councilman shall be elected by the legal voters of each ward.

b Resigned February 11, 1862, and C. W. Lindlag elected February 25, 1862, to fill the vacancy.

c Superseded by Joseph A. Stellwagon, October 8, 1861.

d Resigned July 23, 1861.

e Resigned November 12, 1861, and Fred. Nirdlinger elected December 7, 1861, to fill vabancy.

1863.

Mayor—F. P. Randall.
Clerk—E. L. Chittenden.
Treasurer—John Conger.
Marshal—Pat. McGee.
Attorney—Joseph S. France.
Market Master—W. D. Henderson. *a*
Assessor—S. C. Freeman.
Civil Engineer—John S. Mower.
Chief Engineer—L. T. Bourie *b*
Street Commissioner—C. W. Lindlag.
Wood Measurer—Patrick Ryan. *c*
Captain Police—E. C. Pens. *d*

ALDERMEN.

Morris Cody,
Henry Monning,
A. F. Schele, *f*
B. H. Kimball,
Edward Slocum, *h*
John S. Harrington, *e*
C. D. Piepenbrink,
Dennis Downey,
H. Nierman, *g*
B. H. Tower.

BOARD OF HEALTH.

Dr. S. Woodworth, Dr. Charles Schmitz, Dr. W. H. Meyers.

a Resigned May 10, 1864, and Thomas D. Beard elected same day to fill vacancy.
b Superseded by Joseph A. Stellwagon, February 9, 1864, and Stellwagon resigned June 14, 1864, and, on same day, Munson Van Geison was unanimously elected to fill vacancy.
c Discharged December 8, 1863, and reinstated December 22, 1863
d Resigned February 4, 1864, and Wm Ward elected March 22, 1864, to fill vacancy.
e Resigned December 8, 1863 and C. Neirelter elected December 30, 1863, to fill vacancy.
f Resigned January 24, 1865, vacancy continued.
g Resigned July 12, 1864, and P. Hoagland elected August 13, 1864, to fill vacancy.
h Resigned April 11, 1863, to except office of School Trustee, and Wm. Waddington elected May 2 1865, to fill vacancy.

1765.

Mayor—J. L. Worden. *a*
Clerk—E. L. Chittenden.
Treasurer—John Conger.
Attorney—F. P. Randall.
Marshal—Pat. McGee.
Assessor—John B. Reckers. *b*
Street Commissioner—P. Falahee.
Civil Engineer—W. S. Gilkison. *c*
Chief Engineer—Munson Van Geison.
Market Master—Thomas D. Beard. *d*
Captain Police—William Ward.
Sealer Weights and Measures————————, *e*

ALDERMEN.

Morris Cody,	A. P. Edgerton,
B. H. Kimball,	Fred. Nirdlinger.
P. S. Underhill,	D. Downey,
P. Hoagland,	H. Monning, *f*
B. H. Tower,	Wm. Waddington.

BOARD OF HEALTH.

Dr. B. S. Woodworth, Dr. I. M. Rosenthal, Dr. T. P. McCullough.

By the Amended Charter approved December 20, 1865, the Civil Engineer and Assessor are appointed by Council, instead of, as heretofore, elected by the people. The offices of Auditor and City Judge were created if by the Council deemed expedient. The terms of Councilmen were changed so that the successors of Councilmen now acting, whose terms expire in May, 1867, shall be elected for one year, and the successors of the Councilmen whose terms expire May, 1869, shall be elected biennially.

a Resigned September 11, 1866. Same day B. H. Tower was elected President of Council, and Benjamin Saunders chosen acting Mayor.

b Resigned October 10, 1865, and A. C. Prohasco appointed December 27, 1865, to fill vacancy.

c Resignation presented March 12, 1867, and laid on the table and C. S. Brackenridge appointed deputy.

d Superseded May 8, 1866, by William Kanning.

e The office of Sealer Weights and Measures abolished by Council in 1864.

f Resigned June 19, 1866, having received the nomination of County Treasurer, and David Hoit elected August 4, 1866, to fill vacancy.

1867.

Mayor--Henry Sharp.
Clerk--E. L. Chittenden.
Treasurer—C. Piepenbrink.
Attorney—R. S. Robertson.
Marshal—William Linderman.
Assessor—George Fisher.
Street Commissioner—William H. Briant.
Civil Engineer—Charles S. Brackenridge
Chief Engineer—Joseph B. Fry. *a*
Market Master—William Kanning. *b*
Captain Police—William Ward.

ALDERMEN.

John Arnold,	*George Dewald*, *
B. H. Kimball,	Fred. Nirdlinger,
J. C. Bowser,	A. P. Edgerton,
George Link,	B. W. Oakley, *c*
Morris Cody,	*M. Hogan*, *
W. T. McKean,	*John Taylor*, *
John Cochrane,	*George Jacoby*,
Joseph March,	William Waddington.

BOARD OF HEALTH.

Dr. B. S. Woodworth, Dr. I. M. Rosenthal, Dr. T. P. McCullough.

By the Amended Charter approved March 14, 1867, the Civil Engineer, Assessor and Street Commissioner were appointed by Council.

At the May election 1867, the 6th, 7th, and 8th Wards were constituted, and at special elections held therein May 25, 1867, elected their Councilmen,—*in italics*,—who having drawn lots for term office, resulting in the gentlemen marked with a (*) drawing the long term.

At the May election in 1868, the 6th, 7th, and 8th Wards held election of one Councilman each, to serve two years, resulting in the choice of N. C. Miller from 6th, Geo. Jacoby from 7th, and Geo. Link from 8th.

a Superceded by Hiram Poyser, May 26, 1868.

b Superceded by Wm. Schneider, May 26, 1868.

c Mr. Oakley having removed from the 3d Ward, his seat was declared vacant, and John B. Krudop elected in his seat, and qualified November 12, 1867.

1869.

Mayor—F. P. Randall.
Clerk—Sam. P. Freeman.
Treasurer—Christian Piepenbrink.
Attorney—Allen Zollars.
Marshal—Pat. McGee.
Assessor—E. C. Pens.
Street Commissioner—B. L. P. Williard.
Civil Engineer—C. S. Brackenridge.
Chief Engineer—Thomas Mannix.
Market Master—Wm. Schneider.
Captain Police—1869—F. R. Limecooly.
" " 1870—Pat. McGee.

ALDERMEN.

J. C. Bowser,	George Doerfler,
T. Hogan,	J. R. Prentiss,
G. W. Brackenridge,	M. Hedekin,
George Jacoby,	M. F. Schmetzer,
O. E. Bradway,	J. D. Hance,
George Link,	Henry Trier,
A. H. Carier,	T. J. Hutchinson,
N. H. Miller,	William Wadington.

BOARD OF HEALTH.

Dr. I. M. Rosenthal, Dr. A. J. Erwin, Dr. W. H. Meyers.

1871.

Mayor—F. P. Randall.
Attorney—Allen Zollars.
Treasurer—John A. Droegemeyer.
Clerk—Sam. P. Freeman.
Civil Engineer—C. S. Brackenridge.
Chief Engineer—Thomas Mannix.
Marshal—Charles Uplegger.
Captain Police—1871—D. Meyer.
" " 1872—M. Singleton.
Market Master—Wm. Schneider.
Street Commissioner—B. L. P. Williard.

ALDERMEN.

O. E. Bradway,	John Bull,
A. H. Carier,	L. Dessauer,
Wm. Fisher,	J. S. Goshorn,
Tim. Hogan,	Samuel Hanna,
O. P. Morgan,	John Schoepf,
John Stoll,	Jacob Shryock,
William Tegtmeyer,	Conrad Tremmel,
B. H. Tower,	P. S. Underhill,
G. H. Wilson,	William Wadington.

1873.

Mayor—C. A. Zollinger.
Attorney—L. Newberger.
Clerk—Sam. P. Freeman.
Treasurer—John A. Droegemeyer.
Civil Engineer—C. S. Brackenridge.
Chief Engineer—Frank B. Vogel.
Marshal—Christopher Kelly.
Captain Police—M. Singleton.
Market Master—Wm. Schneider.
Street Commissioner—Henry Trier.

ALDERMEN.

O. E. Bradway,
John Bull.
L. Dessauer,
Samuel Hanna,
James Lillie,
Charles McCulloch,
John Schoepf,
Henry Schnelker,
William Tegtmeyer,
Jacob Becker,
A. H. Carier.
Tim. Hogan,
George Jacoby,
O. P. Morgan,
H. N. Putnam,
John Stoll,
Conrad Tremmel,
G. H. Wilson.

Carbonized Cement Pipe Works

Opposite Pittsburgh, Fort Wayne & Chicago Railroad Depot.

FORT WAYNE, IND.,

MANUFACTURE AND SELL

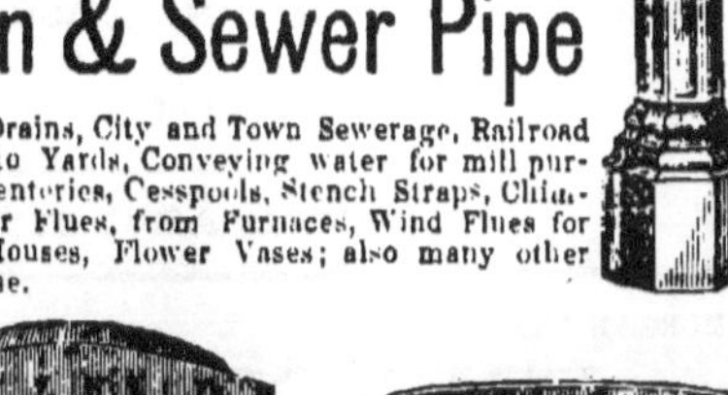

Cement Drain & Sewer Pipe

Which are used for House Drains, City and Town Sewerage, Railroad Culverts, Sluices, Driveways into Yards, Conveying water for mill purposes, Drainage for Parks, Cementeries, Cesspools, Stench Straps, Chimneys, Wells, Ash Safes, Cold Air Flues, from Furnaces, Wind Flues for Manufacturing, Flues for Hot Houses, Flower Vases; also many other purposes for which they are in use.

(Drain Pipe.)

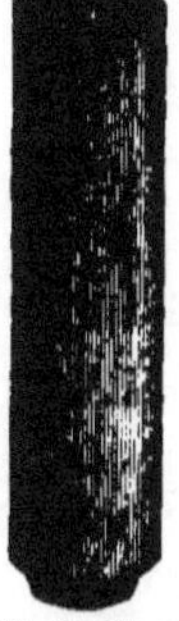

(Drain Pipce)

(Sewer Pipe.)

(Well Pipe.)

HENRY WILLIS, General Manager.

KERR MURRY,

Engineer, Millwright,

Founder and Manufacturer of

Steam Engines, Boilers, Iron and Brass Castings,

GRIST, LINSEED OIL AND SAW MILLS.

Practical Builder and Contractor for the erection of Gas Works, manufacturer of all the Latest and best Machinery.

Works East side Calhoun street, opposite Railroad Depots.

FORT WAYNE, INDIANA.

FORT WAYNE

MACHINE WORKS.

J. H. BASS,

Manufacturer of

STEAM ENGINES, BOILERS,

Flued or Tabular, all sizes.

Saw and Grist Mill Machinery

AND MILL FURNISHING GOODS.

Sole agents for Judson's Celebrated Steam Governors and Stillwell & Pierce's Patent Heater and Lime Extractors.

CAR WHEELS,

Chilled Tyres, Locomotive Cylinders, and all kinds of Railroad and Car Castings, Building Columns, Grates, Railings, &c., made to order. Engines, Boilers and general machinery promptly repaired. Competent millwrights always on hand to furnish drafts and specifications, and superintend putting up our mills. Special attention is called to our line of

WOOD WORKING MACHINERY,

Consisting in part of Wisill's Improved Spoke and Axle Handle Lathes, Felloe Saws, Stave Cutters, Heading Jointers, Equalizing Saws, &c.

Street Directory.

Baker, west from Calhoun next south of Brackenridge.
Barr, south from Calhoun next east of Clinton.
Barr (North), from canal north to St. Mary's river.
Bass, from Fairfield avenue east to Hoagland avenue, next north of Colerick.
Berry (East), from Calhoun east to Canal, next north of Wayne.
Berry (West), from Calhoun west of College, next north of Wayne.
Brackenridge, west from Calhoun, next south of Douglas avenue.
Brandriff, west from Webster to Hoagland avenue, next south of Melitta.
Broadway avenue, south from canal to corporation line, next west of Fulton.
Buchanan, east from Lafayette to Hanna, next south of Lasselle.
Butler (East), from Calhoun east to Lafayette, next south of Williams.
Butler (West), from Calhoun west to Fairfield avenue, next south of Williams.
Calhoun, south from canal to corporation line, next west of Clinton.
Calhoun (North), from canal north to St. Mary's river, next west of Clinton.
Canal, south from canal to Wayne, Piepenbrink's Addition.
Cass, south from canal to Berry, next east of Ewing.
Cass (North), from canal north to St. Mary's river, next east of Ewing.
Centre, south from canal basin to Fair, next west of Cherry.
Charles, east from Lafayette to Hanna, next south of Wallace.
Charley, east from Hanna to corporation line, south of Samuel.
Cherry, south from canal basin to St. Mary's river, next east of Centre.
Chicago, west from Calhoun to College, next north of P., Ft. W. & C. Railway.
Chute, south from Maumee Road to Lewis, next east of Division.
Clay, south frdm Canal to Lasselle, next east of Lafayette.
Clinton, south from canal to Butler, next east of Calhoun.
Clinton (North), from canal north to St. Mary's river, next east of Calhoun.
Colerick, west from Hoagland avenue to Fairfield avenue, next south of Bass.
Columbia (East), from Calhoun east to canal, next north of Main.
Columbia (West), from Calhoun west to Harrison, next north of Main.
College, south from Berry to Chicago, next west of Rockhill.
Comparet, south from Wayne to Maumee road, next east of King.
Court, south from Main to Berry, east side Court House Square.
Creighton avenue (East), from Calhaun to Hanna, corporation line.
Creighton avenue (West), from Calhoun west to Broadway Avenue, corporation line.
Dawson, west from Calhoun to Hoagland avenue, next north of Williams.
Division, south from Maumee Road to Lewis, next east of Harmer.

Douglas avenue, west from Calhoun to McClellan, next south of Lewis.
Duck, east from Calhoun to Barr, next north of Water.
Edsall, south from Main to Berry, next west of Jackson.
Elm, south from Maumee Road to Lewis, next east of Ohio.
Erie, east from Francis, next north of Wayne.
Ewing, south from canal to George, next east of Griffith.
Ewing (North), from canal north to St. Mary's river, next east of Griffith.
Fair, east from St. Mary's river, next south of Kekionga.
Fairfield avenue, south from George to corporation line, next east of Hoagland avenue.
Force, south from Herndon to corporation line, next east of Hanna.
Fox, north and south from Henry, next east of Miner.
Francis, south from canal to Railroad, next east of Hanna.
Fulton, from canal south to Jefferson, next east of Broadway.
Garden, from Washington south, next west of Nelson.
Gay, south from Railroad to Charley, next east of John.
George, continuation of Brackenridge, west of Broadway.
Grand, south side of T., W. & W. Railway, west from Calhoun to Kansas.
Grant, east from Gay to Thomas, next south of Wallace.
Griffith, south from canal to George, next east of Fulton.
Griffith (North), from canal north to St. Mary's river, next west of Ewing.
Grove, south from canal to Lewis, next east of Walter.
Guthrie, north side of T., W. & W. Railway to Lavina avenue.
Hamilton, east from Calhoun to Lafayette, next south of Murray.
Hanna, south from canal to corporation line, next east of Monroe.
Hanover, south from canal to Lutheran College Grounds, next east of Grove.
Harmer, from canal south to Lewis, next east of Francis
Harrison, south from canal to corporation line, next west of Calhoun.
Harrison (North), from canal north to St. Mary's River, next west of Calhoun.
Hendricks, west from Fairfield avenue, next south of Pritchard.
Henry, continuation of Dewald, west to Broadway avenue.
Herndon, east from Hanna to Railway, next north of Wallace.
Highland, east from Calhoun to Webster, next north of Dawson.
Hoagland avenue, from T., W. & W. Railway south to corporation line, next east of Fairfield avenue.
Holman, east from Calhoun to Hanna, next south of Montgomery.
Hood, south from Pritchard to Wall, next east of West.
Horace, west from John, next north of Samuel.
Hough, east from Clay to Hanna, next south of Holman.
Jackson, south from canal to Chicago, next west of Van Buren.
Jefferson (East), from Calhoun east to Division, next south of Washington.
Jefferson (West), from Calhoun west to Garden, next south of Washington.
John, south from Herndon to Charley, next west of Gay.
Johnson, south from Dawson, next eas of Hoagland avenue.
Jones, east from College, next south of Wilt
Kansas, from Railroad south to Melitta, next west of Webster.

Kekionga, east from St. Mary's river, next south of Spruce.
King, from Wayne street south to Maumee road, next east of Harmer.
Lafayette, south from canal to corporation line, next east of Barr.
Lasselle, east from Lafayette to Hanna, next north of Buchanan.
Lavina avenue, from Taylor south to Guthrie, west of Metz.
Lewis (East), from Calhoun east to corporation line, next south of Jefferson.
Lewis (West), from Calhoun west to Ewing, next south of Jefferson.
Lillie, south from Maumee road, next west of corporation line.
Locust, west from Fairfield avenue, next south of T., W. & W. Railway.
Locust Alley, east from Calhoun to Harrison, next north of Water.
McClellan, from Lewis south to Chicago, next west of Webster.
McCulloch, south of Maumee road to Lewis, next east of Grove.
Madison, east from Barr to Division, next north of Lewis.
Maiden Lane, south from canal to Berry, next west of Harrison.
Main (East), from Calhoun east to canal, next north of Berry.
Main (West), from Calhoun west to corporation line, next north of Berry.
Maumee, east from Calhoun to Clinton, next south of Holman.
Maumee Road, east from Harmer to corporation line, nexr south of Washington.
Mechanics, south from Canal Feeder to Fair, next west of Cherry.
Melitta, west from Harrison to Hoaglaud avenue, next south of Grand.
Metz, south from Cherry to Guthrie, next west of Broadway.
Mill, east from canal basin to Fulton, north side canal.
Miner, north and south from Henry, next east of Broadway.
Monroe, from canal south to Lasselle, next east of Clay.
Montgomery, east from Barr to Francis, next south of Lewis.
Morrell, south from P., Ft. W. & C. Railway to Wall, next east of Hood.
Murray, from Calhoun to Lafayette, next north of Hamilton.
Nelson, from Washington south to Jones, next west of College.
Nirdlinger avenue, west from Broadway, next south of Wall.
Oak, east from Division to Ohio, next south of Maumee road.
Oakley, from Taylor south to Henry, next west of Fairfield avenue.
Ohio, south from Maumee road to Lewis, next east of Chute.
Oliver, south from P., Ft. W. & C. Railway, next west of Thomas.
Osage, south from canal basin to Main, next west of Mechanics.
Park, east from Cherry to Osage, next north of Main.
Pearl, west from Harrison to Fulton, next south of Canal.
Pine, south from T. W. & W. Railway to Taylor, next west of Fairfield avenue.
Pittsburgh, from Clay east to Hanna, next south of Hough.
Plum, from Water north to St. Mary's river, next west of Harrison.
Pontiac, east from Lafayette to Hanna—corporation line.
Poplar, west from Hoagland avenue to Oakley, next south of Walnut.
Prince, north and south from Bass, next east of Fairfield avenue.
Pritchard, west from Fairfield avenue to Rockhill, next south of Wilt.
Railroad, east from Calhoun to Clinton, next south of Maumee.
Reed, north side canal, Reed's addition

River, east and west from north Van Buren, Reed's addition.
Rockhill, south from Main to Pritchard, next east of College.
St. Clair, south from Lasselle to corporation line, next east of Lafayette.
St. Francis, from Lafayette east to Hanna, next south of Buchanan.
Samuel, east from Hanna, next south of Horace.
Smith, from P., Ft. W. & C. Railway south, next east of Gay.
Spruce, east from St. Mary's river, next south of Main.
Spy Run avenue, commencing at bridge, east end Water, running north on west side St. Joe river.
Sturgis, west from Fulton, next south of Jefferson.
Summit, east from Division to corporation line.
Suttenfield, from Lafayette east to Hanna, next south of Taber.
Taber, east from Lafayette to Hanna, next south of Creighton avenue.
Taylor, from Fairfield avenue west to Lavina avenue, next south of Locust.
Thomas, south from P., Ft. W. & C. Railway, next east of Oliver.
Toledo, east from Lafayette to Hanna, south side P., Ft. W. & C. Railway.
Union, from Berry south to Pritchard, next west of Jackson.
University, south from Main to Maumee road, next east of Comparet.
Van Buren, south from canal to Pritchard, next west of Broadway.
Van Buren (North), from canal north to St. Mary's river, Reed's Addition.
Virginia, east from Lafayette to Hanna, next north of Wallace.
Wall, west from Broadway, next north of Nirdlinger avenue.
Wallace, east from Lafayette to P., Ft. W. & C. Railway, next south of Virginia.
Walnut, west from Fairfield avenue, next south of Taylor.
Walter, south from Wayne to Maumee road, next east of University.
Washington (East), from Calhoun east to Grove, next south of Wayne.
Washington (West), from Calhoun west to Garden, next south of Wayne.
Water (East), from Calhoun east to Clay, next north of canal.
Water (West), from Calhoun west to Fulton, next north of canal.
Wayne (East), from Calhoun east to Hanover, next north of Washington.
Wayne (West), from Calhoun west to College, next north of Washington.
Webster, south from Berry to corporation line, next west of Harrison.
West, from Pritchard south to Chicago, next west of Hood.
Williams, west from Calhoun to Fairfield avenue, next south of Dawson.
Wilt, from Broadway west to Nelson, next south of Jefferson.

Bloomingdale Street Directory.

Barthold, north from Railroad to Canal Feeder, next east of Wefel.
Bowser, west from Wells, next north of High.
Clark, from High north, next east of Barthold.
Douglas, west from Wells, next north of Bowser.
Fifth, east from Wells to North Calhoun, next south of Sixth.
First, east from Wells to Railroad, next south of Second.

Fourth, east from Wells to North Calhoun, next south of Fifth.
High, west from Wells to St. Mary's avenue, next north of Railroad.
Langohr, west from Wells, next north of Douglas.
Marion, from High north to Douglas, next west of Wells.
North Calhoun, from Third north to Canal Feeder, next east of North Harrison.
North Cass, from Railroad north to Sixth, next east of Wells.
North Harrison, from First north to Sixth, next east of North Cass.
Orchard, north from High to Douglas, next west of Marion.
Polk, west from Railroad to Canal Feeder.
St. Mary's Avenue, from Canal Basin north to Canal Feeder, west of Wefel.
Second, east from Wells to Railroad, next south of Third.
Sixth, east from Wells to North Calhoun, next south of Canal Feeder.
Third, east from Wells to North Calhoun, next south of Fourth.
Wefel, north from High, next west of Barthold.
Wells, north from St. Mary's River to Feeder Canal, next west of North Cass.

Boundaries of Wards.

First Ward—Comprises all that part of the city lying between Lafayette and Monroe streets, north of railroad tracks and south of river.

Second Ward—Comprises all that part of the city lying between Lafayette and Calhoun streets, north of railroad tracks and south of river.

Third Ward—Comprises all that part of the city lying between Calhoun and Ewing streets, north of railroad tracks and south of river.

Fourth Ward—Comprises all that part of the city lying west of Ewing and east of Broadway, north of railroad tracks and south of river.

Fifth Ward—Comprises all that part of the city lying west of Broadway and north of the T., W. & W. Railway track.

Sixth Ward—Comprises all that part of the city lying west of Calhoun and south of the T., W. & W. Railway track.

Seventh Ward—Comprises all that part of the city lying east of Calhoun and South of both railway tracks.

Eighth Ward—Comprises all that part of the city lying east of Monroe street and north of the T., W. & W. Railway track.

Ninth Ward—Comprises all that part of the city lying north of St. Mary's River and south of the Wabash & Erie Canal Basin.

Justices of the Peace in Allen County.

Lafayette Township—Samuel H. Ambler and J. B. Daws. Terms expire in 1876.

Adams Township—Samuel Cleveland. Term expires in 1874. John Dougal. Term expires in 1876. O. D. Rogers. Term expires in 1876.

Washington Township—Henry Elbert and John P. Hedges. Terms expire in 1876.

Jefferson Township—John Nail. Term expires in 1874. Nicholas Ladig. Term expires in 1876.

Jackson Township—Charles Noyes and William Keller. Terms expire in 1876.

Monroe Township—William Dickerson. Term expires in 1874. Martin S. Morrison, A. A. Baker and M. S. Baker. Terms expire in 1876.

Madison Township—Silas Work. Term expires in 1876.

Marion Township—Hiram Coleman. Term expires in 1874. John Brown. Term expires in 1876.

Cedar Creek Township—J. W. Bead. Term expires in 1874.

St. Joe Township—John Brown and Luke Levanaway. Terms expire in 1876.

Milan Township—D. M. Frisby. Term expires in 1874. Eli Ringwalts. Term expires in 1876.

Scipio Township—H. W. Hyde. Term expires in 1874.

Springfield Township— ——— Cosgrove and M. B. Hall. Terms expire in 1874.

Maumee Township—Robert Shirley. Term expires in 1875. Edward Foster. Term expires in 1876.

County and City Officers.

Court House Square, between Calhoun and Court and Main and Berry streets.

Judge of the Circuit Court—Robert Lowry, Judge of the Tenth Judicial District. Term expires in 1876.

Judge of the Criminal Circuit Court—Joseph Brackenridge. Term expires in 1875.

County Clerk—William S. Edsall. Office in the Court House. Term expires in 1874. Deputies, C. W. Edsall, Criminal Circuit Court; Willis D. Maier, Circuit Court.

Sheriff—J. D. Hance. Office in the Court House. Term expires in 1875. Platt J. Wise and Henry Lankenau, Deputies.

Auditor—H. J. Rudisill. Office in the Court House. Term expires in 1874. F. W. Kuhne, Deputy.

Treasurer—John Ring. Office in the Court House. Term expires in September, 1875. C. M. Barton, Clerk.

Recorder—John Koch. Office in the Court House. Term expires in June, 1875. D. P. White, Deputy.

Surveyor—W. H. Goshorn. Office in the Court House. Term expires in 1874.

Coroner—A. M. Webb. Term expires in October, 1874.

Commissioners—Jacob Hillegass, John Begue and J. C. Davis. Office in the Court House. Meet quarterly.

Court House Janitor—A. M. Webb.

Superintendent of the Poor House—John Spice.

School Examiner—James H. Smart.

Mayor—Charles A. Zollinger. Office in City Hall.

City Clerk—Sam P. Freeman. Office in City Hall.

City Treasurer—John Drœgmeyer. Office in City Hall.

City Marshal—Christopher Kelly. Office in City Hall.

Civil Engineer—Charles S. Brackenridge. Office in City Hall. Wm. Manthey, Assistant.

Board of Health—Drs. W. H. Myers, I. M. Rosenthal and John M. Josse.

Assessor—Henry Steup.

Township Officers.

Trustee—J. Hill, sr. Term expires in October, 1874. Office over Wagner's drug store, Calhoun street.

Justices of the Peace—Adam H. Bittinger. Office northeast corner of Main and Calhoun streets, opposite the Court House. Term expires in 1874.

Jas. E. Graham. Office No. 7 East Main street. Term expires in 1876.

Wm. Stewart. Office No. 58 Calhoun street. Term expires in 1876.

Daniel Ryan. Office on Court street, opposite Court House. Term expires in 1874.

John Dolan, jr. Term expires June 23, 1876.

NOTARIES PUBLIC.

Maier Willis D.
Wilson F. H.
Colerick Phil. B.
Blystone Isaac
Hayes Frederick
Ruthrauff William H.
Wise Platt J.
McCulloch C. M.
Hertig Charles M.
Redelsheimer David S.
Swift Bayless
Bloomhuff Thomas M.
Lumbard Sidney C.
Crane Calvin D.
Zollars F. T.
Furste F. L.
Granger Horace
Colerick Thomas W.
O'Rourke Edward
Rayhouser G. I. Z.
Heiber Frederick
Newberger Lewis
Gottshall M. V. B.
Carier A. H.
Bloomhuff S. H.
Mohr John Jr.
Philley Milton S.
Bursley G. E.
Crane George D.
Curtis John F.
Crabb Cyrus
Myers D. H.
Bossler H. H.
Hillegas J. D.
Randall F. P.
Meegan Thomas
McLain David
Lombard Joseph
Fisher D. C.
Smart Stephen F.
Withers W. H.
Purman A. A.
Barton C. M.
Jennison William T.
Bayless Sol. D.
Tons Henry
Hench Samuel M.
Hartman Homer C.
Jones George W.
Shaffer John
Tresselt Christian
Williams H. M.

POPULATION AND WEALTH OF THE UNITED STATES.

The following Table shows the Area, Population, Assessed Valuation of the Real and Personal Property of the United States and Territories, and the Progress of Railroad Construction during the past ten Years :

STATES AND TERRITORIES	Area in square Miles.	Population.		Assessed Valuation.		Miles R. R.	
		1860.	1870.	1860.	1870.	1862.	1872.
States.							
Alabama	50,722	964,201	996,992	$ 432,198,762	$ 155,592,595	805	1,671
Arkansas	52,105	435,450	484,471	180,211,330	94,528,843	38	258
California	188,981	379,994	560,247	139,654,667	269,644,068	23	1,013
Connecticut	4,674	460,147	537,454	341,250,976	425,433,237	630	820
Delaware	2,120	112,216	125,015	30,929,685	64,787,223	127	227
Florida	59,268	140,424	187,484	68,929,685	32,480,843	402	466
Georgia	58,000	1,067,286	1,184,109	618,232,387	227,219,519	1,420	2,108
Illinois	55,410	1,711,951	2,539,891	389,207,372	482,899,575	2,998	5,904
Indiana	33,809	1,350,428	1,680,637	411,012,424	663,455,044	2,175	3,529
Iowa	55,045	674,913	1,191,792	205,166,985	302,515,418	731	3,160
Kansas	81,318	107,209	364,399	22,518,232	92,125,861		1,760
Kentucky	37,600	1,155,684	1,321,011	528,212,693	409,544,294	567	1,123
Louisiana	41,346	708,002	726,915	435,787,265	253,371,880	335	539
Maine	31,776	628,279	626,915	154,380,388	204,253,780	505	871
Maryland	11,184	687,049	780,894	297,135,218	423,834,918	408	820
Massachusetts	7,800	1,231,066	1,457,351	777,157,816	1,591,983,112	1,285	1,606
Michigan	56,451	749,113	1,184,059	163,533,005	272,242,917	853	2,235
Minnesota	83,531	172,023	439,706	32,018,773	84,135,332	....	1,612
Mississippi	47,166	791,305	827,922	509,472,912	177,278,890	862	990
Missouri	65,350	1,182,012	1,721,295	266,985,851	556,129,969	838	2,580
Nebraska	75,995	28,841	122,993	7,426,949	54 584,616	....	827
Nevada	112,000	6,857	42,491	.....	25,740,973	....	593
New Hampshire	9,280	326,073	318,300	123,810,089	149,065,290	661	790
New Jersey	8,320	672,035	906,096	296,682,492	624,868,971	633	1,265
New York	47,000	3,880,735	4,382,759	1,390,464,638	1,967,001,185	2,728	4,470
North Carolina	50,704	992,622	1,071,361	292,297,602	130,378,622	937	1,190
Ohio	39,964	2,339,511	2,665,260	959,869,101	1,167 731,697	3,100	3,740
Oregon	95,244	52,465	90,923	19,024,915	31,798,510	4	159
Pennsylvania	46,000	2,906,215	8,521,791	719,253,335	1,319 236,042	3,000	5,113
Rhode Island	1,306	147,620	217,353	125,104,305	244,278,854	108	136
South Carolina	29,385	703,708	705,606	489,319,128	183,913,337	973	1,201
Tennessee	45,600	1,109,801	1,258,520	382,495,200	253,782,161	1,253	1,420
Texas	237,504	604,215	818,579	267,792,334	149,732,929	451	865
Vermont	10,212	315,098	330,551	84,758,619	102,548,528	562	675
Virginia	40,904	1,219,630	1,225,163	657,021,336 (Virginia and West Virginia)	365,439,917	1,379	1,490
West Virginia	23,000	376,688	442,014		140,538,273	361	485
Wisconsin	53,924	775,881	1,054,670	156,226,169	333,209,838	961	1,725
TOTAL STATES	1,950,171	31,183,744	38,113,253	$11,984,576,538	$14,021,297,071	32,120	59,587
Territories.							
Arizona	113,916	......	9,658	....	$ 1,410,295	....	.. .
Colorado	104,500	34,277	39,864	....	17,338,101	....	392
Dakota	147,400	4,837	14,181	....	2,924,489	....	..
District of Columbia	60	75,080	131,700	$41,084,945	74,271,693	*	*
Idaho	90,932	......	14,999	....	5,292,205	....	....
Montana	143,776	......	20,595	....	9,943,411	....	....
New Mexico	121,201	93,516	91,874	20,838,780	17,784,014	....	..
Utah	80,056	40,273	86,786	4,158,120	12,565,842	....	375
Washington	69,994	11,594	23,955	4,394,735	10,642,863	....	....
Wyoming	93,107	......	9,118	....	5,516,748	....	498
TOTAL TERRITORIES	965,032	259,577	442,730	$70,476,580	$157,689,661	....	1,265
Agg'gate United States	2,915,203	31,443,321	38,555,983	$12,050,053,118	$14,178,986,732	32,120	60,852

*Included in the railroad mileage of Maryland.

G. R. & I. Railroad.

STATIONS.	MILES.
Distance from Fort Wayne, by rail, to	
Junction	1
Wallen	8
Huntertown	12
Bruces	17
Swans	18
Avilla	22
Kendallville	28
Rome City	35
Wolcottville	38
Lagrange	47
Lima	52
Sturgis	56
Notawa	65
Air Line Crossing	67
Mendon	72
Portage Lake	75
Vicksburg	80
Kalamazoo	93
Plainwell	104
Martin	110
Bradley	112
Wayland	115
Ross	119
Grand Rapids	141
D. & M. Crossing	144
Rockford	155
Edgerton	158
Cedar Springs	162
Pierson	169
Maple Hill	173
Howard City	175
Morley	181
Lower Big Rapids	190
Upper Big Rapids	167
Paris	202
Ashton	215
Clam Lake	238
Linden	241
Wexford	244
Manton	251
Walton	259
Kingsley	269
Mayfield	272
Traverse City	285

C., R. & Ft. W. R'y.

STATIONS.	MILES.
Distance from Fort Wayne, by rail, to	
Adams	1
Hoagland	8
Williams	15
Decatur	18
Portland	24
Ridgeville	32
Winchester	43
Snow Hill	70
Lynn	76
Newport	79
Parry	86
Richmond	91

Ft. W., M. & C. R'y.

STATIONS.	MILES.
Distance from Fort Wayne, by rail, to	
Wabash Junction	3
Indianapolis Road	5
Ferguson	7
Sheldon	11
Ossian	14
Greenwood	17
Engleville	19
Murray Road	20
Bluffton	24
Worth. Crossing	31
Keystone	35
Montpelier	38
Hartford	47
Bowser	50
Eaton	54
Shidlers	56
Royerton	59
Muncie	65
West Mills	69
McCowens	71
Pleasant Hill	72
Allens	75
Summit	78
N. C. Junction	80
New Castle	83
Piersons	86
Corwins	88
New Lisbon	90
Gilberts	94
Cambridge City	96
Milton	98
Lockport	101
Beesons	103
Connersville	108

Ft. W. J. & S. R'y.

STATIONS	MILES.
Distance from Fort Wayne, by rail, to	
Academie	6
Huntertown	10
Stoners	12
New Era	16
Auburn	23
Waterloo	28
Pleasant Lake	37
Angola	42
Fremont	50
State Line	54
Camden	58
Reading	64
Bankers	69
Jonesville	75
Wilson	94
Jackson	100

P., Ft. W. & C. R'y.

(Fort Wayne and Pittsburgh.)

STATIONS.	MILES.
Distance from Fort Wayne, by rail, to	
Maples	10
Monroeville	16
Dixon	19
Convoy	25
Van Wert	32
Delphos	45
Elida	48
Lima	59
Lafayette	67
Ada	74
Washington	81
Dunkirk	83
Forest	90
Kirby	95
Upper Sandusky	102
Nevada	110
Glenville	115
Bucyrus	119
Robinson	125
Crestline	131
Mansfield	144
Wooster	185
Massilon	210
Canton	218
Alliance	236
Salem	250
Enon	275
New Brighton	281
Rochester	294
Allegheny	319
Pittsburgh	320
Harrisburgh	665
Baltimore	658
Washington	683
Philadelphia	751
New York	796
Boston	887

T., W. & W. R. R.

(Fort Wayne and Toledo.)

STATIONS.	MILES.
Distance from Fort Wayne, by rail, to	
New Haven	6
Woodburn	16
Antwerp	23
Cecil	30
Emerald	33
Defiance	43
Oakland	53
Napoleon	58
Liberty	65
Washington	69
Whitehouse	77
Maumee City	86
C. & T. Crossing	93
Toledo	94

P., Ft. W. & C. R'y.

(Fort Wayne and Chicago)

STATIONS.	MILES.
Distance from Ft. Wayne to	
Arcola	9
Columbia City	17
Larwill	27
Pierceton	31
Kosciusko	33
Warsaw	40
Selby	45
Atwood	46
Etna Green	50
Bourbon	53
Plymouth	64
Donelson	71
Hamlet	79
Davis	85
Hanna	89
Wannatah	95
Valparaiso	104
Wheeler	111
Hobart	115
Liverpool	118
Clarke	124
Casselo	128
Robertsdale	132
South Chicago	136
I. C. R. R. Junction	139
Archer Avenue	141
Chicago	148
San Francisco	2559

T., W. & W. R. R.

(Fort Wayne and Danville.)

STATIONS.	MILES.
Distance from Ft. Wayne to	
Prairie Switch	6
Roanoke	15
Huntington	23
Antioch	29
La Gro	36
Wabash	42
Kellers	47
Peru	56
Waverly	62
Logansport	71
Clymers	77
Burrows	81
Rockfield	85
Delphi	92
Colburn	97
Buck Creek	100
Wild Cat	...
Lafayette	108
Lafayette Junction	110
Wea	116
West Point	118
Independence	125
Attica	130
Williamsport	133
West Lebanon	138
Marshfield	142
State Line	147
I., B. & W. Junction	154
Danville	155

Public Buildings, Halls, &c.

Anderson's Block, northwest corner of Broadway and Jefferson

Aveline House Block, southeast corner of Calhoun and Berry

City Hall, in Market House, east side Barr, between Wayne and Berry

Burgess Block, southeast corner of Court and Main

Colerick's Opera House, north side of Columbia, between Clinton and Barr

Court House, on Public Square

Covenant Hall, east side of Calhoun, opposite Keystone Block.

Ewing Building, southwest corner of Main and Harrison

Firemen's Hall, northeast corner of Court and Berry

Hamilton's Block, west side of Calhoun, between Main and Berry

Hamilton's Hall, in Hamilton's Block.

Keystone Block, southwest corner of Calhoun and Columbia

Masonic Hall, northwest corner of Calhoun and Berry

McDougall's Block and Hall, northwest corner of Berry and Calhoun.

Miner Block, northeast corner of Main and Clinton

Odd Fellows' Hall, over the Post Office

Phœnix Block, northwest corner of Main and Calhoun

Post Office, east side of Court, between Main and Berry

Robinson's Block, west end of Columbia

Sentinel Block, southwest corner of Calhoun and Wayne

Templar's Hall, northwest corner of Calhoun and Berry

Townley's Block, northeast corner of Columbia and Calhoun

Turner Hall, Ewing block, southwest corner Main and Harrison

Union Block, northwest corner of Main and Clinton

UNITED STATES GOVERNMENT.

July 1, 1873.

THE EXECUTIVE.

ULYSSES S. GRANT, of Illinois, *President of the United States*........................Salary $50,000
HENRY WILSON, of Massachusetts, *Vice President of the United States*................ " 10,000

THE CABINET.

HAMILTON FISH, of New York, *Secretary of State*..................................Salary $10,000
GEORGE S. BOUTWELL, of Massachusetts, *Secretary of the Treasury*.................. " 10,000
WILLIAM W. BELNAP, of Iowa, *Secretary of War*.................................... " 10,000
GEORGE M. ROBESON, of New Jersey, *Secretary of the Navy*.......................... " 10,000
COLUMBUS DELANO, of Ohio, *Secretary of the Interior*.............................. " 10,000
GEORGE H. WILLIAMS, of Oregon, *Attorney-General*.................................. " 10,000
JOHN A. J. CRESWELL, of Maryland, *Postmaster-General*............................. " 10,000

THE JUDICIARY.

SUPREME COURT OF THE UNITED STATES.

SALMON P. CHASE, of Ohio, *Chief Justice*, [*Deceased April* 1873.]........................Salary $8,500

NATHAN CLIFFORD, of Maine,	*Associate Justice*	STEPHEN J. FIELD, of California,	*Associate Justice.*
NOAH H. SWAYNE, of Ohio,	" "	WILLIAM M. STRONG, of Pa.,	" "
SAMUEL F. MILLER, of Iowa,	" "	JOSEPH P. BRADLEY, of N. J.,	" "
DAVID DAVIS, of Illinois,	" "	WARD HUNT, of N. Y.,	" "

Salary of Associate Justices, $8,000. Court meets first Monday in December, at Washington.

MINISTERS TO FOREIGN COUNTRIES.

ENVOYS EXTRAORDINARY AND MINISTERS PLENIPOTENTIARY.

Country.	*Capital.*	*Ministers.*	*Salary*	*Appointed.*
Austria	Vienna	John Jay, N. Y	$12,000	1868
Brazil	Rio Janeiro	James R. Partridge, Md	12,000	1871
Chili	Santiago	Joseph P. Root, Kansas	10,000	1869
China	Pekin	Frederick F. Low, Cal	12,000	1869
France	Paris	Elihu B. Washburne, Ill	17,500	1869
Great Britian	London	Robert C. Schenck, Ohio	17,500	1870
Italy	Florence	George P. Marsh, Vt	12,000	1861
Mexico	Mexico	Thomas H. Nelson, Ind	12,000	1869
Peru	Lima	Francis Thomas, Md	10,000	1872
Germany	Berlin	George Bancroft, Mass	17,500	1867
Russia	St. Petersburg	James L. Orr, S. C	12,000	1872
Spain	Madrid	Daniel E. Sickles, N. Y	12,000	1869

MINISTERS RESIDENT.

Country.	*Capital.*	*Ministers.*	*Salary*	*Appointed.*
Argentine Republic	Buenos Ayres	Julius White, Ill	$7,500	1869
Belgium	Brussels	J. R. Jones, Ill	7,500	1869
Bolivia	Cochabamba		7,500	1869
Costa Rica	San Jose	Jacob B. Blair, W. Va	7,500	1868
Denmark	Copenhagen	M. J. Cramer, Ky	7'500	1870
Ecuador	Quito	E. Rumsey Wing, Ky	7,500	1870
Greece	Athens	John M. Francis, N. Y	7,500	1871
Guatemala	Guatemala	Silas A. Hudson, Iowa	7,500	1869
Hawaiian Islands	Honolulu	Henry A. Pierce, Mass	7,500	1869
Honduras	Comayagua	Henry Baxter, Mich	7,500	1869
Japan	Yedo	C. E. DeLong, Nevada	12,500	1869
Netherlands	Hague	Chas. T. Gorham, Mich	7,500	1870
Nicaragua	Nicaragua	Charles N. Riotte, Texas	7,500	1869
Paraguay	Asuncion	[See Uruguay]	7,500	
Portugal	Lisbon	Chas. H. Lewis, Va	7,500	1870
San Salvador	San Salvador	Thomas Biddle, Penn	7,500	1869
Sweden and Norway	Stockholm	C. S. Andrews, Minn	7,500	1869
Switzerland	Berne	Horace Rublee, Wis	7,500	1869
Turkey	Constantinople	George H. Boker, Penn	7,500	1870
Uruguay and Paraguay	Montevideo	John L. Stevens, Me	11,500	1871
U. S. of Colombia	Bogota		7,500	
Venezuela	Caracas	William A. Pile, Mo	7,500	1869

MINISTERS RESIDENT AND CONSULS GENERAL.

Country.	*Capital.*	*Ministers.*	*Salary*	*Appointed.*
Hayti	Port-au-Prince	E. D. Bassett, Pa	7,500	1869
Liberia	Monrovia	J. Milton Turner, Mo	4,000	1871

CARIER & CAMPBELL'S

FORT WAYNE DIRECTORY

FOR 1873-4.

ABBREVIATIONS USED.

al	alley.	c	corner.	mkr	maker.
atty	attorney.	cab mkr	cabinet maker.	n	north.
av	avenue.	carp	carpenter.	not pub	notary public.
b	between.	clk	clerk.	nr	near.
bar k	bar keeper.	com	commission.	opp	opposite.
bds	boards.	confec	confectioner.	prov	provision.
b h	boarding house	e	east.	propr	proprietor.
bk	book or brick.	eng	engineer.	s	south or side.
b k	book keeper.	h	house.	servt	servant.
bk layer	brick layer.	lab	laborer.	w	west.
bldr	builder.	manuf	manufacturer.	wh	wholesale.
bldg	building.	mer	merchant.	wks	works.

A

ABBOTT WILLIAM T. & Co., Produce and Commission Merchants, Pork Packers, &c., warehouse cor Clinton and Water
ABBOTT WILLIAM T., Produce Merchant, h 213 W. Berry
Abenroth ——, blacksmith, bds Summit City House
Accor Robt., carpenter, h 29 Hood
Adams Mrs. Hannah M., bds 139 W. Main
Adams Richard, lab, bds 161 W. Washington
Adams Wm., Fireman Wabash Shops, bds 76 Dawson
Adams Ida, bds 86 E. Main.
Adams Robt., conductor Wabash Ry., h 114 Fairfield
Adams Wm. H., conductor Pitts. Ry., h 196 Broadway
ADAMS JNO., Prop. Nat. Restaurant and Saloon, 256 Calhoun
Adam Henry, lab, h 43 E. Main.
ADAMS J. B., Eng. Pitts. Road, h 146 W. Wayne
Adams Rodney, Fireman Pitts. Ry., h 35 Buchanan
Adams Henry, lab., h 30 Wells
Adams Wm., Fireman Wabash Ry., bds 66 Chicago
Adkin Armus, conductor Pitts Ry., h 59 Charles
Adler Geo., carpenter, h 13 Wall
Adler Andrew, Expressman, h 61 Wall
ÆTNA LIFE INS. CO., Hartford, Con., Cash Assets $18.000.000, A. H. Carier, Agent

Agster Mary, Widow, h 138 Harrison
Aheren Thomas, lab, h 29 Colerick
Ahsendorf Mrs. E., Widow, h 7 Wert
Aiken Mrs. Allen, h 156 Fairfield
Ainsworth J. M., (Paine, A. & Co.,) Stave Manuf, h 40 Garden
Aker David, Dealer in Fruit Trees, h 203 Barr
AKER DAVID B., Prop. Aker House, 205 Calhoun
Aker Ambrose, Fruits and Nuts, 172 Calhoun
Akers Henry, Student, bds Ft. Wayne College
Akins Mrs. M. J., Milliner and Dress Maker, h 225 Calhoun
Akins Wm. B., carpenter Pitts. Shops, h 225 Cal
Albiston Sarah, widow, bds 108 Harrison
Albers Herman, lab, h 327 Hanna
Albrecht John, Shoemaker, bds 55 W. Wayne
Albrecht John, Shoemaker, bds 133 E. Lewis
Albrecht Peter, Shoemaker, bds 133 E. Lewis
Albert Jules N., Saloon, 88 Barr
Albrecht Luther, Painter, h 54 E. Wayne
Alberroth David, clk, bds 256 Calhoun
Alderman Frank, agt, bds American House
Alexander Thomas, blacksmith Wabash Shop, bds 157 Van Buren
ALEXANDER, D. S., (McNeice & A.,) Gazette Office, h 259 W. Wayne
Algeier Anton, collar Maker, bds 126 E. Washington
Alice Edward, Machinist Wabash shop, bds 64 McClellan
Alliger B. H., brickmaker, h on Maumee
Alink H., lab, h 82 Maumee
Allen Milton, brakeman Wabash Ry., h 84 Fairfield
Allen C. W., carpenter, h 171 W. Wayne
Allen Leyrand, book Keeper, h 157 W. Berry
Allen James, carpenter, Pitts. Shop, bds 162 Montgomery
Alling Lawrence, clk, h 273 E. Jefferson
Allison Chas., bartender at Mayer House
Allen Susan, widow, h 71 E. Main
ALGEIER & BRO., Tinners, store 63 E. Main
Algeier Frank, Tinner, 63 E. Main
Algeier Chas., Tinner, bds 63 E. Main
Allinger H., book Keeper Fruit House, h 140 Calhoun
Alspaugh George, Moulder Bass Foundry, bds 296 Hanna
Alter Peter, carpenter Pitts. Shops, h 21 John
Altekruse Ernst, lab, h 329 Hanna
Alter Jacob, Painter, h 20 Wilt
Alter Nicholas, Grocer, h 27 Force
Altevogt Herman, lab, h 145 E. Lewis
Altenberger B., Teamster, h 183 Montgomery
Altick James, brass Moulder, h 43 E. Main
Alvord Nathan, brass Moulder Pitts. Shop, bds 46 Jefferson
Aman Lewis, Plasterer, h 213 E. Washington

Ames Mylon, lab, bds 60 Chicago
Ames Myron, lab. h 324 Calhoun
Ames George, Teamster, h 16 W. Jefferson
Ames Samuel, Telegraph Operator, bds 16 W. Jeff
Ames Benson, Teamster, bds 16 W. Jefferson
Ames Rufus, Fireman G. R. & I. Road, bds 16 W. Jefferson
AMERICAN EXPRESS CO., Office 77 Calhoun
Amler Frank, clk, bds Robinson House
Ammon Daniel, h 287 W. Wash
Amy Annie, Widow, h 25 Nirdlinger ave
Andruss Geo., Eng. Pitts. Ry., h 69 Douglass ave
Andrews David, boilermaker Pitts. shop, h 209 Barr
Anderson James, wks Pitts. shop, bds 8 Hough
Anderson Calvin, h 123 W. Wayne
Anderson Wm. N., clk. (Mayer Bro. & Co. Drugstore,) h 368 Calhoun
Anderson Mrs. S., h 8 Hough
Anderson E. G. (A. & Douglass,) Grocer, h 198 W. Jefferson
Anderson & Douglass, Grocery and Provisions, 122 and 124 Broadway
ANDERSON COL. W. H. Eng. Vigilant Steam Fire Engine, bds 93 Calhoun
ANDERSON T. P., Dealer in Pianos and Organs, store 98 Calhoun
Andrew Thomas W., (Ellsworth, Andrew & Co., dealers in Carpets,) bds Aveline House
Ane Geo. laborer, bds 76 Wallace
Angell Mrs. Kate, h 166 W. Berry
Angel B. D., Sect. Gas wks., h 216 W. Washington
Ankanbrock Barney, Driver City Mills exp., h 172 E. Washington
Ankenbrock Martin, helper Pitts'gh shop, h 255 E. Wayne
Anthony John C., wks. Pitts'gh shop, bds 98 Montgomery
Anthony Peter, laborer, bds cor Calhoun and Jefferson
APP MATHIAS, Manf. & Dealer in Boots and shoes, store 106 Calhoun
Anwiler Henry, carpenter, h 212 Broadway
App Mathias, Shoemaker, h 104 W. Washington
Archbeck Jacob, laborer, bds 35 Force
Arens Herman, laborer, h 122 Madison
Arentz Geo., Lumber Dealer, bds 58 E. Washington
Arentz Simon, carpenter, bds 58 E. Washington
ARENTZ PHILLIP, Lumber Dealer, h 58 E. Washington
Arland Mrs. A., widow, h 43 E. Water
Arland Mrs. Adelaide, Widow, h 45 Water
Armstrong Mrs. Malinda, h 247 W. Berry
Armstrong M. A., School Teacher, bds 139 E. Washington
Armbouster Chas. Jr., Eng Pittsburgh Ry., h 37 Force
Armbouster Lorenz, laborer, h 69 Buchanan
Armbouster Chas. bds 37 Force
Arment Wm., carpenter, h 141 Barr
Armack Dora, widow, h 20 W. Water
Armstutz Peter, laborer, h 75 Force

Armstutz Joseph, laborer, bds 75 Force
Arnold John, carpenter, h 131 W. Washington
Arntz Jacob, laborer, h 145 Broadway
Arnold Anthony, Furniture Dealer, h 166 Broadway
Arnes B., Teamster, bds 122 Madison
Arnold Clinton, conductor P. Ft. W. & C. Ry. h 200 Broadway
Arndt Jno., Grocery and Saloon, h 22 W. Main
Arvin Andrew, Eng. T. W. & W. Ry., bds 82 Fairfield
Ashley Vincent, cooper, bds 404 Calhoun
Ashley A. J., conductor T. W. & W. Ry., h 282 Harrison
Ashley P. H., conductor Ft. W. M. & C. Road, h 121 W. Washington
Ashley Winfield, Painter, h 138 W. Berry
Ash H. J., Stove Merchant, h 104 E. Main
ASH H. J., Stoves and House Furnishing Goods, store 17 E. Columbia, h 104 E. Main
Atkins Wm., laborer, bds 87 Williams
Aubrey Joseph, laborer, h 29 Duck
Auer D. R., laborer, h 51 Wall
Auer Conrad, Policeman, h 217 Broadway
AUGER CHARLES. Florist, h 453 E. Wayne
Auger Lewis, bds 453 E. Wayne
Augst Lenhart, blacksmith, h 56 E. Madison
Auman Conrad, laborer, h 118 Gay
Auman Chas., laborer, h 28 Orchard
Auman Wm., laborer, h 67 Rockhill
Aunweiler Lewis, carpenter, h 165 Jackson
AURENTZ S. A., Groceries, 151 Broadway, h 137 Broadway
Aurentz Solomon, Grocer, h 151 Broadway
Aurentz Solomon A., Grocer, 137 Broadway
Austin Jno. C., conductor T. W. & W. Ry., h 228 Noel
Austin Joseph, Fireman T. W. & W. Ry. h Calhoun between Wallace and Hamilton
Ausbach Jacob, brakeman T. W. & W. Ry., bds 15 Holman
Austes William J., clerk, bds 10 W. Berry
Aveline John J., Engineer, bds Aveline House
Aveline Mrs. F. S., bds Aveline House
Aveline George J., Accountant, (Shuricks Stave Factory,) bds Aveline House
AVELINE HOUSE, McDonald and Mrs. Aveline props., s e cor Berry and Calhoun
Axe Andrew, conductor G. R. & I. Ry., h 14 Chicago
Axt William, laborer, bds 129 Francis
Axt M. carpenter, h 123 Francis
AYERS H. P., M. D., office in Volmer's Drug Store, h 114 Clinton
AYERS HENRY B., Druggist cor Lewis and Lafayette
Ayers Daniel D., carpenter, h 23 Langohr
Ayers James, conductor P. Ft. W. & C. Ry., bds 343 Hanna

B

Baals Frank, blacksmith, bds 302 W. Jefferson
Baals John L., laborer, h 302 W. Jefferson
Baals George, carpenter Pitts. shop, h 152 Montgomery
Baals August, clerk, bds 152 Montgomery
Baals & Steger, confectionery, 64 Calhoun
Baada Wm., drayman, h 263 E. Jefferson
Babcock W. C., ass't car master Pitts'gh road, h 149 Holman
Babcock Mrs. Fanny, widow, h 99 W. Main
Baber Jacob, carpenter, h 342 Broadway
Baack B., carpenter Pitts. shop, bds 178 Barr
Back Peter, mason, h 1 Walnut
Backer Lorenz, stone mason, h 100 Lasselle
Bacon Danton, dentist, bds 118 Barr
Bachelder J. S., confectioner, h Lillie's Add
Backer Mrs W., widow, h 133 Calhoun
Backler Q., machinist, h 221 Broadway
Bacon J. P., dentist, bds 118 Barr
Bade Fred., shoemaker, h 88 Montgomery
Bade Fred., shoemaker, h 13 Barthold
Bade Henry, laborer, h 17 Barthold
Bademeyer Fred., works Olds & S, h 329 E. Washington
Badge John, blacksmith, bds 82 Fairfield Avenue
Bagley Hugh, shoemaker, h 58 Wells
Baguet Peter, locksmith, h 68 Ewing
Bagley A. G., laborer, bds 203 Calhoun
Bahner Adam, vinegar maker, h 351 W. Main
Bailey Wm. H., fireman Pittsburgh R. R., h 14 Colerick
Baier Nicholas, carpenter, h 35 Brackenridge
Baier Valentine, carpenter, h 35 Brackenridge
Baillie John, blacksmith, h 166 Jackson
Bair John, photographer, bds 10 Harrison
BAKER JACOB & KILIAN, saw mill and lumbermen, E Water
Baker Jacob, (J. & K. Baker,) h 128 E. Main
Baker George, blacksmith, shop 16 Lafayette
Baker Isaac W., clerk, bds 14 Lafayette
Baker Jacob, foreman stave factory, h cor Taylor and Eagle
Baker Conrad, shoemaker, h 193 W. Berry
Baker Charles A., drug clerk, bds 193 W. Berry
Baker Julian, machinist Murray's shop, bds 193 W. Berry
Baker John, (Welch & B.) tinner, bds 193 W. Berry
Baker Daniel, laborer, h 84 Fairfield Av
Baker Kilian, (J. & K. Baker,) h 92 E. Main
Baker John, blacksmith and wagon-maker, h 145 Clinton
Baker Mrs. R., widow, h 175 Clinton
Baker George W., agent for Olds & Son, h 175 Clinton

Bair Amos, conductor P., Ft. W. & C. R'y, h 58 Douglas Av
Baker George, clerk, bds St. Nicholas, 93 Calhoun
Baker R., conductor P. F. W. & C. W., h 196 Ewing
Ball John, engineer P. F. W. & C. R. W., h 55 Grand
Baldwin Albert, engineer T. W. & W. R. W., h — Fulton
Baltes Michael, contractor, h 63 Harrison
Ballauf Edward, drug clerk, bds 202 W Jefferson
Ballman Joseph, drayman, h 30 Nirdlinger
Baldwin Mrs. Anna, hair dresser, 30 E. Columbia
Baldwin Sarah, dress-maker, h 54 W. Wayne
Bandan, Fred, Carpenter, h 105 Wells
Banister Catherine, widow, h 138 Francis
Bande Fred, laborer, h 27 Pritchard
Band Fred, carpenter, bds 48 McClellan
Bannister G., fireman G. R. & I. R. R., bds 138 Francis
Barnes Joseph, laborer, h 165 E. Lewis
Baron John, laborer, h 119 Lafayette
Bargus Martin, carpenter, h 156 E. Jefferson
Barner Charles, carpenter, h 153 Montgomery
Bartels John, carpenter, h 150 Montgomery
Barnes J. B., foreman Wabash shops, h 28 Brandriff
Barrett Fred, boss Street Railroad, h 135 Wells
Bartels John, laborer, h 38 Force
Bartlett J. C., Prof. Indiana Conservatory of Music, bds Hamilton House
Barrows John G., Painter, bds 39 W. Washington
Barbour M. F., bds Hanna House
Barghorn Fred, boiler-maker, h 123 Madison
Baron August, laborer, bds 200 Hanna
Barnes H. N., Rev., Pastor M. E. Church, h 1 Wert
Barcus Isaac, stone-cutter, h 131 W. Water
Bard Samuel, contractor, h 208 W. Berry
Barrett John, laborer, bds 29 Baker
Bard Wm. A., clerk, bds 208 W. Berry
Bard Frank J., drug clerk, bds 208 W. Berry
Barth S., laborer, bds 130 W. Berry
Barr James, livery and sale stable, bds Mayer House
Bartler Robert, laborer, bds Steuben House
Barnum P. G., veterinary Surgeon, h 55 E. Berry
Bartels Henry, carpenter, h 27 Lavinia
Barry William, clerk, bds 49 and 51 W. Berry
Barr John H., clerk Ft. Wayne Eating House
Barbier Peter, saw repairer, h 103 E. Main
Barr George, carpenter, h 35 Hoagland Av
Barr George J., brakeman Pittsburgh R'y, h 230 Lafayette
Bartlett George, laborer, bds cor Calhoun and Wallace
Barren Frank, laborer, h 200 Hanna
Barton Charles M., clerk County Treasurer's office, h 303 W. Washington
Bartholemew H., bds 62 Lillie

BASH SOL. & CO., Dealers in Wool, 49 & 51 Columbia
Bash Solomon, produce merchant, (B. & Co.) h 240 W. Berry
Bash Charles S., clerk, bds 240 W. Berry
Bastian Jacob, laborer, bds 68 E. Washington
Bass Mrs. Eliza, h 147 W. Washington
Bassford Abram, barkeeper, bds 9 E. Wayne
Bassett John, carpenter, h 347 Lafayette
BASS JOHN H., Manufacturer of Car-Wheels, Engines, Boilers, Castings and Mill Machinery, cor. Hanna & Railroad
Bass J. H., h south-east cor. Berry & Griffith
Bass Mrs. Mary Ann, widow, h 332 W. Jefferson
Basler Joseph, laborer, h Lillie's Ad
Bassel Louis, switchman Pittsburgh R. R. yard, bds 16 Chicago
Bassal William, switchman Pittsburgh R. R. yard, bds 16 Chicago
Bastues Michael, h — Montgomery
Battenberg Jacob, tailor, h 133 High
Batt Frank, laborer, h 26 Walnut
Baty Mrs Theodona, h 24 Barthold
Baty William, laborer, bds 24 Barthold
Bauer William, machinist Pittsburgh shops, bds 235 Lafayette
Baughman Newton, fireman P. F. W. & C. R'y, h 28 Buchanan
Baumer Michael, miller, h 19 West
Baughman Jeremiah, foreman Hurd's shop, h 63 Langohr
Bauer Joseph, barber, h 95 Baker
Bangert B., grocer, h 167 Broadway
Bauer Henry, shoemaker, 319 Lafayette
Bayless Sol S., brakeman Pittsburgh R'y, bds 32 E Wayne
Bayless Frank L., brakeman Wabash R'y, bds 32 E. Wayne
BAYLESS SOL. D., Notary Public, Real Estate & Collecting Agt., office 108 Clinton, h 32 E. Wayne
Bayless Nancy, widow, bds 89 W. Water
Bayless Alexander H., drover, h 236 W Jefferson
Beach George, laborer, h 15 Clark
Beamer Edward, teamster, h 127 W. Water
Beard John M., drug clerk, bds 138 W. Wayne
Bear Joseph, brakeman Wabash R'y
Beard Jasmes Q., confectioner, bds 38 Clinton
Beard Thomas D., confectionary and h 38 Clinton
Beaber L. D., carpenter, h 122 Fulton
Beard Hayman S., carpenter, bds 47 W. Water
Bear John, switchman Pittsburgh R'y, bds 16 Chicago
Beach Fred, bds 444 Broadway
Beach John, clk Pittsburgh R'y shops, h 444 Broadway
Beard John, watchman at mill, h 210 W. Main
Beaber A. G., laborer, h 150 Broadway
Beach ——— machinist Wabash shops, h 29 Wall
Beam C. F., engineer P. F. W. & C. R'y, h 131 Holman
Beaver, Miller & Co., dealers in lumber, 17 Grand

Beals, M. M., bds 70 Wells
Beals John H., engineer P. F. W. & C. R'y, h cor Fifth & N. Calhoun
Beach Fred, miller, bds 15 Clark
Beam Mrs. Elizabeth, bds 98 Barthold
Bear Martin, laborer, h 49 Langohr
Beals William, machinist Wabash shop, h 116 Jackson
Beach Frederick, (Morgan & Beach, Hardware) h 133 E. Berry
Beaman Mrs., widow, h 61 Lafayette
Beaver Charles, clerk, h 147 Broadway
Beals William, h 70 Wells
Beals Mrs. Sarah, widow, h 150 W. Jefferson
Bean Ed L., manager at eating house, South Depot
Beckman John, carpenter, h 201 E. Jefferson
BECK JOSEPH R., M. D., Consulting Gynecologist, office Hamilton Hall Block, h 15 E. Washington
Becker Louis, laborer, h 16 Clark
Beckes John, laborer, h 30 Third
Becker Frank, bds 9 Force
Becker Charles, carpenter Pittsburgh shops, h 170 W. Washington
Becker Ernst, bds 34 McClellan
Beckley Stephen, clerk, bds 262 E Wayne
Beckley Isaac, clerk, h 262 E. Wayne
Becquette T. Mrs., widow, h 200 E. Wayne
Bechtold George, plowmaker, bds 91 W. Water
Beck ——— carpenter, bds 170 Lafayette
Beck Henry, laborer, h 13 Wert
Beck Joseph, works Olds & S., h 101 Clay
Becker M., (J. Becker & Co., produce,) h 152 W. Washington
Becker Jacob, (B. Bro's, produce) h 181 W. Wayne
Beck Conrad, laborer, h 34 Force
Beck Jacob, laborer, bds 325 Lafayette
Beck Locus, laborer, bds 293 Hanna
Becker Charles, Blacksmith, bds 11 E. Washington
Beckes Mathias, laborer, bds 30 Third
Beck Frank J., brewer, h 157 Wells
Becker Jacob, laborer, h 129 Wilt
Becker Christian, stone cutter, h 220 W. Berry
Becket Peter, laborer, h 191 E Washington
Becker Henry, carpenter, h 191 E. Washington
Becker John, agent, h 191 E. Washington
Becker Emil, bds 181 W. Wayne
Becker Louis, clerk, bds 181 W. Wayne
Becquett John, sawyer, h 138 E. Main
Becker Fred, blacksmith, h 11 E. Washington
Becker Fred, Jr., blacksmith, bds 11 E. Washington
Beety James, switchman Pittsburgh R'y, bds cor. Lafayette & Wallace
BEEKS JAMES C., attorney at law, office 57 Clinton, h 259 W Wayne

Beeler C., conductor G. R. & I. R R., h 19 Pine
Beese James, brakeman Wabash R'y, bds 59 Grand
Beegan Lizzie, widow, h 6 & 8 Kansas
Beeps Charles, carpenter Pittsburgh shops, h 74 Henry
Beforden August, laborer, h 231 Webster
Beforden S., carpenter Wabash shops, bds 231 Webster
Behr John, filecutter, h 210 W. Main
Beiber Milton, (Stanley & B.,) h 64 Wall
Beinicke Ernst, bds 127 W. Washington
Beierlein George, laborer, h 22 Pritchard
Beierlein John, laborer, h 107 Cass
Beirman Henry, laborer, bds foot W. Water
Bellamy Albert F., painter, h 98 W. Water
Bell R. C., attorney, h 432 Broadway
Belling H., laborer, h 26 Oak
Bell Cecelia, widow, bds 85 E. Jefferson
Bell Frank R., fireman Wabash R'y, bds 5 Barr
Belyea Wellington, bds 138 W Berry
Bell G. L., omnibus driver, h 18 E Wayne
Bentley Geo. W., clerk, h 28 Locust
BENOIT JULIAN, Very Rev., h 171 Calhoun
Benton Mrs. G., h 24 Fairfield ave
Bender George, cooper, h 204 Francis
Bennigan Henry, machinist Pittsburgh shop, h 86 Force
Bender Ernst, laborer, Ft. Wayne eating house
Bennett Adam, fireman T. W. & W. Ry., bds 125 Henry
Benton Winton, watchman T. W. & W. Ry., h 125 Henry
Benke C., drayman, bds 263 E. Jefferson
Benz Adam, laborer, h 253 E. Washington
Benz Adam, laborer, h 253 E. Washington
Benner G. A., sawyer, bds 234 W. Wayne
Benz Conrad, yard boss Wabash Ry., h 202 W. Washington
Bender & Co., cigar mfg., 30 W. Main
Bente Herman, foreman Wabash paint shop, h 155 Griffith
Bentz George, bds 73 N. Cass
Bentz Nicholas, truckman, h 73 N. Cass
Benett E. S., bds 55 William
Bender L., cigar maker, h 168 E. Washington
Bensman Mrs. E., h 74 E. Madison
Bensman Henry, boatman, bds 74 E. Madison
Bensman, William, Boiler maker, h 76 E. Madison
Bennett Mrs. Lavina, h 155 Broadway
Benson Mrs. M., h 122 Ewing
Bennette Abraham, boiler maker Pittsburgh shop h 176 Ewing
Bender Phillip, stone cutter, bds 75 W. Jefferson
Benton Mrs. A., widow, h 60 E. Washington
Bender Jacob, clerk, bds Hanna House
Benz Phillip, h 123 Madison

Bennigan L. H., moulder, h 207 E. Lewis
Bennett Frank, carpenter, h 124 Union
Berberick Joseph, butcher, bds 264 Calhoun
Benning Conrad, grocer, 71 E. Main
Bernard Simeon, sawyer, h 190 W. Main
Berghammer John, cigar maker, bds American House
Berleman Fred, boiler maker h 91 E. Washington
Bermingham John, spoke finisher, h 86 E. Madison
Bercot Joseph, carpenter, h 68 Lasselle
Bernard Joseph, bds 48 Charles
Bernhardt Christian, laborer, h 29 John
Bernhardt Augustus, laborer, bds 33 Jefferson
Berry William B., clerk, 16 W. Berry
Berning Conrad, grocer, cor Barr and Madison
Berger August H., boiler maker Pittsburgh shop, h 186 Montgomery
Berlin Henry, laborer, h 100 W. Walnut
Bergman Sophia, widow h 174 Taylor
Berger Lewis, laborer, h 224 W. Jefferson
Berry John, mason, bds 301 W. Jefferson
Bermer Conrad, painter, h 94 Montgomery
Besanco Frank, laborer, h 180 Hanna
Besson John B., bricklayer, h 136 Monroe
Bethel Elizabeth, widow, bds 189 Ewing
Betzler George, cooper, h 296 Broadway
Beuchner Casper, laborer, h 224 E. Wayne
Beuret Mrs. Mary, h 166 E. Berry
Beverly William, pedler, bds 172 Calhoun
Bichey Joseph, baggage master Ft. W. J. & S. Road, bds Robinson House
Bickler William, laborer, bds 39 Wall
Bickman Henry, shoemaker, h 146 Maumee
Bickness Fred, policeman, h 171 E. Lewis
BIDDLE T. M., Druggist and Dealer in Paints, Oils, and Window Glass, 6 Keystone Block
Biddle T. M., druggist, h 138 W. Wayne
Biddle Richard, bds 99 E. Berry
Biemer George, blacksmith and wagon shop, cor Main and Clay, h 140 E. Main
Biedenweg Gottfried, laborer, h 319 Hanna
Bierly William, wks Olds & S., bds 109 Holman
Bierly David, wks Olds & S., h 109 Holman
Bierbaum Frederick, laborer, bds 52 McClellan
BIEMER GEORGE., blacksmith and Wagon Maker, shop, 3 Clay
Bierman Fred, teamster, bds 91 W. Jefferson
Bieber Enoch, land speculator, h 47 N. Cass
Bieber Milton, (Stanley & B.,) h 64 Wall
Bigelow Francis A., conductor T. W. & W. Ry., h 49 Malitta
Biller Saul D., wks Olds & Sons, bds 209 Barr

Bilser Charles, Brewer, wks at Linker, Hey & Co., h 181 E. Wayne
Binder Ursula, widow, h 20 Poplar
Binckley H. C., conductor P. Ft. W. & C. Ry., h 169 Clinton
Bingman William, fireman P. Ft. W. & C. Ry., bds 219 Lafayette
BIRD OCHMIG, Senator, h 151 Griffith
Birsley Luther, blacksmith, Pittsburgh shop, h 113 Holman
Birsley Samuel, wks Olds & Son, bds 109 Holman
Birkner Charles, stone cutter, h 266 W. Jefferson
Birch Rev. William S., h 67 Brackenridge
Bird Mrs. Mary, h 66 Wilt
Bishing Henry, shoemaker, bds 335 E. Washington
Bishop William, trunkmaker, bds Robinson House
Bismark Frank, Wabash shop, h 289 Hannah
Bishop Clifford, baggage master G. R. & I. Road, bds 14 Chicago
Bishop Alferd, clerk, (Foster Bros.,) bds 86 E. Main
Bishchoff R. A., teacher Concordia College
BITTINGER J. R., Attorney at Law, 5 E. Main
Bittinger J. R., attorney, h 262 W. Washington
Bittel George, laborer Pittsburgh shop, h 234 Francis
Bittenbender Henry, laborer, h 187 W. Washington
Bittenbender Charles, moulder, bds 187 W. Washington
Bitzinger Joseph, laborer, h 436 E. Wayne
Bitner James, laborer, h 120 Butler
Bitner Andrew J., harness maker h 98 E. Jefferson
Bitner John R., machinist Pittsburgh shop, bds 98 E. Jefferson
BITTINGER A. H., Attorney, h 144 Pritchard
Bixler William, teamster, h 29 Marion
Blakesley Edson, conductor P. Ft. W. & C. Ry., h 227 Lafayette
BLACK JOSEPH, Hoop Skirt Manufacturer, h 132 W. Jefferson
Blase Lewis, bakery, 29 W. Columbia
Blaisdell Phillip O., truckman, h 26 Douglass ave
Blackburn George, brakeman P. Ft. W. & C. Ry., bds 19 Hood
Blaisdale M., brakeman G. R. & I. Road, bds 197 E. Jefferson
Blackburn William C., brakeman G. R. & I. Road, bds 19 Hood
BLAKELY WILLIAM, Conductor P. Ft. W. & C. Ry., h 225 W. Jefferson
Blain Scott, fireman, P. Ft. W. & C. Ry., bds 32 Grand
Blakesley L. L., conductor P. Ft. W. & C. Ry., h 67 Baker
Blaxsam John, gas agent, h 87 Montgomery
Blackburn William P. brakeman P. Ft. W. & C. Ry., h 19 Hood
Blackwell George A. engineer G. R. & I. Road, bds 322 Calhoun
Blake L., night watchman, P. Ft. W & C. Ry., h 159 E. Jefferson
Blair David D., moulder, bds Fox House
Black Joseph, hoop skirt factory, 15 E. Columbia
Black C., bds Robinson House
Blakesley Robert W., conductor P. Ft., W. & C. Ry., h 47 Baker
Blaisdell Charles, machinist Pittsburgh shop, h 26 Douglas ave

BLACKBURN ROBERT, Conductor P. Ft. W. & C. Ry., h 11 McClellan
Bley Theodore, yard master Pittsburgh Ry., h 154 E. Lewis
Bleek D. laborer, h 131 Madison
Blee Charles A., laborer, h 39 Grand
Blee Edward, coppersmith Pittsburgh shop, bds 71 Douglass ave
Bloom Andrew, carpenter, bds ———
Block Marx, clothing store, 5 Columbia
Bloomhuff Samuel H., h 70 W. Main
Bloomhuff John, laborer, bds 10 Harrison
Blœkner William, bds 399 E. Washington
Bloomhuff Catherine, h 151 W. Wayne
Bloomhuff William, engineer T. W. & W. Ry., h 16 Wilt
Bloomer T. S. watchman Saginaw road, bds 40 Wells
Bloomhuff F. attorney, h 143 Francis
Blythe David, clerk, h 15 N. Cass
Blyston J. laborer, bds 103 Calhoun
Blythe Delilah, widow, bds 68 W. Main
Boag William, machinist P. Ft. W. & C., Ry., h 78 Brackenridge
Bocksberger Valentine, laborer, h 43 N. Calhoun
Bocksberger Martin, laborer, h 43 N. Calhoun
Bode Augustus, machinist, (J. C. Bowser & Co.,) bds 178 Barr
BOERGER & HOUSE, Vinegar Factory, 76 Barr
Bœster Fred, carpenter, h 164 Griffith
Bœster George carpenter, h 161 Griffith
Bœcker Henry, laborer, h 58 Pritchard
Bœse William, carpenter Pittsburgh shop, h 18 Hough
Bœger Rudolf h 183 E. Washington
Bœrger Florence, trunk maker, bds 183 E. Washington
Bœs Aman, butcher, h 146 E. Jefferson
Bœrger Henry, clerk, h 183 E. Washington
Bœsler Henry Jr., shoemaker, bds 55 W. Wayne
Bœrger Ernst, laborer, bds 74 W. Jefferson
Bœn Peter, laborer, bds 3-5 R. R.
Bœrger Henry, bds 196 E. Jefferson
Bœse Fred, teamster, h 289 W. Jefferson
Bœrger William, carpenter, h 194 E. Washington
Bogue Daniel, h 120 Creighton ave
Bogart David C., express messenger, Richmond Road, h 3 Pine
Bogge William Carpenter, h 52 McClellan
Bogge Frederick, laborer, h 52 McClellan
Bohan John H., h 118 Creighton ave
Bohen Engle, widow, h 111 W. Jefferson
Bohen M., laborer, h 245 E. Jefferson
Bohn B. E., book keeper, bds Robinson House
Bohmer Charles, clerk, bds 171 W. Washington
Bohling William, moulder Bass foundry, h 12 Force
Bohn Christian, printer, h 7 McClellan

BOLTZ & ELY, Groceries, Provisions, Fruits &c., store 90 Calhoun
Boltz George C., gardner, h 111 Wells
Bolling Lemuel, painter, h 73 Wells
Bolling John, brick maker, h 99 E. Madison
Bollman Christian, laborer, h 47 W Lewis
Bolman Christian, machinist, (Olds & Son,) h 167 Jackson
Boltz F. F., (B. & Ely,) grocer, h 250 W. Jefferson
Bolman Henry, teamster, h 92 W. Jefferson
Bolger James P., driver Vigilant Steam Fire Engine, h 61 Clinton
Boldwin Sylvester, cooper, bds 11 Duck
Bollyer Jacob, hostler, bds 25 Barr
Bono Justin, laborer, h 125 E. Lewis
Bonfield Mrs. Mary, h 180 E. Wayne
Bond Steven B., banker, (Allen, Hamilton & Co.,) h Fairfield ave
Bond Charles E. book keeper, bds cor Fairfield and Creighton ave's
Bonnel D. R., telegraph operator, bds Hanna House
Bond H. J., bds Hamilton House
Bond George blacksmith Pittsburgh shop, h 159 Hanna
Bond Charles, bds Creighton ave
Bonter C., conductor P. Ft. W. & C. Ry., bds 60 W. Main
Bonnefoi John, laborer, bds 58 Columbia
Bond A. S., engineer T. W. & W. Ry., h 155 Broadway
Bond Charles D., President Fort Wayne Nat. Bank, h cor Farefield and Creighton
Bond A. L., widow, bds Farefield ave
Bond W. J., druggist, h 190 E. Wayne
Bonner William, saw setter, h 184 W. Main
BOOKWALTER J. Agent Weed Sewing Machine, 130 Calhoun
BOOKWALTER W. S., Dentist, bds 330 Calhoun
Booth Dr. bds 231 Barr
Bookwalter Elias, bds 330 Calhoun
Bookwalter Winfield, bds 330 Calhoun
Boon James, master mechanic, h 91 E. Madison
Bookwalter Josiah, sewing machine agent, h 330 Calhoun
Boph Joseph, laborer, 42 John
Bork Michael, conductor T. W. & W. Ry., h 51 Malitta
Borgamann Christian, boatman, h 35 Lavina
Borgman, William, boatman, h 202 Ewing
Borden Jane, widow, bds 71 W. Wayne
Borden James W., lawyer, bds Hamilton House
Borneman Charles, grocery and provissions, h 98 Harrison
BOSSLER H. H., Real Estate and Insurance Agent, office over Hamilton's Bank
BOSEKER CHRISTIAN, Contractor, h 39 Brackenridge
Bostick John, (B. & Son,) h 108 E. Wayne
Bostick Emanuel, merchant tailor, h 158 E. Wayne
Bostick Eph, clerk, bds 158 E. Wayne
Bosse William, carpenter, bds 9 Buchanan

Boseker Henry, clerk, h 259 W. Jefferson
Boster Henry, mason, h 210 W. Jefferson
Bose William, laborer, h 44 Butler
BOSTICK E. & SON, Merchant tailors, 103 E Columbia
Boss Henry, traveling agent, 43 E. Main
Bosseker Charles, carpenter, h 62 McClellan
Bosler Mrs. Minnie, h 105 W. Main
Both Theodore, (Tresselt & B.,) h 100 E. Jefferson
Bottel Ernst, bds 158 Montgomery
Bott Urbin, laborer, h 56 Taylor
Bothner John, saloon, h 139 Calhoun
Bott E., laborer, h 29 Pine
Bounds James, foreman Olds & Son
Boucquard Joseph, laborer, bds 58 Columbia
Bouse N. laborer, bds 168 Holman
BOURIE LOUIS T., (of Leutz & B.,) Wholesale Wines and Liquors, corner Main and Clinton, h 11 E. Wayne
Bourie Brutus, traveling agent, h 10 E. Lewis
Bourie Desdimona, h 102 E. Lewis
Bouse L., laborer, h 168 Holman
BOWSER J. C. & CO., Fort Wayne Steam Boiler and Machine Works, Water between Calhoun and Harrison
Bowser J. C., (B. & Co.,) h 64 E. Berry
Bowser George W., laborer, h 110 Gay
Bowers Mrs. Maria, h 168 W. Washington
Bowen George, bds 113 Barr
Bowen Lorett, widow, h 113 Barr
BOWSER JEFF C., Attorney, h 104 Lafayette
Bowen William, bds 113 Barr
Bowser Augustus, fireman Pittsburgh, Ft. Wayne & Chicago Ry., h 227 Barr
Bowen Rosette, bds 113 Barr
Bowers, Edward, teamster, bds 164 Harrison
Bowers Miller, prop. Union House, 49 W. Main
Bower & Michaels, barbers, 17 W. Main
Bowers James, painter, bds 268 W. Washington
BOWEN DR. GEORGE W., h 189 Madison
Bowers Joe, well digger, h on Medtz
Bower John F., Union House, h 210 Fairfield
Bower & Miller, (Union House props,) 49 W. Main
Bowser L. book keeper, h 10 W. Water
Bowen Lavina D. W., widow, h 119 E. Washington
Bowen I. carpenter, h 204 Francis
Boyd F. T., conductor Richmond Road, h 84 Force
Boyles R. D., carpenter, h 30 Wilt
BOYD BENJAMIN F., conductor, h 212 Lafayette
BRACKENRIDGE A. M., agent T. W. & W. Ry., bds 269 W. Wayne

Brackenridge Mrs. F. A., h cor Clinton and Washington
Brackenridge E. F., clerk Pittsburgh freight office, bds cor Clinton and Washington
Brackenridge Charles S., City civil engineer, bds cor Clinton & Washington.
Brackenridge Jos. G., P. O. clerk, bds 196 Calhoun
Brackenridge T. K., h 196 Calhoun
Brackenridge E. J., clk Wabash freight office, bds 196 Calhoun
Brackenridge Robt., bds cor Clinton and Washington
Brackenridge Robt, O., bds 23 Douglas ave
BRADLEY J., Foreman Pittsburgh machine shop, h 315 Calhoun
Braener Conrad, Mfg. Boots and Shoes, h 20 Harrison
Branning Ernst, shoemaker, bds 20 Harrison
Brase Fred, teamster, h 75 W. Jefferson
Bradtmiller G. carpenter, h 59 Douglas
Brandt Charles, street buyer h, 34 McClellan
Branger C., wks Pitts shop, h 206 E Washinton
Braun Albert, baker, h cor Calhoun and Railroad
Brackman H., laborer, h 159 Madison
Bradway O. E., molder, Pitts shop, h 266 E Lewis
Brady Geo., car maker, bds 198 Madison
Brannan Julia, widow, h 35 Monroe
Bras John, laborer, bds 111 W Jefferson
Brackenridge Joseph, Att'y and Judge Criminal court, office 57 Clinton
Braun George, baker, h cor Calhoun and Railroad
Brandt Christina, widow, h 45 W Jefferson
Brake Ulrich, drayman, h on Maumee
Brackenridge Geo. W., h 23 Douglas ave
BRANDRIFF, PRESCOT & 'CO., Hardware, Stoves, Iron and Tinners' Stock, 50, 52 and 54 E Columbia
Brand Michael, h 114 Fulton
Braum Geo., bds cor Broadway and Lavina
Brauer, Sr. Conrad, shoemaker, h 148 Ewing
Bracket August, machinist Wabash shop, bds 32 Brandriff
Brauer Jr. Conrad, marble cutter, bds 148 Ewing
Brandmeyer Fred., Foreman Bowser & Co., h 168 Ewing
Bradley J. K., machinist Pitts shop, h 41 Jones
Brandt Fred., carpenter, bds 158 Harrison
Bramer Henry, teamster, h 97 Barr
Braun Jacob, blacksmith, h 192 Griffith
Braun Lewis, laborer, bds 211 Madison
Brandt Henry, molder Bass' foundry, h 161 Hanna
Brandriff A. D. (B. Prescot & Co) h 236 W Berry
Brandenburg A., prop. boarding house, h 92 Montgomery
Brandt Fred, 158 Harrison
Breuchle Henry, tanner, h 165 E Washington
Brames Crist, h 168 E Jefferson
Brames Lewis, Deputy Assessor, h 168 E Jefferson

Braking Chas., laborer, h on Dewald
Bracht Joseph, Engineer Wabash R'y., h 34 Butler
Brandenburg W. H., Fruit and Confectionery, h 116 Calhoun
Brammer Rev. Joseph H., Pastor Cathedral, h 171 Calhoun
Breymeier Henry, blacksmith, h 219 W Jefferson
Brese E. J., pedler, h 169 Jackson
Brenan Anna, bds 86 E Main
Brehm Frank, teamster, bds 186 W Main
Brenton C. F., book keeper, h 220 W Wayne
Brenton Mrs. Eliza, h 220 W Wayne
Breidenstein Mathias, carpenter, h 264 W Washington
Breidenstein S. M., clerk, bds 264 W Washington
Brecht John, Prop bakery, h 48 Columbia
Breler Lazarus, laborer, bds corner Lafayette and Wallace
Breitkrutz August, molder Bass' foundry, bds 28 Force
Breen Jas. grocery, h 16 Lewis
Brenner Geo., printer, bds 13 W Wayne
Brecht John, laborer, h 125 Harrison
Brenner David, saloon, 13 W Wayne
Brew N., engineer Pitts R'y., h 170 Francis
Breimeyer Ernst, mason, h 233 W Jefferson
Bredemeier Henry, laborer bds 52 Wells
Brening Conrad, shoemaker, h 49 W Jefferson
Breese Mrs. Lizzie h 169 Jackson
Brelsford Frank, laborer, h 141 E Washington
Breen Michael, laborer, h 14 Bass
Brewer Richard, Reporter W. U. Telegraph office bds 49 and 51 W Berry
Brehm John F. & Co., meat market, 254 Calhoun
Brehm John F. (J. F. B. & Co.,) butcher, h 254 Calhoun
Brehm John, butcher, bds 254 Calhoun
Breen Jas., groceries and provisions, 176 Calhoun
Brenton Milton H., clk Pitts freight office, 15 Madison
Bredemeier Wm., tailor, h 8 Harrison
Bricker Conrad, laborer, h 251 Webster
Brick Adam laborer, h 156 Wells
Brinsley John, master transportation Muncie Road, h 7 N Cass
Brick Mrs. Ann h 156 Wells
Brickard Conrad, engineer, h 57 Grand
Bright Wm. helper, Bass' foundry bds 161 Holman
Brighty John, brakeman, Wabash R'y. bds 59 Grand
Brighty Henry, conductor, Wabash R'y., bds 59 Grand
Brinkroeger Wm., shoemaker, h 65 High
BRIEL FRED., Prop American House Saloon, bds American House
Brins F. C., laborer, h 224 E Jefferson
Brittingham Wm. B., M. D., h 227 W Washington
Brittingham P. E., fireman, Wabash R'y., bds 227 W Washington
Brink Kate, widow, h 1 E Washington

Brinkrœger Wm., shoemaker, bds 65 High
Brimmer J. H., painter, bds Robinsion House
Briggs Nettie, widow, bds Anderson House
Brown James, stone cutter, bds 86 E. Main
Brown Charly, fireman, Wabash R'y, bds 82 Fairfield ave
Brown S. B., M. D., h 280 W. Berry
Browning Mrs. Edna, bds 218 W. Washington
Browenkent D., shoemaker, h 14 Nirdlinger
Brooks Wm., carpenter, h 120 Union
Brother Irenius bds St. Joseph Academy
Brown Jane, widow, h 43 W. Main
Brown Wm. R., carpentes, h 137 Force
Brobst Jacob, conductor, Pitts R'y, h 99 Gay
Brown E. F., bds Robinson House
Broderick Thomas, laborer, bds 99 W. Water
Broderick Michael laborer, bds 99 W. Water
Brother John, bds St. Joseph Academy
Brother Theophilus, bds St. Joseph Academy
Brother Nesarius, bds St. Joseph Academy
Brown Mathew, saloon, h 243 Calhoun
Brown S. B., dentist, cor Main and Court
Brown Mrs. Allen, h 157 Van Buren
Bronson Andrew A., saloon and billiard hall, 10 and 12 W. Berry
Brown A., cook, h 78 Barr
Brown Geo. F., carpenter, h on Pickway road
Brockerman, Jacob R., plasterer, h 49 Division
Brooks M. H., plasterer, h 249 W. Washington
Brooks T. M., foreman trunk manufactory, h 14 Fairfield ave
Brocking Richard, laborer, h 32 Lavina
Brother Ephraim, bds St. Joseph Academy
Brother Placidus, bds St. Joseph Academy
Brown Jno., blacksmith, h 152 E. Wayne
Brown Matthias, engineer oil mill, bds 129 E. Lewis
Brown Wm., wagon maker (Olds & Son), bds 79 Holman
Brown Jno., cook, wks Aveline House
Brown James, brakeman, Pitts R'y, bds 220 Lafayette
Brophy Wm., blacksmith, bds 25 Barr
Brown John, machinist, Wabash shop, bds 116 Chicago
Brossard John, blacksmith, wks Pitts shop, h 82 Wells
Brossard Geo., blacksmith, h 82 Wells
Brossard Wm., laborer, h 24 Clark
Brown August C., laborer h 42 Fifth
Brooks Henry, carpenter, h W Jefferson
Brown Jas. laborer, Pitts shop, h 216 Lafayette
Brockerman, Lem., brakeman, Pitts R'y, bds 49 Division
Brown A., blacksmith, bds 152 E. Wayne
Brown Arbaham, cook, bds 93 Calhoun
Brown Jno., (Hall & B.,) barber, h 189 Calhoun

BROWN SENECA B., 100 W. Berry
Brown Jno., cook, bds Aveline House
Brooker H. H., traveling agent, bds Central Hotel
Brown I. D., M. D., bds Aveline House
Brown Margaret, widow, h 73 Grand
Brown John, wagon maker, shop 152 Clay h 152 E. Wayne
Brown Alex., wagon maker, bds 152 E. Wayne
Brown Jacob blacksmith, wks 3 Clay
Brossard Geo., blacksmith, h cor Main and Fulton
Brooks Wm. H., M. D., h 110 W. Main
Brown Mrs. Flora, h 116 Chicago
Brown Frank, brakeman, Wabash R'y, bds 17 Taylor
Brown Jane, widow, h 43 W. Main
Brunner Adam, brewer, bds on Taylor
Brucher Michael, policeman h 62 Nelson
Brunn E., laborer, h 28 West
Bruman P., fireman, Wabash R'y, h 247 Webster
Brunner John, shoemaker, h 47 Lavina
Brucher Jacob, stone cutter, h 219 W. Jefferson
Brush Herbert, engineer, Wabash R'y, bds cor Webster st and Douglas avenue
BRUEBACH, G. T., M. D., h cor Washington and Van Buren
Brubaker Michael, saloon, h 42 Wells
Bruns Christian, Sr., h 332 Harrison
Bruns Wm., carpenter, Pitts car shop, h 69 Charles
Brunett Jno., laborer, h 57 Langohr
Brunett Andrew, painter, bds 57 Langohr
Brunner John, laborer, h 78 West
Bruebach Mrs. Emma, h 77 Calhoun, up stairs
Brunka Conrad cigar maker, bds 148 Calhoun
Bruns Christian, Jr., carpenter Pitts shop, h 332 Harrison
Brune Eberhard, laborer, h 190 Griffith
Brumley Chas., baggage man, Muncie road, bds 40 Wells
Brunett Chas laborer, bds 57 Langohr
Bryant Mrs. Annie, h 137 Wallace
Bryant Mary, widow, h 45 Monroe
Bryant Geo. W., laborer, h 45 Monroe
Bryant Alvin, tinner, bds 120 Lafayette
Bryant Elisha, molder, Bass' foundry, bds cor Calhoun and Wallace
Bryant Jas., dealer in fish, h 76 Barr
Bryant Wm. H., h 131 Griffith
Bryant Jos., laborer, h 100 Smith
Bryant Jno., clk., bds 76 Barr
Buck Wm., h 39 Nirdlinger
Bucker Fred, cooper, h 493 E. Washington
Buck Chas., conductor Richmond Railroad, h 188 Hanna
Buchtman Christian, laborer, h 74 Wallace
Buckwalter Lewis, machinist, Pitts shop h 134 Harrison

Buechel Louis, carriage trimmer, h 89 E. Main
Buechel Louis, Jr., painter, bds 87 E. Main
Buck Deitrich, tailor, h 290 W. Jefferson
Bucher Benj., teamster, bds 164 Harrison
Buche Henry, carpenter, Pitts shop, h 298 Hanna
Buckley Henry, blacksmith, Pitts shop, bds 22 Baker
Buck Thomas, foreman, Pitts R'y shops, bds 13 Maumee
Buckheit Adam, carpenter, Pitts shop h 20 Hood
BUCKLES JOHN H., Prop Robinson House, on Harrison
Buchman Wm., carpenter, Pitts. shop, h 131 Holman
Buchfink Mrs. S., h 67 High
Buck Wilson S., agt., h 105 W. Jefferson
Buddemeyer Ernst, carpenter, h 20 McClellan
Budde Herman laborer, h 69 Buchanan
Buerlager G., drayman, h 159 E. Jefferson
Buhler Ferdinand, school teacher, h 111 Griffith
Buhre Nicholas, painter, bds Exchange Hotel
Bulger Martin S., traveling salesman, h 151 Griffith
Bulow Jno., laborer, h 108 High
Bullerman Henry, h 284 W. Jefferson
Bullerman Wm., laborer, bds 83 W. Washington
Buloe Fred, laborer, h 168 Holman
Buuck Wm., carpenter, Pitts shop h 10 Hough
Bundel Isaac, h 253 E. Lewis
Bundel Martin, eng., Ft. W., M. and C. R'y, h 253 E. Lewis
Buuck Conrad shoemaker, h 254 Broadway
Buuck Conrad, shoemaker, shop 154 Calhoun
Buuck Fred, laborer, h 13 Wall
Burt Chas., molder, h 232 E. Jefferson
Burlager Wm., laborer, h 210 E. Washington
Burris Jno., carpenter, h 82 Hanna
Burkholder Joseph, (furniture manufacturer), 80 Pearl
Burgess Henry, office over 1st Nat. Bank
Burland Robt., machinist, Murray & Co's shop, bds 14 Chicago
Burgess Benj., blacksmith, Wabash shop, bds 28 Lavina
Burgeot John, wks Pitts blacksmith shop, h 241 Barr
Burns Patrick, machinist, Wabash shop, h 41 William
Burhenn Edward, butcher, h 104 Calhoun
Burkas Jno. A., clerk, h 77 E. Water
Buret John, laborer, h 87 W. Water
Burgess Francis, machinist, Pitts shop, h 28 Lavina
Burns Patrick, h 16 Bass
Burnes James, laborer, h 11 Bass
Burke Edward, pedler, h 81 Buchanan
Burgoyne John, molder, Bass' foundry, bds 274 Hanna
Burkas John A., clk h 77 Water
Burgess David, carpenter, h 120 Union
Burtic John, brakeman, Saginaw Railroad, bds 120 W. Water

Burbeck Wm., machinist, Wabash shop, h 64 Butler
Burdelman Ernst, expressman, h 1 High
Burk Geo. J., carpet weaver, h W. Walnut
Burgeot Chas., bds 241 Barr
Burington Chancey, eng., Pitts R'y., h 149 Holman
Burlage Geo., expressman, h 137 E. Washington
BURKHOLDER JOS. (Emrick & B.), h 130 W. Jefferson
Bursley Gilbert E., Supt. Street Railroad, h S of Fairfield ave
Burkholder J. H., wood turner, bds 130 W. Jefferson
Busch Anthony, wagon maker, h 365 E. Lewis
Busch John, carpenter, h 247 W. Washington
Buschman Joseph, laborer, bds 11 Force
Buschelman, Ferdinand, h 11 Force
Bushman Mrs. Lizzie, h 141 Lafayette
Bushman Wm., clk., bds 141 Lafayette
Bussa Wm. (B. & Tegtmeyer), saw mill, h 160 Ewing
Butler Geo., laborer, h N. Harrison
Butler John, Ashery, N of canal, bet Lafayette and Clinton
Butler Wm. (book keeper, O. & S.), bds Hamilton House
Butler Mrs. Mary E., h 224 W. Jefferson
Butler Allen, bds 17 Taylor
Butler John, laborer, bds 233 Broadway
Butler Mrs. Kate, h 233 Broadway
Butt Wm., watchman Bass' foundry, h 111 Force
Butler Jas., barber, bds 233 Broadway
Buxton Geo., fireman, Wabash R'y, bds 82 Fairfield ave
Byeron Jacob, machinist, Pitts shop, bds 231 Barr

Cac James A., Sawyer, h 82 Fairfield
Cady Fred, brakeman P., Ft. W. & C. Ry., bds 49 Baker
Caffry John, laborer, h 259 Webster
Calhoun George, brakeman P., Ft. W. & C. Ry., bds 13 Maumee
Calbacher Adam, laborer, h 65 Force
Catliar Lucy, widow, bds 105 W. Berry
Campbell Charles, laborer, h 47 Buchanan
Campbell Charles, brakeman P., Ft. W. & C. Ry., bds 24 Lasselle
Campbell Joseph, Pittsburgh Coppersmith shop, h 47 Buchanan
Campbell George, brakeman P., Ft. W. & C. Ry., h 24 Lasselle
CAMPBELL I. W., General Business Agent, (Carrier & C.,) h 160 E. Berry
Campbell John G., carpenter, bds 193 Barr
Campbell Charles, laborer, h 166 Ewing
Campbell Jesse, laborer, bds Bloomingdale Hotel
CAMPBELL HARRY, Foreman Pittsburg Blacksmith shop, h 157 Montgomery

Campbell Daniel, blacksmith Pittsburgh shop, bds 157 Montgomery
Campbell Daniel, Foreman Wabash blacksmith shop, h 53 Brackenridge
Campbell James, laborer, h 106 Ewing
Campbell Mrs. Sarah, h 292 W. Jefferson
Campbell Thomas, Moulder, (J. H. Bass,) bds 81 Holman
Canida William, brakeman T., W. &. W. Ry., bds 17 Taylor
Canida August, Plasterer, h 82 Smith
CARRIER A. H., Notary, Real Estate and Ins. Agent, office in P. O. Building on Court, h 178 E. Berry
Cartwright L. F., butcher, h 77 Holman
Cartwright John F., laborer, h 71 Baker
Cartwright John, conductor P., Ft. W. &. C. Ry., bds 63 Baker
Cartwright Ely, brakeman P., Ft. W. & C. Ry., h 41 Jones
Cartwright Frank, butcher, h 139 Griffith
Cartwright George, laborer, bds 71 Baker
Cartwright John F., Jr., laborer, h 73 Baker
Cartwright Charles, Agent, h 63 Baker
Carroll John, laborer, bds 24 Colerick
Carroll James, blacksmith, bds 25 Barr
Carroll Elias, Engineer P., Ft. W. & C. Ry., bds 96 Montgomery
Carroll Vinandy, carpenter at car shop, h 24 Colerick
Carroll Patrick, laborer, h 96 W. Water
Carroll Patrick, Night Watchman P., Ft. W. & C. Ry., h 102 Maumee
CARSON W. W., Attorney, office over P. O., h E. Berry
CARNAHAN, SKINNER & CO., Wholesale Boot and Shoe Store, 30-32 E. Main
Carnahan William L. (C. Skinner & Co.), Boots and Shoes, h 176 W. Washington
Carey M., Salesman, h 182 E. Jefferson
Carey Charles, Fireman T., W. & &. Ry., bds 4 Colerick
Carey Mrs. Sarah, h 171 Clinton
Carey Adolphus, laborer, bds 341 W. Washington
Carey Edward, (Root & Co.), bds 171 Clinton
Carey M. J., Painter, bds Aker House
Carey William, Student, bds 236 W. Jefferson
CAREY E. D., Attorney at Law, office 22 Court, up stairs, h 20 Fairfield ave
Carey Frank, laborer, h 24 Lasselle
Carey Thomas, laborer, h 38 Bass
Carter Edward, laborer, bds cor Lewis and Webster
Carter William, mfg. Hot Air Furnaces, Copper, Sheet Iron Ware, 25 W. Columbia
Carman Calib, Machinist P., Ft. W. & C. Ry., h 348 Calhoun
Carnes ———, h 51 Barr
Carpenter Charles, brakeman T., W. & W. Ry., h 305 Harrison
Carpenter D. L., carpenter, h 115 W. Washington
Carpenter Warren, Fireman T., W. & W. Ry., bds 305 Harrison
Carpenter Ernest, laborer, bds 58 Columbia

Carmeny Joseph, Fireman P. Ft. W. & C. Ry., h 313 Lafayette
Cares Charles, laborer, h 206 Hanna
Carrigan James, Machinist Pittsburgh Shop, bds 71 Douglass ave
Carver Kahn K., Engineer T. W. & W. Ry., h 73 Dawson
Carder H. W., wheelmaker, h 147 E. Jefferson
Carney Joseph, Machinist Wabash shop, bds 23 Grand
Carl Albert, Trunkmaker, bds 171 Madison
Carll George S., Undertaker, h 124 E. Berry
Carl John, Foreman Tobacco Factory, bds 94 E. Berry
Carl Patrick, laborer, h 262 Calhoun
Carl John, bricklayer, h 226 E. Washington
Carl Phillip, brakeman P. Ft. W. & C. Ry., bds 264 Calhoun
Carns James, Machinist Pittsburgh Shop, h 31 Hood
Carvic Isaac M., Moulder Bass shop, h 130 Madison
Castle Charles E., laborer, h 271 Hanna
Caskey M. D., laborer, bds 19 Baker
Case Frank, laborer, bds 38 Force
Case W. W., (Humphrey & C.,) Oil Mill, h 219 W. Wayne
Case August, Fireman T. W. & W. Ry., bds 402 Calhoun
CASSO FRANK, Saloon, 36 Barr.
Cannan John K., Machinist Wabash shop, h 61 Gordon
CENTLIVRE CHARLES L., Prop French Brewery, between Feeder and St. Joe River, 1 mile north of city
Center John W., Engineer at Clark and Rhinesmiths, h 61 Mallitta
CENTRAL HOTEL, O'Conell Brothers props., 20-22 E. Berry
Certia Peter, (Eder, C. & Co.,) Brewery, bds Bloomingdale Brewery
Challenger Joseph W., Grocer, 70 Barr
Chambers William, clerk, bds 120 Lafayette
Chamberlain Henry, h 40 E. Jefferson
Chamberlain William H., clerk, bds 40 E. Jefferson
Chamberlain Thomas, Dealer in Fruit and Candy, h 25 W. Washington
Chamberlain Porter, Machinist (at Bass') h 81 Butler
Chamberlain Mrs. Sarah, h 165 Clinton
Chamberlain James, bds 165 Clinton
Chamberlain Richard, Painter, h 163 Clinton
Chapman F., Druggist, bds 82 W. Berry
Chapman B. W., Engineer T. W. & W. Ry., h 277 W. Washington
Chapman Catharine, widow, h 86 Calhoun, up stairs
Chapman Francis, Accountant, h 139 Griffith
Chapman Nathaniel, Engineer Ft. W. M. & C. Road, h 19 N. Cass
Chapman Joe, Fireman T. W. & W. Ry., h 22 W. Jefferson
Chase William H., brakeman P. Ft. W. & C. Ry., bds 220 Lafayette
Chancey Charles, blacksmith, h 51 E. Water
Chancey J. B., blacksmith, h 221 E. Water
Chancey, C. & F., blacksmith and Wagonmakers shop, cor Clinton and
Chancey Frank, blacksmith, h 51 E. Water
Cherry Frank, boilermaker, h 111 E. Madison
Cherry William, boilermaker, Pittsburgh shop, h 128 Clay

Cheviron H., Machinist Pittsburgh shop, h 36 Hough
Cheviron Francis, laborer, h Lillie Ad
Childs Joseph, Express Agt. Ft. W., M. & C. Road, bds 122 W. Jefferson
Chittenden E. L., h 69 W. Berry
Christian John, clerk, h 36 Butler
Christie John B., Machinist, wks Kerr Murry's, h 3 Dawson
CLARK JOSEPH M., Merchant Tailor, Store cor Berry and Clinton, bds Aveline House
Clark Wilson, Transportation Master P. Ft. W. & C. Ry., bds 316 Calhoun
Clark Anna, widow, h 82 Barr
Clark George R., clerk, bds Central Hotel
Clark James, Engineer T. W. & W. Ry., bds 22 Baker
Clark Frederick, Fireman T. W. & W. Ry., h 46 W. Lewis
Clark Joseph, Helper Pittsburgh Round House, bds 198 Lafayette
Clark Walter, conductor P. Ft. W. & C. Ry., bds 316 Calhoun
Clark John, Hackman, bds 94 E. Berry
Clark John H., Dealer in Lumber, h 111 Wayne
Clark Lewis laborer, h 112 Hanna
Clark Victoria, widow, h 5 Brandiff
Clark George, barkeeper, bds 92 Calhoun
Clark Theodore, laborer, bds 109 W. Berry
Clark Joseph, h 138 W. Berry
Clark Sarah, widow, bds 77 Butler
Clark Charles, laborer, bds 79 Holman
Clark Frank, Engineer T. W. & W. Ry., h 67 Grand
Clark George, brakeman T. W. & W. Ry., h 165 Fairfield
Clark Edward, conductor T. W. & W. Ry., h 77 Baker
Clark J. W., Master Transportation on P. Ft. W. & C. Ry., bds Harmon House
Clapp Andrew, Fireman G. R. & I. Road,
Clare Michael, laborer, h 88 Barthold
Clarkson T. F., book Keeper, h 132 W. Wayne
Clauss John, Shoemaker, bds 180 Broadway
Clauss John C., Shoemaker, h 180 Broadway
Claughff Rebecca, Widow, h 146 Maumee
Clear Robert, brakeman P. Ft. W. & C. Ry., bds 160 Holman
Clemment William, laborer, h 18 Brandriff
Clerenger D. R., clerk, h 122 Fulton
Clugson Samuel, carpenter, bds Union House
Coburn Fred, night watch, bds Fox House
Cochrane John, (C., Humphrey & Co.,) h 16 Edasll
Cochrane H. W. engineer, bds 70 E Madison
Cochrane Mrs. Margarett, h 43 Wall
Cochrane James, contractor, h 240 E. Jefferson
Cochrane, Humphrey, & Co., Door, Blind and Sash Mfg., west end Pearl

Cody Maurice, Dealer in Ice, h 13 Barr
Cody Thomas, bds 13 Barr
Cody John H., clerk, bds 13 Barr
Cofman James, bds Aker House
Cogan Phillip, wks woolen Factory, h 100 Columbia
COLERICK, W. G., & H., Attorneys at Law, offices 22 Court, opposite Court House
Colerick Mrs. M., widow, bds 85 E. Jefferson
Colerick Thomas W., Notary Poblic, bds 88 E. Berry
Colerick Walpole, Lawyer, bds 88 E. Berry
Colerick David H., Lawyer, bds 88 E. Berry
Colerick Henry, Lawyer, h 88 E. Berry
Colerick Ed. F., h 401 Broadway
Colerick John A., h 85 Jefferson
Coling Peter, Shoemaker, h 338 Harrison
Collins James, wks at H. Trentman & Co., bds 235 E. Wayne
Coleman John, wks Pittsburgh shops, h 91 Montgomery
Collins Daniel, laborer, bds 20 Chicago
Colson Edward, Saw Mfg., h 333 W. Main
Collins James, laborer, bds 18 Bass
Collar Mrs. L., h 21 N. Cass
Collar Melvin, laborer, bds at 21 N. Cass
Collins George, laborer, h 70 W. Walnut
Cole Samuel D., carpenter, h 291 W. Main
Cole Benjamin, brakeman T., W. & W. Ry., h 92 Chicago
Collins Dennis, laborer, h 58 Baker
Collens John, laborer, h 43 Baker
Compston R. H., clerk, bds 49-51 W. Berry
Compston C. B., Telegraph Operator, bds 49-51 W. Berry
Comincavish Felix, Machinist, Pittsburgh shop, h 25 Holman
Commero Otto, printer, bds 25 Broadway
Comstock John, brickmaker, h cor Hanover and Washington
Compton Charles, brakeman P., Ft. W. & C. Ry., bds 245 Calhoun
Congdon J. E., Agt., h 50 E. Washington
Connier William, blacksmith Pittsburgh shop, h 24 Baker
Connett Martin, blacksmith Pittsburgh shop, h 39 Force
Conklin John, Engineer T., W. & W. Ry., h 136 Jackson
Conn Harry, bds Phillips House, 107 E. Columbia
Conrad Charles, Wood Carver, bds 130 E. Wayne
Congress Alferd, brakeman P., Ft. W. & C. Ry. bds 98 Montgomery
Connally James, laborer, bds 25 Colerick
Conway Mary, widow, h 17 Bass
Conklin Mrs. Elizabeth, h 311 W. Jefferson
Conklin Mrs. Francis, h 311 W. Jefferson
Condon John, bar keeper, bds 93 Calhoun
Conrod M. C., laborer Pittsburgh shop, h 94 Maumee
Conklin Carry, Engineer T., W. & W. Ry., h 184 Henry
Conklin Sidney, fireman Ft. W., M. & C. Road, bds 103 W. Main

Conner John. laborer, h 251 Webster
Conners Patrick, blacksmith Wabash shop, bds 6 Kansas
Conrad John, laborer, h 43 John
Conners Michael, driver Mechanics' Steam Fire Engine, h 60 Clinton
COOMS & Co., Dealers in Iron, Steel, and Heavy Hardware, 38-40-42 E. Main
Coombs Joseph, bds 53 W. Wayne
Coombs Mrs. Elizabeth, h 202 W. Jefferson
Coombs John M., (C. & Co.,) iron mchts., h 263 W. Wayne
Coombs William H., (Coombs, Miller & Bell,) h 53 W. Wayne
COOMS, MILLER & BELL, Attorneys, office 32 E. Berry
Cook C. O., machinist Pittsburgh shop, bds 19 Holman
Cook C., machinist, bds 158 Harrison
Cooper C., drayman, h 25 Wert
Cooper Winfield S., machinist Wabash shop, bds 26 Wert
Cook John R., laborer, bds 231 Barr
Cook E. A., clerk, bds Harrison
Cooper Mrs. E., h 182 W. Washington
Coolican Pat., laborer, h 19 Poplar
Cook Newton, brakeman, T., W. & W. Ry., bds 291 Harrison
Cook Marion, widow, h 291 Harrison
Cook Charles W., clerk Pittsburgh Freight office, bds 291 Harrison
Cook James, fireman T., W. & W. Ry., bds 59 Grand
Cook James, fireman T., W. & W. Ry., bds 73 Grand
Cook Albert, school teacher, h 338 Broadway
Cooper Benjamin, fireman P., Ft. W. & C. Ry., bds 42 Chicago
Corey Joseph A., blacksmith, h 100 Montgomery
Corcoran Thomas, teamster, bds 86 Lewis
Corneille August, h 38 Duck
Corneille John B., clerk, h 47 Water
Corbel Charles, blacksmith, bds 50 W. Main
Corwin Mrs. Teddy A., h 202 Fairfield
Corneille Francis, clerk, h 70 E. Madison
Corcoran Pat., boarding house, 23 Grand
Cosler John, tailor, bds 15 N. Cass
Costilo John, bds 63 W. Water
Cothrell Jared, dining hall and feed yard, 12 Clinton, h 171 E. Washington
Cothrell Mose, teamster, h 94 E. Berry
Cothrell Albert, hackman, bds 94 E. Berry
Cothrell Charles, brakeman, h 152 E. Washington
Cothrell William, laborer, bds 171 E. Washington
Cothrell Mrs. Ann, h 152 E. Washington
Cottingham William, dealer in hot air furnaces and gas fixtures, shop 67 E. Main, h 73 E. Berry
Cottingham & Co., mfg. hot air furnaces, 67 E. Main
Cottingham Samuel, (at Cottingham & Co.,) h 67 E. Main
Courtney L. F., umberella dealer and repairer, h 119 Calhoun

County James, laborer, bds Bloomingdale Hotel
Cour Eugene, fireman Gas House, h 19 Buchanan
Cour Frank, blacksmith, bds 19 Buchanan
Covert Cranson, conductor Ft. W. J. & S. Road, bds 63 W. Wash
Cowan John, wks Pittsburgh shop, bds cor Montgomery
Cox John, h 183 Hanna
CRANE GEORGE D., Attorney at Law, h 56 Douglas ave
Crane William M. Jr., clerk, bds 91 Ewing
Crane L. J., painter, h 215 Hanna
Crane George B., attorney, h 56 Douglass ave
Crane William M., attorney at law, h 91 Ewing
Crane Calvin, book keeper, h 144 W. Wayne
Cran Charles Jr., moulder Bass foundry, h 85 Lillie
Cran Edward L., clerk, bds 93 W. Wayne
Cran Robert, moulder at Bass foundry, bds 398 Calhoun
Cran John, carpenter, h 221 Barr
Cran Charles, tailor, h 398 Calhoun
Craig James, harness maker, bds 46 E. Berry
Craig Samuel H., switchman P. Ft. W. & C. Ry., yard, bds 27 Grand
Cragg Thomas, wheel maker, h 175 Lafayette
Cragg Charles, weaver, h 68 Lasselle
Crauser Victor, laborer, bds 58 E. Columbia
Crabbs Cyrus, agt, h 162 Madison
Crance William, laborer, h on Brackenridge
Crawford George T., laborer, bds 208 W. Main
Crawford Joseph, engineer, h 68 E. Madison
Cranston Mrs. Alice, h 58 Douglass
Crance James, laborer, h 104 Gay
Cratzer John, clerk, h 38 Fifth
Cramer Lucinda, widow, h 332 Calhoun
Cramer David, engineer P. Ft. W. & C. Ry., bds 332 Calhoun
Cramer Martin, laborer, h 28 John
Cretzer John, clerk, h Bloomingdale
Cretzer L, broom maker, bds 315 Harrison
Cretzer Elizabeth, widow, h 315 Harrison
Crissenbury Peter S. prop. Phillips House, 107 E, Columbia
Crissenbury Willis W., bds Phillips House
Christ Joseph, shoemaker shop, 155 E. Berry
Critz Henry, brakeman, P. Ft. W. & C. Ry., bds 16 Chicago
Crighton William, machinist, (K. Murry,) h 49 Brackenridge
Critey Daniel, laborer, bds 25 Broadway
Crimmins Patrick, h 51 Wilt
Critchet H. A., brakeman, P. Ft. W. & C. Ry., h 165 Clinton
Cribber Augustus, clerk, bds 22 Madison
Croxton W. F., bds Robinson House
Crocker Wesley, bds 96 Montgomery
Crocker, Israel, engineer, h 96 Montgomery
Crosby George J., machinist, Wabash shop, h 15 Henry

Crosby Mrs. Mary, h 295 W. Jefferson
Crosby William, machinist, Pittsburgh shop, bds 295 W. Jefferson
Crosby Marion, clerk, bds 201 W. Main
Cromwell Joseph W., h 236 W. Wayne
Cromwell Joseph C., clerk, bds 236 W. Wayne
Cruse D. A., painter, h 148 Fairfield
Crumley Gorham, engineer P. Ft. W. & C. Ry., h 42 Chicago
Crumley Jerome, engineer P. Ft. W. & C. Ry., h 31 Grand
Cull Catharine, widow, h 27 Taylor
Cull Edward, laborer, h 94 Chicago
Culberly George, moulder at Bass, h 41 Baker
Culbertson John, fireman P. Ft. W. & C. Ry., bds 151 Barr
Cummings Thomas J. T., model baker patentee, h 29 Grand
Cummings Jerry, brakeman P. Ft. W. & C. Ry., h 170 Wallace
Cummings George labores, bds 264 Calhoun
Cummings Judith L., widow, prop. Pensylvania House, 264 Calhoun
Cumpston D. B., widow, bds 49-51 W. Berry
Cummer Albert, machinist, h 103 W. Washington
Cumpston C. T., h 49-51 W. Berry
Cumminsky John, wks P. Ft. W. & C. Ry., bds 152 E. Wayne
Cummings Nathaniel, watchman P. Ft. W. & C. Ry., bds 19 Baker
Cunningham John, carpenter, h 107 Wilt
Cunningham John, carpenter, h cor College & Wells
Current S. S., laborer, bds 42 Butler
CURRIER CHAS., Manager W. U. Telegraph office, h 168 Griffith
Currier Charles H. telegraph operator, 6 E. Berry
Curry John, finisher, wks Hattersley, bds 49 Grand
Curry Michael, brakeman, bds 49 Grand
Curry Frank, laborer, h 49 Grand
Curtis John F. blacksmith, (Bass foundry,) bds 150 Griffith
Curtis M. E. (clerk at Bass foundry,) bds 347 Hanna
Curtis Martin, blacksmith Pitsburgh shop, h 347 Hanna
Curtis J. J., Auditor's office clerk, bds 347 Hanna
Curtis John F., clerk at Bass shop, bds 150 Grffith
Curtis F. clerk, h 95 Ewing
Curley John, fireman P. Ft. W. & C. Ry., bds 22 Baker
Cushing Timothy, bds 26 Wallace
Cushing Michael Jr., moulder, bds 16 Wallace
Cushing Michael, laborer, h 26 Wallace
Custer Edward, laborer, bds 145 Broadway
Cutshall Joseph, wks Pitsburgh Round House, h 103 Wilt

D

Dahl Chas., baker, bds 62 E Main
Daily Jas. W., clk, h 15 Sturgis
Daily Daniel, lab wks Bass' foundry, bds 179 Hanna

Dailey Chas. E., mach Wabash shop, bds Fulton
Dailey Mrs. Laura A., h Fulton
Dailey Thomas, lab, h 140 Barr
Dailey Simon, h 247 Webster
Dailey Jno., lab, bds 332 W. Main
Dailey Andrew, trunk maker, bds Steuben House
Daim H., fruits and confectionery, cor Columbia and Clinton
Dale Daniel, shoemaker, bds 170 Lafayette
Dalton Edmond, carpenter, h 32 Wilt
Dalton Jas., lab, h 18 Bass
Dalton Timothy, lab, h 19 Colerick
Daly Wm., lab, h 12 W. Washington
Daly T. C., peddler, bds Central Hotel
Dammier Wm., h 61 Douglas ave
Dammeyer Henry, blacksmith, Pitts shop, h 201 Ewing
Dammon J. M., lab, bds Fairfield ave
Dan Fred., carpenter, h 108 Douglasave
Daniels H. A., clk., Coombs & Co., h 117 E. Wayne
Darrow, P. Mrs., widow, bds Fairfield ave
Darrow Geo., (Snyder & D.) h cor First and Harrison
Darker Martha, widow, h 77 Butler
Daugherty Thomas, trunk maker, bds 39 Water
Daugherty Marcella, widow, bds 92 E. Main
Davenport L. C., drug clk., bds Mayer House
Davenport David, lab, bds 88 W. Water
DAVIS, A., Manager Howe Sewing Machine Co., 72 Calhoun
Davidson Jas., lab, h 18 Walnut
Davidson Wm., mach, Wabash shop, h 49 Locust
Davis Ames, agt Howe Sewing Machine, h 148 E. Lewis
Davis Wm., Mason, bds 14 W. Jefferson
Davis Wm. H., (Davis & Bro., Book Binders,) h 49 E. Jefferson
Davis Alfred A., carpenter Pitts shop, h 125 Monroe
Davis H., eng Pitts R'y, h 224 E. Jefferson
Davis E. T., clk bds 197 E. Lewis
Davis Byron, painter, Pitts shop, h 212 Lewis
Davis J. C., freight agt. Pitts R'y, h 117 Hanna
Davis & Bro., Book Binders, Miller's block, up stairs
Davis Joseph, turner, bds Steuben House
Davis Chas., h 75 Webster
Davis W. T., eng., h 308 E. Wayne
Davis Frank, mach Wabash shop, bds 213 Fairfield ave
Davis H. M., lab, bds W. Jefferson
Davis Geo., painter, h 32 Monroe
Davis P. D., clk, bds 148 E. Lewis
Davis Villroy, agt model baker, h 29 Grand
Davis Samuel T., speculator, h 65 Langhohr
Davis Frank, lab, bds 14 W. Jefferson
Davis Chas., (Davis & Bro., Book Binders,) bds 49 E. Jefferson

Dawson John, bds 105 W. Berry
Dawson C. N., Cashier Merchants' Nat. Bank, h 244 W. Berry
Dawson Michael, well digger, h 231 Lafayette
Dawson Chas., bds 231 Lafayette
Dayton Wm., painter, h 120 W. Wayne
Day Henry, cigar maker, bds 99 E. Washington
Day Christoff, painter, h 99 E. Washington
Day Henry, painter, h 137 W. Water
Deak Herman, lab, bds 223 W. Washington
Deak John H., eng., h 323 W. Washington
Deam Alexander, huxter, h 16 Madison
Decker Oliver, shoemaker, wks 32 E. Main, bds Exchange Hotel
Decker John, lab, h 287 E. Wayne
Deeter John W., eng., J. & S. Railroad, h 322 Calhoun
Deeter Jas. M., eng., Pitts R'y., h 150 W. Wayne
Degrattery James, clk, Morgan & Beach, h 90 E. Lewis
De Groff S. V., clk, bds Robinson House
Degitz Chas., cigar maker, h 93 Barr
Degitz Chas., Sr., cigar manufacturer, h 15 Colerick
Degitz Henry, cigar maker, bds 15 Colerick
Degitz Chas., Jr., cigar maker, bds 15 Colerick
Degan Patrick, wks Pitts shop, h 247 Clay
Dehart Abraham, lab, h 39 Wall
Dehart Robert, conductor Wabash R'y, h 165 Broadway
De Haven Abraham, teamster, h 331 W. Jefferson
De Haven Elizabeth, widow, bds 24 Jones
De Haven Allen, expressman, h 24 Jones
Dehne Wm., h 142 Madison
De Haven Mrs. Elizabeth, h 282 Broadway
De Haven David, printer, bds 282 Broadway
Dehne Ernst, carpenter, h 142 Madison
De Haven Harrison, wks Pitts shop, h 107 Holman
DEININGER U., Notion Store, h 161 W. Washington
Deitrich Davis, wks Olds & Son, h 237 Barr
Deininger, Jos., Sr., tailor, h 161 W. Washington
Deihl Hugh M., air brake repairer, Pitts shop, h 49 Harman
Deimer Jos., tanner, h 367 W. Main
De la Camp Jno., architect and eng., h 108 Maumee
Delzel Mrs. Elizabeth, h 173 W. Jefferson
Dellingham A. J., turner, h 23 Baker
Delano Thomas, lab, h 16 Sturges
Denio Mrs. C., hair dresser, 12 E. Columbia
Denny Frances, widow, 223 E. Jefferson
Denter Michael, stone cutter, bds 105 High
Denney Geo., clk, bds 21 and 23 E. Main
Denner Benjamin, switchman Muncie Railroad, h 188 W. Main
Denter Jno. M., tailor, h 105 High
Dennis Anthony, brakeman, Wabash R'y, bds 5 Bass

Depner Geo., clk, 10 E Berry
Depew S. Ann, widow, h 148 Madison
Depler G. W., conductor, Pitts R'y, h 182 Jackson
Deppen Augustus, bds 12 W Main
Derome Soloman, lab h 88 E Main
Despres Victor, lab h 73 Lasselle
Dessauer Louis, h 90 W Main,
DESSAUER L. & CO., Manufact'r of, and Dealer in Havana and Domestic Cigars, 23 Calhoun
De Turk L., blacksmith, bds 10 Harrison
De Turk Henry, lab, h 14 Melitta
Devaux Frank, wood turner, lab, h 52 Lasselle
Devaux Xavier, lab, h 23 Lasselle
Deveny Martin, lab, h 76 Baker
DE WALD GEO. & CO., Dry Goods Store, 1 Columbia
De Wald Henry, stoves and tinware, 36 Clinton
De Wald Geo. W., merchant, (D. & Co.,) h cor De Wald and Hanna
De Wald Frank, lab, bds 31 Force
Dewald Henry, tinner, h 19 Fairfield
Dewald Michael, lab, bds 31 Force
Dewald Loenard, shoemaker, h 281 E. Washington
Dewald George, h 130 Fairfield
Dewald Anthony, clk, bds 130 Fairfield
Dewald Nicholas, Grocery and Saloon, 28 Clinton, h 404 Calhoun
DeWitt Laura Mrs., bds 113 E. Main
Detzer Martin, Druggist, bds 56 Douglas ave
Dial E., fireman, Wabash R. R., h 17 Taylor
Dicke Henry, clk, bds 38 W. Jefferson
Dickmeier William (Dickmeier & Lausman), Grocer, bds 109 W. Water
Dick Daniel, eng G. R. & I. R. R., h 85 Butler
Dickenson Robert, Telegrapher, Wabash Office, bds 18 Colerick
DIDIER JOSEPH C., dealer in Groceries, Provisions and Liquors, h 66 E. Columbia
Didier Francis, Grocery and Provision Store, cor Barr and Columbia
DIDIER JOS. C., Groceries and Provisions, 66 E. Columbia
Dierstein Christian, grocer, h 4 Fairfield ave
Dierstein Harry, carpenter, h 336 Harrison
Diers Henry, fireman, Wabash R. R., bds 28 Locust
Diebold Joseph, lab, h 275 E. Washington
Diedrich Jacob, lab, h 142 Fairfield
Dierstein Christine Mrs., h 115 Fairfield
Dierstein Anton, wagon maker, h 37 Wall
Diem Chas., Saloon, 127 Calhoun
Diem Christian, h 135 Calhoun
Dierstein Conrad, grocer, h —— Broadway
Dierstein Samuel, carpenter, h 36 Williams
Diether Louis, book-keeper, bds 128 Griffith
Diether John (H. & Co.), harness maker, bds 128 Griffith

Diether Chas., lab, h 128 Griffith
Dierstein Anton, wagon maker, cor W. Main and Ewing
Dierkes F. W., basket maker, h 74 Barthold
Diffendorfer Benjamin O., machinist Pitts shop, h 187 Barr
Dignan Lawrence, switchman Pitts yard, h 90 E. Lewis
Dignan Rosette, widow, h 79 Holman
Dillon Floyd, machinist Pitts shop, bds 153 W. Washington
Dillon Mrs. Ann, h 153 W. Washington
Dills Wm. H., attorney, bds Exchange hotel
Dilschneider Matthias, h 180 Griffith
Dillmain Peter, cooper, h 23 Wert
Dinkler Margaret, widow, h 271 E. Washington
Dinklager Herman, drayman
Dinklager George, clk, bds 353 Main
Dinkler Elizabeth, widow, h 241 E. Washington
Dirrumus Peter, lab, bds cor Lafayette and Wallace
Dirkes Frank, collar maker, bds 100 Laselle
Dirkes August, drayman, h 100 Laselle
D'Isay Isaac, h 107 Lafayette
Disson Susan, widow, bds 278 Webster
Distmus Edward, fireman Pitts R'y, bds 98 Montgomery
Ditcher William, marble cutter, bds 10 Harrison
Dittol Albert, ice dealer, h 7 Monroe
Ditner C. B., lumber measurer, 88 Calhoun
Dixon Daniel B., clk, h —— Langohr
Dixon John, lab, bds 30 Malitta
Dix Seth, hackman, h 97 E. Barr
Dornte William, cigar maker, bds 79 Calhoun
Dothage Mrs Sophia, h 23 Wilt
Dothage Dina, widow, h 70 Webster
Douglass W. V. (Anderson & Douglass), grocer, bds 262 W. Jefferson
Douglass William B., conductor Pitts R'y, h 262 W. Jefferson
Dowings Henry, lab, h 40 Jones
Downey Edward, bds 170 W. Jefferson
Downey Dennis, lab, h 170 W. Jefferson
Downey John, bds 170 W. Jefferson
Downing Spencer, brakeman Wabash R'y, bds 17 Taylor
Dow David, lab, h 39 Taylor
Doyle John, lab, h 63 Hanna
Dochsteiner William, upholsterer, h 265 W. Jefferson
Dodge Charles, tinner, h 42 McClellen
Dodge Ann, widow, h 22 Madison
Dodez & Rockhill, proprietors City Grocery Store, 37 and 39 W. Main
Dodez G. C. (Dodez & Rockhill), grocer, h 264 W. Wayne
Dodge A., day clerk at Mayer House
Dodgson John L., clk, h 116 E. Wayne
Dœlker Jacob, butcher shop 70 Calhoun, h 66 Wells
Dœlker John, bds 66 Wells

Dœrfler George, h 241 Barr
Dolton James, lab, bds 262 Calhoun
Donovan Thomas, lab, h 72 Baker
Donovan Timothy, eng G. R. & I. R. R., h 133 E. Main
Donnel William, lab, h 42 Butler
Donovan Jeremiah, bds 95 E. Main
Donehoe Daniel, lab, bds 20 Locust
Doriot Jules, moulder Bass' Foundry, h 56 Charley
Doriot Emil, carpenter Pitts shop, h 75 W. Washington
Doriot Lemuel, carpenter Pitts shop h 42 Lasalle
Dorr Theodore, bds 64 W. Main
Dorman Henry, carpenter Pitts shop, h 118 Wallace
Dorain W. F., brakeman Pitts R'y, bds Robinson House
Dorr A. K., h 64 W. Main
Dorr E. K., bds 64 W. Main
Dorr E. K. (E. K. & Bro.), 22 W. Berry
Doyle Patrick, carpenter, h 172 Montgomery
Doyle Thomas, carpenter, bds 186 Montgomery
Doyle Mrs Mary, bds 17 Baker
Drake Lenora, widow, h 93 W. Wayne
Drake Frederick J., post office clerk, bds Mayer House
Drake J. T., brakeman Wabash R'y, bds 227 Lafayette
Drake Clara A., teacher, bds 138 Lafayette
Drager Charles, watch maker, h 89 Barthold
Draker John, bds 39 Pearl
Draker John (Draker Bros.), livery, h 149 W. Berry
DREIER & BRO., Druggists and dealers in Paints, Oils and Window Glass, cor Columbia and Calhoun
Dreier Henry, lab, h 9 Buchanan
Dreier Anton, brewer (Linker, Hey & Co.), h 181 E. Wayne
Dreier William, moulder (J. C. Bowser & Co.), bds 178 Barr
Dreier Charles, blacksmith Pitts shop, bds 178 Barr
Dreier Henry, of Dreier & Bro., bds Exchange hotel
DREW JNO. W., Oyster Ocean Dining Hall and Saloon, 74 Calhoun
Drew William, ice dealer (Cody & Co.,) h 288 W. Main
Dressel Henry, carpenter Pitts shop, h 158 Montgomery
Dressel George, helper Pitts Round House, h 158 Montgomery
Dresser Ella, bds 115 Barr
Drerer George, carpenter, bds 265 E. Lewis
Driscoll Ed., sr., bds 274 Calhoun
Driscoll Ed., jr., Saloon and Restaurant, 274 Calhoun
Driftmeier Ernst, carpenter Pitts shop, h 131 Monroe
Driver Albert, brakeman Wabash R'y, bds 67 Wilt
DRŒGEMEYER JOHN A., City Treasurer, h 70 W. Washington
Droud Jacob, peddler, h 241 Calhoun
Dromley James, lab, bds 222 Lafayette
Dromley Edward, farmer, 222 Lafayette
Droste Diedrich, plasterer, h 100 W. Jefferson

INDIANA

ESTABLISHED IN 1858.

A TRI-WEEKLY AND WEEKLY GERMAN PAPER,

has a large Circulation not only in Indiana but also in almost every State of the Union and is an exellent medium for advertising.

J. D. Sarnighausen,

PUBLISHER & PROPRIETOR.

TERMS:

Tri-Weekly, $4.00 Per Annum, in Advance.
Weekly, - - $2.00 Per Annum, in Advance.

ENGLISH AND GERMAN

JOB PRINTING,

Promptly and Neatly executed at the Lowest Rates.

OFFICE:

N. E. Corner of Columbia and Clinton Streets,
FORT WAYNE, IND.

Drucker Henry, lab, h 66 W Washington
Druhot Joseph, moulder Bass' Foundry, h 28 Force
Dryas Christian, wks Bass' Foundry, bds 197 Lafayette
Dubois John B., agent, h 213 Lewis
Ducet I., lab, bds 70 E. Madison
Dudley James, fireman Pitts R'y, h 28 Buchanan
Dudenhœfer P. H., carriage maker, h 336 E. Wayne
Dudenhœfer Conrad, mason, h 407 E. Wayne
Dudenhœfer Philip, carriage maker, h 336 E. Wayne
Duffy Patrick, lab, bds 3 and 5 Railroad
Duffy Mrs. Louise, h 98 Barthold
Duiter Christian, tailor, bds 105 High
DUKEMAN & GUMPPER, Sample Room, 84 Calhoun
Dukeman August (Dukeman & Gumpper), saloon, bds 84 Calhoun
DUMM ROBERT D., Chief Editor Sentinel, bds 93 Calhoun
Dumer Matthias, harness maker, bds 288 W. Main
Dunne William, clk, h 16 Lewis
Dunbar William, eng Pitts R'y, h — Wallace
Dunn Charles W., teamster, h 50 Pearl
Dunn William, machinist Wabash shop, h 6 Brandriff
Dunn James, clerk, bds American House
Dunshee C. J., clk Pitts Freight Office, bds Hanna House
Dunn James, bds Central Hotel
Dunn Robert, boiler maker (K. Murry), h 14 Brandriff
Durfee William A., eng Wabash R'y, h 153 Van Buren
Durnell Chester, fireman Pitts R'y, bds 151 Barr
Durdrow Mrs Ledy, h 120 W. Water
Dustman Frank, lab, h 43 Grand
Dutcher John, carpenter, h 78 E. Madison
Dwelly Charles, machinist Pitts shop, h 157 Holman
DWENGER, RIGHT REV. JOSEPH, Catholic Bishop, h 171 Calhoun
Dyer Thomas, eng Pitts R'y, h 273 W. Jefferson

E

Eagy John H., conductor Grand Rapids R. R., h 377 Hanna
Eaken Mrs. M. A., h cor Jackson and W. Wayne
Earl William, eng P., F. W. & C. R. R., h 169 E. Wayne
Early John, fireman Pitts R'y, h 133 Madison
Earle Mrs. Elizabeth, h 31 Charles
Earson John, fireman Pitts R'y, bds 47 Bass
Eaton James, lab, h 140 High
Eaton James, fireman Wabash R'y, bds 17 Lavina
Eberly Daniel, miller, h 40 Fifth
Eberhart William, mason, h 115 Wilt
Eberwein C., lab, wks John H. Bass, h Pickway road

Ebner Lorenz, carpenter Pitts shop, bds 152 E. Lewis
Ebner George, wks Pitts shop, bds 152 E. Lewis
Ebner Jacob, wks Pitts shop, bds 152 E. Lewis
Ebright Joseph, machinist Pitts shop, bds Fox House
Eghelberger Samuel, lab, h 3 Dawson
ECKERT, FREDERICK & CO., butchers and meat store, 60 Calhoun
Eckert John (Eckart & Ortmann) cigar manufacturer, h 23 Lewis
Eckert Sophia, widow, h 93 Barr
ECKERT & ORTMANN, manufacturers and wholesale and retail dealers in Cigars and Tobacco, 85 Calhoun
Eckert Frederick, butcher, h 75 Barr
Eckart Joe, lab, bds 252 E. Wayne
Eckart William, street car driver, bds 252 E. Wayne
Eckart Jacob, lab, h 252 E. Wayne
Eckels W. J., clk, bds 215 W. Washington
Eckels James, carpenter Wabash shop, h 215 W. Washington
Eckerle Albert, brewer, h 96 Broadway
EDER, CERTIA & CO., Bloomingdale Brewery, Bloomingdale, on Feeder Canal
Eder Henry (E. Certia & Co.) Brewery, h 108 Wells
EDGERTON A. P., President Gas Works, h 154 W. Berry
Edgerton E. C., bds 87 W. Wayne
EDGERTON, JOSEPH K., Ft. W. S. P. Co., office 87 W. Main, h 59 W. Wayne
Edgerton Henry H., Treasurer Gas Works, h 148 W. Berry
Edgerton Bela, bds 154 W. Berry
Edgar William H., h 114 W. Main
Edler Frank, music teacher, h 93 Ewing
Edmonds William, street buyer, h 21 N. Cass
Edmonds William, blacksmith Pitts shop, h 166 Madison
EDSALL, WILLIAM S., Allen County Clerk, bds Aveline House
Edsall E. P., clk County Clerk's Office, bds Hanna House
Edsall C. W., clk County Clerk's Office, h on Maumee
Edsall Joseph W., County Clerk's Office, bds 254 W. Jefferson
Edwards Daniel, carpenter Pitts shop, h 167 Jackson
Edwards David, blacksmith, bds 58 Columbia
Edwards George, bds 155 Hanna
Egeter George, cabinet maker, h 124 Harrison
Eggerman David, shoemaker, bds 66 E. Main
Eggerman William, shoemaker, bds 104 W. Washington
Eggerman Peter, shoemaker, h 54 W. Washington
Eggerman David, shoemaker, h 81 W. Washington
Ehinger Otmar, carpenter, h 112 E. Jefferson
Ehinger Charles, lab, h 113 Barthold
Ehinger Michael, h 113 Barthold
Ehinger Joseph, carpenter, bds 113 Barthold
Ehinger John, drayman, h 204 Madison

Ehinger B., tailor, h 10 Nirdlinger
Ehlert Frederick, switchman Wabash R'y, h 325 W. Jefferson
Ehle Edward, brick mason, h 271 W. Washington
Ehle Frank, lab, bds 142 Broadway
Ehle Ernst, lab, h 27 West
Ehle Nicholas A., cigar manufacturer, h 142 Broadway
Ehrman F., collar maker, h 32 Jones
Ehrman Matthias, sr., teamster, h 349 W. Jefferson
Ehrman George, lab, h 82 Wilt
Ehrman Charles, blacksmith, h 339 W. Jefferson
Ehrman John M., carpenter, h 82 Wilt
Ehrman Andrew, shoemaker, h 22 Pritchard
Ehrman Henry, teamster, h 69 W. Lewis
Ehrman Charles M., blacksmith, 104 W. Main
Ehrman & John, collar manufacturers, 116 W. Main
Eickoff John, bds 130 E. Wayne
Eickoff Charles, wks Bass' Foundry, bds 130 E. Wayne
Eickoff Francis. wks Pitts Car Shop, h 130 E. Wayne
Eider August, lab, bds 22 John
Eider Peter, lab, h 22 John
Eilert Charles, bds 178 Barr
Eisenacher Frederick, carp, bds 65 Wall
Eislen John, carp, h 435 and 437 Lafayette
Eising John, lab, h 73 Force
Eix Augustus, lab, bds 60 W. Washington
Eix Sophia, widow, h 60 W. Washington
Eix William, drayman, h 319 W. Main
Elder James, carp, bds 10 Harrison
Eldred John D., conductor Wabash R'y, h 44 Chicago
Elet Mrs. Elizabeth, h 124 W. Jefferson
Elliott Cecil, telegraph operator, bds Robinson House
Elliott Margaret, widow, h 220 Lafayette
Elliott Samuel, carp, h 332 W. Jefferson
Eligson Henry, tailor, h 19 Clark
Ellenwood Horace, Master of Transportation Pitts R'y, h 127 Wallace
ELSNER JOE, propr Hoop Skirt Factory, 15 E. Main
Elsner Joseph, propr Bazaar, Main street, bds 86 E. Main
Elstner William C., book-keeper, bds 182 Broadway
Ely George (Boltz & Ely), grocer, bds 123 W. Wayne
Embry Mrs. E. h 187 Griffith
Embry Arthur, clk, bds 336 Broadway
Embry Lewis, time clk Wabash shop, 336 Broadway
EMBRY JAMES S., grocer, &c., h 132 Fairfield
Embry Edward, clk, h 227 E. Washington
Embry Arthur, clk, h 227 E. Washington
Eme C. F., dry goods (Rohs, Eme & Reinking), h 175 E. Wayne
Emerson T. M., Genl Ticket Agent Ft. W. M. & C. R'y, bds 49 and 51 W. Berry

Emerson Herman, drayman, h 14 Colerick
Emmerson George, lab, bds 181 Madison
Emmil Casper, wks Linker, Hey & Co., h 181 E. Wayne
Emmil John, blacksmith, bds 44 Monroe
Emmerson Allen, teamster, h 181 Madison
Empie T. B., clk, bds 202 W. Jefferson
Empie William, agt Wabash R'y, h 316 W. Jefferson
Empie Thomas, clk, bds 202 W. Jefferson
Emrick A. J., dealer in Furniture, h 22 W. Water
Emrick Henry, lab, h 183 Madison
Endlig Peter, lab, h 373 Lafayette
Engelking Mrs. M., widow, h 136 Barr
Engelking Mrs. Louisa, h 125 High
Engelking Henry, lab, h 167 Van Buren
Engelking Henry, lab, bds 125 High
Englert George, machinist Wabash shop, h 49 Taylor
Englert George, machinist Wabash shop, h 157 Broadway
Englert George, cooper, bds 18 Nirdlinger ave
Englert Frank, cooper, h 18 Nirdlinger ave
Engle William, fireman Muncie R'y, h 200 Broadway
Engel M., Prof. Concordia College
Engel Alexander, brakeman Muncie R'y, bds 120 W. Water
Engle William, carp, h 147 Henry
Engor Nelson C., cabinet maker, bds 30 Walnut
Englehart Abraham, cooper, bds 408 W. Main
Englen William L., conductor Wabash R'y, bds 27 Grand
English Thomas, lab, h 347 Hanna
Enright John, lab, h cor Lewis and Webster
Epple John, carp Pitts shop, h 37 Wilt
Eppstein Mayer, h 54 W. Berry
Erdman, Rev. William J., Pastor Second Presbyterian Church, h 89 W. Main
Erdel Valenitn, blacksmith Pitts shop, h 302 Hanna
Erdel Lewis, lab, bds 42 Charles
Ernsting Frederick, lab, bds 16 Clark
Ernsting Charles, lab, h 16 Clark
Ersig William, wks oil mill, h 75 E. Jefferson
Ervin John, h 12 Harrison
Erwin Joseph, Sewing Machine agt, h 27 Taylor
ESSIG ADAM P., propr Summit City House, 39 Water
Esmond George, h 306 Calhoun
Etchey Frank, carp, h 41 Wefel
Etzold William, machinist Wabash shop, h 46 Douglas ave
Evans & Co., A. S., wholesale dry goods and notions, 28 and 30 E. Berry
Evans M. A., Mrs., widow, h 60 Maiden Lane
Evans Nathan, merchant, h 79 West Main
Evans S. C., Prest. Mer. Nat. Bank, h 105 W. Berry
Evans John K., h 147 W. Berry

Evans Edwin, h 174 W. Wayne
Evans George, machinist, Wabash shop, bds 3 and 5 Railroad
Evans George, bds 126 E. Main
Evans & Co., A. S., wholesale dry goods, 33 and 35 Clinton, h 126 E. Main
Evans John, wks A. S. E. & Co., bds 126 E. Main
Evans Mrs. Emma, h 227 Lafayette
Evers Henry, lab, h 73 Force
Ewald Max, bds 119 Holman
Ewing Mary C., widow, h 88 W. Wayne
Ewing John, lab, bds 157 High

F

Fahlsing Mrs. C., h 159 E. Lewis
Fahlsing Conrad h 393 W. Main
Fahlsing Wm., street car driver, h 133 Wallace
Fairfield Jas., h 75 Melitta
Fairbank Clark, (Taylor, Fairbanks & Co.), bds 77 Douglas ave
Fairbank Rev. John B., Pastor Plymouth Church, h 228 Fairfield ave
Falconer Richard, machinist, bds 71 Williams
Falconer Richard C., clk, bds 71 Williams
Faling Frederick, Foreman Baker's saw mill, h 102 Water
Falbey Daniel, section boss, Pittsburgh R'y, h 18 Chicago
Falk Leopold, liquor dealer, 11 Harrison
Falconer John, blacksmith, h 71 William
Fallen Peter J, lab,.bds 259 Webster
Falls Daniel M., (Bowser & Co.), h 153 W. Wayne
Falker Frank, clk, bds 93 Calhoun
Falk ———, h 55 Barr
Farmer John, bds American House
Farnan Jas., baggage man, Richmond road, bds 72 Wallace
Farnan John, molder, bds cor Calhoun and Wallace
Farrar Ward B., Propr. Burglar and Fire Alarm, h 134 Lafayette
Farley Sarah, widow, h 81 Holman
Farrer Geo. H., bds 134 Lafayette
Farnan Owen, blacksmith, Pittsburgh shop, bds cor Calhoun and Wallace
Farnan Owen, h 305 Lafayette
Farber Fred, lab, h 197 Hanna
Fater George, barber, bds American House
Faude J. J., clk, bds Robinson House
Faust Frank, box maker, h E. Washington
Faulner Frank lab, h 33 Laselle
Fay Jas. A., atty., office over 1st National Bank
Fay Ezra, carp, h 63 Third
Fay Samuel, fireman, Wabash R'y
Fechtman Daniel, school teacher, h 234 W. Jefferson

Fecher J. P., lab, h 80 Buchanan
Fedeli Jerolomes, fresco painter, bds 86 E. Main
Fee Thos. W., (Griebel & F.), h 65 Clinton
Fehling Fred, fireman, h 102 E. Water
Feiler, William, carp, h 196 E. Jefferson
Feiler Frederich, lab, bds 196 E. Jefferson
Feist Peter, lab, h 70 E. Jefferson
Felehee Michael, lab, h 17 Brandriff
Felger John, hatter, bds 190 W. Jefferson
Felger Peter, carp, h 190 W. Jefferson
Felts Charles E, teamster, bds 259 E. Washington
Felts D. L., wks Olds & Son, bds 259 E. Washington
Felts Louisa, widow, h 259 E. Washington
Feustel Augustus (Mayor's clk), h 27 Wall
Ferckel Martin, saloon, h 23 Clinton
Ferber Jno., lab, bds Steuben House
Ferry Mrs. Caroline, h 130 W. Main
Ferriter Richard, brakeman, Pittsburgh R'y, h 83 Holman
Ferguson B. F., lab, h 196 W. Washington
Ferry Frank J., eng. Grand Rapids and Indiana R. R., bds 60 Chicago
Ferris Frank, conductor, Pittsburgh R'y, bds 74 Douglas ave
Fessel Mrs. Minnie, h 165 Broadway
Fetter Martin, lab, bds 205 E. Washington
Fetter Mary, widow, h 205 E. Washington
Fick Otto, M. D., office cor Clinton and Main
Fickle George, watchman, Pittsburgh shop, bds 205 Calhoun
Fiegel Charles, wagon mkr, h 54 Wells
Fiegel Fred, blacksmith, h 144 Wells
Fiegel Fred, brewer, Bloomingdale Brewery
Fiegel Robert, lab, bds Bloomingdale Hotel
Fike Cyrus, mail driver, h 75 Lafayette
Filson Robert C., commission mer., h 204 W. Berry
Fink Frank, molder, h 176 E. Jefferson
Finein Edward, cooper, bds 6 Kansas
Finey Michael, lab, h 18 Melitto
FINK CHARLES, Undertaker, h 55 W. Main
Fink Fred, brakeman, Wabash Ry., h 88 Fairfield ave
FINKENBUIER J. S., Manager Singer Sewing Machine Manuf Co., office 60½ Calhoun
Finlay William M., machinist, Wabash shop, h 418 Broadway
Finn Thomas, lab, h 287 E. Washington
FIRST NATIONAL BANK, J. D. Nutman, Pres., cor Court and Main
Fischer George, carp, h 162 Griffith
Fischer Henry, bds 63 W. Water
FISHER D. C., Insurance Agent, office with John Hough, bds Hamilton House
Fish Benjamin, fireman, P., Ft. W. and C. R. R., h 167 E. Lewis

Fisher R. J., b. k, h 177 W. Wayne
Fisher Albert, brakeman, Pittsburgh R'y, bds 260 Calhoun
Fisher O. G., train boy, Grand Rapids Railroad, bds 203 Calhoun
Fisher Isaac, butcher, h 135 W. Washington
Fisher Emanuel, butcher, bds 135 W. Washington
Fisher A., carpenter, h 265 E. Washington
Fisher Fred, machinist, Organ Factory, h 196 Fairfield ave
Fisher George W., plasterer, h 250 E. Washington
Fisher D. C., clk, bds Aveline House
Fisher Michael, carp, Pittsburgh shop, h 85 E. Berry
Fisher A., h 201 Hanna
Fisher John H., eng, Pittsburgh R'y, h 333 Hanna
Fisher Robert J., J. H. Bass' office, h 177 W. Wayne
Fisher Jacob, bds 180 Montgomery
Fisher Dave, agent, bds Aveline House
Fisk William W., clk, h 209 W. Jefferson
Fitzgerald M. M., day clk Exchange Hotel
Fitzgerald John, machinist, (K. Murry), bds 251 Webster
Fitzgerald Edward, train dispatcher, G. R. & I. R. R., bds 49 and 51 Sturgis
Fitzgerald Patrick, lab, bds 231 Barr
Fitzgibbons & Knoder, barber shop, 276 Calhoun
Fitzgibben Michael, barber, bds 92 Baker
Fitzgibben Margaret, widow, 92 Baker
Fitzmorris Bridget, widow, h 58 Baker
Fitzpatrick Michael, lab, h 20 Chicago
Fitzpatrick James, laborer, bds 262 Calhoun
Fitzpatrick Barth, lab, h 26 Bass
Fitzsimmons Patrick, h 39 Lasselle
Fitch Otis, lab, bds 33 Francis
Fittle Fred, teamster, bds 57 W. Lewis
Flanders James, eng, Wabash R'y, h 25 William
Flaherty Patrick, lab, h 59 Gay
Flaherty Patrick, lab, h 179 W. Jefferson
FLEMING WILLIAM, (Dumm & F.), Sentinel, h cor Berry and Rockhill
Fleming Luke M, clk, Sentinel office, bds cor Berry and Rockhill
Fleming Mrs. Sarah, (at Wm. Fleming's), cor Berry and Rockhill
Fleming Thomas, sawyer, h 329 W. Washinton
Fleming R. E., h 158 W. Berry
Fleming John G., eng, Pittsburgh R'y, h 282 Webster
Fletter Samuel C., lab, h 30 Bass
FLETCHER & POWERS, Livery and Proprs. Omnibus Line, 18 E. Wayne
Fletcher J. F., A. J. Barr's Livery Stable, h 17 E. Main
Fletcher Charles, Fletcher & Powers' Omnibus and Hack Line, h 18 E. Wayne
Fletcher Steven, lab, bds 29 Pearl

Fletcher C. C., (Miller & F.), Grocer, h 72 Cass
Fleack Anton, wks P., F. W. & C. R'y, h 171 E. Lewis
FLEDDERMAN JOHN G., Merchant Tailor, h 27 E. Main
Fleider Christian, lab, bds 23 Harrison
Fleiger Joseph, lab, h 93 W. Washington
Fleischer Edward, barber, h 38 Wall
Fleckinger Edward, (Agt. Olds & Son), bds 141 E. Berry
Flich Joseph, butcher, h 325 Lafayette
Flickinger John, fireman, Wabash R'y, bds 73 Grand
Flinn G. A., bill poster, bds 55 E. Berry
Flinn Charles M., blacksmith, bds 55 E. Berry
Flinn George, lab, h 55 E. Berry
Flood Michael, lab, Pittsburgh shop, h 5 Wert
Flynn Dennis, lab, h 33 Buchanan
Flynn James, machinist, Wabash shop, h 235 Barr
FOELLINGER J. M., Dealer in Foreign and Domestic Groceries, Wines and Liquors, cor Calhoun and Main, h 235 W. Main
Fœllinger Martin, clk, h 130 Harrison
Fœllinger Jacob, Boots, Shoes, etc., 6 Phœnix Block, Calhoun, h Fairfield ave,
Fogarty C. D., blacksmith, bds 9 Pearl
Fogerty Edward, blacksmith, h 13 Harrison
Foley Jerry, lab, h 34 Baker
Folwell, Mrs. Elizabeth, h 182 Jackson
Fontaine Eugene, Smoke Stack Manuf., h 178 E. Lewis
Fontaine A., Smoke Stack Manuf., bds 178 E. Lewis
Fontaine Henry, machinist, Pittsburgh R'y, bds 178 E. Lewis
Foote James, (Peck & F.,) Confec., store 67 Calhoun
Fort Wayne Gas Works, A. P. Edgerton Pres., E. Water
Foote Wm. A., (Keller & F.,) cigar manuf., bds 100 Barr
FORT WAYNE PAPER MILL, 3 miles N. E. of city, office 57 Columbia, Freeman & Barnett Proprs
Fort Wayne Ricker Little Washer Manuf. Co., office cor Columbia and Clinton
FORT WAYNE CONSERVATORY, A. K. Virgil, Principal, E. Main
FORT WAYNE NATIONAL BANK, Chas. D. Bond, Pres., J. D. Bond, Cashier, J. C. Woodworth, Assistant Cashier, cor Clinton and Main
FORT WAYNE GAS LIGHT CO., cor Barr and Water, A. P. Edgerton, Pres., B. D. Angell, Manager
FORT WAYNE STEEL PLOW MANUF. CO., cor Main and Maiden Lane, office 59 W. Main, Nelson & Co., Proprs.
FORT WAYNE TRUNK FACTORY, H. Lingenfelser, Propr., 10 Columbia
Fort Wayne Office Muncie and Cincinnati Railroad, 26 E. Wayne
FORD CHARLES, Propr. Fort Wayne Tobacco Works, 51 and 53 E. Berry

FORT WAYNE STEAM IRON WORKS, J. C. Bowser & Co., Manufs. Steam Engines, Boilers, Saw and Grist Mills, W. Water, b Calhoun and Harrison
Forkefer John, lab, bds 63 E. Water
Ford Andrew, fireman, Pittsburh R'y, h 145 Holman
Fording Peter, brakeman, Wabash R'y, h 40 William
Fording Isaac, conductor, Wabash R'y, h 26 William
Forker August, carp, h 47 William
Forrest William, barber, h 19 N. Cass
Ford James, tailor, bds 113 E. Main
Fortriede Lewis, shoemaker, h 32 W. Main
Ford William, lab, 140 High
Fordney George M., Molder, (J. H. Bass') h 192 Lafayette
Forsythe Mrs. Lizzie, 401 Broadway
Forest John, printer, bds 46 E. Jefferson
Forbach George, h 393 E. Wayne
Ford William O., clk, bds 245 E. Lewis
FOSTER BROS. & CO., Dry Good Store, 16 Columbia
Foster William, postal clk, Wabash R'y, h 87 Montgomery
Fosdick Edward, mail agent, Muncie Railroad, bds 122 W. Jefferson
Foster Lee D., brakeman, Grand Rapids Railroad, bds cor Lafayette and Wallace
Foster Abner, helper in Pittsburgh shop, bds 220 Lafayette
Foster Andrew, mer. tailor, 62 Calhoun
Fowles John, (N. B. Young & Co.), h 103 E. Washington
Fowler George, (Moderwell & Fowler), h 25 Brackenridge
Fowler Benjamin B., conductor, Muncie Railroad, h 40 Wells
Fowler Susan B., teacher of drawing and French, bds Hamilton House
FOX GEORGE, Confectionery Store, 25 E. Main
Fox Joseph, clk, bds 25 E. Main
Fox Phœbe, widow, bds 9 E. Wayne
Fox Francis, blacksmith, h 156 Wallace
Fox Joseph, confec., (at G. Fox's), h Taylor
Fox August, gardener, h Taylor
Fox James, lab, h Langohr
Fox J. R., machinist, (Bass' shop), h 25 Summit
Fox James, coal dealer, h 58 McClellan
Fox Louis, clk, bds 25 E. Main
Fox William, Propr. Fox House, 258 Calhoun
Fox Eli, fireman, bds 258 Calhoun
Fraley Michael, blacksmith, Pittsburgh shop, bds 20 Chicago
Frame Prosper, plasterer, h 30 Lasselle
France William, carp, h 27 Smith
France Mrs. Margaret, h 370 Lafayette
France Joseph, lab, bds 370 Lafayette
France Harry, bds 10 McClellan
FRANCE JOSEPH, Att'y at Law, h 10 McClellan
Frank Max, Frank & Thanhouser, Dry Goods, h 46 W. Berry

Frank Augustus, shoemaker, bds 178 Barr
Frank Mrs. Margaret, h 313 W. Main
Frank Charles, shoemaker, h 220 W. Main
Franklin B., lab, h 134 Madison
Frazier William, brakeman, Pittsburgh R'y, h 30 Force
Fransdorf William, blacksmith, h 19 Clark
France Abraham, teamster, h 137 Henry
Francis Thomas P., machinist, Wabash shop, h 32 Brandriff
Franks H. J., machinist, Bass' shop, h 116 Creighton ave
Frary Henry, lab, h on Francis
FRANK & THANHOUSER, Dealer in Fancy and Staple Dry Goods, 7 Keystone Block
Frank Charles, coffin maker, bds 142 E. Wayne
Frank Henry, lab, bds cor Ewing and W. Berry
Frank N., cigar maker, bds 21 and 23 E. Main
Frank Joseph, clk, bds 142 E. Wayne
Frank Mrs. H., h 142 E. Wayne
Franks Jasper, painter, h 105 Wells
Francisco John, fireman, Wabash R'y, bds 59 Grand
Francisco William, eng, Wabash R'y, h 42 Taylor
Francisco Charles, eng, Richmond Railroad, bds 322 Calhoun
Freiburger Simon, h 97 W. Berry
FREDERICKSON, JACOB, Saloon, h 8 Force
FREIBERGER I., Saloon, 24 E. Berry
Freinstein, Moritz, tailor, h 13 E. Wayne
Fredrickson George, lab, bds 192 Montgomery
FRENCH, HANNA & CO., (R. Morgan F., Charles H. and Oliver W. Jefferds), Proprs. Summit City Woolen Mills, Manufacturers of Cloths, Satinets, Jeans, Tweeds, Flannels, Blankets, Yarns, etc., also Dealers in Wool. S. S. Water, b Barr and Lafayette
Frech Henry, brewer, bds on Taylor
Freiburger L., (F. & Bro.), h 155 W. Wayne
Frederickson John, milkman, h 49 Langohr
FREEMAN A., Propr. Main Street Exchange, 18 W. Main
Freeman Safford, patent right, bds 152 E. Washington
Freeman Samuel. clk, bds 21 and 23 E. Main
Freeman Mrs. Sophia, h 98 Ewing
FREEMAN & BARNETT, Proprs. Paper Mills, 57 Columbia
Freeman M. D., h 180 W. Wayne
Freeman Samuel C., Justice of Peace, h 139 W. Main
Freeman Samuel P., City Clerk, h 146 W. Berry
Freinstein M., tailor, h 179 E. Washington
Fredrickson Christoff, h 109 Wells
Freiburger S. & Bro., Dealers in Leather, 24 E. Main
Fresch George, machinist, bds 184 E. Jefferson
Freed Calvin, brakeman, Pittsburgh R'y, bds 16 Chicago
French R. M., (Woolen Mills), h 144 E. Washington
French Broak, organ maker, bds Anderson House

French Charles G., contractor, h 90 E. Wayne
French Carrie, bds 90 E. Wayne
Friese Frank, h 8 John
Fricke William, carp, h 29 Lavina
Fritze William, cabinet maker, bds 25 Broadway
Fritag August, lab, h 19 Walnut
Fricke Henry, h 175 Lafayette
Frike Anthony, mason, h 17 Lavina
Fritsche Julius, lab, 18 Hough
Friederich Jacob, h 415 Lafayette
Frietzsche John W., M. D., h 152 Griffith
Friday Henry, drayman, h 1 Brandriff
Friday Henry, h 15 Colerick
Frost George, brakeman, Wabash R'y, bds 75 Baker
Frohsmith John, shoemaker, h 93 Buchanan
Frohsmith John, Jr., lab, bds 93 Buchanan
Frohsmith Max, lab, bds 93 Buchanan
Fronfield R., h 20 W. Water
Frœlich Charles, lab, h 66 Nelson
Frost Charles, brakeman, Wabash R'y, bds 106 Chicago
Frost James, fireman, Wabash R'y, bds 106 Chicago
Frost Benjamin, h 106 Chicago
FRY JACOB & SONS, Tanners, corner W. Main and Cherry
Fry Jacob, (J. & Co.), tanner, h 296 W. Main
Fry Henry William, (Fry & Bro.), tanner, h 361 W. Main
Fry John, h city limits, W. Main
Fry Franklin, carp, h city line, W. Main
Fry Joseph, (Fry Bros.), tanner, h 305 W. Main
Fry Jacob, blacksmith, bds Union House
Fry Harry, conductor, Wabash R'y, h 299 Harrison
Fuchs Bernard, carp, h 21 Walnut
Fuchs George, grocer, h 167 E. Jefferson
Fuchs F. J., h 13 Force
Fuller William, lab, h 42 W. Jefferson
Fuller D. W., conductor, G., R. & I. R. R., bds Exchange Hotel
Furguson William, M. D., h 126 Harrison
Furste Francis L., clk, h 22 W. Wayne
Furthmiller John J., h 57 Douglas ave
Futter Martin, varnisher, h 135 Cass

G

Gable Frank, clk, h 87 E. Washington
Gable Philip, blacksmith Bass' shop, h 74 Lillie
Gable Christian, h 40 Madison
Gable Hannah, widow, h 65 Harrison
Gablenz Charles, eng Pitts R'y, h 202 Francis

Gacke August, blacksmith, bds 47 Wayne
Gæger August, lab, h 5 Hood
Gaffney Edward, lab, h 33 Bass
Gaffney William, bakery and eating house, 270½ Calhoun
Gagney Henry, conductor Wabash R'y, bds 59 Grand
Gahn William, blacksmith, shop and house 157 W. Main
Gair Joseph, blacksmith Wabash shop, h 118 Union
Gains Elizabeth, widow, h 30 E. Columbia
Gallmeier Ernst, carp, bds 137 High
Gallmeier Frederick, lab, bds foot W. Water
Gallmyer William, carp, h 136 Francis
Gallagher Thomas, switchman Pitts. R'y, bds cor Lafayette and Wallace
Galing Herman, lab, bds 127 W. Wayne
Galland Henry, wks wood train, h 305 Hanna
Gallmeyer C., moulder, bds 165 Ewing
Gamble Joseph, lab, bds cor Lewis and Division
Gans Louis, lab, h 3 Marion
Ganshorn Peter, lab, h 25 Nirdlinger
Garrett F. C., drayman, h north of E. Wayne
Gardiner David, peddler, h 40 Taylor
Garrison Albert, lab, h 18 Colerick
Garrison Charles A., fireman Wabash R'y, h 117 William
Garrison John, fireman Pitts. R'y, h 76 Butler
Garwood Joseph, clk, h 29 Butler
Garte Samuel, lab, h 63 E. Water
Gardener Anthony, saloon, h 274 Hanna
Gardner & Morey, Tobacconists, 120 Calhoun
Gardner W. R., lab, bds 203 Calhoun
Gard B., M. D., 128 Calhoun
Garzner John P., clk, h 50 Wall
Gard B., M. D., h 215 W. Wayne
Gardner John, tobacconist, bds 92 E. Washington
Gartley Samuel, plasterer, bds 92 Montgomery
Gardner M. W., eng Wabash R'y, h 18 Fairfield ave
Gass August, blacksmith Bass' shop, h 62 Lillie
Gass Joseph P., lab, Bass' shop, h 92 Lillie
GASPER MATTHIAS, Saloon and Restaurant, h 250 Calhoun
Gates Nathan, saddler, bds 39 Water
Gates William, conductor Pitts. R'y, bds 2 McClellan
Gates Mrs. E., notion store, h 120 Broadway
Gates Abraham, conductor Ft. W., M. & C. R'y, h 2 McClellan
Gates D. S., exp. mess. G. R. & I. R'y, bds Robinson House
Gavin James, wks gas factory, h 239 E. Washington
Gavin Robert, miller City Mills, h 8 Harmer
Gavin Robert, h 194 Madison
Gaylord William, eng Richmond R'y, bds 322 Calhoun
Gaylord Henry, clk, bds Robinson House
Geary James, bds Phillips House, 107 E. Columbia

Geary James, lab, bds 58 E. Columbia
Gebhart George, harness maker, h 143 Francis
Gebhart Charles, eng, bds Bloomingdale Hotel
Gebet C., moulder, bds 112 Hanna
Geddis William, clk, bds Central Hotel
Geerken Frederick, lab, h 80 E. Madison
Geerken Henry, boiler maker, bds 80 E. Madison
Geen Mrs. Francis M., doctress, h 139 W. Main
Geissman Eliza, widow, h 40 Locust
Geiger Charles, school teacher, h 125 E. Jefferson
Geiss Jacob, grocer, h 355 Lafayette
Geismar Adolph, clk, bds Robinson House
Gelzeman Ernst H., carp, h 48 Water
Geller George, lab, h 6 Hood
Georgan Stephen, cigar maker, h 141 Lafayette
Gephard William, mason, h 205 Madison
Gerry William, jr., bds 36 Wayne
Gerry William, h 36 Monroe
Gerlach Jacob, lab, h 173 Harrison
Gerke Frederick, lab, bds 21 Gay
Gerber Conrad, lab, h on Francis
Gerard Anton, helper Pitts. shop, h 126 E. Lewis
Gerard Mrs. Ann, h 184 Griffith
Gerke H. F., grocer, h 209 Lafayette
German Adam, bds 30 Madison
GERARDIN HYPOLITE, Saloon, 28 E. Columbia
Gerardin Mrs. Theressa, grocery store, h 314 Lafayette
Gerlak Lewis, lab, bds 213 W. Washington
Gers Philip, grocer, h 115 Fairfield
Getz John, shoemaker, h 173 Griffith
Geye Herman, shoemaker, bds 424 E. Wayne
Geye Henry, shoemaker, h 424 E. Wayne.
Gibson Frank, carp, h 38 Oak
Gibson James, lab, h 341 W. Washington
Gibson Daniel, book-keeper, h 59 Brackenridge
Gibson Joe, carp, h 190 Montgomery
Gick George, clk, h 154 Clay
Giesler Christian, cigar maker, bds 148 Calhoun
Giese Mrs. W., h 2 Fairfield ave
Gilbert John, drug clerk, h 246 W. Washington
Gilby John, lab, h 16 Williams
Gillespie James, baggage master Saginaw R'y, h 34 Cass
Gilmartin Edward, telegraph repairer, h 31 Williams
Gilman & Fletcher, dress makers, 17 E. Main
Gill Josiah, carp, h 67 Wilt
Gilchrist Christopher, hair dresser, 26 E. Columbia
Gilbert Joseph, lab, h 165 Jackson
Gilliland & Medsker (James G. & I. N. M.) grocers, cor Lewis & Laf.

Goodman F. X., jr., painter, bds 11 Columbia
Good Daniel, moulder Wabash shop, bds 67 Malitta
Good John, moulder Wabash shop, h 67 Malitta
Good Caroline, widow, h 6 McClellan
Goodrich W. W., mail agent, bds 205 Calhoun
Goodwin & Holdt, barbers, 131 Calhoun
Gooven Henry, carp, h —— W. Main
Goodwin Anson, barber, bds 3 Pine
Goodhue George, eng Wabash R'y, bds 82 Fairfield
Goodenough George, eng Pitts. R'y, bds 233 Lafayette
Goodnow Charles, fireman G. R. & I. R'y, bds 126 E. Lewis
Goodman Charles, clk, bds 11 Columbia
Goodman F. X., saloon, 11 Columbia
Goodrich William, mail agent Richmond R'y, bds 203 Barr
Goodwin William, clk, bds 49 and 51 W. Berry
Goodwill J. P., gardner, h Hanna farm
Gorell S. R., conductor Pitts. R'y, bds Exchange Hotel
Gorgas N., clk, bds 46 E. Jefferson
Gorham Jesse, lab, h 12 Orchard
Gordan William, bds 26 McClellan
Gorrell A. C., brakeman Wabash R'y, h 67 Wilt
Gorham Charles E., General Manager Pitts. R'y, bds Hamilton House
Gordan Hough, lab, bds 100 W. Berry
Gorsline Sylvester L., brakeman Muncie R'y, h 198 Lafayette
Gordan Samuel, lab, h 63 Water
Gors Peter, lab, h 49 Walnut
Gorham Charles D., Superintendent Western Division Pitts. R'y, bds Hamilton House
Gorham Thomas, brakeman Pitts. R'y, bds 285 Hanna
Gorwin Lewis, h 24 Fairfield ave
GOSHORN W. H., County Surveyor, office in Court House, bds at Mayer House
Goshorn Jacob S., bridge contractor, h 14 Force
Gossett John W., traveling agent, h 25 Lewis
Gottshall George M., agt., bds 80 Baker
Gotshall M. V. B., attorney, h south on Hoagland ave
GOULD GEORGE, manufacturer and dealer in furniture and mattresses, h 72 Columbia
Gould Theodore, fireman Pitt.. R'y, bds 98 Montgomery
Gouty T. A., wks planing mill, h 244 W. Washington
Graham J. S., plasterer, h 254 W. Wayne
Graham Mrs. Margaret, h 59 Wilt
Graffe George W., tinner, h 26 W. Jefferson
Graffe Charles F., tinner, h 24 W. Jefferson
Granemeier Theodore, druggist, bds 118 Barr
Graf John N., machinist Pitts. shop, h 208 Lafayette
Graff Marx & Son, wholesale liquor dealers, 18 W. Columbia
Grahl Clemens, German teacher, h 196 Barr

Gilliland James G. (G. & Medsker), h 97 Montgomery
Gilbert James B., blk smith, h 169 Griffith
Gilbert William H., saddler, bds 169 Griffith
Gilbert A. L., telegrapher Wabash office, bds 18 Colerick
Gilliland James, Prof., propr store cor Lafayette and Lewis, h 97 Montgomery
Gillett James H., fireman Richmond R'y, h 32 Buchanan
Gintner Charles A., tinner, bds American House
Glanson Patrick, lab, bds 20 Chicago
Glass Mrs. Nancy, h 141 W. Water
Glaser Caroline, widow, h 13 W. Jefferson
Glendinsing Charles, fireman Pitts. R'y, bds 98 Montgomery
Gleason Myron, bds 54 W. Main
Glessner Mrs. Hester, h 303 W. Washington
Glesen Edward, baker, h 195 Hanna
Glover W. H., photographer, bds Exchange Hotel
Glutting Jacob, saloon 76 E. Columbia, h 15 W. Washington
Glutting Andrew, bds 15 W. Washington
Glusenkamp William, lab, bds 58 W. Lewis
GLYNN MATTHIAS, Livery and Sale Stable, 53 E. Main
Glynn Mrs. Jane, h 98 Ewing
Goble Samuel, lab, bds 18 W. Washington
Goble Stephan L., lab, bds 18 W. Washington
Gocke Anthony, salesman, B. T. & S., h 47 W. Wayne
Godfrey Albert, moulder at Murray & Co.'s, bds 109 Holman
Godfrey James T., eng Wabash shop, h 160 Henry
Godfrey Mrs. Sarah, h 292 W. Jefferson
Godown John M., civil eng, h 77 Douglas ave
Godown Johnson, h 77 Douglas ave
Goddard H. R., wks Olds & S., h 243 Clay
Godfrey Walter, moulder Bass' Foundry, bds 109 Holman
Godfrey J., brakeman Wabash R'y, bds 305 Harrison
Gœble Peter, sr., h 155 Holman
Gœble Mrs. C., h 219 Lafayette
GŒRIZ A., Dr., office 30 Columbia
Gœtja John, saloon, h 183 Calhoun
Gœglein John, wood dealer, h 246 Broadway
Gœglein Valentine, teamster, bds 246 Broadway
Gœbel Peter, jr., stone cutter, bds 155 Holman
GŒRIZ ADOLF, M. D., office 30 E. Columbia, h 365 Lafayette
Gœte George, trunk maker, bds 75 Buchanan
Gœriz Lewis, bds 365 Lafayette
Golden Margaret, widow, h 38 Malitta
Goldsmith, George, fireman Muncie R'y, bds 120 W. Water
Golden Patrick, lab, h 34 Smith
Golden H. A., lab, bds Union House
Golden Mary M., widow, h 8 Bass
Goodman B., tinner Pitts. shop, bds 11 Coumbia

Grage William, water wagon, h 15 Sturgis
Graham Charles, lab, h 109 Barthold
Gray James, conductor Pitts. R'y, h 64 Williams
Granneman Christian, carp, bds 19 Barthold
Gray Mrs. Anna, h 29 E. Main
Graham James E., Justice of Peace, h 2 Hoagland ave
Graham William H., painter, shop 231 Calhoun
Graybill Daniel, carp, bds 205 Calhoun
Graffe George W. & Co., tinner, 132 Calhoun
Graffe Frederick (G. W. G. & Co.), h 134 Calhoun
Grafmiller Christian, Ass't Supt. Street R'y, h 260 Calhoun
Graves Ora, stone cutter, bds 282 Broadway
Grathans Henry, carp, h 194 E. Wayne
Granger Horace, student, bds 164 E. Wayne
Granger Noah, insurance agent, h 164 E. Wayne
Graham, George W., lab, h 103 Barr
Graf John, lab, h 20 Buchanan
Graff M., h 113 W. Wayne
Graff M. L., bds 113 W. Wayne
Graf Philip, lab, bds 20 Buchanan
GRAHAM WILLIAM H., painter, h 13 Hamilton
Graffe Henry C. (Mayer & G., jewelers), h cor Fulton and W. Jefferson
Grage Frederick, lab, h 185 W. Jefferson
Granneman Charles, lab, h 302 Harrison
Granneman H. G., fireman Wabash carpenter shop, h 301 Harrison
Green Harley, book-keeper, bds 221 W. Wayne
Green Charles W., bds cor Ewing and Berry
Green Miss Mary A., h cor Ewing and Berry
Greer John, carp, h 30 Walnut
Green George, eng Wabash R'y, h 70 Baker
Grebben James M., carp Pitts. shop, h 29 Douglas ave
GRENAMIER & CO., proprs People's Drug Store, h 128 Calhoun
Greensfelder Gustaf, grocer, h 206 Broadway
Greensfelder Josiah, cashier Fruit House, bds 206 Broadway
Green S., lab, h 281 E. Washington
GREGG JAMES S., M. D., h 176 E. Wayne
Green George, bds 86 Main
Greves Joseph, carp, bds 101 Wallace
GREENE G. G., insurance agent, bds 328 Lafayette
Greer John, wks Olds & S., bds 457 Lafayette
Grenomllet Jacob, h 305 Hanna
Green William H., bds cor Ewing and Berry
Green ———, carp, bds 25 Broadway
Green Corydon, wheat buyer, h 221 W. Wayne
Greibel William, teamster, bds 174 Taylor
Griebel William, cabinet maker, bds 58 E. Jefferson
Griffee Walter C., hostler, bds American House
Grimme John H., h 19 W. Wayne

Grimmerson James, lab, bds 3 and 5 Railroad
Griebel Louis, Griebel & Fee, furniture, h 58 E. Jefferson
Grimm John, teacher, h 275 W. Washington
Grim Ferdinand, wks Wabash Freight House, h 163 E. Jefferson
Griebel Lewis, teamster, h 55 Wells
GRIEBEL & FEE, manufacturers and dealers in furniture, 47 E. Main
Griswold ——, cabinet maker, bds 170 Lafayette
Griese Frederick, clk, bds Steuben House
Grieb John, tailor, h 182 E. Lewis
Grimme John C., clk, bds 19 W. Wayne
Griebel William, collar maker, bds 53 Water
Griebel A. L., local editor, h 148 W. Wayne
Griffith Levi, carp, h 207 Broadway
Griffith Catherine, widow, h 241 Webster
Griffith Lafayette, fireman Wabash R'y, h 118 Fairfield
Griffith William E., clk, h 274 W. Jefferson
Griffiths James M., carp, h 76 Chicago
Grote Mrs. Mary, h 297 W. Jefferson
Grosjean August, lab, h 86 Smith
Grout Lavina, widow, h 74 Douglas ave
Grout Allison E., express messenger G. R. & I. R'y, bds 74 Douglas ave
Grosjean Frank, plasterer, bds 86 Smith
Grout William E., druggist, bds 74 Douglas ave
Grout Mary A., widow, h 74 Douglas ave
Grove Maxwell J., boiler maker, h 106 E. Berry
Gross Christine, clk, h 136 Calhoun
Gross Mrs. Pauline, h 163 Van Buren
Groves Daniel, lab, h 95 W. Water
Gronauer William G., h 96 Ewing
Gruber Joseph, conductor Pitts. R'y, h 231 W. Jefferson
Gruber Valentine, h 53 Taylor
Gruber Anthony, eng, h 52 Walnut
Grund Philip R., blacksmith Pitts. shop, h 176 Henry
Gruber Michael, tailor, h 18 Wilt
Grund Frederick, stone mason, h 59 Melitta
Guenther H., barber, shop 24 Court
Guetler Matthew, clk, bds Robinson House
Gugenheim J. H., clk, bds 173 W. Washington
Guilford A., barber, bds 68 Barr
Guillman Joseph, carp, h 35 Wilt
Gumppers C. C. (Dukeman & G.), saloon, h 84 Calhoun
Gunkel L., h 40 Nirdlinger ave
Gun George, conductor Wabash R'y, bds 73 Grand
Gun L., brakeman Wabash R'y, bds 73 Grand
Gurtz Bernhart, lab, h 55 E. Water
Gust John, blacksmith, h 170 High
Guthrie Frank, printer, h 261 W. Jefferson

Guthdermuth George, h 38 Wilt
Guthdermuth Henry, blacksmith Pitts. shop, h 38 Wilt
Gutermuth ———, baker, bds Steuben House
Gutermuth J. G., lab, h 167 Van Buren
Guttermuth Casper, turner, h 59 W. Jefferson
Guth Frederick, h 20 Hanna
Gweiner Michael, tanner, h 47 Wells
Gyer John, lab, bds 25 Barr

H

Haas Lewis, clk, h 125 Cass
Haag Mrs. Louisa, h 329 W. Washington
Haaselhorst H., mustard manuf., h 256 E. Washington
Haberkorn Henry, machinist, Pittsburgh shop, h 395 Lafayette
Haberkorn Emil, machinist, Pittsburgh shop, h 136 Harrison
Habecker Elias, carp, h 16 Sturges
Hable Andrew, shoemaker, h 172 Taylor
Hackens Andrew, lab, h 73 Brackenridge
Hadley John, brakeman, Pittsburgh R'y, bds 59 Grand
Haentschel Clement, teacher, bds 234 W. Jefferson
Haffner Christian, bakery, cor Harrison and W. Berry
Hagarty James, lab, h 34 Baker
Hageman William, Sr., lab, h 188 Broadway
Hageman William Jr., cigar maker, bds 188 Broadway
Hagedorn Herman, clk, Pittsburgh freight house, h 128 Chicago
Hagan Timothy, Councilman 6th Ward, h 11 Grand
HAIBER FRED, Notary, h 64 Wells
Hake Frank, (H. & Co.), ashery, h 45 N. Calhoun
Hall & Brown, barber shop, 189 Calhoun
Hally Martin, bds 323 Lafayette
Hall Charles, fireman, Pittsburgh R'y, bds 22 Madison
Hall Andrew S., boot and shoe manuf., 16 W. Main
Hall Susan A., widow, h 94 Barr
Hall James E., carp, h Creighton ave
Hall S. T., eng, Pittsburgh R'y, h 128 E. Lewis
Hallaner Daniel, gorcer and provision mer, h 214 Calhoun
Halm M. F., brewer, Bloomingdale brewery
Hall Charles, fireman, Pittsburgh R'y, bds 197 E. Jefferson
Hallaka Henry, lab, h 116 Fairfield
Hall A. S., boots and shoes, 14 W. Main, h 132 E. Main
Ham John J., clk h 10 Henry
Hambrock F., lab, Bass' foundry, h 209 Hanna
Hamilton Mrs. Elizabeth, h 16 Wallace
HAMILTON & CO., Coffee and Spice Mills, 30 Clinton
Hamilton William, bds 73 E. Berry

Hamilton Allen, machinist, Pittsburgh shop, bds 118 Barr
Hamilton Mrs. Allen, widow, h cor Clinton and Barr
HAMILTON ANDREW H., h head of Clinton
Hamilton M., (Heustis & Hamilton), h cor Lewis and Clinton
Hamilton F., bds Hanna House
Hamilton John, baggage master, Pittsburgh R'y, h 151 W. Wayne
Hamilton Ann, widow, Propr. Hamilton House, h 103 W. Berry
Hamilton Miss L., Hamilton House
Hamrood Andrew, machinist, Pittsburgh shop, h 60 E. Washington
Hamsher Benj. F., eng, Pittsburgh R'y, h 45 Butler
Hamrecht George, cigar maker, h 44 Douglas
HAMILTON ALLEN & CO., Bankers and Exchange Dealers, W. S. Calhoun, opp. Court House
HANCE J. D., Sheriff Allen County, office in Court House
HANUM DANIEL, Propr. Occidental Billiard Hall and Saloon, 83 Calhoun, h 93 Wayne
Hanley Rudolph, wks Pittsburgh shop, bds 98 Montgomery
Harvey William, fireman, Wabash R'y, bds 82 Fairfield ave
Handheim John J., machinist, Wabash shop, h 12 Mc Clellan
Hansen Joseph, lab, h 208 W. Main
Handler Peter, mason, h 37 Walnut
Hankinson Peter, carriage trimmer, h 25 Butler
Hanley J. H., blacksmith, Wabash shop, h 217 Broadway
Handman William, lab, bds 224 E. Jefferson
Hanna Robert, machinist, Bowser's foundry, h 17 N. Cass
Hanna Oliver, clk, bds cor Lewis and Division
Hanna Henry, Jr., bds 135 E. Berry
Hannen James, cooper, bds 29 Butler
Hannan Mrs. Mary, h 25 Baker
Hanna Joseph, bds 135 E. Berry
Hanna H. C., h 135 E. Berry
HANNA SAMUEL T., Dealer in Real Estate, h 109 W. Berry
Hanna Charles, (French, Hanna & Co., woolen mills), h 64 E. Jefferson
Hanna Hugh T., bds cor Lewis and Division
Hanna Mrs. Lizzie, widow, h cor Lewis and Division
Hanson R. C., gas fitter, h 48 E. Main
Handsh Simon, h 408 W. Main
HARPER & CO., Hat and Cap manufs., and Dealers in Furs, 3 Phœnix Block
Hartman George B., (L. R. H. & Co.), bucket manufacturer, h 161 W. Washington
Harton James, lab, bds 104 E. Madison
Hartman Mrs. Eliza, h 161 W. Washington
Hartman Rev. D. P., bds 241 W. Wayne
Hartman Adolph, lab, h 35 Maumee
Hartman Amos, cooper. h 138 W. Main
Hartman B. S., dentist, bds 241 W. Wayne
Hartman L. R., cashier First Nat. Bank, h 241 W. Wayne

Harvey J., eng, bds 70 E. Madison
Hartmeyer Fred, collar maker, h 163 E. Jefferson
Harrison William H., h cor Fairfield ave and William
Hartung Ludwig, h 284 W. Jefferson
Hartnett Richard, lab, 68 Baker
Hardesty William, bell boy at Mayer House, bds same
Hartshorn, J. S., eng, Wabash R'y, h 65 Garden
Harris Mrs. Hannah, h 18 Pine
Harrington E. B., carp, h 17 Henry
Hartshorn S. J., lab, h 15 Lavina
Hardendorf, John, millwright, h 245 W. Wayne
Harter John, teamster, h 95 W. Water
Harkemeper William, clk, bds 21 and 23 E. Main
Harrison Charles, baggage master, Richmond R. R., bds 205 Calhoun
Harding Daniel L., ass't civil eng, Pittsburgh R'y, h 235 W. Jefferson
Hartstein Lewis, lab, h 344 Broadway
Hartshorn S. J., bds 65 Garden
Hart J. R., agt. Wheeler & Wilson Sewing Machine, h 112 E. Wayne
Hartman Mrs. Ann, h 104 E. Madison
Harring Theodore, fireman, Wabash R'y, h 119 William
Harper James P., hatter, h 59 Barr
Harrison Joseph, lab, bds 39 Water
Hartman John, lab, h 59 Water
Hartnett James, lab, h 25 Baker
Harrison William, machinist, Pittsburgh shop, h 199 Barr
Harrison Charles, brakeman, Richmond R. R., bds 203 Barr
HARTUNG CHRISTIAN, Mer. Tailor, and Gents' Furnishing Goods, 82 Calhoun
Hartman William H., eng, Wabash R'y, h 15 Holman
Hartman Isaac, cooper, h 334 Hanna
Hartsuff William D., clk, bds 341 Hanna
Hartman Christian, lab, h 53 W. Jefferson
Hartung Gottholt, tailor, bds 284 W. Jefferson
Harkless William H., fireman, Grand Rapids R. R., h 320 Hanna
Hartnett William, lab, h 52 Baker
Hartung Christian, tailor, h 284 W. Jefferson
Hartung Emil, tailor, bds 284 W. Jefferson
Harper James, hats and caps, h 163 E. Wayne
Harrison Robert, machinist, Pittsburgh shop, h 265 Hanna
Hartman Herman, lab, h 126 E. Washington
Harmeyer William, lab, h 47 First
Harwell George, cabinet maker, h 235 Lafayette
Harper James & Co., manufs. silk hats, 11 E. Columbia
Harries John & Co., Fort Wayne file works, 126 Calhoun
Harmon Daniel J., clk at Harmon House
Harris J. L., carpenter, bds 264 Calhoun
HARMON HOUSE, Harmon Daniel, Propr., 284 Calhoun
Harmon Samuel W., cigars and tobacco, 276 Calhoun, bds Harmon House

Hartman John, lab, h 59 E. Water
Hartman George, lab, bds 59 Water
Harrison Frank, eng, Wabash R'y, bds 76 Dawson
Harter George, lab, bds 170 W. Main
Harter Joseph, blacksmith, shop and h 170 W. Main
Harris John, hardware &c., h 152 Holman
Harris George, h 252 E. Lewis
Harris Amos, lab, bds 76 Wallace
Hartman L. R., (L. R. H. & Bro.), bucket manuf., h 161 W. Washington
Harmeyer Fred, collar maker, bds 57 W. Water
Hassinger William, brakeman, Grand Rapids R. R., bds 203 Calhoun
Hastmeyer C. W., sewing machine agt., h 120 Chicago
Haskell Washington, com. mer., and agt. for Maltby's oysters, 65 E. Columbia
Hass Jacob, lab, h 72 Wallace
Hasty John, fruit stand, h 114 Calhoun
Hasty S. W., clk, bds 114 Calhoun
Haskell Wash, com. mer., bds 92 Calhoun
HATERSLEY A., Plumber and Gas Fitter, 48 E. Main
Hattersley William, clk, bds 173 W. Wayne
HATTERSLEY ALFRED, Propr. Fort Wayne Brass Works, Plumber, Gas and Steam Fitter, 48 E. Main, h 73 W. Wayne
Hathaway John, h 91 Wilt
HANSER OTTO, Director Concordia College
Hauss David, (Bœrger & H.), vinegar works, h 243 W. Washington
Hauble Charles, machinist, Wabash shop, h on Taylor
Hausbach Jacob, lab, h 38 Henry
Haurand B., lab, bds Union House
Hauser Mrs. R., widow, h 208 Hanna
Hausman William, blacksmith, Pittsburgh shop, h 208 Monroe
Hauenstein Julius, shoemaker, h 189 W. Main
Hawes D., manuf. window shades, 59 Columbia
Haverly Anthony, blacksmith, Pittsburgh shop, h 170 Madison
Haxby James, att'y, bds 144 E. Berry
Hayes Thomas, lab, h 25 Colerick
Hayes John, lab, bds 24 Charles
Hayes Charles fireman, Wabash R'y, bds 74 Douglas ave
Hayes Charles A., student at law, 34 E. Berry
Hayes James, night watch, Muncie round house, bds 40 Wells
Haynes Frank, eng, Wabash R'y, h 29 Melitta
Headford Saul, cabinet maker, h 186 Clay
Heaber Barbara, widow, 10 E. Berry
Hebert Peter, eng, Pittsburgh R'y, bds 230 Calhoun
Hebbiser George, brakeman, Wabash R'y, bds 59 Grand
Hebert Oliver, eng, Pittsburgh R'y, h 167 E. Wayne
Heck John T., lab, h 333 E. Washington
Hecker Henry, lab, h 385 E. Wayne
Hecht Joseph, carpenter, bds 28 Locust

HECKER GEORGE M., Grocer, 110 Wells, h 112 Wells
Hecker George, eng, h 29 Pearl
Hedinger Jacob, shoemaker, bds 319 Lafayette
Hedges Thomas J., carpenter, h 323 W. Main
Henderhorst Ernst, lab, bds 136 Francis
HEDEKIN HOUSE, Wolf and Wagner Proprs, 25 Barr
Hedekin Thomas, h 82 E. Washington.
Hedekin Ellen C., widow, h 95 E. Main
Hegerer C. Stewart Concordia College
Hehnlein Michael, lab, h 183 W. Jefferson
Heilbronner Abraham, dealer in hides &c., h 62 W. Main
Heit Alex., butcher, h 74 Wells
Heinlen William, machinist, (K. Murry), h 304 Harrison
Heidenrich E., lab, h 26 Henry
Heibler Jane T., widow, h 189 Ewing
Heit Christian, clk, bds, 93 Calhoun
Heine Mrs. C., h 96 E. Madison
Heil Fred, lab, h 104 W. Walnut
Heibner John, lab, h 323 Lafayette
Heinling Mrs. Fred, h 321 Lafayette
Heitwinkel Henry, carp, h 54 W. Wayne
Heilbronner Samuel, h 56 W. Wayne
Heine Fred, painter, Wabash shop, h 139 Wallace
Heingardner Martin, tailor, shop on Clinton, Union Block, h 155 W. Main
Heidelbrecht Henry, dry goods, bds 152 W. Jefferson
Heidelbrecht & Schwartz, dry goods, 142 Broadway
Heineman Fred, wks at Bass' shop, h 161 Hanna
Heiney N., clk, h 253 E. Jefferson
HEINGARTNER MARTIN, Mer. Tailor, and Gents' Furnishing Goods, 34 Clinton
Heilbronner A., h 62 W. Main
Heine Frederick, carp, Pittsburgh shop, h 52 Douglas ave
Heinlen Emanuel, machinist, Pittsburgh shop, h 158 Griffith
Heit Mrs. Josephine, h 188 Griffith
Heke Herman, drayman, h 156 E. Washington
Heldt Gorge, barber, h 69 High
Helm Theodore, carp, h 174 Henry
Held Ferdinand, molder, Bass' foundry, h 153 Hanna
Heldt John M., razor grinder, h 78 High
Heller William L., cabinet maker, bds 220 Lafayette
Helmkamp Henry, carp, h 240 W. Washington
Held Adolph, molder, (J. H. Bass), bds 189 Barr
Helmuth G., h 25 W. Washington
Hemphill David, fireman, Pittsburgh R'y, bds 332 Calhoun
Henkennis Frank, teamster, h 22 Douglas
Henderson George, lab, bds Bloomingdale Hotel
Hencey Henry, carp, h 53 High

Heuer Ernst, helper, bds 147 E. Lewis
Henkel Phil, foreman vinegar works, h 119 Lafayette
Henry Joseph E. clk, h 139 Clay
Hennings August, lab, bds 92 E. Madison
Hennesy Alex, lab, h 34 Third
Henschen Henry lab, h 164 Ewing
Henshen William, lab, wks Pittsburgh shop, h 222 Francis
Henry William H., wheat buyer, h 94 Jackson
Henry H. H., h 195 W. Main
Henderson Louisa, bds 104 E. Wayne
Henschen George H., lab, Bass' foundry, bds 222 Francis
Henderson S. C., machinist, Pittsburgh shop bds Hanna House
Hench Samuel, att'y at law, bds Robinson House
Henderson Henry, machinist, Wabash shop, bds 40 Madison
Henderson George, clk, bds 23 Madison
Henderson William, h 23 Madison
Henderson John A., carp, h 100 Columbia
Henderson Angeline M., propr. boarding house, 86 E. Main
Hennesy Dennis, lab, bds 34 Third
Henderson A. R., sup. woolen factory, h 115 E. Wayne
Hennings Fred, h 92 E. Madison
Henkel Charles, music teacher, bds 119 Lafayette
Hepburn A., painter, bds 25 Barr
Herring John lab, h 71 Douglas
Hergonrather Mrs. Maggie, h 43 Nirdlinger
Herr George, h 64 McClellan
Hertig C. M., lawyer, bds Mayer House
Hermann Alex, M. D., h 177 Montgomery
Herrington John, Sr., carp, h 68 Dawson
Hersh George, student, bds 261 W. Wayne
Herman Mrs. Regina, h 99 Lasselle
Henman Michael, carpenter, h 99 Lasselle
Herschen Henry, lab, Pittsburgh shop, bds 222 Francis
Hering Peter, lab, 15 West
Hermsdorfer Adam, shoemaker, h 281 W. Jefferson
Hermsdorfer George A., boot and shoemaker, 33 E. Main
Hersh William, student, bds 261 W. Wayne
Herr Jacob, machinist, h 72 Lasselle
HERBST FREDERICK, Saloon and Boarding House, h 3 and 4 Railroad
Herwer Valentine, lab, h 24 Clark
Hesemeier Henry, mason, h 15 Lavina
Hess John, expressman, h 71 Douglas
Hesner Henry, lab, h 5 Marion
Hesner Charles, lab, h 5 Marion
HEUCHLING THEODORE, M. D., h 76 W. Berry
Heuer John, clk, bds 55 W. Wayne
Heuer Herman, shoemaker, h 55 W. Wayne

Heuer Christian, lab, h 107 Force
Hey Ernst, clk, bds 92 Barr
Hey Amandeus, (Linker & Co.), h 181 E. Wayne
Hickman James, fruits and candies, 133 Calhoun
Hess N. W., plow maker, h 12 Fairfield ave
Hesemeier Henry, mason, h 24 W. Jefferson
Hettler Christoff, bds 167 Holman
Hettler Godtlieb, lab, 84 Charles
Hettinger E. B., bds 140 Barr
Hettler Mrs. Kate, h 145 E. Lewis
Hickman E. grocer, 54 Barr
Hickman Samuel, bds 54 Barr
Hickman S., bds 54 Barr
Hickman & Bro., grocers, store 98 Barr
Hienholz Kohlman, carp, h 37 Bass
Hight E., clk, h 37 Henry
Hight Eugene, Machinist, h 131 Lafayette
Hight H. A., theatrical, h 113 Lafayette
Higgins F. P., eng, h 143 E. Jefferson
Higgins C., train dispatcher, Pittsburgh R'y, bds 49-51 W. Berry
Hight Eugene, Jr., coppersmith, bds 131 Lafayette
Hight H., Jr., bds 113 Lafayette
HILL, C. L., Wholesale and Retail Dealer in Pianos, Organs, and General Musical Merchandise, 52 and 54 Calhoun
Hill Madison, street buyer, bds 82 W. Berry
Hill Jacob, bar keeper, bds 93 Calhoun
Hill Henry, h 181 Jackson
Hill Mrs. M. W., h 199 W. Wayne
Hilbrecht Henry, Jr., machinist, (Bowser & Co.), bds 228 W. Jefferson
Hilbrecht Henry, blacksmith, h 228 W. Jefferson
Hilker Charles, carp, Pittsburgh shop, h 137 Francis
HILDEBRAND WILLIAM, grocer, and provision mer, 201 Calhoun
HILT FRED & CO., harness makers, 117 E. Main
Hillier W., blacksmith, bds 10 Harrison
Hilgeman Fred, lab, h 180 Ewing
Hill John E., Jr., miller, bds 82 W. Berry
Hill Daniel, lab, h west of Wells
Hill David, policeman, h 62 Douglas
Hilton James, machinist. bds 87 William
Hille William, lab, h 41 Walnut
Hilgeman Fred, carp, h 399 E. Washington
Hilgeman Fred, lab, h 18 McClellan
Hill O. G., h 278 W. Jefferson
Hild Henry, carriage painter, h 52 W. Jefferson
Hillmann Fred, lab, h 69 Buchanan
Hill Mrs. Barbara, h 158 W. Main
Hilgeman Henry, lab, h 184 Ewing

Hilgeman William, carp, h 180 Ewing
Hilker Fred, lab, h 175 Washington
Hill John, brakeman, Pittsburgh R'y, bds 54 Chicago
Hilgeman Henry, Sr., eng, h 91 W. Jefferson
Hilgeman Henry, Jr., clk, bds 91 W. Jefferson
Hild, Henry, painter, h 39 W. Jefferson
Hill Joseph, mason, h 62 W. Lewis
Hill Mary, widow, bds 34 W. Water
Hiller William, cabinet maker, bds 220 Lafayette
Hilgeman William, carp, h 216 E. Washington
Hilt John, lab, h 26 Baker
Hildebrand Fred, carp, h 33 Jefferson
Hilt Fred, harness maker, (H. & Co.), bds 26 Baker
Hilliker William, fireman, Pittsburgh R'y, bds 17 Holman
HILL JOHN E., Township Trustee, h 82 W. Berry
Hill John H., h cor Lewis and Harrison
Hinker Charles, blacksmith, Pittsburgh shop, h 42 Charles
Hinton William, brakeman, Wabash R'y, bds 30 Baker
Hinds Theodore, fireman, h 36 Brandriff
Hinman Edwin, h 14 W. Wayne
Hinton Samuel, fruits and nuts, 210 Calhoun
Himbert John, drayman, h 16 Hood
Hines John, lab, bds 49 Baker
Himmelsbach W., bds 82 W. Berry
Himbert Michael, drayman, h 14 Lavina
Himmelbach William, 16 W. Berry
Hinman H. F., carp, h 43 Union
Hinkle Oscar N., conductor, h 79 Douglas ave
Hinkley Mrs. F. M., widow, bds Hanna House
Hinton John, conductor, Pittsburgh R'y, bds 30 Baker
Hinton Samuel, fruit stand, h 30 Baker
Hirschfelder L., mason, h 360 E. Wayne
Hislop Catherine widow, h 120 Butler
Hisner William, carp, h 108 Jackson
Hitt Mrs. R. J., h 349 W. Jefferson
Hitzman Fred, lab, h 36 Lavina
Hitzman George, policeman, h 20 Summit
Hitchcock, Mrs. A., h 12 Marion
Hitzman Gottleib tailor, h 49 Wilt
Hitzman Christian, clk, bds 66 Douglas
Hitzman Henry, clk, bds 49 Douglas ave
Hitzeman William, clk, bds 66 Douglas ave
Hith Jacob, eng, Pittsburgh car shop, h 204 Lafayette
HOAGLAND & TRESSELT, Proprs. City Mills, Manufs. of Flour, and dealers in all kinds of grain, cor Clinton and Water
Hoagland James E., miller, bds 106 W. Berry
Hoagland A. V., clk, bds Robinson House
Hoagland Plinny, (Hoagland & Tresselt), city mills, h 106 Berry

Hockstetter William, lab, h on W. Washington
Hockemeier Charles, lab, h 317 W. Washington
Hock Fred, bds 11 E. Main
Hochtmeier Ernst, lab, h 196 Ewing
Hockaday Debora, widow, h 59 Grand
Hoch William, saloon, h 321 Lafayette
Hockemeyer Henry, carp, bds 111 W. Jefferson
Hochemeier Fred, night watchman, bds 92 E. Madison
Hodgdon William A., Prof. Indiana Conservatory, h 166 Montgomery
Hoesch David, carpet weaver, bds 31 W. Columbia
Hoffman A. E., (Hoffman Bros.), h 186 W. Wayne
Hoffman Bros., manufs. chair stuff &c., cor Main and Van Buren
Hoffman Elizabeth, widow, h 9 Hood
Hoffman Daniel, varnisher, h 293 W. Jefferson
Hoffman Mrs. Susan C., h 219 W. Washington
Hoffman John, steward at Gentral Hotel
Hoffmeister Henry, cooper, h 12 Wells
Hofer Charles H., clk, Bloomingdale Hotel
Hoffman Mrs. Mary, h 190 W. Main
HOFFMAN J. R. & CO., Patent Saw Mill Manufs., cor Main and Van Buren
Hoffman Newton, millwright, h 190 W. Main
Hoffman George, wagon maker, h on E. Washington
Hoffman George, wagon maker, wks 3 Clay
Hoffman Christian, eng, Wabash R'y, bds 50 Melitta
Hofferman Michael, stave joiner, bds 6-8 Kansas
Hoffer John G., carp, h 37 N. Cass
Hoffman Henry, (H. Bros.), bds 166 W. Berry
Hoffman Eli, (H. Bros.), h 186 W. Wayne
Hoffman William H., (H. Bros.), bds 166 W. Berry
Hofman John A., carp, Pittsburgh shop, h 31 Force
Hofman Martin, turner, Pittsburgh shop, bds 31 Force
Hoffer Andrew, butcher, h 26 Baker
Hoffer I. N., carp, h cor Monroe and Madison
Hoffman Charles, wks Muncie Railroad, h 122 Clay
Hoff Anthony, lab, h 101 Wells
Hogan Timothy, saloon, 269 Calhoun
Hogan John, lab, h 17 Brandriff
Hogan Michael, foreman, Pittsburgh yard, h 133 Fairfield ave
Hogan Hugh, machinist, bds 121 E. Washington
Hogarth Thomas, fireman Pittsburgh R'y, h 203 Hanna
Hohmeicer D., bds 66 E. Main
Hohnhaus John, lab, bds 211 Madison
Hohing John J., machinist Pitts shop, h 27 Poplar
Hohnhaus George, carp, bds 65 Wall
Hohnhaus Peter, cabinet maker, h 65 Wall
Hohing John G., machinist Pitts. shop, h 27 Poplar
Hohenstein Leonard, lab, h 160 E. Washington

HOLLINGER ELIAS, carp, h Hanna Farm
Hollinger Jacob, bds Hanna Farm
Hollenger Jacob, carpenter, bds 98 Montgomery
Hollenger Daniel, lab, h 104 Columbia
Holzwarth Edward, blacksmith, 48 W. Main
Holtke Frederick, lab, h 214 W. Jefferson
Holterman Frederick, lab, bds 153 Madison
Hollman Frederick, carp, h 7 Hood
Holmes George, lab, bds 545 Calhoun
Holmke Edward, shoemaker, 182 Calhoun
Hollenbeck William, carp, h 148 Calhoun
Holt Benjamin, boiler maker Wabash shop, bds 188 Henry
Holland John, boiler maker Wabash shop, h 32 Butler
Holbrock Herman, carp Pitts shop, h 96 Fairfield
Holt Thomas, boiler maker Wabash shop, h 150 Fairfield
Holiehan Agneu, coppersmith Wabash shop, h 69 Grand
Holton T. J., student, bds 177 W. Wayne
Holsworth George, teamster, h 199 Broadway
Holmes William I., conductor Pitts R'y, h cor Smith and Grant
Holt William S., book-binder, h 39 Baker
Holmes J., stock yard, h 18 Gay
Holmes George, stock yard, bds 18 Gay
Holmes B., stock yard, h 296 Hanna
Hollister A. J., cigar maker, h 17 W. Jefferson
Hollingsworth Mrs. A. N., widow, h 99 E. Berry
Holsworth Addison, clk, h 158 W. Wayne
Holt John, boiler maker Wabash shop, h 188 Henry
Honick Henry, carp, h 127 Montgomery
Honick A., lab, bds 156 E. Jefferson
Hoober James, h 20 Harrison
Hood Thomas N., printer, h 223 E. Jefferson
Hood Mrs. E., widow, h 223 E. Jefferson
Hood William E., teller First Nat. Bank, h 246 W. Berry
Hoover Abram, carp Pitts shop, h 91 E. Lewis
Hops Robert W., plasterer, h 50 Butler
Horstmeier Gottlieb, carp, h 5 Broadway
Horton William, insurance agent, h 31 E. Main
Horstman Frederick, tailor, shop 146 Calhoun
Horstman ———, carpr h 203 Hanna
Hockemeier Henry, lab, bds 317 W. Washington
Horstman Frederick, tailor, h 59 E. Wayne
Horstmyer William, tailor, bds 264 E. Washington
Horstman John, lab, bds 274 E. Washington
Horstmeyer William, carp, h 179 Ewing
Horstmeyer Lewis, carp, h 13 Wall
Hornung Jacob, moulder Bass' foundry, h 10 Force
Hornung George, prop. Summit City Brewery, 69, 73 and 75 Harrison
Horton E. A. (McCartney & Co., grocers), h 16 Douglas ave

Hornung John J., conductor Pitts. R'y, bds 94 E. Berry
Hostman Nicholas, cooper, bds 36 Force
Hostman Christian, painter Wabash shop, h 86 W. Jefferson
Hostman C., jr., bds 88 W. Jefferson
Hosey L., machinist Pitts. shop, bds 71 Douglas ave
HOUGH JOHN, attorney, land and loan agent, 32 E. Berry, h 127 W. Wayne
Housman Z. T., M. D., 128 Calhoun
Housman Z. T., M. D., h 54 W. Main
Houser John, bds 137 E. Jefferson
Houghton L. S., clk, h 154 W, Jefferson
Houser William, machinist at Bowser & Co.'s, h 37 Gay
Houser Samuel L., conductor, h 137 E. Jefferson
Howe Mrs. Allen, bds 221 W. Wayne
HOWE SEWING MACHINE COMPANY, A. Davis, manager, 72 Calhoun
Howes D., manufacturer of lap window shades, 59 Columbia, bds 79 E. Main
Howey A. B., clk Pitts shop, bds 38 McClellan
Howley Thomas, blacksmith, h 30 Malitta
Howard John, prof. of music, bds Hanna house
Howenstein John, traveling agent bds 50 E. Wayne
Hoyt Moses C., conductor Pitts. R'y, bds 47 Baker
Hubler Abraham, lab, bds 134 Monroe
Hubler Thomas, wks Olds & Son, bds 231 Barr
Hubler Benjamin, wks Olds & Son, bds 231 Barr
Huber Nicholas, painter, h 81 E. Berry
Hubbel Joseph, eng Saginaw R'y, bds 63 Wells
Hubbard C. S., harness maker, bds 105 Wilt
Hubbard Alexander, sewing machine agent, h 105 Wilt
Hubler A., lab, bds 58 Columbia
Hubler Mrs. Nancy, h 241 E. Wayne
Huber George, butcher, h 159 Barr
Hubbard Mrs. M., widow, bds 79 E. Wayne
Hucksoul August, lab, bds 38 Force
Hudry Nicholas, carp, h 186 Montgomery
HUESTIS & HAMILTON, wholesale grocers, 83 and 85 Columbia
Huestis A. C., wholesale grocer, (H. Hamilton & Co.), h 205 W. Berry
Huestis C. D., book-keeper, bds 205 W. Berry
Huff Hiram, watchman Wabash R'y, h 23 Melitta
Hughs E., moulder Bass' foundry, h 179 Hanna
Hughes James C., foreman Pitts. boiler shop, h 100 E. Lewis
Hughs James, lab, h 25 Walnut
Hughs Daniel, lab, h 40 McClellan
Hull Lewis O., painter, bds 278 Broadway
Hull Wesley, inventor patent rights, h 278 Broadway
Hull Sylvester, painter, bds 278 Broadway
Hulse Thomas, fireman Pitts. R'y, h 228 Francis

Hulse William L., machinist, h 185 W. Wayne
Humphrey, Mrs. Jane, h 171 W. Berry
Humphrey B. S., fireman, bds 104 Barr
Humbert E., lab Wabash freight house, h 18 Oak
Humphrey George (Cochrane, H. & Co.), h 175 W. Berry
Humphrey James, carp, bds 175 W. Berry
Humphrey Matthew, bds 171 W. Berry
Humbert James, wks oil mill, bds 86 E. Main
Humphrey William S., oil mill (H. & Case), h 142 Montgomery
Huntsberry Jacob M., painter, works at Stanley, Bieber & Co.'s, bds 71 Dawson
Huntsberry James A., varnisher, wks at Gould's, bds 71 Dawson
Hunt Patrick, teamster, h 6 Smith
Hunt James, teamster, bds 6 Smith
Hunt Edward, lab, h 6 Smith
Hunting William H., engineer Organ Factory, h 16 Henry
Hunt John, plasterer, bds 6 Smith
Hunt Thomas, porter at Mayer House, bds Mayer House
Huntsberry John B. peddler, h 71 Dawson
HURD O. D., sash manufacturer, h 142 W. Jefferson
Hurd Mrs. Nancy, h 142 W. Jefferson
Hurd Charles, clk, bds 142 W. Jefferson
Hurd Oscar, book-keeper, bds 142 W. Jefferson
Hurlburt Benjamin, carriage maker, h 389 Calhoun
Husener William, carp, h 108 Jackson
Huser Lewis, shoemaker, bds 19 Pritchard
Hussel John, lab, h 200 W. Washington
Hutzel Daniel, druggist, bds 299 W. Main
Hutchenson A., plasterer, bds 227 E. Jefferson
Hutchenson R., street buyer, h 227 E. Jefferson
Hutzel Frederick, lab, bds cor Lafayette and Wallace
Hutchinson Thomas G., gang boss Pitts. shop, h 43 Brackenridge
Hyatt Harvey, fireman Pitts. R'y, h 86 Montgomery

I

Iba Mrs. Elizabeth, h cor Fairfield and Colerick
Iba George, fireman Wabash R'y, bds cor Fairfield and Colerick
Ibas E., lab, h 25 Nirdlinger
IDDINGS H., pension agt, cor Main and Harrison, bds Mayer House
Ide John, blacksmith, h 14 W. Jefferson
ILER & BROBST, druggist, 143 Calhoun
Iller Lewis, brakeman Pitts. R'y, bds 343 Hanna
Iler Julius C. (Iler & Brobst), druggist, bds 143 Calhoun
Imboyt Adam, turner, bds 80 Chicago
Imboyt Dorathea, widow, h 80 Chicago
Imrie John B., contractor, h 150 Griffith

INDIANA CONSERVATORY OF MUSIC, Bartlett, Secretary, cor Main and Court
Ingraham T. J., eng Wabash R'y, h 51 W. Lewis
Irey Alfred K., clk U. S. Express, bds 186 Griffith
Irey Mrs. Sarah, h 186 Griffith
Irwin John W., insurance and real estate agent (with Irwin and Lumbard), 241 W. Main
Irwin John S., M. D., h 241 W. Main
Irwin Thomas, h 169 W. Jefferson
Irwin Edward D., conductor Pitts. R'y, bds Exchange Hotel
Isabey Louis C., lab, h 47 Buchanan
Israel Henry, lab, bds 127 W. Washington
Iten Mrs. Catherine, h 47 Buchanan
Ives George, eng Pitts. R'y, h 45 Grand

J

JACOBY & WIEGAND, contractors and builders, manufacturers of sash, doors, blinds and dressed lumber, cor Virginia and Murray
Jacoby George (J. & Co.), h 78 Wallace
Jacoby Frederick, carp, h 103 Wallace
Jacquot Augustus, lab, bds 58 Columbia
Jackson Mrs. D. D., h 245 Calhoun
Jackson William T., train despatcher Pitts. R'y, h 164 Broadway
Jackson Kerby C., eng Pitts. R'y, h 55 Brackenridge
Jackson J. H., agent, bds Robinson House
JACOBS & SON, boot and shoe store, Calhoun, opp Keystone Block
Jacobs John H., (Jacobs & Son, boots and shoes), bds 50 E. Berry
Jacob William, shoe merchant, h 50 E. Berry
Jacob Frederick, painter, h 68 W. Washington
JACOBS CHARLES W., propr Union Bakery, 62 E. Main
Jacobs James, lab, bds 117 Calhoun
Jacobs Thomas K., brakeman Pitts. R'y, h 11 Gay
Jacobs Arnold C., clk, bds 120 Lafayette
Jacobs Mrs. B., h 100 E. Madison
Jacobson Elkan, h 107 W. Main
Jacobson Victor, clothing merchant, h 136 W. Wayne
Jæbker Frederick, machinist (Olds & Son), bds 127 Montgomery
Jahn Nicholas, carp Wabash shop, h 17 Hood
James Daniel H., teamster, h 102 Williams
James William H., teamster, bds 102 Williams
James Joseph, painter, bds 20 W. Jefferson
James Jesse M., lab, bds 102 Williams
Jantz Charles, lab, h 113 High
Jantz Christian, lab, h 19 Barthold
Jarisch Christian, lab, bds 81 Wells
Jasper Frederick, lab, h 124 Harrison

Jasper Frederick, carpenter Pitts. shop, bds 51 W. Washington
Jasper Frederick, jr., carpenter, bds 51 W. Washington
Jasper Rudolf, carpenter, h 51 W. Washington
Jeffords O. W. (Woolen Mills), h 131 E. Wayne
Jeffries Mrs. Susan, h 172 W. Main
Jefferds Amelia, widow, h 102 E. Lewis
Jeffries L. Q., editor *Sentinel*, bds Central Hotel
Jenkins J. D., bds Robinson House
Jenkinson Joe, clk, bds 49 and 51 W. Berry
Jennison William, attorney at law, bds Hamilton House
Jenrich John, brakeman Pitts. R'y, bds 49 Baker
Jennison Mrs. Mary, h 219 W. Wayne
Jenkins Frederick D., drug clk, bds 138 Broadway
Jenks Edward, fireman Wabash R'y, bds 292 W. Jefferson
Jerman A. S., h 63 W. Water
Jerome Ann, widow, h 5 Brandriff
Jobst Alexander, lab, h 140 Douglas
Jobst Bruno, cooper, h —, west of Wells
Jobst Amant, butcher, h 327 Lafayette
Jocquel Louis, bds 15 W. Washington
Jocquel J. J., lamp oil dealer, h 168 Calhoun
Jocquel Louis, book store, 170 Calhoun
Johnson Frederick, lab, bds 63 Baker
Johns G., saddler, h 205 Lafayette
Johns Alfred, harness maker, h 19 Monroe
Johnston M., cooper, h 346 E. Wayne
John Edward, collar mf., h 333 W. Washington
Johnson Lorer, conductor G. R. & I. R'y, h 26 Wert
Johnson William, brakeman, bds 330 Calhoun
Johnson Iaaac, watchman Pitts. shop, h 21 Taylor
Johns Dell, brakeman Pitts. R'y, bds 196 Ewing
Johnson William, lab, bds 93 W. Washington
Johnston William (book-keeper Coombs & Co.), bds Hamilton House
Johnson James, lab, bds 100 Fairfield
Johnson John, lab, h 309 W. Washington
John A., lab, h 248 E. Jefferson
Johnson H., blacksmith, h 256 E. Washington
Johnson H., blacksmith Pitts. shop, bds 197 E. Jefferson
Johnson John, eng Ft. W., M. & C. R'y, bds Exchange Hotel
Johnson Elias, peddler, h 15 Douglas ave
Johnson Mary E., bds 91 E. Main
Johnson Hulda, widow, h 91 E. Main
Johnson Mary A., widow, bds 87 Barr
Johnson Thomas, brakeman Pitts. R'y, bds 82 Barr
Johnson A., bds 346 E. Wayne
Johns Alfred, jr., harness maker, bds 19 Monroe
Johnston William, cooper, bds 346 E. Wayne
John Nicholas, tailor, h 19 Pritchard

Johnson George Y., fireman Pitts. R'y, h 54 Chicago
John Human, book-keeper, bds 19 Pritchard
Johnson Horace, watchmaker and jeweler, h 252 Calhoun
Johns G., harness maker, h 140 Calhoun
Johnson Elias, tin and glassware dealer, 253 Calhoun
John A. S. & Son, mfg harness, 69 E. Main
Jones John, jr., machinist Wabash shop, h 64 Butler
Jones Thomas, clk Wabash office, h 30 Pine
Jones Ann, widow, h 228 Lafayette
Jones Edward, brakeman Wabash R'y, bds 123 Williams
Jones George M., fireman Wabash R'y, bds 20 Locust
Jones Harvey P., printer, bds 49 and 51 W. Berry
Jones Joseph H., M. D., h 329 W. Jefferson
Jones Mary, widow, bds 53 W. Water
Jones Mrs. Christine, h 161 W. Washington
Jones S. A., widow, bds 20 Harrison
Jones William A., attorney at law, bds Hamilton House
Jones Edward, eng Pitts. R'y, bds 137 Wallace
Jones John, lab, h 109 W. Jefferson
Jones Nancy, widow, bds 49 Harmer
Jones Charles E., clk, bds 146 Jackson
Jones George W., book-keeper, h 146 Jackson
Jones Charles, leader of band, h 114 Lafayette
Jones Frederick, hack driver, bds 18 E. Wayne
Jones William A., barber, h 152 Barr
Jones Frank, clk, bds 250 Calhoun
Joost Albert, music teacher, bds 82 W. Berry
JOSSE JOHN M., M. D., office Wagner's drug store, h 138 Wells
Josse George, druggist, h 18 Maiden Lane
Joslin William, agt Coombs & Co., h 175 Clinton
Jordan H. C., bds Central Hotel
Jourdain C., grocery and saloon, h 98 Maumee
Joyce Mark, mason, bds 245 Calhoun
Judkins H. B., eng, h 213 Broadway
Judkins James, machinist Pitts. shop, h 88 E. Lewis
Jungeblodt William, clk bds 21 and 23 E. Main
Jupp George, book-keeper, h 87 E. Washington

K

Kaag Frederick, agt, h 108 Harrison
Kaag Jacob clk, h 109 Barr
KABISCH JULIUS, saloon, 12 W. Main
Kabisch Rudolf, butcher, h 182 Fairfield
Kabisch Mrs. Louisa, h 182 Fairfield
Kætler William H., bucket turner
Kagle Mrs. ———, dress maker, 128 Calhoun

Kaiser Charles, lab, h 14 Gay
Kaison Ernst, helper Pitts. shop, h 186 E. Lewis
Kaiser ———, lab Pitts. shop, bds 293 Hanna
KALBACHER ANTON, dealer in provisions, &c., 286 Calhoun, h 234 E. Wayne
Kall A. L., fireman Pitts. R'y, h 38 Williams
Kalbacher Martz, bds 151 Barr
Kallehan William, lab, h 83 Williams
Kamphues Henry, clk, bds 57 E. Main
Kampe Adolf, clk, h 52 W. Lewis
Kammeier Conrad, watchman Wabash shop, h on Dewald
Kammeier Henry, lab, h 21 Barthold
Kamp George, mach Pitts. shop, h 32 Colerick
KAMM J. J., postmaster, h 112 E. Main
KANE JAMES M. & BRO., wholesale and retail dealers in Yankee notions, fancy goods, toys, &c., Calhoun, opp Keystone Block
Kane Thomas, clk, bds 264 Calhoun
Kana John, mason, h 88 Henry
Kane Alfred, eng Wabash R'y, bds 28 Locust
Kane Patrick H. (Kane & Bro.), h 66 W. Main
Kane James M. (Kane & Bro., notion store), h 50 W. Berry
Kane Hannah, widow, bds 50 W. Berry
Kanning William, h 59 E. Wayne
Kanne Frederick, contractor, h 33 Madison
Kanne Henry, clk, bds 33 Madison
Kanning Frederick, blacksmith, bds 99 E. Madison
Kanning Mrs. Sophia, h 99 E. Madison
Kappeln J., blacksmith, h 312 E. Wayne
Kappel Henry, lab, h 349 E. Lewis
Karber Peter, machinist Pitts. shop, h 290 Harrison
Karst Charles, foreman Lingenfelser's trunk factory, bds American House
Kassens Nicholas, jr., lab, bds 161 E. Washington
Kassens Nicholas, sr., bds 161 E. Washington
Kassack William, lab, h E. Washington
Katt August, clk, bds 135 Madison
Katt C., mason, h 135 Madison
Kaufman Christian, butcher, h 1 Broadway
Kavanaugh James, street car driver, bds 260 Calhoun
Kavanaugh Thomas, lab, h 62 Griffith
Kayser Christian, h 127 Madison
Kayser Mena, widow, h 127 Madison
Kayser Frederick, shoemaker, h 139 Madison
Kayser Conrad, millwright, h 35 First
Kayser Frederick, tailor, h 9 N. Cass
Kayser & McNulty, boots and shoes, store 117 Lafayette
Kay John, lab, bds 140 Holman
Kayser Prederick (K. & McNulty), h 139 Madison
Kearns Luther, lab, h 141 Force

Keagan Frank, fireman Pitts. R'y, h 402 Calhoun
Keanly Frederick, street car driver, h 323 Hanna
Kearman John, bds 100 Montgomery
Keaton John, lab, bds 20 Chicago
Keagle Catherine, widow, h 8 Colerick
Keefer Henry, clk, h 201 Barr
Keegan P. H., eng Pitts. R'y, h 155 W. Washington
Keegan Thomas, moulder Bass' Foundry, bds 274 Hanna
Keegan James, machinist, bds 121 E. Washington
Keever William, bds American House
Keever William H., collar maker, bds American house
Keegan William, boiler maker, bds 121 E. Washington
Keffe Catherine, widow, h 69 Holman
Kegelman Julius, upholster, h 271 W. Washington
Kegstein Joe, lab, bds 3 and 5 Railroad
KEIL, A. C., drug store, 128 Broadway, h 138 Broadway
Keil D. S. (Keil & Bro.), book store, bds 248 W. Wayne
KEINZ PHILIP, saloon, &c., h cor Lafayette and Wallace
Keil Frederick W., book store, h 248 W. Wayne
Keil Lewis D. (K. & Bro., bds 248 W. Wayne
Keifer C., stone cutter, h 25 Wert
Keil Conrad, shoemaker, h 149 Wells
Kelly Michael, saloon, 270 Calhoun, bds Harmon House
Kelly William H., brakeman, h 287 E. Washington
Kettler Conrad, upholster, bds 205 E. Jefferson
Kettler Lizzie, widow, h 205 E. Jefferson
Kellogg Douglas, clk, bds 106 Jackson
Kellogg Mrs. Lizzie, h 73 High
Kelly Patrick, lab, h 11 Walnut
Keller Henry, blacksmith Pitts. shop, h 25 Williams
Keller & Co., stone cutters and builders, cor Griffith and Pearl
Kelly James, boiler maker, bds 120 W. Water
Kelly John, lab, 17 Bass
Kelly John, lab, bds 313 Harrison
Keller Charles, sr., file cutter, h 224 W. Main
Kelly Timothy, lab, h 18 Brandriff
Kelpler Gerge, lab, h 26 Gay
Keller Joseph, cigar manufacturer, h 203 E. Wayne
Kelker Anthony, eng Pitts. R'y, h 174 Griffith
Kelly Thomas, lab, h 108 Douglas
Keller Charles, lab, bds 285 Hanna
Keller Amos, lab, h 102 Wallace
Kelsey James T., bds 22 Harrison
Kelling Frederick, ice dealer, h 83 W. Washington
Kelker George, foreman Pitts. shop, h 184 Francis
Kelker Samuel, eng Pitts. R'y, bds 98 Montgomery
Keller Sebastian, stone cutter, h 313 W. Washington
Kelly William B., brakeman Pitts. R'y, bds 19 Hood

Kelly J. S., bds Phillips House, 107 Columbia
Kelker Henry, eng., h 232 Lafayette
Kelker Mary, widow, h 98 Montgomery
Keller Charles, jr., file cutter, bds 244 W. Main
Keller Cassimer, expressman, h 19 Nirdlinger
Kelker John, blacksmith Pitts. shop, h 78 Force
Kelly Oliver, brakeman Pitts. R'y, h 16 Holman
KELLER & FOOTE, cigar manufacturers, 100 Barr
Keller Samuel, marble cutter, bds 50 E. Washington
Kelley Christopher, City Marshal, h 47 E. Washington
Kellenberger Mrs. Frances, widow, h 65 E. Wayne
Kempf William, grocer and baker, h 17 High
Kemp R. L., blacksmith, bds 104 Barr
Kemp Robert S., blacksmith, bds 25 Barr
Kenneth John. lab, h 19 Baker
Kendel John H., yard master Pitts. R'y, h 64 Chicago
Kennedy William, conductor G. R. & I. R'y, bds 13 Maumee
Kenney Dennis, lab, bds 20 Chicago
Kensill George, machinist, bds 150 E. Jefferson
Kensill John C., boiler maker, h 150 E. Jefferson
Keough William, agent, bds 64 Barr
Keplinger J. A., eng. Pitts. R'y, h 61 Chicago
KERR, W. J., attorney, office northwest cor. Main and Calhoun, h 154 Griffith
Kerr Joseph M., carp, 120 W. Water
Kerr B. M., clk, h 15 E. Jefferson
Kern Jacob F., book-keeper, bds Robinson House
KESTEL P., dealer in musical instruments and notions, also agent for Ætna Sewing Machine Co., 76 Calhoun
Kessens C., carp, h 35 Maumee
Kessans William, h 170 E. Washington
Kessler Frederick, butcher, h 88 E. Wayne
Ketcher M., widow, bds 104 W. Washington
Ketscher John, lab, h 23 Charles
Kether Emily P., widow, h 200 E. Wayne
Ketchum Walter, blacksmith, h 162 Calhoun
Ketchum Harison, blacksmith, bds 162 Calhoun
Kettler William, clk, bds 205 E. Jefferson
Ketker Frederick, blacksmith Pitts. shop, h 18 Lavina
Ketchum Walter, blacksmith, h 104 Columbia
Keutz Simon, moulder Bass' Foundry, bds 8 Force
Keys John Monroe, h 70 Williams
Keys Thomas H., brakeman Pitts. R'y h 197 E. Lewis
Key Herbert, wks Olds & Son, bds 79 Holman
Keys Taylor, conductor Wabash R'y, bds 19 Holman
Keys A. B., brakeman Wabash R'y, bds 19 Holman
Keys Jane, widow, h 19 Holman
Kibler Charles, clk, bds 11 E. Main

Kibler Abraham, cooper, bds 29 Butler
Kiefer George, h 27 Wall
Kierspe Charles, machinist Wabash shop, h 39 Locust
Kiefer Henry, clk, h 185 Ewing
Kiefer George, carp, bds 27 Wall
Kiefer Christian, carp, bds 27 Wall
Kiefer Philip, lab, h 27 Wall
Kiefer Jacob, carp, h 34 Wall
Kiefhaber George, lab, h 22 Pritchard
Kiefer Adolph, tinner, bds 185 Ewing
Kiefer Jack, lab, bds cor. Clinton and Washington
Kikly Frances, widow, h 90 Chicago
Kikly H., brakeman Wabash R'y, bds 90 Chicago
Kilpatrick Oscar D., lab, h N. Harrison
Killkinny John, lab, bds 203 Calhoun
Kiley Mary, widow, h 33 Colerick
Kiley John, switchman Pitts. R'y, bds 33 Colerick
Killian Joseph, lab, bds 76 Wallace
Kimball I. E., brakeman Pitts. R'y, h 43 Lavina
Kimball Mrs. Ann L., h 43 Lavina
Kimball Samuel, teacher of music, h 126 Williams
Kimball Frederick, h 126 Williams
Kimmel Michael, lab, h 257 Hanna
Kimball B. H., carp, h 29 West
Kintz Alexander, mason, h cor Fourth and North Harrison
Kinnan John M., h 392 Calhoun
Kinney Michael, lab, h 23 Henry
Kinlein Adam, lab, h 90 Fairfield
Kincade B. F., carp, h 53 E. Madison
King I. D., blacksmith, bds 104 Barr
Kinsey J. J., barber, bds American House
King John, harness maker, h 41 Harrison
King Moses, lab, h 229 E. Wayne
Kintz John, carp Pitts. shop, h 174 Montgomery
King George E., machinist Pitts. shop, h 125 Montgomery
Kintz John, policeman, h 293 Hanna
Kinner August, lab, bds 76 Wallace
King John, brick mason, bds 98 Montgomery
Kincade William, eng. Wabash R'y, h 10 Wert
King V., lab, h 265 E. Washington
Kirchhoff Mrs. Caroline, h 157 Broadway
Kirkley Richard, conductor Wabash R'y, bds 77 Baker
Kirkley William, yard master Wabash R'y, bds 77 Baker
Kirchner Gottlieb W., lab, h 43 Wilt
Kirbach Frederick, lab, h 47 Buchanan
Kirk Margaret, widow, bds 188 Lafayette
Kirchhoffer Alexander, lab, bds 231 Barr
Kirchner Mrs. Paulina, h 237 Lafayette

Kiser Diedrich, lab, h 148 Broadway
Kiser Ellis, draftsman, bds 70 W. Wayne
Kiser Charles, machinist, bds 70 W. Wayne
Kiser Byron, clk, bds 70 W. Wayne
Kiser Peter, h 70 W. Wayne
Kiser Wayne, bds 70 W. Wayne
Kiser Anthony, tailor, h 252 W. Jefferson
Klahen John J., furniture manufacturer, shop 42 and 44 W. Main
Klenke Conrad, lab, h 58 W. Lewis
Kley Frederick, jr., bds 240 W. Main
Klee John, painter, h 378 E. Washington
Kleiner John, painter, h 147 Griffith
Klein John, lab, h 263 Hanna
Kleinhanz John, blacksmith, bds 91 W. Water
Kleinnegees Henrietta, widow, 170 Lafayette
Klett Jacob, lab, h 24 Hood
Kleinegees Mattie, bds 170 Lafayette
KLEY FREDERICK, sr., cooper, h 240 W. Main
Kley Charles, cooper, bds 240 W. Main
Kleinmuller Henry, blacksmith, h 55 E. Madison
Kleinschmidt ———, lab, h 19 W. Washington
Klein Karl, lab, h 75 Lafayette
Kline Jacob, grocery store, 30 Columbia
Klix Pauline, widow, 31 E. Main
Klippert George, baker, 62 E. Main
Klinkel Michael, brakeman Pitts. R'y, h 202 Ewing
Klinger Isaac, teamster, h 57 W. Water
Kliber Mrs. Barbara, h 297 Hanna
Kliber Sebastian, brakeman Wabash R'y, bds 297 Hanna
Klingenberger John, car inspector Pitts. R'y, h 65 Charles
Klingman John, lab, h 373 Lafayette
Kline Frederick, clk, h 1 Sturgis
Kline Peter, bds 118 E. Berry
Klingenberger Mrs. M., h 190 E. Lewis
KLOTZ & WELTON, provision store, 372 Calhoun
Klotz Daniel, provision store (Klotz & Co.), h 372 Calhoun
Klopper Henry, lab, h 19 Wilt
Klugg Gregor, shoemaker, h 196 Hanna
Klug Martin, carp, h 293 E. Wayne
KNAPP ISAAC, dentist, office cor Clinton and Berry, h on Fairfield Avenue
Knapp Albert, wks Wabash R'y, h 20 Locust
Knapp William B., dentist, bds Fairfield
Knecht D., carp., h 22 W. Jefferson
Knecht Samuel, knitting machine agent, h 118 Broadway
Knecht Frank, lab, h 11 High
Knight John, book agent, bds Exchange Hotel
Knight Thomas, carp. Pitts. shop, bds 219 Lafayette

Knowder George, painter Pitts. shop, h 43 Brackenridge
Knothe Julius, h 51 E. Jefferson
Knowel Henry, machinist Wabash shop, h 33 Wilt
KOCH MRS. MARGARET, notions and fancy goods, 152 Calhoun
Koch Anton, lab, h 57 W. Lewis
Koch Christian, street buyer, bds 45 W. Jefferson
Koch John (Swartz & Co.), harness maker, bds 152 Calhoun
KOCH JOHN M., Recorder of Allen County, h 150 Calhoun
Kochs Frank, lab, h 27 High
Koch John, lab, bds 111 W. Water
Koch Christian, carp., h 72 Brackenridge
Kochel Richard, engineer Bloomingdale Mills, bds Bloomingdale Hotel
Koch Adam, lab, h 34 John
Koch Anton, h 58 W. Lewis
Koch Frederick, shoemaker, bds 72 Brackenridge
Koch J. B., grocer, h 124 E. Washington
Koch Henry, cigar maker, h 57 E. Wayne
Koch John W., tailor, h 119 Lafayette
Kœgel Christian, carp., shop 46 Lavina, h cor Broadway and Lavina
Kœster Christian, sr., h 151 Harrison
KŒNIG REV. EDWARD, h 138 W. Washington
Kœster John, shoe shop, 160 Calhoun
Kœster Bernard, lab, bds 160 Calhoun
Kohlman Conrad, lab, h 11 Marion
Kohn William, shoemaker, h 217 E. Jefferson
Kohles Gottlieb, mason, h 385 E. Wayne
Kohles August, h 90 Maumee
Kohrman Andrew, tailor, h 314 E. Wayne
Kohlmann Jacob, watchman, h 147 E. Jefferson
Kolb John A., chair maker, h 81 Montgomery
Kolb George A., lab, h 202 W. Wayne
Kolthoff Frederick, lab, h 11 Wall
Komp Daniel, carp., h 141 Henry
Konig William, boiler maker (Bass'), h 333 E. Washington
Koop Mrs. Mary, h 88 Fairfield
Koons Andrew, eng. Pitts. R'y, h 212 Francis
Koop Henry, lab, bds 88 Fairfield
Kookerly Joseph, blacksmith, bds 152 E. Wayne
Kopman Frederick, lab, bds 53 W. Jefferson
Kopman Henry, lab, bds 53 W. Jefferson
Kopp Michael, lab Bass' Foundry, h 167 Hanna
Kortrey Mrs. K., widow, h 84 E. Wayne
Korte Frederick, carp., h 177 E. Lewis
KOVER & RIVERS, painters, shop cor Main and Calhoun, up stairs
Kover O. J., painter, h 39 W. Washington
Kramer William, moulder, h 348 E. Wayne
Kramer William, lab, h 147 Madison
Krack A., teamster, h 325 E. Lewis

Krauskopf Henry, bds 213 Madison
Kranz Peter, painter, bds 20 Wilt
Kramer Charles, lab, h 32 Lavina
Krackman M., painter, h 344 E. Wayne
Kratzsch Charles, clk, bds 15 W. Wayne
Kranmer Otto, clk, bds 34 W. Washington
Kratzsch Herman, h 15 W. Wayne
Kramer Bernard, clk at J. G. Fledderman's, h 49 E. Madison
Kraft Frederick, carp., h 317 Lafayette
Kranzman Henry, h 129 Monroe
Krack B., lab, bds 325 E. Lewis
Kramer Matthias, slate roofer, h 465 Lafayette
Kratzsch Frederick, lab, h 345 E. Lewis
Krah C., mason, h 95 Ewing
Kramer Henry, h 95 Wilt
Krammer C., clk, bds 348 E. Wayne
Krackman J., painter, h 385 E. Wayne
Krabbenschmiedt E., lab, bds 178 Barr
Krackman Frederick, painter, bds 344 E. Wayne
Kraus David, butcher, bds 92 W. Main
Krefft Conrad, lab, h 181 Jackson
Kresz E., lab, h 133 Henry
KREADY JOHN, proprietor St. Charles Saloon and Restaurant, 26 W. Main
Kreft Frederick, lab, h 333 E. Lewis
Kremer John, slate roofer, h 74 Wallace
Kressler John, hack driver, h 90 Hanna
Kress Melcher, lab, h 29 Pine
Krimmel Christian, carp. Pitts. shop, h 55 Douglas ave
Kridler C., lab, h 184 Montgomery
Krieg George, lab, h 9 Wert
Krickeberg Christian, helper Bass' Foundry, bds 18 Hough
Kronmiller Leonard, cooper, h 103 Cass
Kronemiller George, lab, h 43 Taylor
Krontz Joseph, lab, h 282 W. Jefferson
Krock John, carp., h 95 Clay
Krock George, sawyer, h 95 Clay
Krœzinger Christian, lab, h 149 Wells
Krull R., lab, h 266 E. Washington
Kruse Ernst H., lab, h on Dewald
Krudop John B., contractor, h 29 W. Jefferson
Krudop John, lab, bds 263 W. Wayne
Kruse John F., h 20 Wall
Kruse Henry, carp., h 415 E. Wayne
Krutzsch F. W., machinist Pitts. shop, h 71 Webster
Kruse Christian, lab, bds 178 Barr
Kruse Henry, machinist Pitts. shop, h 161 Montgomery
Krueger A. C., clk, bds Robinson House

Kucher Rev. John, h 195 W. Washington
Kuffman Jacob. carp., h 202 Lafayette
Kuhne F. W., Deputy Auditor, h 124 W. Jefferson
Kuhfuss Julius, machinist Wabash shop, bds 18 Colerick
Kuntz Adam, butcher, h 273 W. Main
Kuntz Jacob, machinist Wabash shop, h 270 W. Jefferson
Kuntz George, upholster, h 292 W. Jefferson
Kunfer Owen, carp., bds 3 Dawson
Kunker E., machinist, h 138 E. Wayne
Kuntz Allen W., printer, bds 104 Barr
Kurtis Charles, brakeman Pitts. R'y, bds 49 Baker
Kurtz Margaret, widow, h 65 Melitta
Kuttner Joe, carp. Pitts. shop, h 239 E. Jefferson
Kyle Abraham, pump maker, h 218 Broadway

L

Lacks Lizzie. widow. h 205 E. Washington
Laepple Christian, carp, Pittsburgh shop, h 51 Grand
Laemuel John, potter, shop, 295 W. Main
Lafin John, lab, h 315 Hanna
Lafrenz Henry, h 294 W. Jefferson
Lafin Michael, lab, bds 315 Hanna
Lageman Henry, lab, h 9 Buchanan
Lageman Rudolph, lab, h 34 Buchanan
Lahmeier John,
Laidlaw, P. B.. slate roofer. h cor John and Samuel
Laible Gottleib, candy maker, (Trentman, Wolke & Co.), bds 4 Wayne
Lamb Charles, bds 121 E. Washington
Lamley Moses, (L. & Rosenthal), h 128 W. Wayne
Lamb David, supt. Wabash water works, h 181 Fairfield ave
Lampker Mary, widow, h 19 W. Washington
Lemer Charles, plasterer, h 162 Calhoun
Lamley & Rosenthal manuf. vinegar and cigars, 69 Columbia
Lamboley John B., saloon and boarding, h an Lafayette, opp. Comparet's mill
Lamb George, fireman, Pittsburgh R'y, bds 233 Lafayette
Lambard L., agt., bds 82 W. Berry
Landsman Fred, grocer, 18 Harrison, h 11 N. Cass
Langohr John, lab, h 129 Wells
Lancaster Charles, molder, (Bass' foundry), bds 137 Wallace
Lannest John, carp, h 142 E. Washington
Lang Peter, lab, h 176 E. Washington
Lang Harry P., h 12 Melitto
Lanigan Patrick, watchman, Pitsburgh R'y, bds 33 Brackenridge
Landis Mrs. Mattie, h 125 Calhoun
Lang Edward, foreman *Sentinel* job office, bds 71 Douglas ave

Lang A. J., (Geo. DeWald & Co.), bds W. Berry.
Langenbacher Mathias, lab, 21 Wall
Landon William H., barkeman, Wabash R'y, h 309 W. Jefferson
Langohr Andrew, bakery, 139 Broadway
Lang John, clk, h 4 Marion
Langley John, farmer, h 3 Bass
Lang George, barber, h 30 Wells
Lang Lenard, eng, Wabash R'y,
LANGARD JOSEPH, Saloon and Boarding House, h 58 and 60 Columbia
Langheinrich Mrs. Frederike, h 13 Francis
Laman Ann, widow, h 43 W. Berry
Laman Edward, lab, bds 43 W. Berry
Laman Augustus, lab, bds 43 W. Berry
Lankenau Frank, carp, Wabash shop, h 80 W. Jefferson
Lancaster Robt,, fireman, Pittsburgh R'y, bds 137 Wallace
Lancaster John, machinist, Pittsburgh shop, h 137 Wallace
Lange William, lab, h 288 W. Jefferson
Lange Fred, machinist, bds 48 McClellan
Landraft Mary, widow, h 189 Ewing
Landgraf John, lab, h 81 Force
Lange H. F. B., clk, bds Robinson House
Lankenau Henry, Deputy Sheriff, h 84 W. Jefferson
Lapp Henry, baker, bds cor Harrison and Berry
Larwill John S., manager Agricultural Works
Larwell John S., Propr. Agricultural Works, h 89 E. Berry
Larrofee Thomas, eng, Pittsburgh R'y, h 197 Barr
Lasse J. T., ins. agt., h 130 W. Wayne
Lasse F. B., M. D., bds 130 W. Wayne
Lase Henry, carp, h 41 Douglas ave
Lattimer Phillip, bucket turner, bds 39 Water
Lauer Justin, carp, h 13 John
Lauderbach Charles, pedler, h 111 Force
Laur Conrad, lab, h 116 Maumee
Lauer Henry, mason, h 17 Nirdlinger
Lauer William lab, h 287 E. Washington
Lauer Peter, lab, h 289 E. Washington
Lauer Joseph, carp, bds 293 E. Wayne
Lauer Ferdinand, sausage maker, h 88 E. Wayne
Lauer B., (Schele & Lauer), h 15 E. Wayne
LAURENT JOHN & SON, Wholesale Dealers in Wines and Liquors, and Manufs. of Mineral Water, 29 and 31 Barr
Lauer Paul, saloon, h 150 Barr
Lau Thomas, h 122 Calhoun
Lau Julian, clk, bds 122 Calhoun
Laufferty Isaac, (McDougal & Laufferty, brokers), h 75 W. Berry
Laubscher Ludwig, architect, office cor Harrison and Main, h 41 Wells
Laurent Anthony, (J. L. & Son), h 29 and 31 Barr

Laughlin William, bds 457 Lafayette
Laufferty Alex., bds 75 W. Berry
Laufferty M. J., merchant, h 97 W. Wayne
Laughlin Samuel W., millwright, h 249 E. Lewis
Lauer John A., night watchman, Pittsburgh R'y, h 241 E. Washington
Laveley Lewis, cooper, bds 408 W. Main
Lawrence Robt. B., express agt., h 99 E. Wayne
Lawrence Alex., eng, Pittsburgh R'y, bds 16 Chicago
Laykoff Nicholas, Boston Bakery, 209 Broadway
Layer Martin, switchman, Pittsburgh yard, h 59 Lasselle
Lazzarini Amadeus, frescoer, h 37 Barr
Leach John, fireman, Pittsburgh R'y, h 84 Henry
Leach John S., carp, h 16 Poplar
Leach William, boiler maker, Wabash shop, h 52 William
Leach Albert, brakeman, Wabash R'y, bds 73 Grand
Leach James, machinist, Pittsburgh shop, h 140 Holman
Leach John T., boiler maker, Pittsburgh shop, bds 140 Holman
Lebenberger John, carp, Pittsburgh shop, h 297 Hanna
Lechler Anthony, agt., bds 46 E. Jefferson
Lechler Henry, agt., bds 46 E. Jefferson
Lechtman H., lab, h 157 Ewing
Lee Frank, brakeman, Pittsburgh R'y, bds 402 Calhoun
Lee E., Boss, Pittsburgh car shop, h 232 E. Lewis
Leeson John, foreman, Pittsburgh shop, h 96 E. Wayne
Lee Louis H., foreman, Pittsburgh freight office, h 16 Chicago
Lee George, lab, bds 112 Hanna
Leeke George, fireman, Pittsburgh R'y, bds 232 E. Lewis
Leffler Henry, h 66 W. Jefferson
Lefferts Walter, brakeman, Wabash R'y, bds 55 Melita
Lefferts Montgomery, brakeman, Wabash R'y, bds 55 Melitta
Legras Joseph, h 14 Lafayette
Legras Margaret, widow, h 14 Lafayette
Legitt Charles, baggage master, bds 29 Pearl
Legget James, (L. & Bro.), livery, h 176 Griffith
Legget R. A., (L. & Bro.), livery stable, bds Exchange Hotel
Legras Augustus, clk, bds 66 Columbia
Legras John, lab, bds 14 Lafayette
Lehrman John, wks Pittsburgh shop, bds 100 Montgomery
Lehnert Augustus, cooper, bds Bloomingdale Hotel
Lehnenke Fred, machinist, h 86 Chicago
Lehman Jacob, brakeman, Wabash R'y, h 48 William
Lehman George, brakeman, Pittsburgh R'y, bds 54 William
Lehman Jacob, lab, h 54 William
Lehman Charles, lumber merchant, h 127 E. Washington
Lehman David, pedler, h 162 Lewis
Lehmeyer Henry, saloon, 195 Lafayette
Lehr Jesse, plasterer, h 163 Clinton
Lehsing John, blacksmith, h 314 E. Wayne

Lehmeyer Daniel, carp, h 232 W. Washington
Lehmeyer Henry, lab, h 180 Montgomery
Lehman John, painter, h 220 E. Washington
Lehman Mrs. Ada, h 122 W. Jefferson
Leifels Joseph, Professor of Music, h 239 Barr
Leinker Ernst, lab, bds 19 Marion
Leikauf, C., lab, bds 23 Hood
Leinker Henry, cabinet maker, h 19 Marion
Leisring Charles, mason, h 17 Wefel
Leicken H., lab, h on E. Washington
Leichner Conrad, bds Steuben House
LEICHNER JOHN, Saloon on Main, opp. Court House, h 35 Douglas ave
Leichner Charles, clk, bds American House
Leikauf Nick, Propr. Boston Bakery, h 23 Hood
Leighton George W., barber, bds 76 Columbia
Leimkohle Fred, policeman, h 90 Barr
Leikoff John, butcher, 94 Barr
Leinsbole Henry, lab, bds 4 W. Water
Leichner William, saloon, 35 E. Main
Leichner R., bds 35 Douglas ave
Leikauf Fred, switchman, Wabash R'y, bds 23 Hood
Leimon Charles, clk, h 255 E. Lewis
Leidolf Conrad, clk, bds 170 Lafayette
Leinkoof Theodore, brakeman, Wabash R'y, bds 23 Hood
Leith J. D., bds Robinson House
Lemkuler Casper, lab, h 324 Hanna
Leaviger Gottlieb, saloon, h 135 and 137 Calhoun
Lenhart F. L., Mrs., widow, h 157 Hanna
Lencker John, brakeman, Pittsburgh R'y, h 236 Lafayette
Leonhardt Henry, lab, 344 Broadway
Leonard William, gunsmith, h 49 W. Water
Lepper Christopher, bds 77 Water
Lepple Gottleib, lab, h 17 Poplar
Lepper C., bds 77 E. Water
Lepper Henry, carp, h 242 E. Jefferson
Lepper F., carpenter, bds 242 E. Jefferson
Lester Mrs. Ann, bds 118 Jackson
Lester James, machinist, Wabash shop, bds 150 W. Jefferson
LEUTZ FRED, h 58 W. Wayne
LEUTZ, BOURIE & CO., Wholesale Wine and Liquor Dealers, Miner Block, cor Main and Clinton
Leutz Henry, lab, h 108 Force
Leuz Ernst, bds 21 Gay
Leuz Jackson, h 21 Gay
Levi August, pedler, h 67 W. Main
Levi David, pedler, h 16 Madison
Levan John, clk, bds 22 Madison

Levan John, clk, bds 197 Jefferson
Lewis Silvester, agt., bds 89 W. Water
Lewis D. M., h 157 High
Lewis Charles, lab, bds 63 Wells
Lewis William, h 129 E. Lewis
Lewis John, machinist, bds 129 E. Lewis
Lewis, Dr., h 79 E. Main
Lewis George, bds 402 Calhoun
Lewis William, conductor, Pittsburgh R'y, bds 322 Calhoun
Lewis Bayless A., city dyer, h 106 W. Water
Lichtrin William, clk, bds 92 Barr
Lichtenberg John, carpenter, bds 115 Barr
Lichtsinn C., lab, bds 157 Ewing
Lidley Nelson, machinist, Pittsburgh shop, h 321 Harrison
Lieveman R., saloon keeper, bds 85 E. Wayne
Lieb Henry, plasterer, h 81 E. Madison
Lillie John, h 67 College
Lillie George, bds 67 College
Lillie Henry, bds on Piqua road
Lillie Mary, widow, h on Piqua road
Lillie James, (Lillie & Co., lime dealers), h 87 Cass
Lillie John Jr., clk, h 39 Second
LILLIE JAMES & CO., Manufs. and Dealers in Lime, Cement, &c., 1 Calhoun, on canal
Link Adam, bds Exchange Hotel
Linderman John, helper, Wabash shop, h 197 Lafayette
Lineker Valentine, brewer, h 16 Monroe
Lindlag C. W., h 115 W. Washington
Lintz Anthony, street car driver, bds 12 E. Columbia
Lintz Martin, clk, bds 12 E. Columbia
Lindman Joe, bds 84 W. Main
Linker Henry E., butcher, h 46 W. Berry
Lindlag Jacob, teamster, h 115 W. Washington
Linch Mrs. Catherine, h 40 Lasselle
Linderman Henry, carp, Pittsburgh shop, h 100 Wilt
Linderman Lewis, bds 100 Wilt
Lintz Delia, widow, h 12 E. Columbia
Lindman Fred, tailor, h 25 William
Lincoln Charles, helper, Pittsburgh shop, h 117 Holman
Lininger Peter, lab, h 105 Gay
Lininger Jacob, brakeman, Richmond R. R., h 105 Gay
Lintz Martin, clk, bds 225 W. Washington
Lindeman Daniel, teacher, h 245 W. Washington
Lintz Mrs. Delia, h 225 W. Washington
Lintz Anthony, street car driver, bds 225 W. Washington
Linenberg C., machinist, h 22 Hood
Linderman William, carp, h 48 Water
Link George, carp, h 236 E. Jefferson

Linch John, lab, h 5 Hoagland
Ling George W., clk, h 328 Lafayette
Linker Valentine, (L. Hey & Co.), h 8 Monroe
Lingenfelser, Emile, trunk maker, bds American House
Lingenfelser, John Jr., trunk maker, bds Robinson House
Lingenfelser John Sr., bds 31 Columbia
LINGENFELSER HENRY, Manuf. of Trunks, Valises, etc., 10 W. Columbia, (old 117), h 157 E. Wayne
LINCKER, HEY & CO., Brewers, cor Monroe & Wayne
Lipes T., fireman Wabash R'y, bds 197 E. Jefferson
Liscom John, brakeman, Saginaw R. R., bds 120 W. Water
Lissing G., lab, bds 266 E. Washington
Little Albert N., painter, Pittsburgh shop, h 194 Lafayette
Littlejohn William, blacksmith, Wabash shop, h 54 Walnut
Little George L., h foot of Water
Litt George, pedler, bds Fox House
Little George, lab, h 38 Gay
LOAG & BROWN, Dentists, office Keystone Block, over Nirdlinger's Palace of Fashion
Loag G. W., dentist, h 20 E. Washington
Lœbking Charles H., policeman, h 33 Jefferson
Lœther Gotlieb, lab, bds Bloomingdale Hotel
Logan Scott A., switchman, Wabash R'y, h 312 Harrison
Logg William, carpenter, h 196 Fairfield ave
Logan Jane, widow, h 312 Harrison
Lohman Joseph, clk, bds 46 W. Wayne
Lomont Adolph, moulder, h 16 Marion
Lombard Eugene, machinist, h 231 E. Jefferson
Long Henry, h 53 High
Long John E., fireman, Pittsburgh R'y, h 129 Wallace
Lonergan J. B., machinist, Wabash shop, h 313 Hanna
Longaker M. P., clk, Pittsburgh freight office, bds 16 Chicago
Long John, conductor, Pittsburgh R'y, h 20 William
Long Robt. J., fireman, Pittsburgh R'y, h 31 Baker
Lonergan Margaret, widow, h 164 Madison
Long Mason, bds 93 Calhoun
Loos Henry, h out lot Hamilton's add
Loock Walter, clk, bds American House
Lordier Augustus, saloon, 20 Clinton
Lord Alonzo, brakeman, Muncie R. R., bds 40 Wells
Lordier Phillip, shoemaker, h 22 Baker
LORDIER PHILLIP, Manuf. and Dealer in Boots and Shoes, 88 Calhoun
LOSEE JOSEPH T., General Insurance Agent, office over Post Office, h 130 W. Wayne
Loustrum Nelson, lab, bds at B. H. Sliger's
Louttit James, wheel maker, (O. & Son), h 337 Lafayette
Loucks E. H., fireman, Pittsburgh R'y, bds 333 Hanna

Lovett Michael, lab, bds 20 Chicago
Lovell James, moulder, (Bass' foundry), bds cor Calhoun and Wallace
Lowinsky Herman, clk, bds 136 W. Wayne
Lowrie Hattie D., widow, h 106 W. Wayne
LOWRY ROBERT, Judge Circuit Court, h 251 W. Main
Lowry Robt., Jr., collector, Gas Co., bds 252 W. Main
Loyd Mal., Clerk, bds W. Berry.
Loyer Stephen, lab, h 323 Hanna
Luckel Conrad, bds 36 Colerick
Lucke Christian, lab, bds 178 Barr
Luce David, eng, Grand Rapids R. R., bds 60 Chicago
Lucken Barney, lab, bds E. Washington
Ludlum S. S., Editor *Journal*, h 68 Barr
Luers J., lab, bds 171 Calhoun
Luhrman Christian, Jr., teamster, h 213 W. Washington
Luhrman Christian, Sr., h 213 W. Washington
Luhrman William, teamster, 213 W. Washington
Luhman William, tailor, h 21 High
Lukens A. T., b. k., bds 259 W. Wayne
Lukub Andrew, lab, h 31 Lasselle
Luley Frank, lab, (Bass' shop), h 2 Jones
Luley Phillip, lab, h 279 Hanna
Luley F. J., carp, h 171 E. Jefferson
Lumbard Lucien, agt. Grover & Baker's sewing machines, 16 W. Berry
Lumbard Joseph, life insurance agt., h 344 W. Jefferson
Lumbard Sanford, ins. agt., h 99 W. Main
Lumbard Mrs. A,. h 99 W. Main
Lumbard Eugene, machinist, Pittsburgh shop, h 95 Montgomery
Lumbard S. C., ins. agt.. h 133 W. Wayne
Lund Hans, draftsman, (Bass' shop), bds
Lunger James, sawyer, h 84 Van Buren
Lund Hans, draftsman, (Bass' foundry), h 151 Holman
Lupton Jos., lab, h 140 W. Main
Lurwig A. labr, bds 266 E. Washington
Lurwig Jno., well digger, bds 266 E. Washington
Luther Jacob, fireman Pittsburgh R'y, h 40 Force
Lye J. M. bds 98 Montgomery
Lyles Jno. A., blacksmith, h 226 E. Lewis
Lyman Wm., brakeman Wabash R'y., bds 13 Poplar
Lynn Lewis, carpenter h 203 W. Washington
Lyne Wm., Lyne & Markey florists, h 29 W. Lewis
Lye J. M., clerk, bds Central Hotel
Lypes R. F. fireman Wabash R'y., bds 22 Madison
Lynch Thomas, bds 12 Kansas
Lynch John., laborer, h 103 Lafayette
Lynch John, carpenter, bds 103 W. Main
Lynch Mrs. Mary, h 103 W. Main
Lynch John, helper Wabash Round House, h 202 Lafayette

Lytle Charles, bds 146 W. Berry

M

Maag William F., foreman *Staats-Zeitung*, h 56 Nelson
Mack Lawrence, of Mack Bros., bds Mayer House
Mack Samuel, of Mack Bros., bds Mayer House
Mack Brothers, dealers in ready made clothing, 26 E. Columbia
Madden John, boiler maker Wabash shop, bds 6 Kansas
Madigan Bridget, widow, h 48 Baker
Madison William, machinist Pitts. shop, h 193 Montgomery
Madison William, jr., machinist Pitts. shop, bds 193 Montgomery
Madison Christian, fireman Wabash R'y, bds 122 W. Jefferson
Maganus, William, eng. Pitts. R'y, h 30 Butler
Mahurin M. B., book-keeper, bds 219 W. Main
Mahany Timothy, brakeman Pitts. R'y, bds 198 Lafayette
Mahrt Conrad, harness maker, h 8 Clark
Mahan James (Francis & Mahan), bds 176 W. Jefferson
Maher James, brakeman Wabash R'y, bds 4 Colerick
Mahan Mrs. Bridget, h 176 W. Jefferson
Mahr William, lab, bds 98 Columbia
Maier John A. (A. H. Carrier), h 315 E. Wayne
Maier John G., ex-Township Trustee, h 76 Lafayette
Maier Willis D., Deputy County Clerk, h 254 W. Jefferson
Maier Frederick, lab, h 7 Clark
Major David, asst. foreman Pitts. Round House, h 43 Charles
Makepeace Samuel D., printer, wks *Sentinel* office
Malloy Thomas, fireman Wabash R'y, bds 402 Calhoun
Malloy Edward, eng. Wabash R'y, bds 402 Calhoun
Malone Patrick, lab, h 51 Wilt
Malon Thomas, fireman Pitts. R'y, h 18 Melitta
Maley Patrick, lab, h 54 Melitta
Malon John, lab, h 102 Chicago
Malley E., fireman Wabash R'y, bds 68 Chicago
Malone Peter, lab, bds 39 Lavina
Malone Charles, lab, bds 39 Lavina
Malley Irwin, fireman Wabash shop, h 76 Dawson
Maloy James, boiler maker, wks Wabash shop, bds 23 Grand
Malle Henry, book-keeper, bds 187 E. Jefferson
Mallo Charles, wagon maker, h Calhoun, bet. Wallace and Hamilton
Mannuel Jules, clk, h 238 E. Wayne
Manthey John, lab. h 191 W. Main
Mansdorfer Jacob, glue mfg., h 29 Nirdlinger
Mannanrich Edward, wks Pitts. shop, h 92 Montgomery
Manthey William, civil eng., h 64 Maumee
Mannanrich Henry, tailor, h 92 Montgomery
Mangeot John, h 14 Lafayette

Manahon John, moulder at K. Murry's, bds 61 Kansas
Manor Joseph, carp, bds 110 Chicago
Manahon Michael, lab, bds 6 Kansas
Mannweiler Christian, blacksmith Pitts. shop, h 23 Poplar
Mansdorfer Mrs. Kate, h 29 Nirdlinger
Mannian Anthony, lab, bds 30 Melitta
Mangen Bridget, widow, h 3 Walnut
Manning Nelson, fireman Wabash R'y, bds 18 Walnut
Mangan Anthony, lab, h 78 Baker
Mank Marion, brakeman Pitts. R'y, bds 49 Baker
Manock Mrs. Caroline, h 121 W. Wayne
Manock Edward, driver, bds Centlivre Brewery
Mannier Margaret, widow, h 36 Barr
Manaray John, carp., h 177 E. Jefferson
Mangels C., mason, h 147 E. Lewis
MANIER MARGUERITE (Manier & Casso), 36 Barr
Mandelin A., lab, bds Exchange Hotel
Manyon Thomas, brakeman Pitts. R'y, bds 3 and 5 Railroad
Mannix Thomas, shoemaker, h 10 Holman
Manock Simon (M. & Kester), tanner, h 143 W. Wayne
Mansfield John, lab, bds cor. Calhoun and Wallace
Mann William, carp. Pitts. shop, h 105 Wallace
Manor Alexander, collar maker, bds 103 W. Main
Manier Francis, grocer, h 231 E. Jefferson
Manheimer Anthony, clk, bds 97 W. Wayne
Mapes Benjamin, lab, h — Taylor
Maples D. W., propr. Hanna House, cor. Barr and Washington
Martin Eliza, widow, h 28 Williams
Martin Frederick, carp., bds 57 Wilt
Marhanka Henry, lab, h 309 W. Washington
Martin George, clk, bds 206 W. Washington
Martin Anthony, book-keeper, bds 206 W. Washington
Martin Mrs. M., h 206 W. Washington
Martin J., moulder at K. Murray's, bds Kansas
Martin Henry, lab, h 41 N. Cass
Marion Frank N., conductor Pitts. R'y, h 65 Williams
Marsh Albert, fireman Pitts. R'y, h 66 Butler
Marhenke Frederick, shoemaker, h 147 High
Markman Charles, cabinet maker, bds 30 Walnut
Martin Barney, lab, h 52 Baker
Martin William, house mover, h 225 Broadway
Marr George, printer, bds Robinson House
MARKLEY, SCHRADER & CO., manufacturers and wholesale and retail dealers in boots and shoes, 4 Keystone Block, Calhoun
Marshall M. S., druggist, h 119 E. Wayne
Markley Lawrence, baggage master T., W. & W. R'y, h 344 Calhoun
Marhanke Christian, lab, h 110 E. Madison
Martin William, eng. Wabash R'y, h 33 Taylor

Marbelius Elizabeth, widow, bds 75 E. Jefferson
MARINE REV. A., Pastor Berry Street M. E. Church, h 26 W. Berry
Markey Willis J. (Lyne & M., florists), bds 29 Lewis
Martin Mrs. Jane, h 115 W. Water
Marts Jacob, carp., h 332 W. Main
Martin Mrs. Ann, h 133 Fairfield
Martin Dietrich, lab, h 57 Wilt
Martin Terrence, blacksmith, h 359 Hanna
Marz Nicholas, carp., h 57 W. Jefferson
Mason Louis J., dentist, bds 91 Williams
Mason William J., tress hoop manufacturer, bds 41 W. Lewis
Mason Richard, jr., bds 41 W. Lewis
Mason, Andrew, cooper, bds 240 W. Main
Mason John, tress hoop manufacturer, bds 41 W. Lewis
Masbaum Mrs. Kate, h 140 E. Washington
Mason Lewis J., dentist, bds 91 Williams
Mason John F., carp., h 91 Williams
Mast Louis, barber, bds cor. Barr and Jefferson
Mason Richardson, cooper, h 41 W. Lewis
Matsch Christian, h 240 W. Washington
Matheny Andrew, pattern maker Wabash shop, h 220 W. Jefferson
Mathena William N., lab, h 8 Cass
Mattoon Groover J., eng. Wabash R'y, h 83 Butler
Match William, machinist Pitts. shop, h 145 Holman
Mathews Stephan, merchant tailor, 141 Calhoun
Maurer Jacob, wks Meyer Bros. & Co., h 39 Harmer
Max Mrs. T., h 200 W. Washington
Maxfield Sarah, widow, h 37 Duck
MAYER HOUSE, cor. Calhoun and Wayne, W. H. Murtagh, propr.
Mayland Frederick, lab, h 236 W. Washington
May William brakeman Wabash R'y, bds 47 Bass
Mayers P., teamster, h 165 Ewing
Mayer Mrs. Jane, h 160 W. Wayne
Mayfield John, fireman, bds 88 W. Water
Mayer Frederick, M. D., h 105 Barr
MAYER & GRAFFE, jewelry store, 22 E. Columbia
Mayer Joseph M., book-keeper, bds 47 E. Jefferson
Mayer Lawrence, teamster, h 47 E. Jefferson
Mayer Louis, tailor, h 80 Montgomery
MAYER GEORGE J. E. & F. VOIROL, watch makers and jewelers, 29 E. Main
Mayer Charles, watch maker, h 27 W. Wayne
Mayer William, machinist Wabash shop, bds 111 W. Jefferson
Medsker J. N. (Gilliland & M.), bds 97 Montgomery
Meehan James, fireman Pitts. R'y, h 24 Locust
Meek William H., lab, h 319 W. Main
Meegan Thomas, time-keeper Pitts. shop, bds 179 Clinton

Meegan T. J., clk Pitts. shop, h 158 Madison
Meegan Eugene, clk, bds 40 E. Lewis
Meehan Mary, widow, h 13 Maumee
Meger Lewis, lab, h 113 High
Mehlos Christopher, insurance agent, bds Steuben House
Mehon Samuel, painter, bds American House
Mehre Lewis, shoemaker, h 201 E. Washington
Meier Henry, helper, 3 Clay
Meier Diedrich, cooper, h 89 Wells
Meier Charles, carp., h 149 Ewing
Meier Frederick, lab, h 33 W. Lewis
Meinzen William, lab, h 141 Madison
Meier William, tailor, h 200 E. Jefferson
Meinzer H., tailor, h 153 Madison
Meier William, shoemaker, h 48 McClellan
Meiser Herman, lab, h 40 John
Meier Henry, blacksmith, h 76 W. Washington
Melching Albert, harness maker, bds 42 High
Melching Mrs. Charlotte, h 42 High
Melheison Mrs., widow, h 57 Williams
Mellinger Jacob, lab, h 45 W. Main
Meloy Rosa, widow, bds 15 E. Jefferson
Mendenhall Rev. M. H., h 195 W. Wayne
Menze William, tailor, h E. Washington
Mendaham William, fireman Pitts. R'y, bds 55 Douglas
Menze Frederick, lab, h 239 Lewis
Mensch Henry, clk, h 153 Ewing
Menze Frederick, lab, bds 329 E. Lewis
Mennewish Frederick, carp. Pitts. shop, h 178 Barr
Mensch Mrs. E., widow, h 14 W. Jefferson
Menwiler Christian, barber, 271 Calhoun
MERCHANTS' NATIONAL BANK, cor. Calhoun and Main
Merz Theodore, carp., bds 25 Pine
Merz Joseph, carp. Pitts. shop, bds 25 Pine
Merz Peter, carp., h 196 E. Lewis
Meredith William, lab, bds 150 W. Jefferson
Merrigan John, lab, h cor. Calhoun and Wallace
MERGEL RHEINHART, grocery store, h 94 W. Main
MERGENTHEIM A., propr. Ladies' Bazaar, 21 Calhoun, bds at Robinson House
Mertgens B., lab, h 224 E. Jefferson
Messing & Zollinger, plow and wagon manufs., 15 E. Water
Metcalf John, transportation master G. R. & I. R'y, h 52 Williams
Metzgar Isaac, bds 91 E. Lewis
Metsker Joseph, plasterer, h 241 E. Washington
Metzinger Andrew, eng. G. R. & I. R'y, bds 60 Chicago
Mettler P. J., city assessor and grocer, h 303 Lafayette
Metley Frederick, cooper shop on E. Water, h 11 Duck

Methley John, book-keeper (K. Murry), h 14 Brandriff
Metheany Milton, supt. C., R. & Ft. W. R'y, bds 74 E. Lewis
Meyerson R., bds 31 W. Main
Meyer Andrew (M. & Graff), h 29 W. Wayne
Meyer D., Deputy Marshal, bds 178 Barr
Meyer Meier, wks spoke factory, bds 39 Water
Meyer Henry, blacksmith, bds 178 Barr
Meyer Margaret, widow, h 335 E. Washington
Meyer Henry, trunk maker, bds 335 E. Washington
Meyer Frederick, tinner Pitts. shop, h 61 W. Lewis
Meyer William (Meyer Bros. & Co.), h 22 W. Washington
MEYER BROTHERS & CO., wholesale and retail druggists, No. 2 Keystone Block and 9 Columbia
Meyer Ann Mary, widow, h 447 E. Wayne
Meyers Almina, widow, h 64 McClellan
Meyer William, machinist, bds 447 E. Wayne
Meyer Louis, tailor, h 76 Montgomery
Meyer William, lab, h 28 Hood
Meyer Henry, h 28 Hood
Meyers Bryan, moulder Bass' Foundry, h 29 Hough
Meyers Ernst, butcher, h 213 Lafayette
Meyers George, moulder Bass' Foundry, h 29 Hough
Meyers John F., cooper, h 28 Douglas
Meyer Henry, carp. Pitts. shop, h 308 Harrison
Meyer William, lab, bds 335 E. Washington
Meyer Frederick, tailor, h 99 Wilt
Meyer Frederick, barber, h 81 Brackenridge
Meyer Henry, h 100 Harrison
Meyer William, machinist Wabash shop, bds 100 Harrison
Meyer Frederick, lab, h 27 Poplar
Meyerson L., bds 173 W. Washington
Meyerson Philip, clk, h 173 W. Washington
Meyers Lewis L., barber, bds cor. Barr and Jefferson
Meyer Nicholas, plasterer, h 183 E. Jefferson
Meyers Henry, carp. Pitts. shop, h 181 E. Lewis
Meyers Frederick, propr. city water wagon, h 66 Douglas ave
Michaels Charles, upholster, bds 297 W. Jefferson
Michaels Herman, lab, h 297 W. Jefferson
Michaels Daniel, varnisher, bds 297 W. Jefferson
Michael Andrew, lab, bds 168 E. Washington
Mickow John, carp. Pitts. R'y, h 133 E. Lewis
Mickels George, wagon maker, h 235 E. Jefferson
Michels Herman, barber, bds 89 W. Lewis
Middendorf B., brick mason, h 140 E. Washington
Miller George, clk, h 62 E. Madison
MILLER BROTHERS, dealers in groceries and provisions, 2 Harrison
Miller William, saloon, h 96 Broadway

Miller Charles T., tinner, bds 96 Wilt
Miles Charles, eng. Pitts. R'y, h 221 W. Washington
Miller Ray, machinist Pitts. shop, h 281 W. Washington
Miller Christian, lab, h 14 Wert
Mills Theodore, painter, h 199 W. Wayne
Miller Frederick, carp., bds 224 W. Washington
Miller Michael, carp., h 224 W. Washington
Miller Mary T., widow, h 57 Williams
Miller Nathaniel (Miller & Bro., grocers), h 187 Griffith
Miller William, firmean Wabash R'y, bds 49 Williams
Miller Ernst, boiler maker Wabash shop, h 51 Williams
Miller Daniel M., bds Aveline House
Miller Charles, helper, h 133 E. Washington
Miller George A., bds 294 Calhoun
Miller Jerry, car inspector on Wabash R'y, bds 316 Calhoun
Miller Christian, grocer, h 54 Wells
Miller Henry D., fireman Pitts. R'y, h 33 Williams
Miller Lewis, carp. Pitts. shop, h 49 Williams
Miller Joseph, carp., h 86 High
Miller Christian, cigar maker, bds 49 Williams
Miller William (M. & Fletcher, grocers), h 61 Cass
Mills Thomas, machinist Wabash shop, h 65 Williams
Miller Oscar, brakeman Ft. W. M. & C. R'y, bds 40 Wells
Miller C. H., watchman B. M. & Co., h 55 William
Miller Edward, hatter, bds 96 Wilt
Miller Theodore, tinner, bds 96 Wilt
Miller Mrs. E., widow, h 36 McClellan
Miller F. E., bds 57 Garden
Miller K. B., traveling agent, h 57 Garden
Millhouse Samuel, carp., bds 332 W. Main
Miller Ernst, lab, bds 74 W. Jefferson
Miller John H., lab, h 99 W. Water
Miller J. J., clk, bds 210 W. Jefferson
Miller Mrs. Martha, h 116 W. Jefferson
Miller Peter, lab, h 31 Brandriff
Miller Casper, book-keeper, bds 116 W. Jefferson
Miller Henry A., bar keeper, bds 9 E. Wayne
Miller R. E., lab, bds Union House
Miller D. B., carp., bds Union House
Miller Joseph A. (Bower & M.), Union House, 49 W. Main
Miller William C., carp, h 129 E. Lewis
Miller Lewis W., painter, bds 129 E. Lewis
Miller Jacob, chair maker, h 294 Calhoun
Miller Frederick, lab, h 5 Force
Miller John J. h 79 E. Washington
MILLER & BŒRGER, manufacturers and dealers in horse collars, leather and findings, 76, 78 and 80 Clinton
Miller William H. H. (Coombs Miller & Bell, lawyers), h 40 Douglas ave

Miller William, bds 200 E. Washington
Miller Olga, widow, bds 260 Washington
Miller Charlotte, widow, h 249 E. Jefferson
Miller Charles, lab, h 10 Lavina
Miller Peter, blacksmith Pitts. shop, h 116 Creighton ave
Miller William, lab, h 307 Calhoun
Miller Charles H., carp. Wabash shop, h 37 Bass
Miller Clemens, lab, h 49 Locust
Miller Harmon, lab, h 74 W. Jefferson
Miller John M., dealer in furniture, store 50 and 52 E. Main, h 52 E. Jefferson
Miller Peter, bds 187 Jackson
Miller John, eng. Pitts. R'y, bds 13 Maumee
Miller Augustus, wks S. S. Smick, bds 64 Barr
Miller Charles, baker, bds 29 W. Columbia
Miller Martha, widow, h 23 Barr
MILLER FREDERICK, druggist, bds Central Hotel
Miller C., clk, bds 52 E. Jefferson
Miller Robert, lab, bds 264 Calhoun
Miller William, brakeman G. R. & I. R'y, bds 264 Calhoun
Miller Andrew, brakeman G. R. & I. R'y, bds 264 Calhoun
Miller Martha, widow, h 23 Barr
Millhouse Davidson, lab, h 332 W. Main
Miles David, tobacconist, h 100 E. Washington
Miner L. R., fireman Ft. W., M. & C. R'y, bds 86 Montgomery
Miner Byrum D., agent, h 62 Douglas ave
Miner L., fireman Muncie R'y, bds 40 Wells
Miniker Ernst, carp., h 75 W. Washington
Miner William, brakeman, h 106 E. Madison
Miner James M., teamster, h 364 Broadway
Miner William G., lab, h 72 Pearl
Mischo Nicholas, lab, h 33 Pritchard
Misner James (M. & Murphy), painter, h 14 Cass
Mischo Mrs. Catherine, h 158 Broadway
Misner & Murphy, painters, 84 Barr
Misner George, painter, bds Central Hotel
Misner Seymour, eng. Pitts. R'y, h 102 Wallace
Mitchell Robert, fireman Wabash R'y, h 20 Locust
Mitchell M. A., drayman, h 189 High
Mitchell William, switchman Pitts. R'y, bds cor. Lafayette and Wallace
Mitchell William W., 16 W. Berry
Mitchell James, carp., h 20 W. Jefferson
Mobley Vernon, brakeman Wabash R'y, bds 28 Williams
Mobley Margaret, widow, h 28 Williams
MODERWELL & FOWLER, shirt makers and dealers fine furnishing goods, cor. Calhoun and Berry
Moderwell Mrs. B., h 51 Wilt
Moddus George, lab, bds 21 Buchanan

Moddus William A., carp. Muncie R'y, bds 21 Buchanan
Moddus John, millwright, h 21 Buchanan
Mœllering Henry, machinist Pitts. shop, h 55 E. Lewis
Moffatt Hamilton, lab, h W. Main
Mœllering William, mason, h 120 Montgomery
Mohring John, jr., lab, bds 30 Lasalle
Mohring John, sr., lab, h 30 Lasalle
Mohr Louis, h 238 E. Washington
Mohler S., gas fitter, bds 73 E. Berry
Mohr Joe, book-keeper, bds 64 Columbia
MOHR JOHN, manufacturer of boots and shoes, h 64 Columbia
Mohr John, cashier Allen Hamilton & Co.'s Bank, bds 64 Columbia
Moltz James, train despatcher Pitts. R'y, h 194 Hanna
Mollenkoff John. wagon maker, bds 158 Griffith
Molahan G., lab, h 100 E. Madison
Molnan John, h 111 Wilt
Molhan Thomas, fireman Wabash R'y, bds 111 Wilt
Molidor Adam, lab, h 7 John
Momer Lewis, moulder Bass' Foundry, h 180 E. Lewis
Momer John, machinist Bass' Foundry, h 174 E. Lewis
Momer Joseph, clk, h 133 W. Main
MONNING HENRY (Trentman, Monning & Son, Spice Mills), h 143 E. Wayne
Monning John B. (Trentman, Monning & Son, Spice Mills), bds 143 E. Wayne
Montgomery Noah, carp., h 26 Williams
Monroe George, moulder Bass Foundry, h 5 Grand
Monroe Mrs. Ann, h 89 Cass
Monehan D. (Monehan & Harper, hat store), bds 235 E. Lewis
Monehan Martin, lab, bds cor. Fairfield and Creighton
Monroe William, conductor Pitts. R'y, bds 285 Hanna
Monroe Samuel, fireman Grand Rapids R'y, bds 285 Hanna
Monroe William, cooper, bds 39 Water
Monroe Mary E., widow, h 69 E. Jefferson
Monrey Henry, blacksmith, bds 66 E. Main
Moor David E., eng., bds 10 Harrison
Moor David H., eng. Pitts. R'y, h 34 Chicago
Moore John W., eng. C. Humphrey & Co., h 133 E. Washington
Moore George, helper Pitts. shop, bds 107 Holman
Moor William, brakeman, bds 330 Calhoun
Moorhead Mary E., widow, h 137 Barr
Moor John S., conductor Pitts. R'y, bds 212 Lafayette
Moor John, lab, h 31 Brandriff
Moon W. S., mach. Wabash shop, h 272 W. Jefferson
Moon George, bds Hanna House
MOON GEORGE, sr., U. S. Revenue Collector, office 57 Clinton
Moon George, jr., Deputy Revenue Collector, office 57 Clinton
Morison R. G., clk (Rohs' dry goods store), h 172 E. Berry

Moran Peter, ice dealer, h 201 E. Wayne
Morse Stanley B., bds Hamilton House
Moran William, lab, bds 201 E. Wayne
Moran W., railroader, bds 229 Lafayette
Morgan George, barber, h 283 W. Jefferson
Morehouse H. B., clk Pitts R'y, bds 218 W. Washington
Morrison George, wks A. Hattersly, bds 12 Lafayette
Mores James, brakeman Wabash R'y, h 68 Butler
Morris Julius, lab, bds Bloomingdale Hotel
Moritz John M., h 79 W. Berry
Morell Edward, mach. Bass' shop, h 17 Gay
Morneiser John, painter, h 263 Hanna
Morris Rosa Ann, widow, bds 105 W. Berry
Moritz Elizabeth, widow, bds 79 W. Berry
Morey Hannah, h 103 W. Jefferson
Morgenthaler Peter, clk, h 85 W. Main
Morell Henry, shoemaker, h 11 W. Jefferson
Morritz Albert, hackman, bds 25 Barr
Morell C. G., shoemaker, bds 10 W. Wayne
Morell George, lab, bds 20 Chicago
Morell Christian L., h 10 W. Wayne
Morss S. E., City Editor *Gazette*, h — Lafayette
Morgan O. P. (Morgan & Beach), h 40 E. Washington
Morgan George W., painter, h 15 E. Jefferson
MORGAN & BEACH, hardware store, 19 and 21 Columbia
Mosbaum George, lab, bds 140 E. Washington
Mosshammer John, lab, h 84 E. Wayne
Moss Frederick, lab, bds 20 Chicago
Mortz, George, tailor, h 40 Second
Mower I., bds 129 E. Lewis
Mowrey Henry, shoemaker, h 115 Wells
Moyer George, saloon, h 45 Wells
Moyer David, lab, bds 80 Barr
Moyer H. L., printer, bds 160 W. Wayne
Muck Charles, moulder Bass' Foundry, bds 28 Force
Mudge J. C., carp., h 43 Wall
Mudge John A., carp., bds 43 Wall
Mudge F. Frank, fireman Pitts. R'y, bds 186 Jackson
Mudge S. R., eng. Pitts. R'y, h 186 Jackson
Mueller William, lab, bds 3 and 5 Railroad
Muhlenbruch William, carp., h 152 W. Jefferson
Muhlenbruch D., carp., h 213 E. Jefferson
Muhlenbruch G., wagon maker, h 173 Holman
Muhlenbruch G., carriage maker, h 173 Holman
Muhlenbruch Charles, wagon maker, bds 213 E. Jefferson
MUHLFEITH JOHN, renovating establishment, 174 Calhoun, h 58 Wells
Muhler Charles (Wilson, Schuckman & Muhler), h 27 W. Berry

Muirhead John, clk, bds 61 Brackenridge
Muirhead Mrs. R., widow, h 61 Brackenridge
Mulcahy Edward, fireman Wabash shop, h 31 Colerick
Muller Charles, pattern maker, bds 6 Gay
Muller Ferdinand, lab, h 35 Francis
Muller William, lab, h 96 W. Jefferson
Muller N., lab, h 296 E. Washington
Muller Henry, mach. Pitts. shop, h 20 Marion
Muller Fred., moulder, bds 20 Marion
Muller Fred., mason, h 8 Summit
Mulday Andrew, bds 100 Montgomery
Muldoon Margaret, widow, h 86 E. Lewis
Muldoon William, cooper, bds 11 Duck
Munson C. A., bds 182 W. Washington
Munch Philip, teamster, h 34 Third
Munch Nicholas, carp. Pitts. shop, h 230 E. Wayne
MURTAGH W. H., propr. Mayer House, cor. Calhoun and Wayne
Murray Kerr, machine shop, h 147 W. Wayne
Murphy John, blacksmith Wabash shop, h 25 Taylor
Murphy Johanna, widow, h 7 Colerick
Murphy George, lab, h 11 Colerick
Murphy John, lab, h 237 Clay
Murray Amasa, mach. Pitts. shop, bds 235 Lafayette
Murry James, mach. Wabash shop, bds 322 Calhoun
Murphy James, lab, bds 11 Melitta
Murphy S., eng., G. R. & I. R'y, h 155 Hanna
MURPHY ROBERT W. (Foster Brothers' dry goods store), h 74 W. Main
Murphy Bernard, moulder, h 59 Force
Murphy Michael, lab, 171 Madison
Murphy Nellie, widow, h 72 W. Main
Murphy David, lab, bds 25 Broadway
Murphy David, lab, bds 19 Baker
Murphy A. N., painter, h 108 Barr
Murphy James, lab, bds 19 Baker
MYERS WILLIAM H., M. D., h 157 W. Wayne
Myers Fred. W., barber shop, 243½ Calhoun
Myers W. H., contractor, h 100 Fairfield
Myers James D., lab, h 27 Duck
Myers Mrs. Barbara, bds cor. Fulton and W. Jefferson
Myers George, carp., h 60 Wilt
Myers Anthony, bds 60 Wilt
Myers William, blacksmith Pitts. shop, h 98 Williams
Myers Ellis, fireman Pitts. R'y, h 114 Fairfield
Myers Frank, painter, bds 183 E. Jefferson

Mc

McBain George, fireman, Richmond R. R., bds 205 Calhoun
McCarthy James, boarding house, 290 Calhoun
McCauley John H., prop. hat store, h 92 E. Washington
McCAULEY & CO., Hatter, 76-78-80 Clinton, store, 4 E. Columbia
McCULLOCH & RICHEY, House Furnishing Store, 3 E. Columbia
McConnell W. A., clk, bds 197 E. Jefferson
McCain Margaret, widow, h 64 E. Jefferson
McClean Peter, dyer, works woolen mills, h 41 Water
McCamsey A. M., lab, h 155 Harrison
McConnell Andrew, bridge builder, h 40 Brandriff
McCutcheon Edward, conductor, Wabash R'y, h 5 Bass
McCartney John, lab, bds 10 Harrison
McCaffrey Thomas, lab, h cor Webster and Dawson
McClain James, bds 232 E. Jefferson
McCormick John, fireman, Wabash R'y, bds 82 Fairfield ave
McCollam John, eng, Muncie R. R., h 154 Broadway
McCumsey Kate, widow, h 155 Harrison
McCulloch Thomas P., Dr., h 34 Douglas ave
McCoy Thomas, boiler maker, Wabash shop, 21 Nirdlinger
McClure Andrew, eng, Wabash R'y, h 50 McClellan
McClure D. B., millwright, 225 W. Main
McCulloch Frank, brakeman, Pittsburgh R'y, bds 220 Lafayette
McClellan J. R., fireman, Pittsburgh R'y, h 234 Lafayette
McCelicet Phillp, lab, bds 79 Holman
McCartney John, grocer, h 154 Griffith
McCay Thomas, boiler maker, Wabash shop, bds 6 Kansas
McCann John, policeman, h 65 Grand
McClain George, boiler maker, Pittsburgh shop, h 195 Barr
McCartney Parrick, eng, Wabash shop, h 3 Colerick
McCarthy Bartholomew, lab, bds 3 Colerick
McCaffrey William, wheelwright, bds 70 E. Madison
McCarthy Timothy, molder, (Murry's foundry), bds 290 Calhoun
McClaren William, fireman, Muncie R. R., bds 63 Wells
McCarty Mary, widow, h 50 Baker
McConahy Albert, brakeman, Pittsburgh R'y, bds 63 Baker
McCarty Dennis, eng, Pittsburgh R'y, h 106 Wallace
McCreary B. F., blacksmith, h 160 E. Jefferson
McCurdy A. R., clk, h 38 Lavina
McConnell J. W., attorney at law, bds Robinson House
McCulloch Fred, (McC. & Richey, hardware), h 164 W. Berry
McCord George S., carp, h 188 Ewing
McDorman Mary J., widow, h 65 E. Wayne
McDonald John, brakeman, Pittsburgh R'y, bds 54 E. Wahington
McDonald James B., mason, h 54 E. Washington
McDermut Nancy, widow, h 28 E. Wayne

McDermut Whitney printer, bds 28 E. Wayne
McDermut Wilson, E., printer, bds 28 E. Wayne
McDermot Roger, plasterer, bds 20 Chicago
McDonald R. T., b. k., bds 54 E. Washington
McDonald Mrs. Johanna, h 17 Baker
McDermot John, brakeman, Pittsburgh R'y, bds 20 Baker
McDermott Joseph, blacksmith, Pittsburgh shop, h 41 Gay
McDermott James, moulder, Pittsburgh shop, h 317 Calhoun
McDowel William, cooper, bds 408 W. Main
McDonald Stephen, brick layer, bds 39 Water
McDonald H. D., eng, Pittsburgh R'y, bds 79 Douglas ave
McDOUGAL & LAUFERTY, Brokers, McD. Block, Calhoun
McDougal John, merchant, bds Aveline House
McDONALD DONALD, Propr. Aveline House, (McD. & Mrs. Aveline), S. E. cor Berry and Calhoun
McDonald W., lab, bds Robinson House
McEwen Theodore, agt., h 53 Baker
McElfatrick J. A., carp, h 107 W. Main
McElfatrick Mrs. Eva, h 103 W. Main
McFerran Milton, eng, Pittsburgh R'y, bds 132 Lafayette
McFee William carp, h 58 Nelson
McFEELY D. R., Oyster Bay Saloon and Restaurant, cor Calhoun and Wayne
McGee Mary, widow, h 35 W. Main
McGrady William, plasterer, h 106 E. Madison
McGoff Peter, plasterer, bds Exchange Hotel
McGuire Owen, telegraph repairer, h 18 Baker
McGinney William, lab, bds 58 Columbia
McGeehon John, brakeman, Pittsburgh R'y, bds 285 Hanna
McGuire Jane, widow, bds 71 Douglas
McGinnis Patrick, brakeman, Wabash R'y, bds 23 Grand
McGrady David, plasterer, bds 134 Monroe
McGuire Terrance, eng Wabash R'y, bds 6 Kansas
McGuire Thomas, lab, h 110 Chicago
McGlasslon Mrs., widow, h 21 Melitta
McGrady John, mason, h 142 W. Main
McGrath Thomas, lab, h 8 Bass
McIntosh Mary Ann, widow, h 118 Barr
McIntyre Patrick, lab, bds Union House
McKinley John, cutter, h 152 E. Wayne
McKinnie Frank, b. k., bds Ft. Wayne Eating House
McKINNIE HENRY, Propr. Ft. Wayne Eating House, h at R. R.
McKINNIE ALEXANDER, bds Ft. Wayne Eating House
McKenzie Robt., moulder, (Bass' foundry), h Lillie's add
McKellar Alexander, machinist, Wabash shop, bds 64 McClellan
McKenzie Mrs. Sarah J. bds 138 Broadway
McKendry Daniel, ass't eng., in office, h 11 Melitto
McKeon James, lab, h 4 Colerick

McKenzie & Keel, dry goods mer., 130 Broadway
McKean James, brakeman, h 68 Butler
McKean William T., foreman, machine shop, h 184 E. Jefferson
McKag William, lab, h 28 Walnut
McKay Neil, contractor, h 134 W. Main
McKinley Perry, lab, h 46 Wells
McKenzie George, machinist, Wabash shop, h 121 Butler
McKindrey Thomas, conductor Wabash R'y, h 103 Williams
McKeg James, conductor, Pittsburgh R'y, bds 49 Baker
McKnight James, blacksmith, Pittsburgh shop, h 40 Lasselle
McKinzie C., lab, h 89 Lasselle
McLean Peter, boss dyer, woolen mills, h 41 E. Water
McLochlin pattern maker, bds 147 W. Washington
McLain B. P., h — Ft. Wayne College
McLaughlin Daniel, lab, h 65 W. Lewis
McLaflin John, wks Pittsburgh shop, bds 100 Montgomery
McLochlin James, bds 12 Cass
McLaughlin William, pattern maker, Wabash shop, h 117 Holman
McLain Allen Dr, bds 69 Garden
McLain George H., baggage master, Pittsburgh R'y, bds Ft Wayne College
McLaughlin Christ, moulder, h 127 Monroe
McLain Patrick, h 232 Jefferson
McMullen Mrs. M., h 188 E. Washington
McMellen James, lab, bds 116 E. Madison
McManus Thomas, lab, h 32 Baker
McManigal J., lab, h 31 Pearl
McMahon S., conductor, Pittsburgh R'y, h 208 Broadway
McMullen Mary, widow, h 124 Union
McMillen John, lab, h 87 William
McMillen John, machinist, Wabash shop, h 90 Wilt
McMillen Mary, widow, h 228 Francis
McMullen William H., painter, h 188 E. Washington
McNulty John, plumber, wks Hattersley's, bds 12 Colerick
McNulty Ann widow, h 12 Colerick
McNulty William, (Kayser & McN.), h 87 Montgomery
McNulty James, wks woolen factory, h 100 Columbia
McNamara Christopher, lab, bds cor Lafayette and Wallace
McNulty Thomas, lab, h 89 W. Lewis
McNiece R. G., (WcN. & Alexander), *Gazette* office, bds 259 W. Wayne
McNulty William, shoemaker, shop on Lafayette, h 88 Montgomery
McNamarah Thomas, lab, h 11 Melitto
McNair Charles, carp. and contractor, h 56 Henry
McNarny, Thomas, lab, h 84 Baker
McNamary Peter, lab, h foot of Baker
McNut John, h 39 Douglas ave
McNally John, carp, h 105 Wallace
McNamara W., foreman, spoke manuf., bds 457 Lafayette

McNamara Mrs. Susan, h 457 Lafayette
McNamara Monroe, carp, bds 457 Lafayette
McPhail, William, foreman Wabash round houses h 192 Ewing
McQuiston John, h 159 W. Washington
McQuiston, A. P., clk, bds 159 W. Washington
McVey Michael lab, h cor Fifth and N. Calhoun
McWilliams Edmond, piano and sewing machine agt., bds 86 E. Main
McWilliams Joseph, civil eng., bds Mayer House

N

Nanamaker S. S., drug clk, h 150 W. Jefferson
Nagel Frederick, lab, h 99 W. Jefferson
Nagel Martin, machinist, Wabash shop, bds 99 W. Jefferson
Nagel Fred, jr., machinist, Wabash ahop, bds 99 W. Jefferson
Nahrwold Fred, lab, h 25 Wilt
Nahrwald Conrad, lab, h 267 E. Lewis
Nahrwold Fred, lab, h 319 W. Washington
Nahrwold Christ, helper, h 147 E Lewis
Nahrwold D., carp, h 62 W. Lewis
Nahrwold William, carp, h 29 Wilt
Nave William, carp, bds 101 Wallace
Nave Benjamin, carp, h 101 Wallace
Nees Henry, wood carver, h 76 E. Madison
Neff Jacob, butcher, h 63 E. Water
Neff John J., butcher, h 63 E. Water
Neher Joseph, shoemaker, (Thomas Manix), h 12 Francis
Nehler J. W., clk, bds Steuben House
Neireiter C. D., harness maker, bds 220 W. Washington
Neireiter Casper, manuf. and dealer in harness, trunks, &c., 13 Columbia
Neireiter Conrad, chair maker, h 87 E. Wayne
Neidhart Joseph, carp, h 56 E. Madison
NEIREITER C., Summit City Trunk Manuf., 8 Calhoun, h 137 W. Wayne
Neireiter C. B., harness maker, h 227 W. Washington
Neiman Fred, lab, bds 7 Hood
Nelson Elmore, hatter, h 64 W. Wayne
NELSON WILLIAM R., Lawyer, bds Hamilton House
Nelson M., machinist, bds 64 W. Wayne
Nelson George, (Ft. Wayne Steel Plow Co.), h 67 W. Main
Nelligan Michael, machinist, (K. Murray), bds 47 Douglas ave
NELSON DeGROFF & CO., Dealers in Grain and Seeds, cor Clinton and Columbia
Nerhood John, bds 8 Lavina
Nestel Ed., grocer, h 189 Lafayette
NESTEL DANIEL, Manager Comodore Foote's Troupe, h 203 W. Jefferson

Nestel Daniel jr., carp, bds 203 W. Jefferson
Nestel Phillip, butcher, h 189 Lafayette
Nestel Charles William, (Com. Foote), bds 203 W. Jefferson
Neuffer Lenard, eng, Wabash R'y, h 306 Harrison
Newton, copper smith, shop 189 Calhoun
Neuenschwander Isaac, propr. saloon, h 46 E. Columbia
Newton Orin L., telegraph operator, bds 17 Holman
Newhart, Louisa, widow, h 47 Barr
Newberger Louis, city att'y, 34 E. Berry
Neuberger Charles, millinery store, h 100 W. Berry
Newall Hans, h 16 Locust
Newberger Henry, propr. cigar store, bds 100 W. Berry
NEWBERGER LOUIS, Attorney at Law, bds 21-23 E. Main
Newcomer Christian, night clk at Harmon house
Newberger Mrs. R., millinenry, 14 E. Columbia
Newberger Henry, dealer in cigars and Tobacco, cor Calhoun and Main
Newell Charles D., eng, Pittsburgh R'y, h 258 W. Jefferson
Nicholas Mrs. Rebecca, bds 117 W. Washington
Nichols John, fireman, Pittsburgh R'y, bds 35 Buchanan
Nichols James, lab, h 110 W. Water
Nicter Otto, moulder, h 158 Broadway
Nidermeier Paul, lab, h 24 Lasselle
Nieman T. H., grocery and saloon, 274 E. Washington, h 272 E. Washington
Niebergall Henry, baker, Concordia College
Nies Charles, turner, h 36 Wall
Nieman Gottlieb, h 49 Douglas ave
Niemeier Henry, teamster, h 153 Madison
Nieter H., lab, bds 178 Barr
Nierman Martin, bds 43 W. Water
Nierman Herman, h 46 W. Water
Niebel Mary, widow, h 1 Bass
Nieman F. W., carp, bds 170 W. Washington
Nies Henry, file cutter, bds 139 Madison
Nighthefer William, grocer, h 337 Lafayette
NILL E. H. & CO., Druggists and Apothecaries, 80 Calhoun, Nill's Block
Nill Henry, shoemaker, h 117 Wells
Nill Conrad, shoemaker, h 117 Wells
Niles H., teamster, bds 57 W. Water
Nill George, shoemaker, bds 31 W. Columbia
Nill Ed. H., (E. H. Nill & Co.), h 34 W. Washington
Nill H., (Nill & Bro.), shop, 31 Columbia
Nill S., Mrs., widow, h 31 W. Columbia
Nill Conrad, (E. H. Nill & Co.), h 34 W. Washington
Nimann John, mason, h 180 E. Washington
Ninde L. M., att'y, 16 W. Main
Nirdlinger Fred, h 31 Main

NIRDLINGER JACOB, Manuf. and Jobber of Clothing, Furnishing Goods, Hats and Caps, 1 Keystone Block
Nirdlinger Frederick, clk, bds Mayer House
Nirdlinger Max, at Palace of Fashion, h 82 W. Main
Nirdlinger Samuel, clk, bds 50 W. Water
Nirdlinger Joe, clk (Root & Co.'s dry goods house), bds 50 W. Water
Nirdlinger Eli, bds 31 W. Main
NISH & CASSO, musicians, 36 Barr
Nish George, painter, h 106 Francis
Nitsche Clara, widow, h 12 W. Jefferson
Nixon Alfred, school teacher at Public School No. 8, h 282 Harrison
Nix Valentine, shoemaker, h 80 E. Jefferson
Noble Lyman, gardner, h old Pickway Road
Nobles Nancy, widow, h 13 Poplar
Noble John, brakeman Richmond R'y, bds 243 Clay
Nohe William, shoemaker, h 19 Nirdlinger
Nohe Joseph, h 167 Broadway
Nolan James, fireman Pitts. R'y, h 140 Francis
Noll John C. (Orff & Co., dry goods), h 245 E. Lewis
Noll Alfred, clk, h 235 E. Lewis
Noll Frank, clk, h 241 E. Lewis
Noll Martin A. (C. Orff & Co., dry goods), h 201 W. Main
NOLL MARTIN, manufacturer and dealer in boots and shoes, 22 Clinton
Nolan John, lab, h 22 Charles
Noll Peter, painter Pitts. shop, h 46 Butler
NOLL MARTIN, boots and shoes, h 146 E. Wayne
Noll George, lab, h 241 E. Lewis
Noll B., book-keeper, h 28 Douglas ave
Noll Edward, accountant, bds 146 E. Wayne
Noll John, clk, bds 146 E. Wayne
Nolan James, fireman, h 78 E. Madison
Nonamaker Solomon, drug clk, bds 150 W. Jefferson
Norton Herschel, fireman Wabash R'y, bds 38 Melitta
Norwald Charles, lab, h 265 E. Lewis
Norton Mrs. L. E., widow, bds Anderson House
Nolestein Joseph, hack driver, bds 18 E. Wayne
Nolestein E., lab, h 141 Force
Novelty I., bds cor. Harrison and Chicago
Noy Edward, lab, h 103 Williams
Nuby Frank, turner, bds Fox House
Nulf Philip, brakeman Wabash R'y, bds 13 Poplar
Nulf Levi, lab, h 13 Poplar
Nulf George A., brakeman Wabash R'y bds 13 Poplar
Nuraugh Louis, tinner, bds 69 E. Jefferson
Nutman John, shoemaker, h 225 E. Wayne
Nuttman Joseph D., jr., bds 130 W. Berry
Nuttman Joseph D., sr., Prest. First Nat. Bank, h 130 W. Berry

Nye Mrs. J., widow, h 80 Barr

O

O'Brien Dennis, supt. of canal, h 225 W. Washington
O'Brien Patrick, section boss Wabash R'y, bds 20 Chicago
O'Brien C., Mason, bds 165 Ewing
O'Brien William, yard master Ft. W., M. & C. R'y, h 50 Melitta
O'Conners Bridget, widow, h 116 Francis
O'Conner J., blacksmith Pitts. shop, h 46 Baker
O'Conner Joseph M., agent, h 92 W. Water
O'Conner Michael, wks Bass' Foundry, bds 72 Wallace
O'CONNELL & BROTHER, proprs. Central Hotel, E. Berry, opposite Court
O'Connell Daniel (O'C. & Bro., Central Hotel), h 203 E. Wayne
O'Connell John (O'C. & Bro.), Central Hotel
O'Heran John, lab, h Lillie ave
O'Homas George, brakeman Pitts. R'y, bds 245 Calhoun
O'Neil Melcena, widow, h 57 Williams
O'Neil Daniel, fireman Wabash R'y, bds 59 Grand
O'Neil Thomas, bds 231 Barr
O'ROURKE EDWARD, Attorney at Law, office over First Nat. Bank, h 24 McClellan
O'Rourke William, moulder, h 235 E. Jefferson
O'Rourke John, conductor Pitts. R'y, h 109 Wallace
O'Rourke C., bds 24 McClellan
O'Rourke P. S., supt. Mich. Lake Shore R'y, h 30 McClellan
O'Rourke Charles, tinner, bds 235 E. Jefferson
O'Rourke John C., conductor Pitts. R'y, bds 30 McClellan
O'Ryan Patrick, carp., h 42 Baker
O'Shaughnessy James, constable, bds 20 Chicago
O'Shaughnessy Thomas, painter, bds 19 Baker
O'Shaughnessy Margaret, widow, h 23 Colerick
O'Shaughnessy Michael, lab, bds 23 Colerick
O'Shaughnessy John, lab, bds 23 Colerick
O'Shaughnessy Martin, lab, h 4 Colerick
Oakley C. B. (O. & Son), h 126 W. Main
OAKLEY & SON, dealers in harness and saddlers' hardware, 29 E. Columbia
Oberhelman William, sewing machine agent, h 309 W. Washington
Oddon Joseph, clk, h 204 E. Wayne
Oddon Joseph F., clk, h 68 Columbia
Oelschlager Fred., tailor, bds 100 W. Jefferson
Ofenloch John H., painter Pitts. shop, h 134 Francis
Ofenloch Valentine, painter Pitts. shop, h 32 Force
Ogdon Robert, wks A. Hattersly, h 20 Lafayette
Oget John J., agent Howe Sewing Machine, bds 98 Montgomery

Ohm Mrs. C., h 133 W. Water
Ohnhaus Mrs. S., h 135 E. Jefferson
OLDS N. G. & SON, spoke and wheel manufacturers, cor Lafayette and Railroad
Olds N. G. (O. & Son, spoke mfs.), h cor. Ewing and W. Berry
Olds Henry J. (O. & Son, spoke mfs.), h cor. Ewing and W. Berry
Olds John D. (O. Son), bds 71 W. Wayne
Olds Jay B., bds cor. Ewing and W. Berry
Olds Charles, bds cor. Ewing and W. Berry
Oldroyde T. B., kook-keeper, bds 130 W. Jefferson
OMNIBUS OFFICE, Fletcher & Powers, proprietors, 71½ Calhoun
Openshaw George, mach. Pitts. shop, h 32 Charles
Oppenheimer Jacob, street buyer, bds American House
Oppenheimer A., dealer in hides, &c., h 54 W. Berry
Oppenheimer Fred., street buyer, bds 54 W. Berry
Oppelt Joseph, eng., h 14 Fulton
Orbison Henry, ticket agent, Ft. W., J. & Saginaw R'y, bds American House
Orban Michael, lab, h 106 Butler
Orel Joseph, book binder, bds 204 E. Lewis
ORFF JOHN, Empire Mills, W. Main
ORFF C. & CO., dry goods store, 5 and 7 E. Columbia
Orff Gottlieb, carp., Pitts. shop, h 150 Clinton
Orff Henry, music teacher, h 232 E. Washington
Orff Christian (C. Orff & Co., dry goods), h 4 W. Water
Oriel Joseph, wagon maker, h Calhoun, bet. Wallace and Hamilton
Orme E. J., stone cutter, h 68 W. Main
Orr Peter, bds W. Walnut
Orr Michael, butcher, h W. Walnut
Orr John W., eng., h 28 Butler
Orr Joseph H., clk Ft. Wayne Nat. Bank, bds 28 Butler
Orr & Berberich, butchers, 272 Calhoun
Orrison John, fireman Pitts. R'y, h 225 Barr
Orthen Joseph, lab, h 38 John
Ortlieb George, saloon, h 21 E. Washington
Ortman Charles, saloon, h 86 Barr
Ortman Henry, cigar maker, h 59 Third
Ortman Theodore, cigar manuf., h 36 Monroe
ORTLIEB GEORGE, lager beer saloon, 78 Calhoun
ORTMANN H. W., cigar manuf. and residence 49 Calhoun
Orvis Mrs. Harriet, h 130 W. Main
Osgood Henry, brakeman Wabash R'y, bds 23 Grand
Ostermann L., drayman, h 235 E. Washington
Ostermann Charles, lab, bds 81 Wells
Ostermann John H., cooper, h 180 E. Washington
Ott Francis, painter, h 81 E. Berry
Ott John, plasterer, bds 113 E. Main
Otting William, baker, bds 29 W. Columbia

Otten H., lab, bds 210 Washington
Otten Lucas, lab, h 34 Gay
Otten Otto H., lab, bds 34 Gay
Out Peter, lab, h 27 Langohr
Overly Thomas, teamster, h 117 Wilt
Overly John, lab, h 23 Jones
Owens Peter, stave jointer, bds 6 Kansas
Owens Owen, conductor Pitts. R'y, bds 198 Lafayette
Owens M., boiler maker Wabash shop, h 319 Herrison

P

Pace Nathan L., clk, h 80 Harrison
Page William D., foreman *Gazette* job office, h 103 Lafayette
Pageler Fred, wheelmaker, (Olds & Son), h 177 Montgomery
Pagnard Augustus, lab, 58 Columbia
Pantlind Henry, drives American Express wagon, h 204 E. Wayne
Pape William, h 137 High
PARAMORE S. H., Lumber Dealer, office 183 Calhoun
Parisot Louis, watchman, h 205 Barr
Parisot Joseph, lab, h 322 Hanna
Parker Charles, bds 40 Garden
PARKER H. C., Agt., bds Hamilton House
Parker Henry, fireman, Pittsburgh R'y, h 17 Holman
Parks William, lab, h 210 W. Main
Parks Augustus cooper, bds 63 W. Water
Parrot Peter, carp, Pittsburgh shop, h 27 Oak
Passage Levy, lab, h 278 Broadway
Passe Charles, machinist, (Bass' shop), bds 137 Francis
Passinot Joseph, machinist, Pittsburgh shop, h 405 Lafayette
Passinot Peter, brakeman, Pittsburgh R'y, 53 Buchanan
Passmore Charles, fireman, Wabash R'y, bds 82 Fairfield ave
Paton L., bds Mayer House
Patten William, contractor, h 53 W. Water
Patten Jesse, policeman, bds Exchange Hotel
Patten Charles, 98 Columbia
Patterson George, brakeman, Wabash R'y, h 309 W. Jefferson
Patterson Oliver, machinist, (wks Olds & Son), bds 205 Calhoun
Patterson C. E., agt., bds Central Hotel
Patterson ———, turner, (Olds & S.), h 72 Wallace
Paul William, grocer, 21 W. Columbia
Paul William, grocer, h 38 W. Jefferson
Paul Frederick, machinist, Pittsburgh shop, h 298 Harrison
Paul Charles, lab, h 47 High
Paulsen Daniel, miller, h 88 Barthold
Payne Elizabeth, widow, h on Hanover, foot of Wayne
Payne John, miller, bds on Hanover, foot of Wayne

Payner George, Dr., bds American House
Pease ———, bds Hanna House
Pearson C. H., drayman, h 309 W. Main
Peggeon Nicholas, lab, h 64 Melitta
Pelz August, lab, bds 237 Lafayette
Peltier James C., clk, Wabash freight office, h 162 Montgomery
Peltier L. jr., b. k., bds 49 E. Lewis
Peltier Louis, (Peltier & Carll, undertakers), h 49 E. Lewis
PELTIER & CARLL, Undertakers, 17 W. Wayne
Pence Levi, lab, h 117 Calhoun
Penington Henry, lab, bds Union House
Pequignot Francis, h 27 Buchanan
PEQUIGNOT JOSEPH, (Langard & Co.), bds 58 and 60 Columbia
Perry George H., fur dealer, bds Mayer House
Perry Joseph, baggage master, Richmond R. R., bds Aker House
Perret Henry, att'y, bds Aker House
Perkins Paul B., (Perkin's Engine Co.), h 62 Fulton
Perry John, eng, Richmond R. R., h 164 W. Wayne
Perry Frank, machinist, Pittsburgh shop, bds 164 W. Wayne
Perry Edgar, gas fitter, bds 164 W. Wayne
Perry Joseph, carp, h 2 Oak
Perrin James, conductor, Wabash R'y, h 92 Fairfield ave
Perkins Mrs., propr. Anderson House, 24 W. Berry
Perkins Engine Company, manuf. Perkin's engines and R'y tank pumps, 16 W. Columbia
Perry Harvey, conductor, Pittsburgh R'y, bds 79 Holman
Perry George W., baggage master, Richmond R. R., bds 203 Barr
Perrin William, brakeman, Pittsburgh R'y, bds 79 Holman
Pesch William, basket maker, h 66 W. Jefferson
Pettit Mrs. L., h 111 E. Wayne
Petit Peter, lab, bds 58 E. Columbia
Peters John, (Peters & Co., box makers), bds 21-23 E. Main
Peters & Co., Fort Wayne Box Factory, office 102 High
Petzinger Mrs. Louisa, h 117 Wells
Petys George, brakeman, Pittsburgh R'y, bds 233 Lafayette
Peters William, clk, Ft. Wayne Eating House
Pittiford E., bds 82 Barr
Peters Fred, lab, h 23 Wilt
Peters Fred, lab, h 20 Lavina
Petgen Elizabeth, widow, h 83 Holman
Pfeifer Joseph, jr., stone cutter, bds Union House
Pfeiffer G. C. & Co., Bloomingdale Mills, h 168 Wells
PFLEIDERER JABOB, Butcher, Meat Market, 110 Calhoun
Phelps George, conductor, Ft. W., J. & S. R. R., h 20 W. Jefferson
Phelps James, brakeman, Pittsburgh R'y, h 25 W. Jefferson
Philabaum David, teamster, h 73 High
Phillabaum George, teamster, h 46 Wells
Phillabaum John, broom maker, h 35 Grand

Philley Milton, student, 129 Lafayette
Philley William, conductor, Richmond R. R., bds 120 Lafayette
Philley Hannah, 120 Lafayette
Philley Eli S., b. k., bds 120 Lafayette
Philley Emily L., bds 120 Lafayette
Philley Milt S., att'y and notary, 16 W. Main
Phillips Michael, lab, h 255 Webster
Phillips Mrs. Elizabeth, h 189 High
Phillips John clk, bds 121 W. Main
Phillips Barney, saloon, h 121 W. Main
Philips Elizabeth, widow, h 209 Lafayette
Phillips George, propr. stage line, h 12 Cass
Pickard Thomas, sup. Bass' shop, h 106 Washington
Pickard T. D., clk, Bass' shop, h 106 E. Washington
Piepenbrink Conrad D., boot and shoe store, 32 E. Columbia
Pierceton George, lab, bds cor Berry and Water
Piel Peter, bds 141 Henry
Pierce Lexas, brakeman, Wabash R'y, h 72 Williams
Pierre Peter, (J. & P. Pierre, dry goods), h 254 W. Washington
PIERCE J. S., Sewing Machine Agt., h 261 W. Wayne
Piepenbrink Crist, clk, bds 253 W. Wayne
Pierce Mrs. Betsy, h 261 W. Wayne
Pierston George, lab, bds 13 Barr
PIETZ J. FERDINAND, Practical Watchmaker and Jeweler, h 66 Calhoun, opp. Aveline House
Pierson Peter, clk, h 119 Wilt
Piepenbrink Conrad D., shoemaker, h 48 W. Washington
Pieper Frederick, machinist, Wabash shops, h 71 W. Jefferson
Pierr Jacob, dry goods, h 96 W. Berry
Pierce Daniel, brakeman, Richmond R. R., bds 203 Barr
Pierce Ernest, machinist, Pittsburgh R'y, h 193 Barr
Pike William, hat store, (Singer & P.), h 134 W. Berry
Pilliot Victor, clk, bds 98 Maumee
Pilgrim Luther, carp, h 229 Lafayette
Piltz Rudolph, baker, bds 195 Hanna
Pingry B., fireman, Richmond R. R., bds 20 Baker
Piper Nettie, bds 115 Barr
Pisano Martin, shoemaker, h 114 Fulton
Pitzel Joe, bds 46 E. Jefferson
Platt Jeremiah, lab, bds 25 Barr
Plattor George, conductor, h 183 Lafayette
Plock Henry, lab, bds 206 W. Jefferson
Plock Mrs. Elizabeth, h 206 W. Jefferson
Pohlman Christian, carp, h 214 W. Jefferson
Polhamus Albert, eng, Pittsburgh R'y, h 169 Montgomery
Poole Emery O., eng, Wabash R'y, h 118 Jackson
Pope Henry, wagon maker, h 23 Barr
Porter A. W., bds Central Hotel

Porter Mrs. Elizabeth, h 39 Lavina
Porter Mrs. Sophia, h 343 W. Jefferson
Porter Edwin conductor, Pittsburgh R'y, h 66 Chicago
Porter Mary M., widow, h 66 Chicago
Porter Charles, clk, Pittsburgh office, h foot of W. Water
Post James, brakeman, Wabash R'y, bds 83 Holman
Pottsgrove William, night watchman, lumber yard, h 242 W. Wayne
Potter Joseph, L., carp. and joiner, h 250 Creighton ave
Potter Joseph, L., carp, 124 W. Main
Potter Thomas, carp, bds 87 Pearl
Potter John, carp, h 87 Pearl
Pothuff William, clk, Ft. Wayne Eating House
Poulson Britton, pattern maker, h 57 N. Cass
Powell John, mason, bds 203 Calhoun
Powers John, (Fletcher & P., omnibus line), h 156 E. Wayne
Powers Emett, bds 156 E. Wayne
Powell David, plasterer, bds 14 Chicago
Poyser Hiram, pattern maker, Wabash shop, h 184 W. Jefferson
Pratt William T., contractor, h 20 Douglas ave
Pratt Norman, cooper, bds 29 Butler
Pratt Allen, brick layer, bds 82 Montgomery
Pranger John William, h 301 E. Washington
Pranger John H., carp, h 301 E. Washington
Pranger B., lab, h 310 E. Wayne
Pranger Ferdinand. painter, bds 68 W. Washington
Pranger Henry, carp, bds 386 E. Wayne
Prescott A. S., (Brandriff & Co.), h 105 Lafayette
Prescott Edwin, (Brandriff & Co.), bds 105 Lafayette
Pressler John, tinner, h 2 Brandriff
Prentiss Joseph R., (Bowser & Co.), h 90 Wells
Prentice Patrick, lab, h 97 Baker
Pritchard Thomas, moulder, Bass' foundry, h 179 Hanna
Prince Thomas, machinist, h 89 N. Calhoun
Priesmeier, William, clk, bds 13 E. Main
Price Thomas W., mail agt., Richmond R. R., bds 46 E. Jefferson
Probasco A. C., canal collector, h 106 E. Main
Prouty, Shordan & Co., wholesale and retail dealers in farm machinery, 61 and 63 E. Columbia
Pross Daniel, bds American House
Puffert A., cooper, h 252 E. Wayne
Pulcipher Charles, brakeman Pitts. R'y, bds 128 Montgomery
Pulver Edward F., bellows maker at Organ Factory, bds 30 Walnut
Purdy William, mail agent Muncie R'y, bds 122 W. Jefferson
Purcill Irwin N., h 10 Harrison
Purdy Dr. T. H., h 151 Ewing
Purman A. A., lawyer, bds 87 Barr
PUTNAM H. N., Councilman, h 117 E. Wayne

Q

QUEEN FIRE INSURANCE CO., of Liverpool and London, cash assets $13,000,000, A. H. Carier, agent
Quicksell Thomas, eng. Pitts. R'y, h 47 Gay
Quidor N. K., eng. Wabash R'y, h 40 Wilt
Quinlan James, stave jointer, bds 6 Kansas
Quinn Bridget, widow, h 38 Chicago
Quinn James, h 107 W. Jefferson
Quinn James, blacksmith, h 142 W. Main
Quinn Michael, lab, h 35 Taylor
Quinn Margaret, widow, h 39 Duck
Quinn Lyman, cooper, h 388 W. Main

R

Raab Fred., grocery and saloon, 44 E. Columbia
Raab John, lab, h 188 E. Jefferson
Raab Fred., butcher, h 175 E. Washington
Raab John, dealer in groceries and provisions, h 112 W. Jefferson
Rabus John, Tailor, h 59 Wells
Rabus Mrs. Magdalena, h 56 Douglas
Rabbitt Mrs. Sarah. h 320 Hanna
Racine Fred. L., collar manuf., shop and house cor. First and Cass
Racine A., collar maker, h 27 N. Cass
RACINE A., propr. collar manufactory, 39 E. Columbia
Racine Theophile, lab, bds 70 E. Madison
Racine Jacob, collar maker, h 88 W. Jefferson
Rademacher Rev. Joseph, h 134 E. Jefferson
Rademacher William, shoemaker, bds Steuben House
Rager R. A., fireman Pitts. R'y, bds 250 Calhoun
Rahe Henry, carp., h 161 Broadway
Rahe Augustus, moulder, bds 161 Broadway
Rainberger William, boiler maker Pitts, shop, bds 92 Montgomery
Raidy David, eng. Pitts. R'y, h 22 Bass
Raifsnyder Sylvester, lab, bds 82 Force
Raifsnyder Jacob, h 82 Force
Rambo B. W., jeweler, h 124 W. Washington
Ramsey James, painter, bds 39 W. Washington
Rank John, sawyer, h 88 E. Madison
Randall T. A., attorney at law, office over First Nat. Bank, bds 159 W. Washington
RANDALL F. P., attorney at law and ins. agent, office 24 Clinton, h 115 E. Berry
Ranke William (R. Yergens & Co., stave manufacturers), h 127 W. Wash.

Rank Gustav, plasterer, h 49 N. Cass
Randell John, lab, bds 25 Barr
Ranke Henry, mach., bds 123 W. Washington
Ranke Fred., mach., h 123 W. Washington
Ranke, Yergens & Co., stave factory, cor. Water and Griffith
Ranzer C. M., carp., bds 195 W. Main
Rapp Christian G., saloon, 24 W. Main
Rapp Snyder, conductor Pitts. R'y, bds 229 Lafayette
Rapp Jacob, carp., h 191 Hanna
Raquet A. C., gunsmith, 20 W. Main
Rassat J. B., lab, bds 171 Calhoun
Rastetter Louis, foreman Olds & Son's machine shop, h 147 Calhoun
Rattray Robert, cigar maker, h 92 E. Jefferson
Rathert Henry, lab, h 212 E. Washington
Rauner Joseph, painter, h 188 Griffith
RAU CASPER, propr. Steuben House, cor. Calhoun and Washington
Rawley A. C., lab, h 9 Bass
RAYHOUSER G. I. Z., h 178 Hanna
Ray Addison, conductor Wabash R'y, bds 172 W. Jefferson
Ray Frank, master mechanic Wabash R'y, h — Dewald
Ray William, bds — Dewald
Ray J. W., printer, bds Robinson House
Ray W., lab, bds 203 Calhoun
READ A. J. (A. J. Read & Son, Livery and Sale Stable), h 16 W. Wayne
Read H. A., Veterenary Surgeon and Infirmary, at A. J. Read's livery stable, h 18 W. Wayne
Read Charles, clk, bds 16 W. Wayne
Reaker Henry, carp., h 53 E. Madison
Read A. J., propr. City Livery and Sale Stable, 18 W. Wayne
Read Moses, corn merchant, h 128 W. Main
Rechenberger Rudolf, mach. Olds & Son, h 103 Wallace
Redelsheimer S., h 48 W. Wayne
Redelsheimer Julius, agent, bds 48 W. Wayne
Redelsheimer Henry, optican, bds 30 W. Washington
Redy William, lab, h 80 Hoagland ave
Redelsheimer David, h 186 W. Washington
Reddy Joe, tailor, h 260 E. Jefferson
Redrip Harry, wks Express office
Reed James L., clk, h 66 Wilt
Reed Isaac N., moulder, h 86 Lillie ave
Reed Daniel J., wks Pitts. shop, bds 100 Montgomery
Reeves John, fireman Richmond R'y, bds 263 Barr
Reese Charles, chair manuf., h 131 Montgomery
Reese Fred., chair maker, bds 131 Montgomery
Reed William, teamster, h 9 Sturgis
Reed Wesley, carp., h 203 Barr
Reed Nancy E., widow, h 151 Barr

Rekers Gerhart, grocer, h 114 W. Washington
Reesely Edward, eng. Pitts. R'y, bds 25 Barr
REFFELT WILLIAM R., carp., h 88 E. Main
Regedenz Charles, clk, Ft. Wayne Eating House
Regans J., night clerk Aveline House
Rehm Samuel, carp., h 205 Broadway
Rehm Christian, lab, h 323 Lafayette
Rehors Fred., carp, Pitts. shop, h 218 E. Jefferson
Rehm Christian, lab, h 247 W. Washington
Rehling Henry, boiler maker Pitts. shop, h 159 E. Lewis
Rehm Mrs. Elizabeth, h 56 Douglas
Rehrer Thomas, eng. Pitts. R'y, h 187 Jackson
Rehm Christian, lab, h 26 John
Rehling Fred., blacksmith Pitts. shop, h 126 Gay
Rehnen Barney, book-keeper, bds 64 W. Wayne
Rehnen Ulrich, mason, bds 64 W. Wayne
Rehnen Henry, mason, bds 64 W. Wayne
Rehsing Augustus, shoemaker, h 60 Clinton
Reiling Philip, porter, Aveline House
Reiter Henry, mach. Pitts shop, h 44 Wall
Reiley Peter, cooper, h 388 W. Main
Reid A. D., plow maker, h 27 Broadway
Reiter Henry, clk, bds 21 and 23 E. Main
REITER GEORGE, manuf. and dealer in cigars, wholesale and retail, 3 Aveline Block
Reidt John, jr., lab, bds 407 E. Lewis
Reinking F., h 173 Ewing
Reinking Ernst, carp., bds 386 E. Wayne
Reiter William, carp, h 49 Wall
Reisor George, wks Olds & Son, h on Pickway Road
Reiter William, lab, h — Taylor
Reidmiller John M., propr. Eagle Brewery, h — Taylor
Reiling Augustus, locksmith, cor. Pearl and Ewing, h 70 Pearl
Reidt John H., lab, h 407 E. Lewis
Reid John. plow mfg, h 91 W. Water
Reinwald Henry, lab, h 82 Williams
Reiter Mrs. Mary, h 134 Monroe
Reitze Charles, carp., bds 255 W. Wayne
Reinhardt M., h 241 E. Jefferson
Reiling F. W., carp., h 68 Nelson
Reineke Fred., musician. h 103 Barr
Reinking Fred., jr., moulder, bds 173 Ewing
Reineke Christian, upholster, h 103 Barr
Reitze Tobias, carp., h 255 W. Wayne
Reinking Diedrich, lab, h 63 W. Jefferson
Reichard Mary, widow, h 281 E. Washington
Reiter Conrad, lab, h 124 Wilt
Reinking William, sr., bds 248 W. Wayne

Rekers G., grocer, cor. Washington and Ewing
Rekers B. J., carp., h 117 W. Washington
Rekers Clement A., h 110 W. Washington
Remmert Herman, pattern maker, h 157 W. Washington
Remsdell Charles, eng. Wabash R'y, bds 50 McClellan
Remar Frank, bds 11 E. Main
Remke Fred., lab, h 47 Wilt
Remmel H. L., drug clk, bds 225 W. Jefferson
Remmert Herman, lab, h 30 Douglas
Remmel K. L., eng. Wabash R'y, bds 316 W. Jefferson
REMMEL A. C., druggist, store 126 Broadway, bds 202 W. Jefferson
Renner George A., paper dealer, bds 58 W. Berry
Renaud Isaac, lab, h 98 Chicago
Rentschler David, h 48 Wall
Renaud Emil, lab, bds 98 Chicago
Renfrew Robert, lab, h 156 Wallace
Rensman Bernard, lab, h 47 Walnut
Renshaw Joseph, moulder at Bowser & Co.'s, h 16 Butler
Renker Charles (Eder, Certia & Co., brewery), bds Bloomingdale Hotel
Renfrew P. K., cooper, h 43 Force
Renner Waldemar, teacher Concordia College, h 96 E. Jefferson
Renfrew B. B., mach. Bass' shop, bds 43 Force
Rensman Martin, h 116 Fairfield
Repine John, conductor Pitts. R'y, bds 316 Calhoun
Repine John, conductor Pitts. R'y, bds Harmon House
Rettew Daniel, brakeman Pitts. R'y, bds 23 Grand
Reynolds John W., candy maker, 47 E. Main
Reynolds William J., candy maker, bds 47 E. Main
Rhine John, lab, h 31 Taylor
Rhinesmith George, foreman Clark & Rhinesmith, h 242 W. Wayne
Rhinesmith John (Clark & Rhinesmith, lumber dealers), bds 231 W. Wayne
Rhinesmith Mrs. Elizabeth, h 231 W. Wayne
Rhinehart Isaac, lab, h 127 W. Water
Rhine Jacob, carp., h 227 E. Jefferson
Rhine Charles, lab, bds 62 Wall
Rhine Fred., lab, h 62 Wall
Rhoads Josiah, cooper, h 39 Duck
Rhodes Samuel, lab, h 1 John
Rhodes D. W., lab, h 24 John
Rhodes Michael, lab, h 389 Hanna
Riaman Augustus, bds 46 W. Water
Riblet H. F., eng. Wabash R'y, h 206 E. Lewis
Richard George, bill poster, Water street
Richard Henry, lab, h 143 Wallace
Rich William, butcher, h 22 Harrison
Rice Englert G., plasterer, bds 92 Montgomery
Richard Henry, bds 77 Holman

Richey Samuel, fireman Pitts. R'y, h 35 Williams
Richards William C., carp., h 48 Cass
Rich George, baggage man Muncie R'y, h 38 Fifth
Rice Joseph, moulder Bass' Foundry, bds 274 Hanna
Richards David, lab, h 89 Lasalle
Richard John, lab, h 284 E. Jefferson
Richard H. F., lab, bds 284 E. Jefferson
Richards John, lab, bds 163 Clinton
Richey Amos (McCulloch & Richey,) h 87 W. Water
Ridley John, barber, bds — Barr
Riley William, conductor Wabash R'y, h 25 Butler
Riley Thomas, conductor Wabash R'y, bds 59 Grand
Riley John, lab, bds 158 Montgomery
Rink George, hostler Phillips House, 107 E. Columbia
Rinewald William F., lab, h 328 Harrison
RING JOHN, County Treasurer, h 26 McClellan
Riordon James, moulder Bass' Foundry, bds 3 and 5 Railroad
Rippe Fred., mason, h 27 W. Columbia
Rippe William, carp., h 56 Wall
Rising John H., cabinet maker, h 123 High
Ritz Lorenz, lab, bds 81 Wells
Ritter Anton, mason, h 67 Wells
Ritter Jacob, mach. Pitts. shop, h 383 Lafayette
Ritter Carl, machinist, bds Steuben House
Rivers Charles (Kover and Rivers, painters), h 65 E. Wayne
Riethmiller John G., lab, bds 28 Eagle
Riethmiller George, lab, h 28 Eagle
Riethmiller Margaret, widow, h 28 Eagle
Ries Philip A., tailor, h 163 E. Jefferson
Riehling Conrad, tailor, h 97 E. Madison
Riedley Anthony, grocery and saloon, cor. Fairfield ave and Poplar
Riedel John, German teacher, h 196 Barr
Rietze W. F., clk, bds Hanna House
Roads Frank, lab, h 21 Poplar
Roach John, lab, h 283 W. Jefferson
Robinson C. H., eng. Wabash R'y, h 189 W. Washington
Robison J. N., fireman G. R. & I. R'y, bds 322 Calhoun
Robertson R. S., attorney, h 179 W. Berry
Roberts Charles B., brakeman Pitts. R'y, bds 23 Grand
Robbins Charles, carp., h 150 Hanna
Robinson Wilson, mach., bds 120 W. Water
Robinson Jesse S., teamster, bds 120 W. Water
Roba Fred., carp., h 55 E. Madison
Robbe Alphonse, clk, bds 31 Barr
Robertson William G., yard master Wabash Ry, h 88 Brackenridge
Robison Arthur, moulder, bds 198 Madison
Robinson Amasa, conductor Pitts. R'y, bds 198 Lafayette
Robinson Edward, bds Robinson House

Roberts George P., bds Aveline House
Roberts W. A., bds Aveline House
Roberts G. P., agent, bds Robinson House
Robison J. H., bds Hanna House
Robison H. H., ins. agent, bds Hanna House
Robertson Charles, moulder, h 198 Madison
Robison D., policeman, h 287 E. Washington
Robinson William, fireman, h 119 E. Lewis
ROBERTSON COL. R. S., attorney at law, office nw. cor. Main and Calhoun, h cor. Broadway and W. Berry
Roberts & Zollinger, mfs. of Fontaine's Improved Locomotive Smoke Stack, 212 Calhoun
Rockhill Mrs. Emily, h 295 W. Wayne
Roche David, lab, bds 60 Baker
Roche James, lab, h 60 Baker
Rochol M., shoemaker, h 19 Harrison
Rockhill J. B., h 3 Broadway
Rockhill William W., grocer, h S. Broadway
Rodenberg George, lab, h 46 Henry
Rodebaugh Adam H., watchman Pitts. shop, h 216 W. Jefferson
Rodeheaver William H., foreman (Olds & Son's Spoke Factory), h 22 Butler
Rodenbeck Fred., boiler maker, h 210 Jefferson
Rodenbeck William, jr., harness maker, bds 67 E. Madison
Rodebaugh T. J., foreman Pitts. paint shop, h 216 W. Jefferson
Rodeman John W., cigar mfg., h 292 Harrison
Robenbeck Henry, lab, h 345 E. Lewis
Rodenbeck William, helper, h 67 E. Madison
Rœbel Henry, mason, bds 68 Ewing
Rœbel Augustus, shoemaker, h 68 Ewing
Rœling John, lab, h 9 Force
Rœmerman Henry, blacksmith Wabash shop, h 143 Broadway
Rœlle Jacob, mach. Wabash shop, h 156 Calhoun
Rœger Christian, lab, bds Steuben House
Rœlle Mrs. Susan, h 156 Calhoun
Rœssler Henry, mach., h 72 W. Jefferson
Rœlle Peter, bds 156 Calhoun
Rogers A. A., carp., h 17 N. Cass
Rogers William, boiler maker h 126 E. Wayne
Rogers John, bds 152 E. Wayne
Rogers Charles, lab, h 42 Barthold
Rohs Henry, merchant (R., Eme & Reinking), h 134 E. Washington
Rohrer John, sr., chair maker, h 36 Wells
Rohrer John, jr., painter, bds 36 Wells
Rohlman William, painter Pitts. shop, h 169 Ewing
Rohle Frank, fireman Wabash R'y, h 127 Harrison
Rohs, Eme & Reinking, dry goods store, 13 E. Columbia
Roller Albert N., fireman Wabash R'y, bds 47 Bass

Rolston James, machinist Wabash shop, h 196 Barr
Rolape John, drayman, h 153 E. Washington
Rolf Fred, lab, h 53 Wall
Rolf Mrs. Minnie, h 53 Wall
Rolf Henry, German teacher, h 196 Barr
Romboldt Gottlieb, lab, h 55 Wilt
Rombke Henry, lab, h 101 Wilt
Rombke Henry, cabinet maker, h 68 E. Madison
Ronny Charles, clk, h on Maumee
Rooney John, eng. P., Ft. W. & Chicago R'y, h 174 E. Berry
Root V., lumber dealer, h 138 E. Berry
ROOT & CO., wholesale and retail dry goods, 90 Columbia
Ropa William, boatman, h 189 W. Jefferson
Rosecrance John, conductor G. R. & I. R'y, h 80 Butler
Rosenberg Joseph, peddler, h 185 Lafayette
Ross George B., eng., h 137 E. Jefferson
Ross Enoch W., shoemaker, bds 3 Dawson
Rossner Julius, tailor, h 137 Henry
Rosington W. W., conductor, bds 117 E. Madison
Rosenthal Albert, traveling agent, h 130 W. Washington
Ross Charles, bds 232 W. Jefferson
Rosenberger Frank, trunk maker, bds 330 Hanna
Rosenberger Henry, clk, bds 330 Hanna
Rosenthal Max, cigar mfg, h 105 W. Wayne
Rosenkranz James, brakeman Wabash R'y, bds 285 Hanna
Rosenberger Charles, painter Pitts. shop, h 330 Hanna
Rost Henry M., h 102 W. Wayne
Ross W. G., traveling agent, bds Mayer House
Rosenberger Charles, cooper, h 176 Fairfield
Rossington Richard, carp., h 59 E. Wayne
Rosenthal E., trader, h 30 W. Washinston
Ross L. E., foreman Olds & Son, h 193 E. Washington
Rosenthal Dr. I. N., h 98 W. Berry
Ross Mr., despatcher Pitts. R'y, bds 49 and 51 W. Berry
Rossington William, h 117 E. Madison
Rossington R. B., telegraph operator, bds 117 E. Madison
ROSENTHAL I. N., physician and surgeon, office over Wagner's drug store, h 98 W. Berry
Ross L. H. & Bro., wooden ware manfs., cor. Ewing and Canal
Rothenbeck Ernst, helper Pitts. shop, bds 168 E. Lewis
Rothenbeck Conrad, helper Pitts. shop, h 168 E. Lewis
Rotheflueh Mrs. Mary, h 160 E. Wayne
Roth Bernard, lab, h 20 Force
Roth Fred., stone cutter, h 37 Wilt
Rothart Christian, blacksmith, bds 178 Barr
Rothschild Solomon (R. & Bro.), h 68 W. Berry
Roughers Mrs. Bridget, h 116 Jackson
Rouner Alexander, lab, h 257 Hanna

Rommary Joe, clk, h 387 E. Wayne
Rowe Joseph, lab, bds cor. Lafayette and Wallace
Rowan Mrs. Rosa, h 161 E. Washington
Rubin Joe, clk, bds 84 W. Main
Rubin Rev. Edward (Rabi Hebrew Synagogue), h 84 W. Main
Rubin Max, bds 84 W. Main
Ruckgaber Joseph, carp. Pitts. shop, h 99 Williams
RUDISILL HENRY J., County Auditor, h on Lima plank road, N. Canal Feeder
Rudolph Fred., mach., bds 170 Lafayette
Rue Nicholas, bds Steuben House
Ruehling Philip, lab, h — W. Jefferson
Ruff William C. F., drug clerk, bds 138 Broadway
Rump Fred., teamster, h 2 Force
Rump Herman, carp., bds 13 Lavina
Rump Ernst, carp, h 13 Lavina
Rumsey Henry, blacksmith (W. and E. Stevens), bds 80 E. Wayne
Rundell Charles, conductor Ft. W., M. & C. R'y, h 19 Williams
Ruppel John, boatman, h — Francis
Ruppel Fabian, mason, h 122 Chicago
Ruppel John, brick mason, h 91 Montgomery
Ruppel Paul, helper Pitts. shop, h 258 E. Wayne
Rupert Ira, ins. agent, h 121 E. Washington
Rupp John, blacksmith Wabash shop, h 253 W. Wayne
Rurode Ernst C. (Root & Co., dry goods), bds Hamilton House
Rush W. A., clk., bds Robinson House
Russell Sarah, bds 23 Baker
Russell William, painter Pitts. shop, h 13 Walnut
Russell William, bds Robinson House
Russell William J., painter Pitts. shop, bds 13 Walnut
Russell James, printer, bds 45 W. Main
Russell Peter, carp., Pitts. shop, h 130 Wilt
RUSSELL WILLIAM R. & CO., dealer in cutlery and guns, 26 Clinton
Rust August, lab, h 40 Charles
Rutan George W., mach. Wabash shop, h 172 W. Jefferson
Ruthrauff William, attorney and clerk First National Bank, bds 79 West Main
Ruthrauff Henrietta, widow, h 79 W. Main
Ruthrauff Henry, bds 79 W. Main
Ryan Bridget, widow, h 17 Bass
Ryan Bridget, widow, bds 44 Chicago
Ryan Cornelius, cabinet maker, h 144 Douglas
Ryan Michael, lab, h 40 Chicago
RYAN DANIEL, Attorney and Justice of the Peace, office on Court, opposite court house, h 390 E. Jefferson
Ryan James, contractor, h 164 Harrison
Ryall John, civil eng. Pitts. R'y, h 324 W. Jefferson

Ryan John, moulder J. H. Bass', bds 81 Holman
Ryan Margaret, widow, h 119 Williams
Ryan Thomas (Mason Bros. & Ryan), h 187 W. Washington
Ryan Patrick, shoemaker, bds 109 W. Jefferson
Ryan Patrick, shoemaker. h 164 Calhoun
Ryan William, bds 187 W. Washington
Ryan William, lab, h 347 Hanna

Sachsstetter John, lab, bds 35 Force
Safon Thomas, mach Bass' Foundry, h 142 Holman
SALLOT V. A., cabinet manuf., 177 Clay, h 164 E. Lewis
Salga C., lab, h 9 Wert
Sallot J. F., h 162 E. Lewis
SALLIER FRANK, brick mfg., h Lillie Addition
Sallier John, lab, bds Lillie's Addition
Sallveau John, lab, bds 134 Monroe
Salfrank John, brewer, bds on Taylor
Sampson George, bds 174 W. Wayne
Sanburn Amos, hack driver, h 305 Harrison
Sauerwein Charles, printer, bds 56 Barthold
Sauerwein Herman, labs h 56 Barthold
Sauerwein Ernst, lab, h 58 Barthold
Sanders George A., h 41 W. Washington
Sanders Ernst, mason, h 103 W. Jefferson
Sandy James, lab, h 80 Harrison
Sander Charles W., dealer in boots and shoes
Sandoe C. W., blacksmith, h 204 E. Lewis
Sanders John, conductor Pitts. R'y, bds Exchange
Sanders Henry, teamster, bds 68 W. Washington
Sanders William, h 86 W. Washington
Sander William, shoemaker, h 107 W. Washington
SARNIGHAUSEN JOHN D., publisher and proprietor of the *Indiana Staats-Zeitung*, office northeast cor. Clinton and Columbia
Sargent William, blacksmith Pitts. shop, h 72 Chicago
Saunders Joe B., mach. Wabash shop, h cor. Harrison and Lewis
Saurs Henry, lab, bds 202 Fairfield
Saurs James T., eng. Wabash R'y, bds 202 Fairfield
Sauers George, dealer in groceries and provisions, 162 Calhoun
SAUSER LOUIS, dealer in watches and jewelry, h 223 Calhoun
Saurs Mrs. Mary Ann, h 202 Fairfield
Saurs Samuel P., eng. Wabash R'y, bds 202 Fairfield
Saurs David, lab, bds 202 Fairfield
Saunders Charles A., dealer in paper, h 58 W. Berry
Saunders John, collar maker, h 325 Lafayette
Saunders Mary Ann, widow, h 208 E. Lewis

Saxton Madam, widow, h 76 Douglas ave
Saxe George A., teacher Concordia College
Sawyer Frank, moulder Bass' Foundry, bds 28 Force
Scarr George, hostler, bds Exchange Hotel
Schaffer William, carp., h 26 Wilt
Schaffer Christian, clk, bds 235 W. Main
Schappman William, grocery and saloon, h 213 Hanna
Schaick John, lab, h 35 Smith
Schaffer William, brewer, bds 75 Harrison
Schalk Matthias, clk, bds 54 E. Main
Schaub Christian cooper, h 73 Force
Schalk John, bar-tender, h cor. W. Main and Fulton
Scharer John, expressman, bds on Erin
Schanck Louis, basket maker, 62 Columbia
SCHAFFER JOS. & CO., auction and commission, 7 E Main
Schack H., file cutter, bds 103 E. Madison
Schack William, shoemaker, h 103 E. Madison
Schafer Daniel, fireman Wabash R'y, h 110 Chicago
Schafer Christian, h 143 Holman
Schabhorst William, lab, bds 8 Orchard
Schabhorst Henry, carp., h 12 Orchard
Schaubhorst Herman, carp., h 8 Orchard
Schack Martin, lab, bds 35 Smith
Schabrack H., lab, bds 256 E. Washington
Schalk Matthias, clk, bds 54 E. Main
SCHENCK CON., St. Nicholas Dining Room and Saloon, ne. cor. Calhoun and Wayne
Schell J. B., cutter, bds Central Hotel
Scheiman Ernst, carp., h 193 Ewing
Scheffer Joseph, cigar box maker, h south on Hoagland
Scheel Henry, lab, bds 120 Lafayette
Scheller Julius, stone mason, h 184 W. Main
Schieffer Gottlieb, lab, h 167 Holman
Schele John B., h 253 E. Jefferson
Scheid Peter, mach. Pitts. shop, h 311 Lafayette
Scheffer William, baker, bds 29 W. Columbia
SCHENCK CON., propr. St. Nicholas Restaurant, h 23 W. Wayne
SCHIEFFER C. & SON, boot and shoe store, 100½ Columbia
Schell James H., lawyer, office over post office, h — Creighton ave
Scheffer Christian, ice dealer, h 193 High
Scherer Andrew, lab, h — Erie
Scheffer John, bds South Hoagland
Schele & Lauer, grocers, 5 E. Main
Schœpf John, wks Wabash shop, h 50 Taylor
Scheumann Fred., carp. Pitts. shop, h 321 Calhoun
Schele Augustus F., h 58 W. Main
Scherer George, baker, bds cor. Harrison and Berry
Scheifer William, bds 99 E. Main

Scherer Frederick, carp. Pitts. shop, h 95 E. Washington
Schele August, mason, h 131 E. Washington
Schele John F., mason, h 180 Griffith
Scherer Christian, lab, h 76 Williams
Scheiman Christian, carp., h 36 Melitta
Scheem William, fireman Pitts. R'y, bds 13 Maumee
Schœrpf Mrs. Delia, h 16 Sturgis
Scheiman Fred., tailor, h 86 E. Jefferson
Scheirer G., carp., h 218 E. Washington
Schell John, tailor, bds 86 E. Main
Schilling Frank, stone cutter, h 255 W. Jefferson
Schick George, Rector Concordia College
Schirmeyer Anthony, lab, h 148 W. Washington
Schieferstein P., butcher, 61 E. Main
Schildmeyer Mrs. L., h 180 W. Jefferson
Schildmeyer Fred., painter, bds 180 W. Jefferson
Schirmeyer Charles, painter bds 148 W. Washington
Schirmeyer L. clk, h 127 E. Jefferson
Schirmeyer Martin, h 127 E. Jefferson
Schieman Frank, boarding house, 81 Wells
Schinoll Gottlieb, lab, h 174 Broadway
Schiefer Diedrich, tinner Pitts. shop, h 135 Montgomery
Schlaudraff L., lab, h — E. Washington
Schmidt William, file cutter, bds 126 Calhoun
Schmidt Jacob, lab, h 33 Wilt
Schmidt Fred., shoemaker, h 32 Wall
Schmidt C., lab, bds 7 McClellan
Schmitz Charles A., M. D., h cor College and Wilt
Schmidt Peter C., carp., h 211 W. Jefferson
Schmidt Andrew, lab, h 12 Hood
Schmidt Christian, butcher, h 76 W. Walnut
Schmidt Charles, mason, h 16 Gay
Schmeiman A., stave cutter, h 255 W. Jefferson
Schmalhaus Fred., fruit stand, &c., h 77 Calhoun
Schmalzrath George, butcher, bds 110 Calhoun
Schmidt Charles, lab, bds 4 Harry
Schmucker Teber, foreman spoke factory, h 309 Lafayette
Schmidt William, brewer, bds 157 Wells
Schmetzer Fred., clk, h 240 W. Washington
Schmidt L., lab, h 211 Madison
Schmidt Mrs. M., h 276 W. Washington
Schmalz Carl, tailor shop, 136 Calhoun
Schmidt Martin, foreman Hornung's brewery, h 162 Calhoun
Schmidt John, teamster, h 339 Lafayette
Schmidt Andrew, plasterer, h 90 Wilt
Schmitz Charles F., officer U. S. Navy, h cor. College and Wilt
Schmidt William R., carp., bds 75 Monroe
Schmidt J. W., tailor and cutter, h 75 Monroe

SCHMUCKLE FRED., Bloomidgdale Hotel, h 132 Wells
SCHNIEDER B. H., proprietor American House, 15, 17 and 19 Calhoun
Schnorberger Christian, mach. Pitts. shop, h 44 John
Schneider Fred., cigar maker, bds 282 W. Jefferson
Schneider John, lab, h 28 Wert
SCHNELKER, BEGUE & CO., Indiana Stave Factory, west side Mets street, north of T., W. & W. R'y
Schneider Gottlieb, tailor, h 52 Wells
Schnabel R. A., local editor *Volksfreund*, bds 170 W. Washington
Schneider William, stone cutter, bds 25 Broadway
Schnelker Henry, brick mason, h 261 E. Wayne
Schneider George, lab, h 282 W. Jefferson
Schneider William, shoemaker, h 104 Webster
Schneider Herman, propr. bakery and eating house, 41 Columbia
Schœpf John F., barber shop, 150 Calhoun
Schone Henry, h 225 E. Washington
Schopman William, grocer, h Lillie Addition
Schœnbein Albert, draughtsman Pitts. shop, h 71 Douglas ave
Schoch Ferdinand, tailor, h cor. Second and Harrison
Schorf Adam, cabinet maker, bds 204 Madison
SCHOTT GEORGE J., druggist, cor. Barr and Washington
Schottman William, carp. Pitts. shop, h 12 Hough
Schrœder F., h 380 E. Wayne
Schrœder John, mason, bds 38 Force
Schrœder Lewis, saloon, 27 W. Columbia
Schram Frank, lab, h 28 Jones
Schreiber John, tailor, h 35 Wefel
Schrader Henry C. (Markley, Schrader & Co.), h 186 Henry
Schreck Agnes, widow, h 81 Holman
Schrœder Henry, lab, h 177 High
Schrage C., tailor, h 214 Madison
Schrader Henry, grave digger, h 141 Francis
Schrader Lewis, h 11 Francis
Schram John, lab, h 463 Lafayette
Schramm Philip, lab, h 37 Force
Schrœder G., tailor and renovator, h 170 E. Jefferson
Schrœder H., student, bds 170 E. Jefferson
Schrœder John, mach., bds 170 E. Jefferson
Schrœder Fred., lab, h 23 Pritchard
Schrack Joseph, carp., h 29 Wilt
Schram Martin, shoemaker, h 129 E. Jefferson
Schuck Lewis, lab, h 94 Smith
Schuster G., fireman Pitts. R'y, h 213 Hanna
Schuster William, lab, bds 208 Hanna
Schuckman H., tinner, (Wilson, Schuckman & Muhler), h 211 E. Washington
Schultz Ferdinand, cooper, bds 408 W. Main

Schultz William, lab, h 108 John
Schultz William, lab, h 103 Force
Schuster, John, lab, h 87 Force
Schultheis John, clerk at James Sommers', bds 41 Douglas ave
Schultheis P., carder, h 211 E. Washington
Schultheis John, carpet weaver, h 211 E. Washington
Schuman R., clk, h 60 E. Wayne
Schumacher John, lab, h 33 Charles
Schuler M., night watchman Pitts. R'y, h 268 E. Jefferson
Schuler John, lab, h 214 E. Jefferson
Schuhler Frank, shoemaker, bds 182 Calhoun
Schulthies T., lab, bds 339 Lafayette
Schumacher Fred., lab, bds 33 Charles
Schumacher Henry, moulder Bass' shop, bds 33 Charles
Schumacher John, lab, bds 38 Force
Schulthes Charles, cutter, h 57 E. Wayne
Schuster Henry, lab, bds 99 E. Madison
Schuckman John, tinner, h 87 E. Jefferson
Schuck Henry, lab, h 106 Butler
Schulz Fred., mason, h 338 Hanna
Schulz William, shoemaker, h 27 W. Wayne
Schulz Peter, boot and shoe maker, 45 E. Main
Schwarz Louis, baker, 62 E. Main
Schwarz George, lab, h 8 Hood
Schwarz Christian, plasterer, h 343 W. Jefferson
Schwegman H. R., clk, h cor. Jefferson and Clinton
Schwarz Henry, plasterer, bds 111 W. Jefferson
Schwarz Charles, German school teacher, h 55 W. Washington
Schwedes Rev. Francis R., Pastor First German Reformed (St. John's) Church, h 59 W. Washington
Schweir William, foreman Bass' Foundry, h 187 Madison
Schwarz Rudolf, h W. Pearl
SCHWARTZ & KOCH, repairers and dealers in saddles, harness and whips, shop 43½ E. Columbia
Schwier Henry, boiler maker, bds 55 E. Madison
Schwegel William, collar maker, h 67 Wells
Schwarz August, teamster, bds 416 Calhoun
Schwarz John A., farmer, h 416 Calhoun
Schwarz William, brakeman Wabash R'y, bds 416 Calhoun
Schwehn Conrad, lab, h 12 Orchard
Schwab John, lab, h 392 E. Wayne
Schwake Henry, school teacher, h 109 Van Buren
Schwier Charles, boiler maker Bass' Foundry, h 174 Montgomery
Scisler George, brakeman Wabash R'y, bds 73 Grand
Sclagel Augusta, widow, bds 149 Ewing
Scott Peter W., conductor Grand Rapids R'y, h 30 Williams
Scott Rev. Walter, Pastor Good Sheperd Church, h 51 Douglas ave
Scott J. C., conductor Ft. W., R. & C. R'y, bds Exchange Hotel

Scott George, mach. Pitts. shop, h 165 Montgomery
Scott William, plasterer, bds 105 Wallace
Scoley John, lab, h 8 Colerick
Scribner Joseph, brakeman Pitts. R'y, h 334 Calhoun
Seargent William, lab, h on Brackenridge
Seabold John, sr., grocer, h 194 Broadway
Seabold, John, jr., clk, bds 194 Broadway
Sears Charles, printer, h 80 Calhoun, up stairs
Sebring James, joiner, bds Union House
Sedgwick John, h 83 Brackenride
Seelman Jacob, lab, bds 23 Nirdlinger
Seeman Charles, lab, bds 48 McClellan
Siemon Rudolph, bds 100 E. Jefferson
Siebold David, grocer, h 121 Wells
Seiman Moses, peddler, h 78 E. Madison
Seibold Gottlieb, lab, h 45 Walnut
Seivers Fred., sewing machine agent, h 10 Henry
Seifert William, brewer, bds Bloomingdale Brewery
Siebold Christian, grocer, h 168 W. Main
Seidler Charles, clk, bds 21 and 23 E. Main
Selle August L., druggist, store 264 Calhoun, h 57 Douglas ave
Selle Augustus, clk, bds American House
Selle Albert, druggist, bds 56 Douglas ave
Self Jasper N., sewing machine agent, h 130 W. Main
Semon Paul, eng., h 82 Jefferson
Sergeant William, lab, h 132 E. Lewis
Sessler William H., eng. G. R. & I. R'y, h 114 Butler
Sessler Peter, conductor Pitts. R'y, h 107 Holman
Setelmeier Mrs. Jane, h 323 W. Main
Shank Christian, cabinet maker, bds 100 Montgomery
Shannon Jacob, lab Aveline House
Shap Matthew, eng. Wabash shop, h 30 Butler
Sharp Thomas, bds 3 E. Water
Sharp Henry, sr., h 3 E. Water
Sharp Henry, jr., bds 3 E. Water
Shafer Oregan, switchman Pitts. R'y, h 294 Calhoun
Shaffer George, lab, h 23 Pritchard
Shaffer Lewis, brakeman Pitts. R'y, bds 92 Montgomery
Shaffer ———, clk, bds 49 and 51 W. Berry
Shaffer William, fireman, h 286 Broadway
Shaffer Jacob, lab, bds 113 E. Main
Shaffer Charles, lab, bds 286 Broadway
Shaffer Daniel, eng., h 44 Hoagland ave
Shaffer Mrs. Elizabeth, h 22 Fulton
Sharf Charles, tinner, bds 204 Madison
Shaughnessy Martin, lab, h 66 Wallace
Shaw V. B., lab, h 25 Smith
Slaw Robert H., mach. Wabash shop, h cor. Fairfield and Colerick

Shaw David J., lab, bds 25 Smith
Shirlenberger William, porter Aveline House
Shea Catherine, widow, h 7 Walnut
Sheppard Charles W., butcher, bds 402 Calhoun
Sheafer William S., carp., bds 187 W. Wayne
Shepherd J. H., widow, dress maker, h 260 Calhoun
Sheppard Thomas, boiler maker, h 189 Montgomery
Sheridan William, carp., h 76 Montgomery
Sherbundy A., h 92 Hanna
Sherbundy A. M., jr., carp., bds 92 Hanna
Shell James, lab, bds cor. W. Berry and Rockhill
Sheper Jacob, shoemaker, bds 133 E. Lewis
Shell Edward, eng. Wabash R'y, h 63 Melitta
Shelby Mary, widow, bds 89 W. Lewis
Sheafer William G., carp., h 187 W. Wayne
Shean Edmund, bds 25 Baker
Shilling Mrs. Mary, millinery, E. Columbia
Shidel Charles, barber, h 198 Fairfield
Shien William, mach. Wabash shop, bds 64 McClellan
Shoemeker Henry, tinner, h 93 Barr
Sholes Eli, brakeman Pitts. R'y, h 118 Fairfield
Shorman G. W., wks Olds & Son, bds 92 Montgomery
Shortey Charles, brakeman Pitts. R'y, bds 245 Calhoun
Sholes William, lab, bds 118 Fairfield
Shortliff Charles, brakeman Pitts. R'y, bds 220 Lafayette
Shorden Stephen, h 61 and 63 E. Columbia
Shordan Daniel, h 19 E. Washington
Shopman Henry, lab, h 139 E. Lewis
Shopman William, teamster, bds 139 E. Lewis
Shoaff Edward, tailor, bds Robinson House
Shoaff Samuel H., manufacturer of harness and saddles, 12 W. Columbia
Shoaff Samuel H., harness maker, h 84 E. Berry
Shoaff W. C., merchant tailor, bds 93 Calhoun
Shoaff John A., photograph gallery, h 153 W. Berry
Shoaff Margaret L., widow, bds 96 Butler
Shorey George, eng. Wabash R'y, h 18 Butler
Shoneberger Joe, lab, bds cor. Main and Barr
Shophorst Fred., lab, bds 105 W. Berry
Shoemaker William, janitor High School, h 191 E. Lewis
Shoemaker James (H. H. & Co.), bds 25 Barr
Shryock Samuel, h 12 Cass
Shrine Daniel, lab, h 348 Calhoun
Shurtleff Walter C., fireman Pitts. R'y, bds 92 Montgomery
Shumacker Adam. boiler maker Pitts. shop, h 212 Broadway
Shunk Charles, druggist, bds 207 E. Jefferson
Shunk Frank, druggist, bds 207 E. Jefferson
Shunk Allen, wks Pitts. R'y, h 207 E. Jefferson
Shuck William H., telegraph operator, h 24 Pine

Shultz William, moulder, h 175 Madison
Shulze Charles E., clk, h 17 Lewis
Shultz John, clk, bds 47 Douglas ave
Shulz Henry, plasterer, h 123 Union
Shurick Frank S., Indiana Stave Factory, bds 49 and 51 W. Berry
SHURICK F. S., stave manufacturer, cor Lafayette and Railroad
Sickmond Herman, tailor, h 101 Wilt
SIDEL EDWARD, h 107 E. Main
Sidla Isaac, eng. Wabash R'y, h 29 Garden
SIEMON & BRO., book store 34 E. Berry
Siemon August F., dealer in books and stationery, h 27 Madison
Siebold Bernard, lab, h 7 Pine
Siebold Christian, teamster, h 126 Calhoun
Siebold George, h cor. Cass and Fourth
Siebold George, carp., h 301 W. Jefferson
Siebold Henry, blacksmith, bds 5 Hood
Siebold Henry, lab, bds 7 Pine
Siebert William, druggist, h 125 E. Lewis
Sigsby Mrs. A., h 15 Lavina
Sihler Rev. William, Pastor German Lutheran (St. Paul's) Church, h 166 Barr
Silvers William, carp., h 19 N. Cass
Simmons John, conductor Wabash R'y, h 7 Bass
Simonson J. H., lumber dealer, h 138 E. Berry
Simson Mart, barber, bds American House
Simons David, brakeman Wabash R'y, bds 59 Grand
Simpson G. W., mach., h 142 E. Jefferson
Simons Gordan, eng. Pitts. R'y, bds 25 Barr
Simons Oscar H., road master Pitts. R'y, h 33 Brackenridge
Simmons Michael, blacksmith Pitts. shop, h 40 Lasalle
SINCLAIR SAMUEL E., attorney at law
Sinclair Thomas, mach. Wabash shop, h 159 Van Buren
Sinclair John, bds 159 Van Buren
Singer & Pike, hat and cap store, 19 E. Main
Singer L. O. (S. & Pike, hatters), h 122 W. Wayne
Singmaster Joseph, watchman Pitts. shop, h 177 Jackson
Singelton Philip, mach. Pitts. shop, bds 29 Baker
Singelton John, lab, h 29 Baker
Singelton Michael, Chief of Police, h 33 Baker
SISTERS OF PROVIDENCE (St. Mary's Academy), cor. Calhoun and Jefferson
Skinner Benjamin (Carnehan & Skinner), h 88 W. Berry
Slate Prof. Engastrimuth, bds 153 E. Berry
Slater John, blacksmith Wabash shop, h 25 Williams
Slater John, lab, h 50 Baker
Slanderhoff L. B., jr., lab, h 174 Taylor
Slagle William, mach. Pitts. shop, h 56 Chicago
Slagle John, mach. Pitts. shop, bds 317 Harrison

Slagle Mrs. J., widow, h 317 Harrison
Sleeper Frank, book-keeper Olds & Son, bds 115 Barr
Sletter L., lab, h 42 Nirdlinger
Slocum George, mach. Pitts. shop, bds 242 E. Lewis
Slocum Edward, h 242 E. Lewis
Slocum Clark, tinner, bds 242 E. Lewis
Slusser Austin, lab. bds 19 Baker
Sma Louis, shoemaker, h 169 Ewing
Smalz John, propr. boarding house, 203 Calhoun
Smart Stephen F., attorney, office 44 Calhoun
Smart James, foreman Wabash blacksmith shops, h 424 Broadway
SMART JAMES H., Supt. Public Schools, h 287 W. Wayne
Smead Albert, lab, h E. Washington
Smenners Daniel, marble cutter, h 161 Barr
SMICK S. S., dealer in agricultural implements, store 22 and 24 W. Columbia, h 64 Barr
Smick M. M., book-keeper (S. S. Smick), bds 64 Barr
Smick William T., clk S. S. Smick, bds 64 Barr
Smied August, clk, bds 234 E. Wayne
Sminers George, stone cutter, bds 47 W. Main
Sminers Henry, stone cutter, h 47 W. Main
Smithy Casper, h 114 E. Berry
Smidt Fred., mason, bds 153 Madison
Smith George W., fireman Pitts. R'y, h 89 Hanna
Smith Daniel, lab, h 44 Wells
Smith Henry, fireman Wabash R'y, h 8 Lavina
Smith A. E., wagon maker, bds 149 W. Main
Smith Henry, teamster, bds 164 Harrison
Smith James S. (Bass & S.), h 96 Butler
Smith Samuel, carp., h 53 W. Lewis
Smith Mrs. Ann, h 41 Lavina
Smith Henry, lab, bds 29 Francis
Smith Martin, bds 75 Harrison
Smith L., carp., bds 63 Harrison
Smith A. T., clk, bds Mayer House
Smith Charles, lab, bds 77 Calhoun, up stairs
Smith Charles H., brakeman Wabash R'y, h cor. Grand and Kansas
Smith George, helper, bds 161 Holman
Smith Joseph, cigar maker, bds 36 Monroe
Smith Charles, theatrical agent, bds 113 Lafayette
Smith Rev. Nathan S., Pastor Third Presbyterian Church, h 21 Brackenridge
Smith Clark, conductor Pitts. R'y, bds 16 Chicago
Smith John, cooper, h 15 Baker
Smith Casper C., eng. Wabash R'y, h 19 Charles
Smith Martin, lab, h 80 Buchanan
Smith Lewis, lab, bds 29 Francis
Smith Peter, lab, h 29 Francis

Smith Dr. S. S., bds 47 Bass
Smith E. B., foreman *Gazette* office, bds 178 W. Washington
Smith Mrs. Sarah, h 124 W. Jefferson
Smith Clarence, book-keeper, bds 124 W. Jefferson
Smith Calvin S., express messenger G. R. & I. R'y, h 41 Lavina
Smith John, moulder, h 343 E. Lewis
Smith Andrew, mach. Bass' shop, bds 343 E. Lewis
Smith William, brakeman Pitts. R'y, bds 92 Montgomery
Smith James, mach. Bass' shop, h 14 Summit
Smith E. C., carriage trimmer, h 11 Monroe
Smith Jane, widow, h 89 Hanna
Smith Robert, hostler (J. C. Davis), bds — Lewis
SMITH C. L., U. S. Express agent, h 54 Jackson
Smith Lorin, news agent at Post office, h 24 E. Washington
Smith Orson, eng. Pitts. R'y, bds 25 Barr
Smith L. H., brakeman Pitts. R'y, bds 74 Douglas ave
Smith Elliott (Smith Bro.'s & Co., marble works), h 340 W. Jefferson
Smith Dr. C. S., h 38 Douglas ave
Snider Augustus, cigar maker, bds 59 Wall
Snider Evan, dentist, h 69 Garden
Snively H. J., carp., h 179 Clinton
Snively Henry J., carp., h 138 Lafayette
Snurr David E., lab, h 153 High
SNYDER & DARROW, North Side Lunch House, cor. First and Harrison
Snyder Evan, dentist, office cor. Harrison and Berry
Snyder Clark, eng. G. R. & I. R'y, h 21 Lavina
Snyder Luther, foreman stave factory, bds 457 Lafayette
Snyder David C., eng. Pitts. R'y, h 293 Harrison
Snyder William, conductor Pitts. R'y, bds 212 Lafayette
Snyder John, conductor Pitts. R'y, bds 212 Lafayette
Snyder George, lab, h 70 W. Walnut
Snyser Peter C., (Bash & Co. produce), bds 240 W. Berry
Snyder Edwin, lab, h 116 E. Madison
Snyder Christian, h 187 Lafayette
Snyder Lewis F., teamster, h 208 W. Main
Sœst Fred., lab, wks Pitts. shop, bds 12 Hough
Solomon Charles, lab, bds 178 Barr
Sommer Gertrude, widow, h 57 W. Jefferson
Sommers John, lab, h 317 Calhoun
Sommers Fred, lab, h 185 Jackson
SOMMERS JAMES, saloon, cor. Calhoun and Baker, h 47 Douglas Avenue
Sommers Michael, bds 47 Douglas ave
Sommers Rheinhart, lab, h 164 Wells
Sommers Carl, photographer, 4 E. Columbia
Sommer Fred., lab, h 44 Douglas
Sommers John, mason, h 33 Grand

Sommer Henry, mach. Pitts. shop, bds 57 W. Jefferson
Sonner Jacob, carp., bds 12 McClellan
Soper Herbert, conductor Wabash R'y, h 55 Melitta
Soper Catherine, widow, h 55 Melitta
Sorvien Samuel H., blacksmith, h 126 Wilt
Sorg Isaac, drug clerk, h 113 E. Madison
Sorg Peter, h 176 E. Washington
Souder Daniel W., carp. Pitts. shop, h 31 Williams
Sours David, lab, bds 102 Williams
Southern Ralph, h 278 Webster
Southern James, eng. Pitts. R'y, 278 Webster
Sovain Philip, lab, bds 12 Clark
Sovain Mrs. Mary, h 12 Clark
Sovain Charles, lab, bds 12 Clark
Sovain Fred., moulder Bass' Foundry, h 121 Douglas
Spaght Samuel, plasterer, bds 69 E. Jefferson
Spangler Joseph, lab, h 375 Lafayette
Spangler Leonard, lab, bds 375 Lafayette
Spang John, conductor Pitts. R'y, h 285 Hanna
Spencer M. V. B., attorney, h 216 W. Wayne
Spencer Mrs. C., widow, h 30 Wert
Spencer Mrs. Ann, h 196 Calhoun
SPENCER & HERTIG, attorneys at law, office Calhoun, opposite Phœnix Block
Spence Mrs. Jane, h 223 W. Jefferson
Spereisen J., blacksmith, h 56 Taylor
Spearing Henry, eng. Wabash R'y, bds 213 Broadway
Spenle Lewis, mach. Bowser & Co., h 114 Creighton ave
SPIEGEL ERNST, grocer, h 36 Nirdlinger
Spiegel G. F., shoemaker, h 315 W. Jefferson
Spiegel Augustus, tailor, h 40 Wall
Spiegel Bernard, clk, bds 40 Wall
Spiegel Gustave, shoemaker, h 315 W. Jefferson
Spitler John, fireman Wabash R'y, h 191 Jackson
Spidel Herman, lab, h 272 E. Jefferson
Spielmann Peter, brewer, h 44 Monroe
Spielmann Peter, brewer, wks Linker. Hey & Co., h 18 Monroe
Spoth Lorenz, lab, bds Bloomingdale Hotel
Spore W. D., lab, h 140 W. Jefferson
Spring John, bds 194 E. Washington
Sprague Mrs. A., widow, h 50 Pearl
Spurrier Dennis, tinner, h 43 W. Main
STAHL & HILLEGASS, attorneps at law, office corner Main and Calhoun, over Merchants' National Bank
STAHL JOHN (Stahl & Hillegass), attorney at law, office over Merchants' National Bank
Staudacher George, lab, h 43 Wilt
Stapleford Henry, auctioneer, 7 E. Main, bds Sturgis House

Starke Charles, lab, bds 63 Water
Staunton James, eng. Muncie R'y, h 24 Cass
Stapleford Francis A., clk, bds Creighton ave
Stahl Christian, lab, h 77 Lasalle
Stanley, Bieber & Co., carriage makers, 106 and 112 W. Main
Stahlhut Charles, teamster, h 145 Ewing
Stahlhut Fred., teamster, h 157 Ewing
Stark Erasmus, lab, h 23 Nirdlinger
Stanley Chauncey, carriage maker (S., Bieber & Co.), h 221 W. Main
Staub A., tinner, bds American House
Stapleford Lavina, widow, h Creighton ave
Stapleford Nelson, bds 336 Broadway
Stahr Charles, lab, bds 3 and 5 Railroad
Stall Edward, fireman Wabash R'y, h 14 Creighton ave
Starkey George, brakeman Pitts. R'y, h 16 Holman
Starkey O. L., painter, h 102 E. Main
Starke Fred., blacksmith Pitts. shop, h 8 Orchard
Stackhouse William, blacksmith, h 71 Wells
Statler A. J., insurance agent, h 119 E. Wayne
Stace William, book-keeper, bds American House
Stahl Fred., lab, h 66 Charles
Stapleford Thomas R., tinner, bds Creighton ave
Stapleford Lucian P., h 87 Barr
Stapleford Clemens, architect, bds 87 Barr
Steinman Mrs. L., h 135 Calhoun
Stemler Philip, tailor at Woodward's, h on Erie
Stegemeier William, wks at spoke factory, h 129 Francis
Stewart Charles, blacksmith Pitts. shop, h 128 Madison
Sterling Robert, bds 206 W. Washington
Stewart R. W., carp., h 264 E. Wayne
Stevens Ephriam (W. & E. Stevens, carriage makers), h 70 Wells
Stewart William H., brakeman Muncie R'y, h 11 N. Cass
Stephan Fred., lab, h 5 Sturgis
Steavans Rupert L., upholster Pitts. shop, h 15 Williams
Steaphan Philip, carp. Pitts. shop, h 26 Hood
Stewart William, mach. Wabash shop, h 5 Henry
Steen Joseph, lab, bds 107 W. Jefferson
Steup Henry, h 106 W. Jefferson
Stellwagon George, eng. Pitts. R'y, h 89 W. Jefferson
Stewart William L., barber, 68 Barr
Stellhorn Charles, boot and shoe shop, 144 Calhoun
Stevens George E., clk Pitts. R'y ticket office, h 138 Clinton
Stellhorn John, carp., h 23 Wilt
Stewart Charles, jr., moulder Bass' foundry, bds 128 Madison
Stellwagon Joe, foreman Pitts. coppersmith shop, h 233 E. Lewis
Stewart Charles, merchants' police, h 123 Wilt
Stephan Julius, carp., h 57 Wall
Stein Fred., lab, h 76 Union

Stegmeier Jacob, carp., h 23 West
Sreinke Mrs. O., h 289 W. Jefferson
Steinke Adolph, varnisher, bds 289 W. Jefferson
Stellhorn Henry, blacksmith Pitts. shop, h 91 E. Lewis
Stetzer Seter, lab, h E. Washington
Stellhorn Henry, baker, bds 33 Jefferson
Stein Mrs. E., h 116 E. Madison
Steger Rudolph, bds 152 Montgomery
Steffy Rev. M. W., h 161 E. Lewis
Steinle Joseph, watchman, h 119 Holman
Steffy Josiah, tinner, bds 161 E. Lewis
Steller Conrad, butchet, h 92 Wilt
Stein Joseph, carp., h 38 Force
Steavens Ellen, widow, h 58 W. Lewis
Steple Jacob, wks Concordia College
Stetlen John, wks Concordia College
Steele William R., publisher of *Vindicator*, h 36 W. Wayne
Stenner Fred. W., clk, h 95 E. Jefferson
Steup Henry, h 105 E. Madison
Stein Peter, shoemaker, h 122 Maumee
Stein Fustave, carp. Pitts. shop, h 142 Jackson
Steinbrenner Mrs. F., h 25 Broadway
Stellhorn Augustus, clk, h 86 W. Lewis
Steinert Michael, butcher, h 18 Harricon
Steinheuser Henry, wagon maker, bds 3 and 5 Railroad
Stern Philip, lab, h 173 Montgomery
Stevens William (W. & E. Stevens), h 15 Clay
Stevens W. & E., carriage makers, 11 and 13 Clay
Stephan Henry jr., carp., bds 109 E. Madison
Stephan Henry, sr., crp., h 109 E. Madison
Steigerwald John A., turner, h 63 E. Madison
Stevens Thomas, agt. Olds & Son, h 141 E. Berry
Stevens Harrison P., bds 22 Baker
Stellhorn Charles, shoemaker, h 133 W. Water
Stein Daniel, carp., Pitts. shop, h 318 Harrison
Sthair Henry, carriage maker, shop 42 and 46 W. Main
Sthair S. W., carriage maker, bds 21 Clay
Sthair John, carriage maker, bds 21 Clay
Stier Mrs. George, millinery and dress making, 32 Clinton
Stites John, carp. Pitts. shop, h 32 Williams
Stiger David, carp, h N. Harrison
Stier George, clk at Orff & Co.'s, h 32 Clinton
Stier Jacob, wks Bass' Foundry, h 106 Lafayette
Stier Henry, street supervisor, h 106 Lafayette
Stier John, h 188 E. Washington
Stier Joseph, moulder, bds 188 E. Washington
Stirling Elizabeth, widow, h 109 W. Washington
Stirling Thomas, lab, bds 109 W. Washington

St. John Spencer, h 47 Baker
ST. MARY'S ACADEMY, Sisters of Providence, cor. Calhoun and Jefferson
Stocking Henry, eng. Wabash R'y, h 126 Ewing
Stokes Catherine, widow, h 348 Calhoun
Stock George, jr., tanner, bds 125 Cass
Stock George, sr., watchman French, Hanna & Co., h 125 Cass
STOCKBRIDGE N. P., book store, 12 E. Columbia, h 225 W. Wayne
Stockbridge C. A., clk, bds 225 W. Wayne
Stockbridge William J., clk, h 225 W. Wayne
Stocking John W., bds 126 Ewing
Stoll Fred., lab, h 48 Walnut
Stoll Henry, teamster, h 25 Second
Stoll Conrad, lab, h 19 Wefel
Stoll Jacob, lab, h 381 Lafayette
Stoner John M., millwright, h 55 E. Water
Stoner John M., miller, bds 55 E. Water
Stone Rev. Dr., Pastor First Baptist Church, bds Hanna House
Stone William E., eng. Wabash R'y, h 70 Douglas ave
Stoler Jacob, fireman Wabash R'y, h 178 Ewing
Stoler Eli, brakeman Pitts. R'y, bds 178 Ewing
Stoler William, lab, bds 25 Broadway
Stonager Fred., lab, h 112 Fairfield
Stoneburner Elias, lab, h 28 Wilt
Stonebrunner Robert, lab, h 24 Williams
Stophlet John, tinner (S. Bros.), bds 322 Broadway
Stophlet Bros., dealers in stoves tin ware, &c, 14 W. Columbia
Stophlet Frank, tinner (S. Bros.), bds 322 Broadway
Stophlet Mrs. Mary, h 322 Broadway
STOPHLET JOSEPH H., architect, office in Hamilton's Block, h 103 E. Washington
Stover Marion, clk, h 145 W. Berry
Storey James, h 16 W. Water
Storr George, conductor Grand Rapids R'y, h 176 W. Jefferson
STOTZ ULRICH, saloon and restaurant, E. Main
Stoder L., bds 98 Columbia
Stout George, carp., bds Union House
Stout Edward F., eng. Wabash R'y, h 19 Madison
Stout E. F., eng. Wabash R'y, bds 28 Locust
Stritmatter Charles, teamster, h 26 Oak
Striker Mrs., h 152 High
Strain Jacob, eng. Muncie R'y, h 50 Douglas
Striker Mrs. Elizabeth, h 123 Wells
Strass Jacob, clk, bds 136 W. Wayne
Strong Henry, shoemaker, h 164 Calhoun
STRODEL MATTHIAS, propr. Union Saloon, 10 E. Berry
Strodel Augustus, clk, 10 E. Berry

Strong Jeremiah, pattern maker (J. C. Bowser & Co.), h 74 Barr
Striker Christian, carp., h 349 W. Jefferson
Striker T. V., carp., bds 349 W. Jefferson
Strahsberg F., ash man, h 269 E. Washington
Strong M. B., conductor Saginaw R'y, h 258 W. Wayne
Strunz Christian, dealer in groceries and provisions, 72 Barr
STRODEL GEORGE, saloon keeper, 54 E. Main
Streider Christian, German teacher, h 166 Barr
Straughn Jesse R., civil engineer, h 87 E. Berry
Strong John H., carp., h 302 W. Jefferson
Stritmatter John, teamster, bds 26 Oak
STRODEL GEORGE, propr. Union Hall Saloon, h 54 E. Main
Struby Charles, professor of music, h 81 E. Jefferson
Strasser Joe, saloon, 28 W. Main
Struver William, grocer, h 66 E. Main
Strope Dennis B., chief of Locomotive Engineers Pittsburgh R'y, h 324 Calhoun
Strange Charles, lab, h 181 Lafayette
Stratton J. R., attorney (Hayden & S.), bds 119 E. Wayne
Strong C., carp., h 243 E. Wayne
Strasburg Christopher, asheryman, h 57 Water
Stratton Joe, mason, h 96 W. Washington
Stratton Charles, printer, bds 96 W. Washington
Strong M. H., eng. Wabash R'y, h 13 Hamilton
Strayer Theodore, fireman Wabash R'y, h 84 Taylor
Strong Cleveland, lab, h 243 E. Wayne
Studer B., carp., h 337 E. Lewis
Stuart Jacob, h 408 W. Main
Stubnatzy Rev. W. S., h 237 W. Jefferson
Stubnatzy Ernst, student, bds 237 W. Jefferson
Stump C. H., agent Howe Sewing Machine Company, h 122 E. Lewis
Stumpp Lewis, lab, h 33 Wall
Studer Wilson Z., conductor Pitts. R'y, h 83 Baker
Stuart Charles, merchants' police, bds 39 Lavina
Stuzenberger Anton, lab, h 187 E. Jefferson
Stuzenberger John, clk, bds 187 E. Jefferson
Stuzenberger Frank, sawyer, bds 187 E. Jefferson
Studhoff Henry, clk, bds 178 Barr
Sullivan Dennis, lab, bds 40 Wells
Sullivan Daniel E., road master Richmond R'y, h 341 Hanna
Sullivan Thomas, mail agent, bds Mayer House
Sullivan Henry, expressman, bds 25 Barr
Sullivan John, cooper, bds 19 Baker
Sullivan C., lab, h 23 Taylor
Sullivan J. R., moulder Bass' foundry, bds 231 Barr
SUMMIT CITY WOOLEN MILLS, French, Hanna & Co., E. Water
Sundheimer Peter, cabinet meker, bds 25 Broadway

Suren John, carp., h 273 E. Jefferson
SUTERMEISTER, DECKER & BOND, architects and builders, and dealers in stone, marble grates, &c., cor. Main and Fulton
Sutermeister Arnold (S., Becker & Bond), h 229 W. Jefferson
Sutton D. C., lab, h 186 E. Wayne
Sutton John, mach. Wabash shop, h 39 Melitta
Swart Amos M., mach., Pitts. shop, h 192 Broadway
Swart Bernard, pattern maker Bass' shop, h 222 Broadway
Swart Henry, carp., bds 152 Ewing
Swartz Frederick, harness shop on Columbia, h 104 Butler
Swain George, plasterer, h 21 Melitta
Swain Bennett, lab, h 211 W. Jefferson
Swain Scott, traveling agent, h 267 W. Wayne
Swain Martha E., widow, h 94½ Barr
Swain John, plasterer, h 21 Melitta
Swain Mrs. E., widow, h 26 W. Jefferson
Swain John, lab, bds 18 Orchard
Swain Charlotte, widow, h 60 W. Main
Swain George, driver Hook and Ladder Co., bds 60 W. Main
Sweeney Abraham, carp., h 139 Griffith
Sweeney Joseph, carp., h 310 Hanna
Sweeney Mrs. Lena, h 33 John
Sweetser Madison, h 113 W. Main
Sweringen Hiram V., M. D., h 231 W. Washington
Sweet Samuel, ticket agent Wabash R'y, h 82 Montgomery
Sweet K. C., eng., h 253 W. Berry
Sweet E. R. traveling agent, bds 282 Broadway
Swinney Thomas W., h west end Jefferson
Swinney William P., brakeman Wabash R'y, bds west end Jefferson
Swift A., h on Erie
Swihart Isaac, conductor Pitts. R'y, bds 285 Hanna

T

Tait George W., lab, h 177 High
Tam Silas, clk, Pittsburgh R'y office, h cor Hamilton and Clinton
Tanneberger George, bds 3-5 Railroad
Tanner Frank, porter, wks Aveline
Tancal M., carp, h 210 E. Jefferson
Tancy Michael, constable, h 42 Melitta
Tapp T., mason, h cor Ohio and Oak
Tarnin August, clk, h 212 E. Wayne
Tarmon Henry, carp, h 179 W. Washington
Tate Rev. C. C., h 168 W. Wayne
TAYLOR, FAIRBANK & CO., Proprs. *Journal*, office over Post Office
Taylor Mary, widow, bds 34 Water

Taylor Charles F., traveling agt., bds 23 Douglas ave
Taylor Robt., saloon, h 136 Barr
Taylor T. S., (Taylor, Fairbanks & Co., *Journal* Printing Office), h 161 E. Wayne
TAYLOR ROBERT S., Att'y at Law, h on Fairfield ave
TAYLOR HENRY C., Restaurant, 52 Barr
Taylor R. W., grain ware house, h 77 W. Wayne
Taylor George W., lab, h 37 Lasselle
Taylor R. W., ware house 26 Pearl
Taylor C. J., (Taylor, Fairbanks & Co., *Journal* Printing Office), bds Robinson House
Taylor William, clk, h 11 Oak
Taylor John, h 244 E. Washington
Taylor Mrs. Margery, h 262 W. Washington
Taylor D. S., h cor Ewing and Berry
Taylor Isaac N., (Nutman & Taylor, lumber dealers), bds 185 W. Wayne
Taylor Lee, h 113 Holman
Tearnorn Thomas, car inspector, h 75 E. Madison
Teeple John, fireman, Pittsburgh R'y, h 41 Gay
Tegeder Henry, carp, bds 100 Harrison
Teghtmeyer Ernst, machinist, Pittsburgh R'y, h 77 Brackenridge
Tegtmeyer Fred, h 24 Wilt
Tegtmeier Fred, lab, Pittsburgh shop, h 12 Summit
Tegtmeyer William, councilman and machinist, h 202 W. Water
Tegtmeier Henry, carp, h 103 W. Water
Tegtmeier David, (T. & Buse, saw mill,) h 109 W. Water
Tegtmeier Christian, lab, bds 297 Harrison
Tegtmier Fred, shoemaker, h 297 Harrison
Tegtmeyer & Bro., shoemakers, 94½ Barr
Teiman William, lab, h 11 McClellan
Tekenbruck Fred, lab, h 142 Broadway
Telford Lorenz, clk, 47 N. Cass
Temme Mary, widow, h N. of E. Wayne
Templar Henry, clk, Wabash office, h 152 W. Wayne
Tenney Ed., eng, Wabash R'y, h 70 Wilt
Tenny C. E., eng, 238 E. Washington
Pence W., fireman, Pittsburgh R'y, h 21 Poplar
Terry J. C., conductor, Wabash R'y, bds 19 Baker
Terry George H., foreman Bass' foundry, h 251 E. Washington
Terrell Frank, machinist, Pittsburgh shop, bds 173 Griffith
Teters William, fireman, Pittsburgh R'y, bds 13 Maumee
Tettlebach Adam, tin roofer, bds 46 E. Jefferson
Thanhouser Samuel, h 24 W. Wayne
Thanhouser Samuel, (Frank & Thanhouser, Dry Goods), Keystone Block
Thain John, mason, h 271 W. Washington
Thesois John, h 117 W. Washington
THIEME J. & BRO., Merchant Tailors, 37 E. Main
Thieme John G., clothing mer., h 53 E. Wayne

Thieme Fred, (J. G. Thieme & Bro.), h 216 W. Berry
THIEME ANDREW, Grocer, h 170 Broadway
Thiel Henry, tinner, bds 75 W. Jefferson
Thile Diedrich, lab, h 186 W. Jefferson
Thompson M., blacksmith, bds 248 W. Wayne
Thompson James, lab, h 204 E. Lewis
Thompson J. R., lab, h 310 Hanna
Thompson Thomas, lab, bds 102 Wallace
Thompson Cornelius, lab, h 102 Wallace
Thompson Charles, lab, bds 213 Broadway
Thompson Henry, inventor, bds Union House
Thompson Nelson, lab, h 114 Chicago
Thomson Mrs. Margaret, h 203 Lafayette
Thomson Joseph, moulder, Bass' foundry, bds 203 Lafayette
Thompson George, moulder, Bass' foundry, bds 203 Lafayette
Thomson Thomas, moulder, Bass' foundry, bds 203 Lafayette
Thomas B. C., fireman, Pittsburgh R'y, bds 22 Madison
Thomas Martin, brakeman, Pittsburgh R'y, h 37 Poplar
Thomas Leonard, printer, *Gazette* office, h 138 Jackson
Thomas Benjamin, fireman Pittsburgh R'y, bds 197 E. Jefferson
Thomas Orion L., printer, h 173 Jackson
Thomas Charles, fireman Pittsburgh R'y, bds 173 Jackson
Thomas Calvin, h 173 Jackson
Thomas G., machinist, Pittsburgh shop, bds 157 Holman
Thorp George B., druggist, h 93 E. Jefferson
Thonlein Charles, tailor, h 363 W. Main
Thornburn Charley, brakeman, bds 330 Calhoun
Thorp William, h 133 Madison
Thorp George B., druggist, cor Barr and Wayne
Thornton Edward, brakeman, Pittsburgh R'y, bds 82 Barr
Thomas M. machinist, Pittsburgh shop, bds 69 E. Jefferson
Thornburg Mrs. L., h 9 N. Cass
Threadgall John E.. lab, h 104 E. Madison
Thrush R., fireman, Pittsburgh R'y, h 246 E. Lewis
Throckmorton J. A., blacksmith, Pittsburgh shop, h 160 Holman
Tibbles John H., chairmaker, h 370 Calhoun
Tieman Fred, carp, Pittsburgh shop, h 57 Wall
Tigar Thomas, h 153 E. Berry
Tiggermann H., well digger, h 183 Montgomery
Tiggerman Theodore, well digger, h 319 Hanna
Tigags Catherine, widow, h 60 W. Washington
Tilford Charles, hack driver, bds 149 Barr
Tilford Harriet J., widow, h 149 Barr
Tilker Charles, carp, h 312 W. Jefferson
Tiner Silas, saddler, bds 25 Barr
Titus Theodore, eng, Pittsburgh R'y, h 17 Holman
Toby W. S., clk, bds Robinson House
Tocterman William F., traveling agt., h 135 W. Wayne

Todd R. J., h 26 W. Water
Todt C., brakeman, Wabash R'y, bds 47 Bass
Todd S. Clay, M. D., bds Aveline House
Tolson Sarah, widow, h 30 Wert
Tompkins D., hatter, bds American House
Tons Henry, ins. agt., with Hough, h 148 W. Wayne
Tons William, trunk maker, bds 148 W. Wayne
Toney Patrick, jr., lab, bds 43 Melitta
Toney Patrick, sr., lab, h 43 Melitta
Toomey Thomas, lab, h 300 E. Wayne
Tooker Mrs., widow, bds 49-51 W. Berry
Torence George, bds 166 W. Berry
Toune William, lab, bds 151 Holman
Toune Julius, boiler maker, (Bass foundry), h 151 Holman
Tower Alex. M. J., painter, bds 96 E. Wayne
Tower Benj. H., frescoer, bds 96 E. Wayne
Tower Agnes, bds 96 E. Wayne
Tower Nancy, widow, h 96 E. Wayne
Tower Margaret, bds 96 E. Wayne
Trauerman Isaac, (Dessauer & Co., cigar manufs.), h 92 W. Main
Traub Louis, harness maker, h 8 McClellan
Trankermon H., plasterer, h 385 E. Wayne
Travis Patrick, conductor, Pittsburgh R'y, bds 49 Baker
Traud James, drayman, h 176 E. Washington
TRENTMAN & SON, Wholesale Grocers, 56-58 Calhoun
Trentman John, clk, bds 72 W. Wayne
Trentman Bernhard, (B. Trentman & Son), h 72 W. Wayne
Trentman B. H., (T. & Wolke, cracker and candy manufs.), h 151 E. Wayne
TRENTMAN, MONNING & SON, Coffee, Spice and Mustard Mills, 59 E. Main
Trentman A. C., (B. T. & S.), h 40 W. Water
TRENTMAN, H. J. & BRO., Queensware, 24 E. Columbia
TRENTMAN HENRY, (H. J. Trentman & Bro.), China Store, h 25 W. Berry
Trentman John, h 151 E. Wayne
Treece James, lab, h 396 Broadway
TRENAM GEORGE, architect, h 162 W. Main
Tretchler Peter, file cutter, h 287 W. Main
Tresselt Charles, dealer in Crockery, China and Glassware, h 88 E. Jefferson
TREMMEL CONRAD, Grocer, Store 238 Hanna, h 281 Hanna
TREESH S. W., dealer in Hard Wood Logs, and Lumber, office 5 E. Main
Tremmel John, blacksmith, Pittsburgh shop, h 34 Force
Tressler Mrs. Anna, h 152 Ewing
Tresler Henry, plasterer, h 152 Ewing
Tressler George, carp, h 102Butler

Treep Mary M., widow, h 104 Barr
Trenelt Herman, lab, bds Steuben House
TRENKLEY & SHERZINGER, Practical Watchmakers, and Jewelers, 80½ Calhoun, Nill's Block
Tressler John, tinner, h 2 Brandriff
TRESELT & BOTH, Queensware Store, 39 E. Columbia
Trepler L., M. D., h 30 Madison
Treep Ann J., widow, h 104 Barr
Tresselt Christian, (Hoagland & Tresselt, proprs. City Mills), h 55 E. Jefferson
Trier Henry, h 111 W. Water
Trimble J. M., conductor, Pittsburgh R'y, h 343 Hanna
Trinkley C., Watchmaker, h 106 W. Washington
Trinkle Marion, conductor, Pittsburgh R'y, h 43 S. Hanna
Trinble Samuel, wks Pittsburgh shop, h 96 E. Lewis
Troutmon Fred, baker, bds Steuben House
Trowbridge Addison teamster, h 122 E. Wayne
Troutman John, teamster, 120 E. Wayne
Truxell Mrs. Lary, h 137 Wallace
Tuckey Charles, brakeman, Pittsburgh R'y, bds 94 E. Berry
Tuckey G., conductor, Pittsburgh R'y, bds 94 E. Berry
Tucker John, moulder, wks Novelty Works, bds 245 Columbia
Tuhrman Charles, shoemaker, h 89 W. Jefferson
Tull Edward H., machinist, wks Pittsburgh shop, bds 4 Melitta
Tully George William, machinist at K. Murray's bds 386 Calhoun
Tully Thomas, eng. Pittsburgh R'y, h 386 Calhoun
Tunison Mrs. N., widow, h 75 Baker
Tunison Harvey G., brakeman, Pittsburgh R'y, bds 75 Baker
Tunison William clk, Pittsburgh R'y, office, bds 75 Baker
Tunnies William, eng. Pittsburgh R'y, h 64 Baker
Turner Harry, bds 104 E. Wayne
Turner Ann, widow, h 104 E. Wayne
Turner John, machinist, Pittsburgh shop, h 44 Webster
Turner Levi, clk, h 89 W. Water
Twoback Mrs. O., h 15 Hough
Tyler Daniel, agt., bds 46 E. Jefferson
Tyler Fred, clk at Coombs & Co., bds 175 Clinton
Tyler John L., Professor of Penmanship, bds Central Hotel
Tyler Franklin, ass't supt. street R. R., bds 268 Calhoun
Tyler Arthur, clk at Meyer Bros. & Co., bds 175 Clinton
Tyler William R.; bds 258 W. Wayne
Tyler Fred, bds 258 W. Wayne
Tyler W. D., bds 142 W. Wayne
Tyler Mrs. Catherine, h 142 W. Wayne
Tyrrell V. B., widow, h 28 Brandriff
Tyrrell Alfred J., fireman, bds 28 Brandriff

U

Uebelheer Phillip, shoemaker, h 56 E. Main
Uebelheer Fred., plasterer, h 44 Lavina
Uhlrick Michael, brewer, bds Bloomingdale Brewery
Uhlm Joseph, stone cutter, h cor. Fairfield ave and Colerick
Uhlman B., pedlar, bds Central Hotel
Ulriclh Mrs. Elizabeth, h 13 Force
Underhay John, painter, bds 219 Lafayette
Underhill P. S., (Smith Bros. & Co., marble works), h 340 W. Jefferson
Underhill F. W., stone cutter, h 87 Wilt
UNDERHILL BRO. & CO., Marble Works, 74 W. Main
Unger Andrew, lab, h 92 Wilt
Unger Gottlieb, lab, bds 46 W. Washington
Unger Louisa, widow, h 46 W. Washington
Updegraff John A., lab, h 14 Maiden Lane
Updegraff H., widow, h 34 Douglas ave
Upnier Fred., carp, h 85 Maumee
Uplegger Charles, policeman, h 146 Broadway
U. S. Express Company, C. L. Smith, agt., 28 E. Main

V

Vail Matilda, widow, h 37 Colerick
Vanalstine William, veterinary surgeon, h 210 Lafayette
Vanalstine Frank, hackman, bds 210 Lafayette
Vancamp Enos, barber, h 119 W. Water
Vander A. C., painter, bds 166 Barr
Vangiesen Margaret, widow, h on Creighton ave
Van Patten Phillip H., eng. Wabash R'y, bds 19 Madison
Van Patten Phillip H., eng. Wabash R'y, bds 28 Locust
Vanstiel Emil, helper, (Bass' foundry), h 119 Holman
Van Sickles Charles, bds 86 E. Main
Van Weert Isaac, conductor, Wabash R'y, h 68 Wilt
Van Winkle H. C., bds Robinson House
Vaughan William B., clk, 26 Main
Vaughn Henry, butcher, h 186 W. Main
Veaugier Xavier, h 12 Sturgis
Vegele Peter, lab, h 53 Walnut
Veith William, brakeman, Pittsburgh R'y, bds 265 E. Wayne
Veith Peter, boatman, h 265 E. Wayne
Veith Frank, blacksmith, bds 265 E. Wayne
Veith Louis, boatman, bds 265 E. Wayne
Verschoone Centil, stone cutter, bds 92 Montgomery
Vestal Eran, brakeman, Muncie R. R., bds 40 Wells
Vincent James, wks woolen mills, bds 52 Barr

Virgil Thomas S., M. D., h 70 Harrison
VIRGIL A. K., Principal Fort Wayne Conservatory, bds 70 Harrison
Vivia Frank, jr, conductor, Pittsburgh R'y, bds 5 Pine
Vivia Frank, sr., lab, h 5 Pine
Vizard M. F., lab, h 23 Brandriff
Vizard Thomas, lab, bds 23 Brandriff
Vizard & Howley, blacksmiths, shop 41 W. Main
Vizard John, blacksmith, Pittsburgh shop, h 14 Melitta
Vogel Frank, (Vogel & Son, mer. tailors), h 57 W. Berry
VOGEL C. G. & SON, Merchant Tailors, E. S. Calhoun, opp. Phœnix Block
VOGEL MRS. C. G., Millinery Rooms, E. S. Calhoun
Vogel Valentine, carp, bds 76 Wallace
Voit Christina, widow, bds 93 Barr
Voirol Emil, clk, bds 268 E. Wayne
Voirol Julius, cigar maker, bds 268 E. Wayne
Voirol Frank, (George J. E. Mayer & F. Voirol, watch makers), h 268 E. Wayne
Voirol Frank, jr., watch maker, (George J. E. Mayer & F. Voirol), bds 268 E. Wayne
Volland Henry, miller, (J. Orff), h 279 W. Washington
VOLLMER DANIEL, Druggist and Pharmaceutist, cor. Calhoun and Berry, h 21 W. Berry
Volmerding F., tailor, h 246 E. Washington
Voors J., carp, bds 84 W. Jefferson
Vorce John, cook, h 26 Holman
VORDERMARK E. & SONS, Wholesale and Retail Dealers in Boots and Shoes, 32 Calhoun
Vordemark Henry, (with V. & Sons), h 161 E. Wayne
Vorholzer M., carp, h cor. Metz and Taylor
Voss Lewis A., bds 20 Wall
Votry Alex., tanner, h 186 W. Wayne
Vredenburgh M. P., carp, h 100 E. Wayne

W

Wade Charles M., mach., h 84 George
Wade Esther, widow, h 16 Holman
Wadge George, wks woolen mills, h 154 Holman
Waddington B., carp. Pitts. shop, h 128 Montgomery
Waddington Walter, carp. Pitts. shop, bds 128 Montgomery
Waddington Joseph, mach. Pitts. shop, bds 161 Holman
WAGNER H. G., druggist and dealer in toilet and fancy articles, 54 Calhoun
Wagner Albert, lab, h 130 Madison
Wagenhalls Rev. Samuel, Pastor English Evangelical Lutheran Church, h 54 E. Wayne

Wagner Robert, wks Olds & Son's, h 164 E. Lewis
Wagner John, carp., h 177 Jackson
Wahmhof William, lab, h 172 Ewing
Wahlschmidt Peter, cigar maker, h 30 W. Main
Wakerley John, carp., h 213 Fairfield ave
Walter Daniel, blacksmith Wabash shop, bds 332 Harrison
Walter E. R., sewing machine agent, h 63 Wells
Walde Fred., tailor, h 219 E. Jefferson
Walde William, wagon maker, h 76 Wallace
Walten J. R., clerk Pitts. freight office, h 51 Baker
Walten C. H., train despatcher G. R. & I. R'y, bds 51 Baker
Walda William, jr., carp., bds 216 E. Wayne
Walten H. B., brakeman G. R. & I. R'y, bds 51 Baker
Walker William, lab, bds 261 W. Jefferson
Walker James, blacksmith, h 32 Hood
Walsh Michael, carp., bds Central Hotel
Waldman Benjamin, saloon, 138 Calhoun
WALTERS D. B., dealer in groceries and provisions, h 207 Calhoun
Walkerman George, wagon maker, h 23 Barr
Walker William, lab, bds 262 Calhoun
Walther Fred. W., piano maker, h 101 Lafayette
Walls J. C., hatter, bds American House
Walkeman George, wagon maker, h 23 Barr
Walker George, stone cutter
Waltemath Charles, policeman, h 138 E. Lewis
Wallace Matilda, widow, h 80 Butler
Waldo Henry, carp., h 126 Chicago
Walsh Martin, peddler, h 124 E. Lewis
Walker Lyman, eng. at Beaver's mill, h 239 E. Wayne
Waltemath Henry, grocer, h 134 E. Lewis
Waddington Mrs. Rosa, h 128 Montgomery
Wallace Frank, boiler maker Pitts. shop, h 153 E. Lewis
Wallace John, boiler maker Pitts. shop, h 153 E. Lewis
Waltemath Henry (Wigman & Co.), h 134 E. Lewis
Wallin Charles H., photographer, bds 49 and 51 W. Berry
Walker Anthony, moulder, h 26 Buchanan
Wallace Fred., cabinet maker, h 124 Harrison
Wallace Michael M., clk at Bass' shop, bds 139Fairfield
Walda William, carp., h 216 E. Wayne
Waltemath L., lab, h 259 E. Lewis
Walters Frank, shoemaker, h 12 Pine
Wallace Andrew, book-keeper, h 139 Fairfield
Walda Henry, carp., h 331 E. Washington
Walda Charles, carp. Pitts. shop. h 329 E. Washington
Walker Mrs. Sarah Ann, h 218 Broadway
Ward John, section boss Wabash R'y, bds 6 Kansas
Warner Augustus, cigar maker, h 128 W. Washington

Warner C. T., eng., h 106 Ewing
Ward Willtam, brakeman Pitts. R'y, h 21 Pritchard
Warren Mrs. M. S., hair store, &c., h 75 Calhoun
Ward H. N., wholesale and retail China, Glass and Queensware, 78 Calhoun, h 233 W. Berry
Wartembe E., wks Baker's saw mill, h 104 Columbia
Warner Mrs. R. W., widow, h 402 Calhoun
Warring Anson F., bds 49 and 51 W. Berry
Washburn G. P., agent Singer Sewing Machine Company, bds Anderson House
Wasserbach John, tailor, h 90 Barr
Wasner John, lab, wks Bass' shop, bds 63 Hanna
Waters Harvey, brakeman, bds 36 Brandriff
Waters Louis, fireman, h 36 Brandriff
Watterman J. H., eng. Wabash R'y, h 118 W. Jefferson
Watermouth Henry, lab, h 43 W. Lewis
Wattles B., eng. Wabash R'y, h 181 Ewing
Waters Mrs. Minerva, h 199 W. Washington
Waters Charles, eng. Pitts. R'y, bds 402 Calhoun
Watrous G. C., master mechanic, h 115 Lafayette
Watson Mrs. M., widow, h 130 Madison
Waugh James R., eng. Pitts. R'y, h 459 Lafayette
Way George, fireman Pitts. R'y, h 46 Hoagland ave
Weaver Thomas, porter at Mayer House, bds at Mayer House
Weaver William, clk., bds 322 Calhoun
Webber Benjamin, mach. h 47 Bass
Webb Frank, moulder Bass' shop, bds 8 Force
Weber Peter, mason, h 308 W. Jefferson
Weber Adam, shoemaker, h 81 Montgomery
Webster John F., fireman Wabash R'y, h 189 Barr
Weber Frank A., grocer, bds 168 E. Jefferson
Weber John J., German teacher, h 43 E. Wayne
Webb Marion, merchant, bds 91 E. Main
Weber Frederick, h 11 Maumee
Webb A. M., janitor Court House, h 234 W. Wayne
Weber John, wks at City Mills, h 275 E. Wayne
Weber Erwin, blacksmith Pitts. shop, bds 413 Lafayette
Weber Andrew, lab, h 413 Lafayette
Weber Henry, tailor, bds 153 Madison
Wedge William, carp. Pitts. shop, h 143 Montgomery
Weet Rodney, moulder, bds 8 Force
Weekly William, moulder Bass' foundry, bds 274 Hanna
Weeks George H., bds 134 Francis
Weeks John H., painter Pitts. shop, h 134 Francis
Wefel Henry, cigar maker, bds Barthold
Wefel John, carp., h 41 Barthold
Wefel William, carp. Wabash shop, bds 213 W. Washington
Wefel Fred., boat builder, h 161 High

Wefel William, tinner, bds 41 Barthold
Weggeman B., carder, bds 224 E. Wayne
Wehrs Fred. (Pfeiffer & Co.), h 156 Wells
Weemer Mrs. G. D., h 159 E. Wayne
Wehmer Miss Minnie, bds 159 E. Wayne
Weidman John, painter, bds 78 Wilt
Weisenburg Daniel, lab, bds 46 Charles
Weigand F. W., lab, h 25 Wall
Weisenberger B., night clerk Mayer House, h 13 Hood
Weisman Jacob, h 14 Hood
Weibel Pladius, cabinet maker Pitts. shop, h 226 W. Jefferson
Weis Manuel, dealer in rags and iron, h on Erie
Weismantel Frank, cigar maker, bds 92 E. Jefferson
Weibke Henry, grocer, 92 Barr
Weil Isaac, dealer in hides, 78 Barr
Weis Nicholas, carp., h 190 E. Lewis
Weil Jacob, street buyer, h 261 Hanna
Weisenburg Mrs. Catherine, h 46 Charles
Weil Nicholas, lab, h 87 Force
Weisenburg George, lab, bds 42 Charles
Weismanfel Peter J., stone cutter, h 114 Jackson
Weilfeldt Henry, moulder, h 11 McClellan
Weismantel Michael, shoemaker, h 114 Jackson
Welkling John, lab, h 44 Taylor
Welch John, lab, bds 29 Walnut
Welch Winny, widow, h 29 Walnut
Welch Barney, lab, bds 29 Walnut
Wells A., dentist, h on Dewald
Wells George, harness maker, h 8 Cass
Welch John H., lab, h Creighton ave
Welsh John, lab, h 27 Brandriff
Weldon Frank, book-keeper Pitts. shop, h 85 Baker
Welker Henry, carp., h 59 Wall
Wells Harvey J., printer, h 206 E. Wayne
Wellenburg Martin, painter Pitts. shop, h 15 Oak
Welsh Garret, watchman, h 71 Holman
Welch Mary A., bds 85 E. Jefferson
Welts Isaac, h 93 Montgomery
Wells Charles M., propr. feed store, h 2 Madison
Welsh Patrick, blacksmith, h 75 E. Water
Welch & Baker, tinners, 184 Calhoun
Welker Daniel, tailor, h 48 Douglas ave
Weller John, butcher, h 123 Harrison
Welch George W., eng. Wabash R'y, h 58 Melitta
Weller Lizzie, bds 97 Barr
Weller Barbara, widow, h 97 Barr
Wells John, blacksmith, h 62 E. Madison
Welton John (Klotz & Welton), h 38 Butler

Welton John (Klotz & Welton), grocer, h S. on Hoagland ave
Wellman Fred., lab, h 112 Jackson
Wellman Henry, carp., bds 108 Jackson
Wemhoff B. stone cutter, h 124 Union
Wemhoff Rev. John, h 391 Hanna
Wente John, lab, h 342 Calhoun
Wente Mrs. W., widow, 90 Barr
WENTE W. L., groceries and provisions, Barr, opposite Market
Wenzel Fred., shoemaker, bds 133 W. Water
Wenzel Ann Mary, widow, h 76 Williams
Wenge John, lab, h 9 John
Wentworth O. M., eng. Wabash R'y, h cor. College and W. Jefferson
Wentworth William, brakeman Wabash R'y, bds cor. College and W. Jefferson
Wenninghoff Rudolph, cigar maker, bds 148 Calhoun
WENNINGHOFF CHRISTIAN, cigar manuf., 148 Calhoun
Wenninger Fred. C., shoemaker, h 266 Calhoun
Wery John H., sr., h 132 Williams
Wery John H., jr., bds 132 Williams
Werk Adam, plasterer, h 263 E. Wayne
Westerhausen George, lab, h 51 Wilt
Weseloh John, student, bds 104 Webster
West Mrs, Rhody, h 210 Fairfield
Westrumb H. C. F., constable, h cor. Wayne and Hanover
Wesel Elizabeth, widow, h 21 E. Washington
Wessel John, eng. Pitts. shop, h 401 Lafayette
Westfall Fred., lab Pitts. shop, h 131 E. Madison
Whalen Hannah, widow, h 18 Bass
Whalen John, moulder Bass' foundry, bds 18 Bass
Whan Joseph, millwright, h 80 Brackenridge
Whalin Edward, lab, bds 262 Calhoun
Whaley Mrs. Hannah, h 9 N. Cass
Wheeler John, fireman Pitts. R'y, h 68 Chicago
Wheeler Nelson, h 258 W. Wayne
Wheeler Luther, eng. Saginaw R'y, bds 92 Calhoun
Whealen Michael, bds 148 E. Lewis
Wheelock Mr., dentist, bds 49 and 51 W. Berry
White W. J., tailor, bds Robinson House
White William, eng. Wabash R'y, h 21 Pine
WHITE J. B., propr. Fruit House, h 60 Barr
White Mrs. Mary, h 235 E. Wayne
White H. K., brakeman Wabash R'y, bds 285 Hanna
White Thomas, lab, bds cor. Calhoun and Wallace
White D. P. Deputy Recorder, bds Hamilton House
White John J., traveling agent, h 206 W. Wayne
Whitney John, h 80 Baker
Whitney W. J., eng. Wabash R'y, h 199 W. Washington
Whitehurst John, bds American House

Whitritt J. H., mach. Pitts. shop, bds Harmon House
Whinery John, mach. Pitts. shop, h 4 Melitta
Whiteley Thomas R., renovator and repairer, h 52 W. Main
Whitehead Mrs. R. A., h 171 W. Washington
Whinery Joseph, eng. Pitts. R'y, h 70 Wallace
Whiche Ferdinand, lab, bds 75 W. Jefferson
Whitfield Robert H., barber, bds 76 E. Columbia
Whittles J., mach. Pitts. shop, h 136 Barr
Whiting Almon, clk Wabash office, bds 47 Melitta
Whitman Henry, mach. Pitts. shop, h 170 Montgomery
Whitehead Arthur, eng. Pitts. R'y, h 316 Calhoun
Whiting Ira M., h 47 Melitta
Whyler Edward, tinner, h 87 E. Main
Wickey Martin clk, bds 75 Harrison,
Wichman Henry, lab, bds 205 E. Washington
Widbrok Henry, lab, h 25 Clark
Wieneke Fred., shoemaker, h 122 Wilt
Wienkelmeyer Henry, h 23 Wall
Wiedman William, lab, bds 78 Wilt
Wiedman Mrs. B., h 78 Wilt
Wiedman Michael, lab, bds 78 Wilt
Wiedelman William, carp, h 386 E. Wayne
Wiest J. D., b. k., bds 63 W. Water
WIEMAN WIILLIAM, Confectionery Store. 11 E. Main
Wiers William, shoemaker, h 133 E. Lewis
Wies Mrs. Caroline, h 237 Lafayette
Wiegand Sebastian, h 339 Lafayette
Wiemeyer William, b. k., bds 49-51 W. Berry
Wies Jacob, carp, h 172 Hanna
Wies Nicholas, carp, h 157 Hanna
Wiegman William, blacksmith, h 403 W. Main
WIGHMAN HENRY, (H. W. & Henry Waltermath), Dealers in Groceries, Provisions and China Ware, and Bakery, 201-203 Lafayette
Wigman Henry, grocer, h 136 E. Lewis
WIGMAN & CO., Grocer, (W. & Waltemath), 101 Lafayette
Wigman Fred., lab, h 200 E. Jefferson
Wihen Jacob, shoemaker, h 33 W. Lewis
Wihe Augustus, carp, h 5 Broadway
Williams D., brakeman, Wabash R'y, bds 47 Bass
Wilson William, b. k., h 114 W. Main
Wiley Thomas, carp, h 398 Calhoun
Wilson Alice, plumber, at Hattersley's, bds 28 Walnut
Williams John H., wagon and carriage shop, h 149 W. Main
Wilson G., clk, bds on Creighton ave
Wilson George, manuf. of saws &c., Calhoun and Lewis
Wilson Frank, att'y, h 180 W. Jefferson
Wilkening Gottlieb, carp, h 30 Lavina

Wilkin Herman, teamster, h 88 W. Water
Wilcox Lester, foreman carpenter shop, Muncie R. R., h 323 Calhoun
Wiburn George, eng. Wabash R'y, bds 592 W. Jefferson
Wilson Jacob L., fireman, Richmond R. R., h 60 Chicago
Wilburt William, eng. Wabash R'y, bds 292 W. Jefferson
Williams John A., lab, bds 82 Baker
Wilson Robert, spinner, bds 13 Monroe
Wilson Charles, carder, bds 13 Monroe
Wilson Oscar J., b. k., Wabash office, h 217 W. Wayne
Wilson John, lab, bds 196 W. Washington
Wilmington William, express driver, (U. S. Ex. Co.), h 337 W. Jefferson
Wilcox Joseph, bds 231 Barr
Willets Isaac, propr. boarding house, 231 Barr
Wilding James, plasterer, h 260 W. Wayne
Wilson Richard, lab, h 23 Barr
Wilson William, conductor, Muncie R. R., h 46 E. Jefferson
Wiley S. J., widow, h 118 Barr
Wilkes Nathan, dealer in notions, 74 Barr
Wilmot J. C., painter and dealer in paints, oil, lead &c., 10 Clinton
WILSON, SHUCKMAN & MUHLER, Dealers in Stoves and tinware, 83 Columbia
Wilson Richard, lab, h 23 Barr
Wilcox Isaac, bar keeper, bds 92 Calhoun
WILSON H. F., Notary Public, Deputy District Att'y, Solicitor of Patents, office over Post Office, h 180 W. Jefferson
Willes Henry, bds Mayer House
Wilson Judson, porter, wks Aveline House
Wilson & Bro., saw manufs., cor. Calhoun and Lewis
Will John, lab, h 33 Williams
Wilkinson John, (Wilkinson & Bro.), 8 W. Columbia
Wilkinson Frank, (Wilkinson & Bro.), 8 W. Columbia
WILKINSON BROS., Saloon, 8 W. Columbia
Williams Samuel, night clk at Exchange Hotel
Wilson Mrs. A. E., widow, bds 225 W. Wayne
Wilder Edwin, propr. Fort House and feed yard, 113 E. Main
Williams Alfred. L., fireman, Pittsburgh R'y, bds 332 Calhoun
Williamson John, coppersmith, Wabash shop, h 37 Langohr
Will Thomas H., blacksmith, Pittsburgh shop, h 117 Butler
Williard, Mrs. R. A., h 45 E. Madison
Wilmot James C., painter, h 222 W. Wayne
Wilder J. H., h 156 W. Washington
William John O., (Wooster, W. & Co., druggists), h 278 W. Berry
Wilt John M., h 306 Calhoun
Williams Jeremiah, drayman, h 39 Grand
Wild Thomas, wood dealer, bds 140 Holman
Wilde Jacob, shoemaker, bds 319 Lafayette
Wild Edmund, wood dealer, h 140 Holman
Williams E. P., (Meyer Bros. & Co., druggists), h 61 W. Berry

Williams J. L., civil eng., h 96 W. Wayne
Williams H. M., lab, bds 102 W. Wayne
Wilson C. H., boss carder, woolen mills, h 13 Monroe
Wilson George H., (Wilson, Shuckman & Co., stoves &c.), h 221 W. Berry
Wilding J. W., jr., plasterer, bds 260 W. Wayne
Wilkins Charles, butcher, bds 116 Broadway
Wilkins Christian, butcher, h 116 Broadway
Wilson Mrs. Amanda, clk Pension office, bds 225 W. Wayne
Winslow Isaac, h 122 W. Washington
WILLIS JOSEPH H., General Manager Carbonized Cement Pipe Works, S. of and opp. Railroad depot
Winters Erastus, lab, h 343 W. Jefferson
Wines Mrs. Elizabeth, h 219 W. Washington
Winter John cigar maker, bds 21-23 Main
Winbaugh Mrs. A. M., h 61 E. Madison
Winkelmeyer, William, moulder, bds 100 Harrison
Winkelmeyer Henry, carp, bds 100 Harrison
Wirich C. J., blacksmith, h on Maumee
Wirsch Peter, lab, h 174 Jackson
Wisel Otis W., agt., h 54 W. Main
Wise A. omnibus driver, bds 18 E. Wayne
Wise Henry A., civil eng., bds Mayer House
Wise Platt J., Deputy Sheriff, h 228 W. Berry
Wise Isaac, lab, h 251 E. Jefferson
Wisner Nicholas, h 112 Creighton ave
Wise Charles D., b. k., bds 228 W. Berry
Witte William, boiler maker, at K. Murray's, bds 49 Williams
Wittley Gottlieb, candy maker, at Wolke & Trentman's bds cor. Fairfield and Poplar
Witman S., lab, h 16 W. Washington
Witherall J. H., bds Fox House
Witerman Ulrich, lab, h 347 Lafayette
Witte William, boiler maker, h 88 Lasselle
Witte Chrisrian, lab, h 27 Charles
Witman Fred., lab, h 275 Hanna
Witte Christian, lab, bds 201 E. Washington
Witte Frank, carp, bds 201 E. Washington
Witrock John, lab, h 168 Holman
Wœbeking Diedrich, file cutter, bds — Broadway
Wœbeking Charles, carp., bds — Broadway
Wœbeking William, carp., h — Broadway
Wœbeking Conaad, carp., h — Broadway
Wœbeking Christian, h 100 W. Jefferson
Wohlford Roseman William, mach., h 36 Colerick
Wohnker Fred., drayman, h 209 E. Washington
WOLKE & TRENTMAN, wholesale dealers and manufs. of confectionery and crackers, 100 Calhoun

Wolke Fred., carp. Pitts. shop, h 21 Force
WOLKE FRANK (W. & Trentman, manufs. of candies and crackers), bds Mayer House
Wolford Jacob, moulder Bass' foundry, bds 3 and 5 Railroad
WOLF A., meat market and sausage manufacturer, 10 W. Main, h 73 W. Main
Wolf Leopold, butcher, bds 73 W. Main
Wolf Michael, lab, h 31 Maumee
Wolf Charles H., conductor Muncie R'y, h 86 Montgomery
Wolf Joseph, mach. Pitts. shop, h 82 Jefferson
Wolf & Kettler, manufs. and wholesale dealers in upholstery and bedding, 76 Clinton
Wolf Paul (W. Kettler), bds 196 Barr
Wolf Daniel (W. & Wagner), h 25 Barr
Wolf Daniel S., clk, bds 25 Barr
Wolf Mrs. M., h 115 E. Madison
Wolf James, car inspector Pitts. shop, h 162 Montgomery
Wolfe Edward, student, bds Fort Wayne College
Wolford William A., mach. Pitts. shop, h foot Hanna
Womer J. D., tailor, bds 104 Barr
WOODMANCY J. F., silver plater, stencil cutter and engraver, 52 Calhoun, up stairs
Woody George W., lab, h 123 Williams
Woodworth Mary, widow, h 19 Brandriff
Wood Isaac N., mach. Wabash shop, h 88 Chicago
Woolsey Hiram, foreman Olds & Son, bds 115 Barr
Woodworth J. C., assistant cashier Fort Wayne National Bank, h 224 W. Wayne
WOOSTER, WILLIAMS & CO., druggists and apothecaries, sw. cor. Calhoun and Main
Woodworth Dr. B. S., office 4 E. Berry, h 234 W. Berry
WOOD W. S., manuf. of picture frames, and dealer in looking glasses, &c., 142 Calhoun
WOODWARD M. E., merchant tailor, clothier and general furnisher, 46 Calhoun, h 134 E. Main
Woodworth D. H., Deputy Postmaster, h 109 Lafayette
Woodworth L., blacksmith Bass' foundry, bds 129 E. Lewis
Woolsey Isaac B., carp., h 115 Barr
Wooden George, cooper, bds 408 W. Main
Woodworth C. B., drug clerk, bds 234 W. Berry
Woodworth B. S., M. D., h 234 W. Berry
Worth Adam, lab, h 75 High
Worthington W. W., supt. Muncie R'y, h 160 W. Washington
Worthington Edward, clk, bds — Harrison
Worch Rudolph, editor Indiana *Volksfreund*, h 78 W. Main
Worch Hugo, printer, bds 78 W. Main
Worden Hon. James L., Judge Supreme Court, h 99 E. Jefferson
Workmast John, clk, Pitts. freight office, bds 60 Maiden Lane

Worden James W., student, bds 99 E. Jefferson
Wort John M., foreman gas works, h 135 E. Main
Worden L. W., carp., bds 221 Lafayette
Worden William, mach. Olds & Son, h 221 Lafayette
Worthington John S., barber, bds Robinson House
Work Robert, h 28 Charles
Worrel Richard, fireman Pitts. R'y, bds 89 W. Jefferson
Worman Jacob, fireman Pitts. R'y, bds 130 Madison
Woulfe Patrick, shoemaker, h 268 Calhoun
Woulfe James & Bro., grocery and provision store, 266 Calhoun
Woulfe James, clk at W. & Bro., bds 35 Melitta
Woulfe Michael (W. & Bro., grocery and saloon), h 35 Melitta
Wren Joseph, h 49 Baker
Wright Helen, widow, h 313 Harrison
Wright Charles, fireman Pitts. R'y, h 313 Harrison
Wright Edward, lab, Pitts. shop, h 87 Holman
Wright F. A., conductor Grand Rapids R'y, bds Harmon House
Wright Alfred, clk at Coombs & Co.'s, bds 175 Clinton
Wright William, brakeman Pitts. R'y, h 64 Williams
Wright Horace, lab, h 192 E. Jefferson
Wright Cobert, bds 106 W. Wayne
Wright Luther, carp. Pitts. shop, h cor Webster and Douglas ave
Wurzberger L. M., dealer in jewelry, bds American House
Wycoff Peter, cooper, bds 408 W. Main

Y

Yakel Matthias, lab, h 32 Henry
Yahr Frank, cabinet maker, h 25 Wall
Yahne John, h 43 Wall
Yanny W., tinner, bds 175 Madison
Yates William, lab, h 35 Bass
Yates John, brakeman Wabash R'y, h 71 Butler
Yergens William, jr., bds 87 W. Washington
Yergens William, mach. J. C. Bowser & Co., bds 178 Barr
Yergens William, sr., h 87 W. Washington
Yenne Gottlieb, h 12 Gay
Yohn Isaac L., boiler maker Pitts. R'y, bds 100 E. Lewis
Yokey J. M., h 169 Broadway
York Cyrus, conductor Wabash R'y, h 3 Harrison
Young Lewis, well digger, h 58 Douglas
Young E., painter, h 191 E. Wayne
YOUNG N. B. & CO., merchant tailors, 9 E. Main, h 218 W. Washington
Young George, nurseryman, h 18 Cass
Young William C., marble cutter, h 171 W. Washington
Young Israel, conductor Wabash R'y, h 56 Baker

Young Lewis, lab, h 191 Jackson
Younkin Charles, h 103 W. Washington
Youngblood Samuel, eng. Monning & Son, h 151 Montgomery
YOUNGBLOOD ROBERT N., propr. City Dye House, bds 63 W. Water
Yudt Charles, lab, h 213 Madison

Z

Zahn Fred., carp. Pitts shop, bds 174 E. Lewis
Zahn Catherine, widow, h 27 Erie
Zahn William, lab, h 212 E. Jefferson
Zauner Matthias, eng. Bass' foundry, h 35 Force
Zekind Dorothea, widow, bds 50 W. Water
Zeller Kilian, lab, h 143 Wells
Zeperlink C., lab, h 259 E. Lewis
Zermuhle Henry, clk, bds 90 Barr
Ziegler Charles, foreman Wieman's Confectionery, bds 11 E. Main
Ziegler Adam, wagon maker, h 113 Wilt
Ziegler Peter, lab, h 44 Force
Zimmerman John, clk, bds Robinson House
Zimmerman & Nohe, shoemakers, h 167 Broadway
Zimmerman Frank E., clk, h 13 W. Jefferson
Zimmerman George, clk, bds 141 Wells
Zimmerman Stephen, shoemaker, h 141 Wells
Zimmerman Mrs. M., h 56 E. Madison
Zimmerman A., cabinet maker, h 63 E. Water
Zimmerman A., groceries and provisions, 57 E. Main
Zimmerman Anton, shoemaker, h 54 Wall
Zimmerly John W., painter Pitts shop h 78 Dawson
Zimmerle S., carp., h 223 Calhoun
Zimmer John G., furniture dealer, 51 E. Main, h 75 Melitta
Zimmer John G., furniture store, h 75 Poplar
Zink John, fireman Pitts. R'y, h 48 Charles
Zink Robert, fireman Pitts. R'y, h 43 Charles
Zink John, drayman, h 41 Locust
Zinn John, lab, bds 408 W. Main
Zinsmeister Fred., clk, bds 118 E. Berry
Zollars Enoch, contractor, h 210 W. Wayne
ZOLLARS & ZOLLARS, attorneys, office cor. Calhoun and Berry
Zollars Frederick (Zollars & Zollars), attorney, office cor. Calhoun and Berry
Zollars Allen (Z. & Z., attorneys), h 17 Brackenridge
Zoller George, h 13 Harrison
Zoller George, lab, h 283 W. Main
Zollinger C. A., hat store (Harper & Co.), h 106 Jackson
Zorbaugh Emanuel, mach. Wabash R'y, h 178 W. Washington

Zorbaugh Emanuel, mach. Wabash shop, h 178 W. Jefferson
Zuber Fred., carp., h 191 E. Wayne

LIST OF STUDENTS AT CONCORDIA COLLEGE.

Andes Peter
Arnold Fred
Bachring Charles
Behrens Fred
Bente Fred
Berge Fred
Berger Fred
Bernthal John
Biewend August
Biltz Theodore.
Birkman Gottlieb
Birkner Henry
Borth John
Bracher Augustus
Brege Fred
Briechter Charles
Brueggman Charles
Bruechner Gottlieb
Brust Fred
Claehn Robt.
Detzer Fred
Detzer Adam
Doenselman William
Dornseif Phillip
Dorsch Casper
Droege Fred
Duerst Melchior
Eirich Adolph
Eisenbliss Fred
Engle Charles
Erk Herman
Frick Julius
Frederick Ernst
Fritze Phillip
Frank Charles
Frosh John
Gans William
Geissler William
Gericke William
Gockel Augustus
Gould James
Griebel John
Griese David
Grimm Augustus
Guenther Charles
Haag George
Hacke Henry
Hæfner George
Hænsgen Augustus
Hafner Charles
Hamm Herman
Hassold Stephen
Heine Theodore
Heinicke Edward
Herancourt Edward
Holls William
Hadekoff George
Husman William
Iben ———
Johann Adam
Johannes George
Johanning Charles
Juengel Herman
Kern Paul
Kœster Christian
Kocee Fred
Krause Julius
Krueger John
Kuechle Harman
Kuehn Christian
Kuehn Gotth
Lamfrecht Theodore
Lange Lewis
Lenke Herman
Leonhardt Edward
Levering William
Luecker William
Mangold Fred
Meyer Charles
Melcher Fred
Merbitz Paul
Mergel Fred

Metz Theodore
Meyer Theodore
Meyer William
Meese Edwin
Mohr Bernhart
Miller William
Miller Charles
Neithammer William
Ostermeier Anton
Otte Fred
Pechtold Christian
Pelzer Edward
Pennskamp Fred
Peterson Emil
Pohlman Lewis
Rabe John
Ranshert Herman
Rehwald Augustus
Riedel Charles
Rodeman August
Rœder Herman
Rœmer Charles
Roshke John
Ross Charles
Saupert Emil
Saxe Alex., jr.
Schafer Henry
Schaible Michael
Schmidt Adam
Schmidt Frank
Schmidt George
Schmidt Charles
Schrœder H.
Schrœder Fred
Schnelke Emil
Schultz Henry
Schulze Lewis
Schum George
Schwan Charles
Siemon Otto
Sievers Ferdinand
Sondhaus Gustav
Speckhardt Herman
Steffen William
Stellhorn Fred
Streckfuss John
Stieter Fred
Stubnatzy Ernst
Theiss Henry
Thieme Trangott
Thieme John
Tresselt Oscar
Van Strohe Fred
Wamesgans Fred
Wamesgans Phillip
Weseloh Henry
Wegel Edmond
Wichman Theodore
Wilder Augustus
Wiltenburgh Henry
Wischmeyer Henry
Weidman Fred
Young Godtfried
Yagel Fred
Yagel Herman

FORT WAYNE
BUSINESS DIRECTORY

BEING A

LIST OF BUSINESS PERSONS, FIRMS, ETC.,

ARRANGED ACCORDING TO THEIR VARIOUS BUSINESS PURSUITS,

FOR LOCATION SEE ALPHABATICAL ARRANGEMENTS OF NAMES.

Attorneys at Law.

Bayless Sol. D.
Bell R. C.
Bittinger Adam H.
Bittinger Jacob R.
Bloomhuff S. H.
Borden James W.
Bowen Daniel
Bowser Jeff. C.
Brackenridge Joseph
Carson W. W.
Colerick D. H.
Colerick E. F.
Colerick Philemon
Colerick W. G. & H.
Colerick Thomas
Coombs, Miller & Bell
Crane William M.
Curtice John F.
Dawson John W.
Du Bois John D.
Edgerton Joseph K.
Fay James A.
France Joseph S.
Graham James E.
Hartman Homer C.
Hayden John W.
Hillegass & Stoll
Hough John
Jennison William T.
Jones William H.
Kerr William J.
Morris & Withers
Newberger Louis
Ninde Lindley M.
O'Rourke Edward
Philley M. S.
Purman Andrew J.
Randall Franklin P.
Robertson Robert S.
Ryan Daniel
Schell James H.
Sinclair Samuel E.
Smart S. F.
Spencer M. V. B.
Taylor Robert S.
Walter W. B.
Whedon D. P.
Westrumb H.
Willson H. F.
Wines W. W.
Worden James L.
Zollars & Zollars.

Agricultural Implements.

Brandriff & Prescott
Fort Wayne Agricultural Works
McCulloch & Richey
Morgan & Beach
Prouty F. D. & Co.
Reid, Warring & Co.
Smick S. S.

Architects.

Laubscher Ludwig
Stophlet Joseph
Trenam George
Goshorn W. S.
Manthey William
De la Camp John
Laubscher William
Wilt John M.

Ale and Beer.

Centlivre C. L.

Auction and Commission.

Scheffer Joseph & Co.

Banks.

Ft. Wayne National Bank
Allen Hamilton Bank
First National Bank
Merchants' National Bank

Boiler Makers.

Bass John H.
Bowser J. C. & Co.
Murray Kerr

Brass Works.

Hattersley Alfred

Brass Founders.

Hattersley Alfred
Murry & Baker

Breweries.

Centlivre L. C.
Eder, Certia & Co.
Hornung John George
Linker, Hey & Co.
Reidmiller John M.

Bridge Builders.

Laubscher Ludwig
McKay & Gosshorn

Broom Manufacturers.

Bechtold Louis
Diedergan Joseph

Boiler Makers.

Bass John H.
Bowser J. C. & Co.
Murry & Kerr

Books and Stationery.

Jocquel Louis
Kiel & Brothers
Siemon & Brother
Stockbridge N. P.

Boots and Shoes.

App Matthias
Bauer Henry
Brœur Conrad
Brinkroeger William
Brunner John
Carnahan, Skinner & Co.
Clauss John C.
Delker John
Foelinger Jacob
Fortreel Louis
Heit Anthony
Helmke Edward
Hermsdorfer George A.
Humphrey Noah
Jacobs W. & Son
Lordier Philip
Mannix Thomas
Markley, Schrader & Co.
Mehre L.
Piepenbrink Conrad
Mohr John
Morrell Charles G.
Noll Martin
Sander Charles
Schiefer C.
Schmidt F.
Schulz Peter
Schulz William
Spiegel Gustave
Stellhorn Charles
Tagtmeyer Frederick & Bro.
Uebelhoer Philip
Vordermark E. & Sons
Woulfe Patrick

Book Agents.

Knight John
Orvis Mrs. Hattie

Book Binders.

Davis & Bro.
Riley, Neff & Dumm

Barber Shops.

Bourn Henry
Brown John W.
Knoder John
Lang George
Meyers F. C.
Meyers F. W.
Michael Fred
Shidel C.
Bower & Michels
Stewart William L.

Basket Maker.

Schanck Louis

Billiard Rooms.

Bronson A. A.
Goodman Francis
Hannum Daniel

Blacksmiths.

Sthair Henry
Baker John
Becker Fred
Brossart George
Brown John
Chovey C. & F.
Farnan Michael
Figel Fred
Fogerty E. D.
Francis & Mahon
Harter Joseph
Mesing & Zollinger
Vizzard & Howley
Welch Patrick

Bakeries.

Blase Louis
Haffner Christian
Holzworth E.
Jacobs C. W.
Kempf W.
Langohr Andrew J.
Leykoff N.
Schwieters Herman
Stellhorn Henry
Wolke & Trentman

Band Saw Mills.

Hoffman J. R. & Bro.

Boarding Houses.

Anderson F. H.
Blythe J. H.
Buckles J. H.
Cothrell Mose
Cummings J. L.
Compston Charles P.
Dean Christ
Erwin John
Fleming Sarah E.
Fox Phoebe A.
French Sarah M.
Hannah House
Hamilton House
Henderson Mrs. Angeline
Herbert Fred
Hackaday Mrs. D.
Houseworth Miss Kate
Iba Mrs. E.
Jackson Mrs. D. D.
Kelker David
Kleinegass Henrietta
McCarthy James
McElfatrick Mrs. Eva
McLaren Mrs. Anna
Manawich Fred
Manier Frank
Manier Mrs. Margaret
Merrigan John
Miller Louis
Moran E.
Pennsylvania House
Philley Mrs. E. H.
Richey Mrs. Sarah
Stapleford Mrs. L.
Sturgis House
Treep Mary
Widman Sebastian

Banks and Bankers.

First National Bank
Fort Wayne National Bank
MacDougal & Lauferty
Merchants' National Bank
Hamilton Allen & Co.

Cloths, Cassimeres, &c.

French, Hanna & Co.

Candy Manufacturers.

Beard Thomas D.
Fox George
Huestis & Hamilton
Wolke & Trentman

Commission Merchants.

Davesac P. & Son
Haskell Washington
Orbison Alexander

Confectioners.

Beard Thomas D.
Brandenburg William A.
Fox George
Hasty John
Landis Mrs. Mattie
Peck & Foot
Smith Lorin
Taylor H. C.
Wieman William
Wolke & Trentman

Contractors.

Allen C. W.
Cochran, Humphrey & Co.
French Charles G.
Kanne F.
Krudop, Mollering & Bro.
KcKee Hugh
Nelson William R.
Paul William
Potter Joseph L.
Reakers B. J.
Sutermeister, Becker & Bond

Cigars and Tobacco.

Dessauer L. & Co.
Degits Charles
Eckert & Ortman
Ehle August
Kabisch Julius
Lamley & Rosenthal
Ortman Henry
Reiter George
Wenninghoff Christian
Ford Charles

Cutlery.

Russell W. R.

Civil Engineers and Surveyors.

Brackenridge Charles S.
Crane Calvin D.
Lowrey Harvey C.
McWilliams Joseph
Williams Jesse L.

Clothing.

Bostick E. & Son
Fledderman John G.
Hartung Christian
Jacobson Victor
Lauferty & Son
Lauferty Max J.
Nirdlinger Jacob
Rothschild & Bro.
Vogel C. G. & Son
Woodward M. E.
Young N. B.

Car Wheels.

Bass John H.

Carpenters and Builders.

Allen C. W.
Cochrane, Humphrey & Co.
Cœgel Christian
Cunningham John
France William H.
French Charles G.
Klug Martin
Link George
Myers James D.
Potter Joseph L.
Pranger J. H.
Sallot J. F. & Son
Wenzel Elias F.

Carpets, Oil Cloths, &c.

Foster Brothers & Co.

Carriage Manufacturers.

Stanley, Bieber & Co.
Stevan Brothers
Sthair H.

Coopers.

Dewald Nicholas
Hoffmeister Henry
Kley Frederick
Meddy Frederick

Carpet Weaver.

Collar Mrs. Luphinia

Coal Dealers.

Bass & Smith
Lillie James
Fox George

Dental Goods.

Biddle T. M.
Vollmer Daniel

Dentists.

Brown Seneca B.
Knapp Isaac
Loag George W.
Snider Evan
Wells Arnold

Dress Makers.

Anderson Miss Anna
Bates Miss J. A.
Clark Mrs. Mary
Crosby Mary D.
Cummings Kate
Cushing Mary
Fletcher Mrs. F.
Gable Hannah
Hollingsworth Mrs. M.
Philley Mrs. E. L.
Strout Mrs. R. A.

Carriage and Wagon Makers' Material.

Coombs & Co.
Olds N. G. & Sons

Chair Manufacturers.

Griebel & Fee
Reese Charles & Co.

Chair Stuff Manufacturers.

Hoffman J. R. & Brothers.

China, Glass and Queensware

Trentman H. J. & Bro.
Tresselt & Both
Ward H. N.
Wigman H. & Co.

Collecting Agents.

Barbour M. F.
Bloomhuff Sol. D.
Bloomhuff S. H.
Bossler H. H.
Graham & Gotshall
Hanna S. T. & H. T.
Ryan Daniel

Children's Carriages.

Schanck Louis
Stockbridge N. P.
Kane James M. & Bro.

Cigar Boxes.

Peters John C.

Drugs, Medicines, &c.

Ayres H. B.
Biddle T. M.
Dreier H. & Bro
Grenemeier J. T.
Kiel A. C. & Co.
Thorp George
Meyer Brothers & Co.
Nill E. H. & Co.
Remmel A. C.
Schott George H.
Selle August L.
Vollmer Daniel
Wagner H. G.
Wooster H. F. & Co.

Dry Goods.

Dewald George & Co.
Evans A. S. & Co.
Foster Brothers & Co.
Frank & Thanhouser
Kiser Peter
Orff C. & Co.
Pierr J. & P.
Rohs, Eme & Reinking
Root & Co.

Dye House.

Jerman A. S.

File Cutters.

Harries & Co.

Fancy Goods.

Black Joseph
Deininger Ulrich
Kane James M. & Bro.
Kratzsch & Schirmeyer
Newberger Mrs. R.
Polak & Cowan

Flour and Feed Stores.

Berger & Miller
Haskell Washington
Kalbacher Andrew
Read Moses
Sedgwick John
Wells C. M.

Flax Mill.

Fort Wayne Flax Mills

Flour Mills.

Beaver D. S.
Cody M. & Son
Hill John E., jr., & Co.
Orff John
Pfeiffer J. C. & Co.
Tresselt, Hoagland & Co.

Fruit Dealers.

Cook Isaac G.
Elliott Joseph
Mensch Frank P.
White J. B.

Fur Dealers.

Bash S. & Co.
Harper James & Co.
Oppenheimer & Becker
Orff C. & Co.

Furniture.

Emerick & Burkholder
Gould George
Griebel & Fee
Hegerhorst & Tegeder
Kapp John & Co.
Klæhn John J.
Miller John M.
Oberhelmann William
Wheeler Nelson
Zimmer J. G.

Grocers—Wholesale.

Huestis & Hamilton
Trentman B. & Son
White J. B.

Grocers—Retail.

Alter Nicholas
Anderson & Douglas
Anderson Robert
Aurentz S. A.
Berning Conrad
Boltz F. F.
Borneman Charles
Breen James
Challenger J. W.
Dewald Nicholas
Didier Francis
Dickmeyer & Landsman
Dierstein Christian
Dierstein Conrad
Dodez & Rockhill
Draker & Brother
Fink Charles
Fœllinger J. M.
Fuchs George
Gaffney C.
Gers Philip
Geiss Jacob
Gerke H. F.
Gilliland & Medsker
Greensfelder Gustave
Gruber V.
Heckman E.
Heiny Brothers
Herbst Frederick
Hickman E.
Hutzel V.
Kempf William
Kiser Peter
Kline Jacob
Klotz & Co.
Koch Barney
Kœster John G.
Mergel R.
Mettler Peter J.
Meyer George
Niedhofer ———
Nieman Gottlieb

Nohe Joseph
Paul William
Phillips B.
Raab John
Raab Frederick
Rekers Gerard
Schaffer George
Schele & Lauer
Siebold John
Spiegel Ernst
Stoner, Wigent & Bro.
Thieme Andrew
Tremmel Conrad
Stuver M.
Weber F. A.
Wente W. L.
White J. B.
Wiebke Henry
Wigman H. & Co.
Woulfe & Bro.
Zimmerman A.

Gas and Steam Fitter.

Hattersley Alfred

Gents' Furnishing Goods.

Bostick & Son
Fledderman J. G.
Hartung Christian
Heingartner Martin
Jacobson Victor
Lauferty I. & Son
Lauferty Max J.
Moderwell & Fowler
Nirdlinger Jacob
Rothschild & Bro.
Thieme J. G. & Bro.
Vogel C. G. & Son
Woodward M. E.
Young N. B. & Co.

Guns, Pistols, &c.

Leonard William
Raquet Christian

German Publications.

Siemon & Brother

Glue Manufacturers.

Smith J. W. & Son

House Movers.

Boerger William
Davenport Frederick

Hot Air Furnaces.

Carter William
Cottingham & Co.

Hair Work and Jewelry.

Denio Madam C.
Gains Eliza
Gilchrist Mrs. M. H.
Warren Mrs. M. S.

Hats and Caps.

Harper James
Harper James & Co.
McCauley J. H. & Co.
Woodward M. E.
Zollinger Charles A.

House Furnishing Goods.

Ash H. J.
McCulloch & Richey
Stophlet & Bro.
Schuckman, Muhler & Co.

Hardware, Cutlery, &c.

Ash H. J.
Brandriff, Prescott & Co.
Coombs & Co.
Harries & Co.
McCulloch & Richey
Morgan & Beach
Russell W. R.

Hide, Pelts, Furs, &c.

Bash S. H. & Co.
Freiburger Simon
Heilbronner A.
Oppenheimer & Becker
Weil Isaac

Horse Shoers.

Brossart George
Chovey C. & F.
Ehrmann Charles
Fogerty E. D.
Francis & Mahon
Mesing Charles W.
Sthair Henry

Hotels.

American House
Aveline House
Exchange Hotel
Fox House
Harmon House
Hekekin House
Mayer House
Old Fort House
Phillips House
Robinson House
Union House
Central Hotel

Hoop Skirts and Corsets.

Black Joseph
Elsner Joe

Horse Collars.

Ehrmann Frederick M.
Miller & Boerger
Racine A.
Racine F. L.

Ice Dealers.

Cody Maurice
Helling Frederick
McLain Patrick

Insurance Agents.

Bossler H. H.
Bowser Jeff. C.
Buck W. S.
Carier A. H.
Crane George D.
Graham & Gotshall
Hanna S. T. & H. T.
Hough John
Irwin & Lombard
Lombard Joseph
Loughlin L. C.
Lumbard Sanford
Randall Franklin P.
Shallcross S. S.
Shoemaker George B.
Stirling John T.
Underhill W. R.
Van Voorkis Frank

Iron Founders.

Bass John H.
Bowser J. C. & Co.
Murray Kerr

Iron, Nails, &c.

Brandriff, Prescott & Co.
Coombs & Co.

Justices of the Peace.

Bittinger A. H.
Freeman S. C.
Graham James E.
Ryan Daniel
Stewart William

Knitting Machines.

Gehring J. D.

Lamps, Burning Fluid, &c.

Embry James S.
Trentman H. J. & Bro.
Tresselt & Both
Ward H. N.

Lap Window Blinds.

Howes & Bookwalter

Looking Glasses.

Miller John M.
Tresselt & Both
Ward H. N.
Wood W. S

Land Agents.

A. H. Carier
Edgerton Alfred P.
Hough John
Randall Franklin P.

Leather Findings &c.

Freiburger S. & Bro.
Miller & Bœrger
Sander & Co.
Schiefer C.
Vordemark E. & Son

Lime and Plaster.

Kanne F.
Keller & Co.
Krudop, Mollering & Co.
Lillie James
Paul William

Locksmith.

Reiling August

Linseed Oil.

Humphrey & Case

Livery Stables.

Barnum Dr. P. G.
Barr James
Glynn Mathias
Read A. J. & Son
Young Jacob

Locksmith.

Reiling August

Looking Glasses.

Miller John M.
Tresselt & Both
Ward H. N.
Wood W. S.

Lumber Dealers.

Ammon Daniel
Arentz Phillip
Beaver, Miller & Co.
Clark & Rhinesmith
Cochran, Humphrey & Co.
Hoffman J. R. & Bro.
Jacoby, Myers & Co.
Nuttman & Taylor

Marble Works.

Smith & Condon
Sutermeister, Becker & Bond
Underhill & Mattison
Underhill Marble and Granite Works.
Young W. C.

Mattrass Manufactory.

Gould George
Smith J. W. & Son
Zimmer J. G.

Mill Machinery.

Bass John H.
Bowser J. C. & Co.
Murray Kerr

Millwright.

Murray Kerr

Meat Stores.

Brehn John F.
Burhn Edward
Coffman Christian
Doelker Jacob
Eckert Fred
Fisher Isaac
Gesler Fred
Kelsey J. F.
Meyer Ernst
Ofenloch & Co.
Schieferstein Phillip
Wilkins Christ
Wolf A.
Yobst A.

Midwife.

Matsch Dorothy

Military Claim Agent.

Kerr William J.

Millinery Goods.

Bates Mrs. J. A.
Black Joseph
Delzell Mrs. S. J.
Horton Mrs. M. A.
Neubeger Mrs. R.
Orff C. & Co.
Phelps Miss Frances
Pierr J. & P.
Shilling M. & Co.
Smith Mrs. L. H.
Stier Mrs. George
Vogel Mrs. C. G.

Mineral Water.

Laurent & Son

Model Baker.

Cummings & Kerr

Musical Instruments.

Anderson T. P.
Hill C. L.
Kestel P.
Stockbridge N. P.

Mustard Manufactory.

Alling Lourens

News Dealers.

Rambo B. W.
Smith Lorin

Newspapers.

Ft. Wayne *Gazette*
Ft. Wayne *Journal*
Ft. Wayne *Sentinel*
Indiana *Staats Zeitung*
Indiana *Volksfreund*

Notions.

Bates Miss J. A.
Black Joseph
DeWald George & Co.
Evans A. S. & Co.
Kratzsch & Schirmeyer
Neuberger Mrs. R.
Pierr J. & P.
Polak & Cowan
Rosenburg & Gans
Rohs, Eme & Reinking

Nursery.

Nelson De Groff & Co.

Occulist and Aurist.

Ayres H. P.

Omnibus and Hack Line.

Fletcher & Powers

Opticians.

Rambo B. W.
Redelsheimer H.

Pump Maker.

Kyle A. P. & Co.

Pianos, Organs &c.

Anderson T. P.
Hill C. L.

Pictures. Picture Frames &c.

Wood W. S.

Planing and Flooring Mills.

Beaver, Miller & Co.
Clark & Rhinesmith
Cochran, Humphrey & Co.
Jacoby, Wiegand & Co.

Plow Manufactory.

Reid, Waring & Nelson

Plumber.

Hattersley A.

Pottery.

Lillie Samuel

Produce Dealers.

Davesac P. & Son
Haskell Wash.
Taylor R. W.

Physicians.

Ayers H. P.
Beck Joseph R.
Brooks William H.
Brubach George T.
Curtice S.
Gard B.
Goeriz Adolph
Gregg J. S.
Gourdeau A. E.
Heuchlin T.
Jones J. H.
Josse John M.
Lewis Edward
McCulloch T. P.
Mayer Charles F.
Medcalf Samuel C.
Morgan W. E.
Myers William H.
Ogle John
Purdy T. H.
Rosenthal Isaac M.
Schmitz Charles
Smith C. S.
Todd S. Clay
Virgil Thomas S.
Woodworth B. S.

Paper Hangings.

Keil & Bro.
Seimon & Bro.
Starkey O. L.
Stockbridge N. P.

Paper Mill.

Freeman & Barnett

Patent Smoke Stacks.

Fontaine & Roberts.

Pedlers' Exchange.

Dillingham A. J.

Periodical Depots.

Rambo B. W.
Smith Lorin

Physicians, Homœpathic.

Bowen George W.
Frietzsche John W.
Leonard P. M.

Painters.

Graham William H.
Kover & Rivers
Miller Louis
Misner J. A.
Murphy A. W.
Ott Franz
Starkey O. L.
Hull L. O.
Wilmot James C.

Paints, Oils, &c.

Ayres H. B.
Biddle T. M.
Bond W. J.
Brandriff, Prescott & Co.
Dreier H. & B.
Kover & Rivers
Meyer Brothers & Co.
Nill E. H. & Co.
Selle August L.
Vollmer Daniel
Wagner H. G.
Willmot James G.
Wooster W. F. & Co.

Paper Hangers.

Kover & Rivers
Starkey O. L.
Hull L. O.
Wilmot James C.

Paper Boxes.

Davis & Brother.

Roofers.

Bramer J. & Brother
Laidlaw Walter
Myers & Gorham

Railroad Contractors.

McKay & Goshorn

Real Estate Agents.

Archer John H.
Bayles Sol. D.
Bloomhuff S. H.
Bossler H. H.
Carier A. H.
Graham & Gottshall
Hanna S. T. & H. T.
Hough John

Restaurants.

Baals & Steger
Cothrel Jarad
Fox George
Kreadly John
McFeely Dennis R.
Schenck Con.
Weiman William

Saddles and Harness.

Johns A. S.
Neireiter C. B.
Schwartz & Co.
Shoaff Samuel H.
Traub Louis

Sash, Doors and Blinds.

Cochrane, Humphrey & Co.
Frohnfield & Todd
Hurd O. D.
Jacoby & Co.
Sallot J. F. & Son.

Sausage Makers.

Eckart F.
Ofenloch Peter
Schieferstein Philip

Slate Roofing.

Laidlaw Peter B.

Saws.

Barbier T. F.
Colson E.
Wilson & Brother

Saw Mills.

Baker J & K.
Busse, Tegtmeyer & Co.

Seed Stores.

Bash S. & Co.
Nelson DeGroff & Co.
Smick S. S.

Sewing Machine Agents.

Anderson T. P.
Davis A
Hill C. L.
Hinman Edwin
Kestel P.
Leach J. W.
Lumbard L.
Perry Joseph
Pierce James S.
Whitney C.

Spice Mills.

Huestis, Hamilton & Co.
Trentman, Monning & Son

Stair Builder.

Ptter Joseph L.

Staves and Headings.

Ranke, Yergens & Co.
Schnelker, Beugnot & Co.

Steam Engines.

Bass John H.
Bowser J. C. & Co.
Murry & Baker

Stone Dealers.

Kanne F.
Keller & Co.
Krudop, Mollering & Co.
Smith & Congdon
Sutermeister, Becker & Bond

Stoves and Hallow Ware

Allgeier & Brother
Ash H. J.
Brandriff, Prescott & Co.
Dewald Henry
Graffe G. W & Co.
Jocquel J. J.
McCulloch & Richey
Wilson, Schuckman & Muhler

Spokes, Hubs, &c.

Olds N. G. & Sons

Tanners.

Breuchle & Co.
Fry Jacob
Manock & Kœster

Tailors, Merchant.

Bostick E. & Son
Clark Joseph M.
Fledderman John G.
Foster Andrew
Grimme John H.
Heingartner Martin
Hartung Christ
Lauferty M. J.
Mayer Louis
Shoaff Wade C.
Stemmler Phillip
Thieme J. G. & Bro.
Vogel C. G. & Son
Woodward M. E.
Young N. B.

Tea Dealers.

Dorr & Bro.
White J. B.

Tin, Copper and Sheet Iron Ware.

Brandriff, Prescot & Co.
Carter William
De Wald Henry
Graffe G. W. & Co.
Jocquel J. J.
McCulloch & Richey
Welch & Baker
Wilson, Schuckman & Muhler

Tin and Glassware.

Johnson E.

Tin Roofers.

Carter William
Wilson, Schuckman & Muhler

Tinners' Stock.

Ash H. J.
McCulloch & Richey
Welch & Baker

Tobacco and Cigars.

Ford Charles, (Wholesale).

Transportation Company.

Empire Fast Freight Line

Trunks, Valises &c.

Lingenfelser H. & Bro.
Neireiter Conrad

Umbrella Maker.

Courtney Lawrence F.

Undertakers.

Fink Charles
Peltier & Carll

Upholsterers.

Gould George
Klaehn John J.
Miller John M.
Zimmer J. G.

Variety Store.

Embry Mrs. J. S.
Kane & Bro.
Kratzsch & Shirmeyer

Veterinary Surgeons.

Barnum G. P.
Read Henry A.

Vinegar Manufactories.

Heilbronner S. & Co.
Henkell Phillip

Watches and Jewelery.

Mayer George J. E. & F. Voirol
Mayer & Graffe
Sauser Louis
Trenkley & Sherzinger

Wagon Makers.

Baker John
Biemer George
Chovey C. & F.
Dierstein A.
Mesing Charles W.
Pope H.
Stevens & Bro.
Williams John H.

Window Blinds and Shades.

Howes David

Wines and Liquors.

Didier J. C.
Fœllinger J. M.
Graff Marx & Son
Laurent J. & Son
Langard & Co.
Leutz, Bourie & Co.
Trentman B. & Son

Wooden Shoemaker.

Mennier N.

Wool Dealers.

Bash & Co.
Falk Leopold
Freiberger Simon & Bro.
French, Hanna & Co.
Oppenheimer & Becker

Woolen Mills.

French, Hanna & Co.

FRENCH LAGER BEER BREWERY

(ON ST. JOE RIVER, ONE-HALF MILE NORTH OF CITY.)

C. L. CENTLIVRE, PROPRIETOR,

FORT WAYNE, INDIANA.

BUY YOUR PLOWS AT THE

FORT WAYNE STEEL PLOW WORKS

A. D. Reid's Old Stand, Corner Main Street and Maiden Lane.

GENUINE CAST STEEL PLOWS

For Sod and General Purposes.

COMBINATION PLOWS,

With Cast Iron or Cast Steel Points,

SINGLE, DOUBLE AND THREE-SHOVEL PLOWS,

New Ground Plows, Road Scrapers, Railroad and Road District Plows.

Call and See the Stock Whether you Buy or Not.

When your plows are worn or need repair, you know where you can have them put in order.

BUSINESS DIRECTORY

OF THE

TOWN OF MONROEVILLE,

AS REPORTED BY J. G. MARRIOTTE.

A. F. BEUGNOT & CO., manufacturers of staves and dealers in flat hoops, A. F. Beugnot and D. Monahan, props.
HELLER & DAGUE, general store, also dealers in produce.
JEAN PIERRE & PETER COLE, groceries, provisions and produce.
DUNHAM & STEELE, dealers in produce.
Baker & Brothers, dry goods, groceries and notions.
Michael L. Baker, Justice of the Peace.
E. G. COVERDALE, attorney, notary public and insurance agent.
M. S. Morrison, Justice of the Peace.
Brown & Meeks, Central Bakery and confectioners.
N. B. Knouse, watchmaker and jeweler.
CHARLES W. ROLLINS, baker and confectioner.
CHARLES W. ROLLINS, druggist.
J. B. WORDEN & CO., druggists and apothecaries, and dealers in stationery and notions.
Empire Stave Company, Heller & Dague, proprietors.
Pacific House, F. V. V. Shell, proprietor; also, collector and attorney at law.
Vanstrouder & Anthony, saddlers and harness makers.
Hon. Mahlon Heller, Representative.
Samuel Pool, dry goods, groceries and notions.
M. & J. Strass, merchant tailors and dealers in men's furnishing goods.
Morris Strass, Postmaster.
Roebuch & Co., dry goods, groceries and country produce.
Maggie F. Eyanson, ladies' furnishing goods, milliner and dress maker.

Thomas Eyanson, merchant tailor.
John Gilchrist, manufacturer and dealer in boots and shoes.
D. A. Ross, shoemaker and repairer.
THE MONROEVILLE DEMOCRAT, the only paper published in the town. Circulation, 1,800. J. D. Foster, editor and proprietor.
Magner & Brantner, undertakers, manufacturers and dealers in household furniture.
N. Scarr & Son, meat market.
D. W. Champer, surgeon.
DANIEL MONAHAN, Trustee of Monroe township.
James Hemphill, stave manufacturer, M. S. Argo, agent.
A. A. Baker, Justice of the Peace, Insurance Agent and Collector.
Jacob Cassady, blacksmith and wagon maker.
J. Dague & Bro.. Monroeville Flouring Mill.
Webster & Weiler, manufacturers of staves and headings, and dealers in rough and dressed lumber
J. B. Niezer & Co., hardware and stoves.
Jonathan Marguardt, broom maker.
Benjamin Vanosdall, constable.
Alexander Argo, marshal.
J. T. Pool, attorney at law and constable.
Jules Simonin, saloon keeper.
W. Connolly, physician and surgeon.
Jacob Engle, physician.
A. Engle, physician.
D. O. Thorp, house and sign painter.
A. S. Wormly, agent Pittsburgh, Fort Wayne & Chicago Railroad.
SILAS WORK, Justice of the Peace and Collecting Agent, Madison Township.

DISTANCES AND RATES OF FARE FROM FORT WAYNE BY RAILROAD.

	Miles	Amount.		Miles	Amount.
Angola, Ind	42	$ 1 45	Massilon, O	210	$ 7 35
Auburn, Ind	23	85	Mansfield, O	144	5 05
Arcola, Ind	9	35	Montpelier, Vt	1095	
Atwood, Ind	46	1 60	Monroeville, Ind	16	60
Altoona, Pa	436	14 00	Maples, Ind	10	40
Allentown, Pa	658	17 50	Maumee City, O	95	3 00
Albany, N. Y	687	17 50	Memphis, Tenn	617	23 10
Augusta, Me	1141		Milwaukee, Wis	233	8 15
Antwerp, O	23	80	Mobile, Ala	1123	36 10
Alliance, O	236	8 25	Nashville, Tenn	425	16 50
Allegheny, Pa	319	11 20	Newark, N. J	745	18 50
Buffalo, N. Y	390	11 80	New Haven, Conn	827	18 75
Baltimore, Md	653	15 56	New Orleans, La	995	35 35
Boston, Mass	887	20 50	New Haven, Ind	6	30
Bourbon Ind	53	1 85	Napoleon, O	59	2 05
Bucyrus, O	119	4 15	New York City, N. Y	751	18 50
Bluffton, Ind	25	1 00	New Castle, Ind	83	3 35
Cincinnati, O	176	5 55	Ossian, Ind	15	60
Cambridge City, Ind	97	3 85	Omaha, Neb	645	24 85
Canton, O	218	7 60	Philadelpdia, Pa	675	16 50
Crestline, O	131	4 55	Peru, Ind	56	2 25
Chicago, Ill	148	5 15	Pittsburgh, Pa	320	11 20
Columbia City, Ind	19	75	Pierceton, Ind	31	1 05
Cleveland, O	207	6 80	Plymouth, Ind	64	2 25
Charleston, S. C	1094	34 75	Paris, Mich	202	6 35
Cairo, Ill	420	15 60	Quincy, Ill	382	14 00
Columbus, O	194	6 10	Raleigh, N. C	1118	
Dayton, O	130	4 50	Richmond, Va	935	
Detroit, Mich	159	5 30	Rochester, N. Y	458	13 20
Danville, Ill	156	6 20	Roanoke, Ind	15	60
Delphi, Ind	92	3 70	Rochester, Pa	294	10 30
Defiance, O	44	1 55	Rome City, Ind	35	1 20
Delphos, O	45	1 55	State Line, Ill	148	5 99
Evansville, Ind	313	11 75	Sturgis, Mich	57	2 00
Forest, O	90	3 15	St. Louis, Mo	382	12 60
Grand Rapids, Mich	142	4 50	Springfield, Ill	268	10 76
Huntington, Ind	24	1 00	Sacramento, Cal	24 1	122 95
Huntertown Ind.	10	42	St. Paul, Minn	663	20 55
Hartford City, Ind	48	1 90	Salt Lake City, Utah	1714	104 35
Hamilton, O	151	4 50	San Francisco, Cal	2559	123 15
Indianapolis, Ind	131	4 60	Savannah, Ga	1005	38 75
Jacksonville, Ill	302	12 00	Tullahasse, Fla	1268	
Jackson, Mich	100	3 25	Toledo, O	94	3 30
Jackson, Miss	813		Terre Haute, Ind	204	7 45
Kalamazoo, Mich	93	3 10	Trenton, N. J	707	18 50
Kendallville, Ind	28	1 00	Troy, N. Y	692	17 50
Leavenworth, Kan	691	23 00	Upper Big Rapids, Mich	198	6 20
Lexington, Ky	334		Upper Sandusky, O	102	3 55
Louisville, Ky	240	9 10	Valparaiso, Ind	104	3 65
La Gro, Ind	37	1 50	Van Wert, O	32	1 10
Logansport, Ind	72	2 90	Watarloo City, Ind	25	1 00
Lafayette, Ind	109	4 35	Wilmington, Del	703	
Larwill, Ind	27	95	Wooster, O	183	6 45
Lima, O	59	2 05	Wanatah, Ind	93	3 30
Lagrange, Ind	47	1 65	Warsaw, Ind	40	1 35
Muncie, Ind	65	2 60	Washington, D. C	681	15 50
Mendon, Mich	72	2 45	Wabash, Ind	42	1 70

BUSINESS DIRECTORY

OF THE

TOWN OF NEW HAVEN.

Bell, Beugnot & Co., dealers in dry goods and notions, on Broadway.
Mack Frederick, boot and shoe maker, on Broadway.
Kleemeier D., merchant tailor, on Broadway.
Lipes Andrew, watchmaker, on Broadway
Dowling B., tinner and dealer in stoves, on Broadway.
Lewis A., painter, shop on Broadway.
Williamson M. F., M. D., on Broadway.
Tenge Henry, manufacturer and dealer in furniture, on Broadway.
New Haven Mills, Powers & Co., proprietors, on Broadway.
DOUGAL ALLEN H., notary public, on Broadway.
Dougal John, Justice of the Peace, corner Main and Broadway.
Eveland S. H., Justice of the Peace, office on Summit street.
Rogers O. D., Justice of the Peace, office on Summit street.
Tilbury James E., constable.
Monahan Cornelius, constable.
Schnelker, Beugnot & Co., stave manufacturers, office on Broadway
Gothe G. & Co., proprietors of the New Haven shingle and planing mills.
New Haven Hotel, on Middle street, J. Taylor, proprietor.
Federspiel & Brother, blacksmiths and wagon makers, Main street.
Sommers Thomas, blacksmith, Main street.
Schnitker A. R., harness maker, on Broadway.
Schuckman N., dealer in groceries and dry goods corner Broadway and Main street.
Simons John W., barber, shop on Broadway.
FISCHER ADAM, saloon, on Broadway.
Crippen & Son, druggists, store on Broadway.

Bilderback J. W., M. D., office on Broadway.
Loos William, manufacturer of cigars, on Broadway.
Frosard A., saloon, on Broadway.
Stark & Stoneman, butchers, shop on Broadway.
St. Nicholas Saloon, N. Schuckman, proprietor, Main street.
Null L. S., M. D., office on Broadway.
Floto W. A., M. D., office on Broadway.
Whitiker & Rogers, dealers in dry goods, groceries and notions, corner Broadway and Main streets.
Knode Robert S., druggist, and dealer in paints, oils, &c., on Broadway.
Meads Thomas & Co., proprietors of the saw mill, office on East Summit street.
Schnelker Hermann, Township Trustee, house corner Main and High streets.
Huth Erwin, boot and shoe maker, on Main street.
Linnerman Frederick, boot and shoe maker, shop on Main street.
Fischer J., butcher, shop on Main street.
Brooks John, butcher, shop on Summit street.
Wolf Charles, saloon, on Grove street.
Thompson M., postmaster, corner of Broadway and High streets.

CHURCH DIRECTORY.

LUTHERAN.

Trinity English Evangelical Lutheran—Corner Wayne and Clinton streets. Rev. Samuel Wagenhalls, Pastor.

St. Paul's, German—On Barr, between Washington and Lewis streets. Rev. Wm. Sihler, Pastor.

Emanuel's German Evangelical—On Jefferson, between Jackson and Union. Rev. W. S. Stubnatzy, Pastor.

St. John's German Evangelical—Southeast corner Washington and Van Buren streets. Rev. John Kucher, Pastor.

REFORMED.

Salem—On Clinton, between Wayne and Berry streets. Rev. C. Baum, Pastor.

St. John's—Southeast corner Webster and Washington streets. Rev. Francis Schwedes, Pastor.

PRESBYTERIAN.

First Presbyterian—Southeast corner Berry and Clinton. Rev. D. W. Moffat, Pastor.

Second Presbyterian—South side Berry, between Harrison and Ewing streets. Rev. W. J. Erdman, Pastor.

Third Presbyterian—Northeast corner Calhoun and Holman. Rev. N. S. Smith, Pastor.

CATHOLIC.

Immaculate Conception Cathedral—East side Calhoun, between Jefferson and Lewis streets. Rt. Rev. Joseph Dwenger, Bishop.

St. Mary's—Corner Lafayette and Jefferson. Rev. Joseph Rademacher, Pastor.

St. Paul's (German)—On Washington, between Griffith and Ewing streets. Rev. Edward Konig, Pastor.

St. Peter's—On St. Francis, between Hanna and Cass streets. Rev. John Wemhoff, Pastor.

METHODIST EPISCOPAL.

Berry Street M. E. Church—Northeast corner Berry and Harrison. Rev. A. Marine, Pastor.

Methodist Episcopal—Southwest corner Broadway and Wayne streets. Rev. J. H. Meck, Pastor.

African M. E.—Corner Wayne and Francis streets. Rev. M. Patterson, Pastor.

Centenary M. E.—Southwest corner Dawson and Harrison streets. Rev. P. Carland, Pastor.

German Church—Northeast corner Washington and Fulton. Rev. John Lambry, Pastor.

PROTESTANT EPISCOPAL.

Trinity Church—Southwest corner Berry and Fulton. Rev. Colin C. Tate, Pastor.

Church of the Good Sheppard—South side Holman, between Calhoun and Clinton. Rev. Walter Scott, Pastor.

BAPTIST.

First Baptist—On Jefferson, between Harrison and Webster. Rev. J. R. Stone, Pastor.

EVANGELICAL ASSOCIATION.

Bethel Church—Northeast corner Clinton and Holman. Rev. J. Schmedle, Pastor.

JEWISH.

Achduth Veshalom—West side Harrison, bet. Wayne and Washington. Rev. Edward Rubin, Rabbi.

CONGREGATIONAL.

Plymouth Church—Northwest corner Washington and Fulton. Rev. John B. Fairbank, Pastor.

Glenwood Chapel—Sunday School. A. C. and D. S. Beaver, Trustees.

Bloomingdale Chapel—Corner Bass and Fourth. A. J. Emerick, J. W. Cromwell and E. T. Williams, Trustees.

Public School Department.

BOARD OF EDUCATION.

Meets first and third Tuesday of each month. Alfred P. Edgerton, President; Pliny Hoagland, Secretary; Dr. John S. Irwin, Treasurer and Secretary *pro tem.*

SUPERINTENDENT OF PUBLIC SCHOOLS.

James H. Smart. Office on East Wayne street, near Calhoun.

SCHOOLS AND TEACHERS.

High School—Building on East Wayne street, near Calhoun. Robert M. Wright, A. B., Principal; Hannah E. Evry and Annie M. Hill, Assistants.

Jefferson School—Building corner Jefferson and Griffith streets. Carrie B. Sharp, Principal; Susan C. Hoffman, Ella F. Clarke, Fannie A. Hatch, Julia D. Brainerd, Maggie S. Cochrane, Frank Hamilton, Elizabeth J. Imrie, Jennie A. Woodworth, Clara Phelps, Rosa Bennett and Lizzie M. Evans, Teachers.

Clay School—Building corner Washington and Clay streets. Mary S. Thompson, Principal; Eliza H. Weed, Mary L. Bickford, Lou. E. Strong, Belle Spore, Ella A. Dresser, Minnie A. Humphrey, Josie Updegraff, Josephine Strong and Emma J. Rupert, Teachers.

Hoagland School—Building corner Hoagland avenue and Butler street. Sarah E. Smith Principal; Ella Embry, Debbie Robertson, Orlinda P. Sinclair, Sallie Updegraff and Anna L. Dillon, Teachers.

Washington School—Building corner Washington and Ewing street. Nettie Mark, Principal; Fannie Clark, Ada Remmel, Sydna Sarbaugh and Zerniah E. McLain, Teachers.

Hanna School—Building corner Wallace and Hanna streets. Maggie McPhail, Principal; Agnes Tower, Teacher.

Harmer School—Building corner Jefferson and Harmer streets. Maggie Armstrong, Principal

Bloomingdale School—Building corner Bowser and Marion streets. Agnes J. O'Conner, Principal; Florence Requa, Teacher.

East German—Building corner Washington and Clay streets. John J. Weber, Principal; Minnie Fero, Teacher.

West German—Building corner Webster and Washington streets. Carl Schwarz, Principal.

Bloomingdale German—Building corner Bowser and Marion streets. Lizzie Sihler, Principal.

Training School—Building on E. Wayne street, near Calhoun. Leonora I. Drake, Principal.

Special Teachers—Susan B. Fowler, drawing and painting; Rev. Edw. Rubin, German; Clara J. Drake, vocal music; John L. Tyler, penmanship.

Janitors—William Shoemaker, Hans Newell, Ernst Bicknell, Ann O'Callahan, Mrs. J. Heck, James Merrigan, John Hoffer and Rudolph Jasper.

Parochial Schools.

St. Augustine's (Catholic) Academy—S. E. Cor. Calhoun and Jefferson, under the auspices of the Sisters of Providence.

St. Mary's (Girl' Dept.)—under the auspices of the Sisters of Notre Dame, S. W. Cor. Jefferson and Lafayette.

St. Joseph's School (Boys' Department)—Southwest corner Lafayette and Jefferson streets. Joseph Buechler and Charles Geiger, Teachers.

St. Paul's School—Corner West Washington and Griffith streets. Jos. Bueler, Teacher.

Cathedral School—Corner Clinton and Jefferson streets. Under the Supervision of the Christian Brothers.

St. Peter's School—On Francis street, between Bass and Hanna. —— Moos, Teacher.

Emanuel's Lutheran—Corner West Jefferson and Union streets.

St. Paul's Lutheran—Corner Barr and Madison streets.

St. John's Lutheran—Corner West Washington and Van Buren streets.

St. John's German Reformed—Corner West Washington and Webster streets.

Fire Department.

Frank B. Vogel, Chief Engineer; Con. Schenck and M. M. Kelly, Assistants.

Alert Hook and Ladder Co. No. 1—House west side of Clinton, cor. East Berry street. Meets first Wednesday in each month at Lafayette Hall, west side Barr, bet. Main and Berry streets. George Strodel, Foreman; A. H. Carier, Secretary.

Mechanics' Engine Co. No. 1—Steam—Northeast corner Main and Berry streets. Byron Kiser, Foreman.

Vigilant Engine Co. No. 2—Steam—Northeast corner Main and Berry streets. Robert Cran, Foreman.

Protection Engine Co. No. 5—Hand—Sixth Ward, south of railroad shops. John Bauman, Foreman.

Rescue Engine Co. No. 6—Hand—Located in Seventh Ward. P. J. Mettler, Foreman.

Hope Hose Co. No. 1—Northwest corner Clinton and Berry streets. Sam. E. Morse, Foreman.

FIRE DISTRICT.

Section 1.—All that part of the City of Fort Wayne embraced within the following limits shall be known as the fire limits of said city, to-wit: Beginning at the intersection of the Wabash and Erie Canal with Ewing street, thence east along said south line of the Canal to the center of Lafayette street; thence south along said Lafayette street to its intersection with Lewis street; thence west along the center of Lewis street to the center of Ewing street; thence north along the center of said Ewing street to the place of beginning.

Location of Cisterns.

1. Intersection Clinton and Wayne streets.
2. " Clinton and Jefferson "
3. " Jefferson and Hanna "
4. " Francis and Madison "
5. " Lavina and Broadway "
6. " Washington and Van Buren streets.
7. East side of Free School, on Clay street.
8. Intersection of Hanna and Wallace "
9. " West and Pritchard "
10. " Prince and Bass "
11. " Lafayette and Montgomery streets.
12. " Barr and Madison "
13. Fronting Engine House on Court street.
14. " Cathedral on Calhoun street.
15. Intersection Wallace and Lafayette streets.
16. " Butler and Hoagland "
17. North side German Catholic church, E. Jefferson St.
18. Intersection Third and Wells streets.
19. Southeast corner Union and Jefferson streets.
20. " " Market House, Broadway.
21. On Holman, east of Calhoun street.
22. On Wallace, " " "

Societies and Associations.

MASONIC.

Masonic Hall, northwest corner Calhoun and Berry streets.

Fort Wayne Commandery, No. 4—Knights Templar; instituted December, 1854. Meets on second Thursday evening in each month.

Fort Wayne Council, No. 4.—Instituted May 5, 1855, Meets on second Saturday evening in each month.

Fort Wayne Chapter, R. A. M., No. 19.—Instituted May, 1851. Meets on first Wednesday evening in each month.

Wayne Lodge, No. 25, F. & A. M.—Instituted March, 1828. Regular meetings Thursday evening on or preceding each full moon. Adjourned meetings Thursday evening of each week.

Summit City Lodge, No. 170.—Instituted May, 1855. Regular meetings on Friday evening preceding full moon. Adjourned meetings Friday evenings of each week.

Home Lodge, No. 342.—Instituted May, 1870. Meets every Thursday evening preceding full moon.

Sol. D. Bayless Lodge, No. 359.—Instituted June, 1867.—Meets every Monday evening.

Ancient and Accepted Scottish Rite—Four Orders. Meets third Thursday evening in each month.

ODD FELLOWS.

Hall east side of Court House, over Post Office.

Fort Wayne Lodge, No. 14.—Instituted October, 1843. Meets every Monday evening.

Harmony Lodge, No. 19.—Institured January 31, 1845. Meets every Thursday evening.

Concordia Lodge, No. 228.—Instituted January 15, 1862. Meets every Wednesday evening.

Summit City Encampment, No. 16.—Instituted November, 1849. Meets first and third Friday evenings in each month.

Independent Order Benai Berith Emack Beracha Lodge, No. 61.—Organized March, 1864. Meets first and third Sunday in each month, in Odd Fellows' Hall, over Post Office. Lewis Newberger, President; Charles Young, Vice President; V. Jacobson, Treasurer; Rev. E. Rubin, Secretary.

I. O. R. M.

Maumee Tribe, No. 23.—Instituted 1871. Meets every Tuesday evening at their hall, southwest corner Berry and Harrison streets. James Ligget, Sachem; J. T. Leach, Chief of Records; George King, Keeper of Wampum.

Chippewa Tribe, No. 26.—(German.) Instituted 1872.

I. O. G. T.

Home Lodge, No. 585.—Meets every Monday evening at Covenant Hall.

Summit City Lodge, No. 14.—Meets every Friday evening at Temperance Hall, corner Berry and Harrison streets.

TYPOGRAPHICAL UNION.

Fort Wayne Union, No. 78.—Meets first Saturday evening in each month, in Temperance Hall, corner Berry and Harrison streets.

O. U. A. M.

Decatur Council, No. 4.—Instituted June, 1870. Meets every Thursday evening at their hall, corner Berry and Harrison streets.

Lafayette Benevolent Society.—Organized 1861. Meets at their hall in Taylor's Block, on Barr street, between Main and Berry, the second Saturday in each month, at 7½ p. m. A. H. Carier, President; A. Parnin, Secretrry; Joseph Didier, Treasurer.

Lafayette Building, Loan and Saving Association.—Meets on Thursday following the 24th of each month, in Lafayette Hall, on Barr street, between Berry and Main. I. W. Campbell, President; Charles D. Barton, Secretary.

Jewish Poor Fund Society.—I. Lauferty, S. Freiburger and Frederick Nirdlinger, Trustees.

Ladies' Hebrew Benevolent Society.—Meets every Thursday. Mrs. F. Freiburger, President; Mrs. Moses Lamley, Secretary.

Indiana Conservatrry of Music.—Burges' Block, corner Main and Court streets. J. C. Bartlett, Secretary.

Allen County Bible Society.—Organized April, 1833. Depository, Keil & Bro., Keystone Block. Meets last Tuesday in each month. F. W. Keil, Treasurer.

Fort Wayne Conservatory of Music.—No. 11½ East Main street. A. K. Virgil, Principal.

Concordia College.—Situated north side Maumee road, under auspices of the German Evangelical Lutheran Synod of Missouri, Ohio and other States. Dr. William Sihler, President.

Lindenwood Cemetery.—Situated on Huntington road, one mile from corporation line. I. D. G. Nelson, President; J. D. Bond, Secretary.

Fort Wayne Gas Light Company.—Organized August, 1855. Works and office on East Water street, between Barr and Lafayette streets. A. P. Edgerton, President.

Y. M. C. A.—Rooms in Hamilton's Building. Reading rooms open every day. A. S. Evans, President; M. V. B. Spencer, Secretary.

Newspapers.

Fort Wayne Sentinel—(Daily and Weekly.) Office, southwest corner Calhoun and Wayne streets. G. W. H. Riley & Co., editors and proprietors.

Fort Wayne Gazette—(Daily and Weekly.) Office, No. 52 Calhoun street. McNiece & Alexander, editors and proprietors.

Indiana Staats-Zeitung—(German, Tri-weekly and Weekly.) Office, northeast corner Columbia and Clinton streets. John D. Sarnighausen, editor and proprietor.

Fort Wayne Journal—(Weekly.) Office, on Court street, opposite the Court House. Thos. S. Taylor, editor and proprietor.

Volksfreund—(German, Weekly.) Office, southwest corner Calhoun street. William Eichelsdorfer, proprietor. Rudolph Worch, editor. Robert Schnabel, local editor.

New Haven Palladium—(Weekly.) Published at New Haven, Ind., by Thomas J. Foster.

Auburn Courier—One of the best weeklies in the State. Published at Auburn, Ind., by T. C. Mays.

U. S. EXPRESS COMPANY'S

Bill Offices in the Western Division.

Adrian........Ohio
Akron........Ohio
Amherst........Ohio
Anna........Ohio
Antwerp........Ohio
Arcanum........Ohio
Archibald........Ohio
Aurora........Ohio
Alton........Ill
Annawan........Ill
Ashland........Ill
Atlanta........Ill
Atkinson........Ill
Auburn........Ill
Arrowsmith........Ill
Anderson........Ind
Antioch........Ind
Arcadia........Ind
Argos........Ind
Attica........Ind
Ackley........Iowa
Ainsworth........Iowa
Albia........Iowa
Algona........Iowa
Allerton........Iowa
Atlantic........Iowa
Avoca........Iowa
Arena........Wis
Avoca........Wis
Adrian........Mich
Albion........Mich
Allegan........Mich
Allens........Mich
Adamsville........Pa
Alexandria........Mo
Ashville........N Y
Atchison........Kan
Austin........Minn
Barry........Ill
Bath........Ill
Bement........Ill
Berlin, Sangamon Co........Ill
Blandinsville........Ill
Bloomington........Ill
Blue Island........Ill
Blue Mound........Ill
Bluff City........Ill
Bowen........Ill
Braidwood........Ill
Braceville........Ill
Bremen........Ill
Brighton........Ill
Bureau........Ill
Burnside........Ill
Bushnell........Ill
Baconburg........Ohio
Belle Center........Ohio
Bellefontaine........Ohio
Belleville........Ohio
Bellevue........Ohio
Belmore........Ohio
Berea........Ohio
Botkins........Ohio
Braceville........Ohio
Bradford........Ohio
Bryan........Ohio
Burbank........Ohio
Burg Hill........Ohio
Brimfield........Ind
Bristol........Ind
Brownsburg........Ind
Brownsville........Ind
Buck Creek........Ind
Buena Vista, Hamilton Co........Ind
Bunker Hill........Ind
Burlington, Rush Co........Ind
Butler........Ind
Bartlett........Iowa
Bentonsport........Iowa
Bloomfield........Iowa
Bonaparte........Iowa
Brighton........Iowa
Brooklyn........Iowa
Burlington........Iowa
Bigelow........Mo
Bonnot's Mill........Mo
Boonville........Mo
Bowling Green........Mo
Brownsville........Mo
Brunswick........Mo
Black Earth........Wis
Boscobel........Wis
Bridgeport........Wis
Brodhead........Wis
Big Rapids........Mich
Blissfield........Mich
Brady........Mich
Bronson........Mich
Burr Oak........Mich

Brownville ... Neb
Brainerd ... Minn
Buffalo ... N Y
Brooklyn ... N Y
Cambridge ... Ill
Camp Point ... Ill
Canton ... Ill
Carlinville ... Ill
Carthage ... Ill
Carrollton ... Ill
Catlin ... Ill
Cayuga ... Ill
Cerro Gordo ... Ill
Champaign ... Ill
Chandlerville ... Ill
Chapin ... Ill
Chatham ... Ill
Chatsworth ... Ill
Chenoa ... Ill
Chicago ... Ill
Chillicothe ... Ill
Clayton ... Ill
Colona ... Ill
Cuba ... Ill
Cairo, Allen Co ... Ohio
Caledonia ... Ohio
Calhoun ... Ohio
Carey ... Ohio
Carlisle ... Ohio
Carthage ... Ohio
Centerton ... Ohio
Ceylon ... Ohio
Cincinnati ... Ohio
Cleveland ... Ohio
Clyde ... Ohio
College Corner ... Ohio
Collins ... Ohio
Columbus ... Ohio
Clayton ... Mich
Clinton ... Mich
Clam Lake ... Mich
Coldwater ... Mich
Constantine ... Mich
Cambridge ... Pa
Cochranton ... Pa
Columbus ... Pa
Corry ... Pa
Cross Plains ... Wis
Carver ... Minn
Columbus Grove ... Ohio
Covington ... Ohio
Crestline ... Ohio
Criderville ... Ohio
Cumminsville ... Ohio
Custne ... Ohio
Calmar ... Iowa
Casey ... Iowa
Centerville ... Iowa
Charles City ... Iowa
Clear Lake ... Iowa
Colfax ... Iowa
Columbus Junction ... Iowa
Conover ... Iowa
Council Bluffs ... Iowa
Cresco ... Iowa
Cicero ... Ind
Connersville ... Ind
Corunna ... Ind
Covington ... Ind
Chambersburg ... Ind
Chesternon ... Ind
Crawfordsville ... Ind
California ... Mo
Camden Point ... Mo
Cameron ... Mo
Canton ... Mo
Carrollton ... Mo

Centralia ... Mo
Chamois ... Mo
Chillicothe ... Mo
Columbia ... Mo
Corning ... Mo
Craig ... Mo
Cakoka ... Mo
Concordia ... Mo
Cedar Springs ... Mich
Davenport ... Iowa
Decorah ... Iowa
Des Moines ... Iowa
De Soto ... Iowa
De Witt ... Iowa
Dexter ... Iowa
Doud ... Iowa
Downey ... Iowa
Drakeville ... Iowa
Durant ... Iowa
Danvers ... Ill
Danville ... Ill
Decatur ... Ill
Delavan ... Ill
Depue ... Ill
Dwight ... Ill
Dayton ... Ohio
Defiance ... Ohio
De Graff ... Ohio
Delta ... Ohio
Daleville ... Ind
Deerfield ... Ind
Delphi ... Ind
Dunkirk ... Ind
Deerfield ... Mich
Detroit ... Mich
Dunning ... Mich
De Witt ... Mo
Dresden ... Mo
Duluth ... Minn
Dunkirk ... N Y
East St. Louis ... Ill
Edwardsville ... Ill
Elkhart ... Ill
El Paso ... Ill
Elmwood ... Ill
Emden ... Ill
Ellsworth ... Ill
Eureka ... Ill
Evanston ... Ill
Edgerton ... Ohio
Elmore ... Ohio
Elyria ... Ohio
Eagle ... Wis
Edgerton ... Wis
Earlham ... Iowa
Eddyville ... Iowa
Eldora ... Iowa
Elkhart ... Ind
Evansburg ... Pa
Edina ... Mo
Findley ... Ohio
Forest ... Ohio
Fostoria ... Ohio
Fredericktown ... Ohio
Freedom ... Ohio
Fremont ... Ohio
Fairfield ... Ind
Farmland ... Ind
Fortville ... Ind
Fort Wayne ... Ind
Fairbury ... Ill
Fairmount ... Ill
Farmer City ... Ill
Fithian ... Ill
Forrest ... Ill
Fairfield ... Iowa
Farmington ... Iowa

Fort Dodge ... Iowa
Forest City ... Mo
Franklin ... Mo
Fulton ... Mo
Faribault ... Minn
Farmington ... Minn
Flowerfield ... Mich
Franklin ... Pa
Freehold ... Pa
Galva ... Ill
Gardner ... Ill
Geneseo ... Ill
Gilman ... Ill
Gibson ... Ill
Girard ... Ill
Godfrey ... Ill
Good Hope ... Ill
Greenview ... Ill
Green Valley ... Ill
Gridley ... Ill
Griggsville ... Ill
Georgetown ... Ill
Glencoe ... Minn
Galion ... Ohio
Garrettsville ... Ohio
Genoa ... Ohio
Gettysburg ... Ohio
Girard ... Ohio
Glendale ... Ohio
Green Spring ... Ohio
Greenville ... Ohio
Gallatin ... Mo
Glasgow ... Mo
Glenwood ... Mo
Gray's Summit ... Mo
Greenwood ... Mo
Grand Junction ... Iowa
Grinnell ... Iowa
Guthrie ... Iowa
Goodland ... Ind
Goshen ... Ind
Grand Haven ... Mich
Grand Rapids ... Mich
Grant, Chatauqua Co ... N Y
Greenville, Mercer Co ... Pa
Harristown ... Ill
Harisburg ... Ill
Havana ... Ill
Henry ... Ill
Highland Park ... Ill
Homer ... Ill
Hopedale ... Ill
Hoopeston ... Ill
Hamilton ... Ohio
Haskins ... Ohio
Havana ... Ohio
Hubbard ... Ohio
Hull Prairie ... Ohio
Huntsville ... Ohio
Huron ... Ohio
Hannibal ... Mo
Harrisonville ... Mo
Hermann ... Mo
High Hill ... Mo
Holden ... Mo
Hopkins ... Mo
Huntsville ... Mo
Homer ... Mich
Hamilton ... Mich
Hillsdale ... Mich
Holland ... Mich
Howard City ... Mich
Hudson ... Mich
Hartford City ... Ind
Hillsboro ... Ind

Huntington ..... Ind
Hastings ..... Minn
Hamburg ..... Iowa
Hampton ..... Iowa
Homestead ..... Iowa
Indianola ..... Iowa
Iowa City ..... Iowa
Ida, Monroe Co ..... Mich
Illiopolis Ill
Independence ..... Mo
Independence ..... Ohio
Indianapolis ..... Ind
Ivesdale Ill
Jacksonville Ill
Jerseyville Ill
Joliet Ill
Jefferson City ..... Mo
Jonesburg ..... Mo
Jamesport ..... Mo
Jackson ..... Mich
Jonesville ..... Mich
Jamestown ..... Ind
Jonesboro ..... Ind
Jamestown ..... N Y
Janesville ..... Wis
Jones' ..... Ohio
Kansas City ..... Mo
Keytesville ..... Mo
Kingsville ..... Mo
Kirksville ..... Mo
Knobnoster ..... Mo
Kent ..... Ohio
Kenton ..... Ohio
Kipton ..... Ohio
Kendallville ..... Ind
Kentland ..... Ind
Kokomo ..... Ind
Kellogg ..... Iowa
Keokuk ..... Iowa
Kalamazoo ..... Mich
Kane Ill
Keithsburg Ill
Kilbourne Ill
Kinderhook Ill
Kennedy ..... N Y
Kenosha ..... Wis
Lacon Ill
La Harpe Ill
Lake Forest Ill
La Salle Ill
Lemont Ill
Leroy Ill
Lexington Ill
Lincoln Ill
Litchfield Ill
Lockport Ill
Latham Ill
Lafayette ..... Ind
Lagrange ..... Ind
La Gro ..... Ind
Laporte ..... Ind
Liberty ..... Ind
Ligonier ..... Ind
Lima ..... Ind
Logansport ..... Ind
Leesburg ..... Ind
Le Roy, Osceola Co ..... Mich
Litchfield ..... Mich
La Rue ..... Ohio
Leavittsburg ..... Ohio
Leipsig ..... Ohio
Lexington ..... Ohio
Liberty Center ..... Ohio
Lima ..... Ohio
Rockland ..... Ohio
La Grange ..... Mo
Lamont ..... Mo

La Plata ..... Mo
Lathrop ..... Mo
Lee's Summit ..... Mo
Lexington ..... Mo
Louisiana ..... Mo
La Belle ..... Mo
Lewistown ..... Mo
Lancaster ..... Mo
Leavenworth ..... Kan
Leroy ..... Minn
Lime Springs ..... Iowa
Linesville ..... Iowa
Lone Rock ..... Wis
Mahomet Ill
Manchester Ill
Manito Ill
Marseilles Ill
Mason City Ill
McLean Ill
Mechanicsburg Ill
Meredosia Ill
Metamora Ill
Milan Ill
Minier Ill
Minooka Ill
Mokena Ill
Moline Ill
Morris Ill
Morrisonville Ill
Mounds Ill
Mt. Pulaski Ill
Mt. Sterling Ill
Murrayville Ill
Monticello Ill
Mackinaw Ill
Mansfield Ill
Milmine Ill
Mansfield ..... Ohio
Mantua ..... Ohio
Marion ..... Ohio
Maumee City ..... Ohio
Miamisburg ..... Ohio
Middletown ..... Ohio
Milford Center ..... Ohio
Milton, Wood Co ..... Ohio
Mingo ..... Ohio
Monroeville ..... Ohio
Mt. Vernon ..... Ohio
Mt. Victory ..... Ohio
Marion ..... Ind
Marsfield ..... Ind
Michigan City ..... Ind
Middlebury ..... Ind
Millersburg ..... Ind
Mishawaka ..... Ind
Monticello ..... Ind
Morristown, Shelby Co ..... Ind
Muncie ..... Ind
Milford ..... Ind
Manchester, Wabash Co ..... Ind
Macon ..... Mo
Macon ..... Mo
Martinsburg ..... Mo
Maryville ..... Mo
Mexico ..... Mo
Miami ..... Mo
Miller's Landing ..... Mo
Missouri City ..... Mo
Moberly ..... Mo
Monroe ..... Mo
Montgomery ..... Mo
Malcom ..... Iowa
Maquoketa ..... Iowa
Marengo ..... Iowa
Marshalltown ..... Iowa
Mason City ..... Iowa
McGregor ..... Iowa

Monona ..... Iowa
Monroe ..... Iowa
Moulton ..... Iowa
Muscatine ..... Iowa
Monticello ..... Iowa
Madison ..... Wis
Mazomaniac ..... Wis
Milton Junction ..... Wis
Milwaukee ..... Wis
Monroe ..... Wis
Muscoda ..... Wis
Manchester ..... Mich
Mendon ..... Mich
Monroe ..... Mich
Morley ..... Mich
Muskegon ..... Mich
Meadville ..... Pa
Mercer ..... Pa
Mill Village ..... Pa
Minneapolis ..... Minn
Moorhead ..... Minn
Napoleon ..... Ohio
Newark ..... Ohio
Newburg ..... Ohio
New Madison ..... Ohio
Newton ..... Ohio
Niles ..... Ohio
North Lewisburg ..... Ohio
Norwalk ..... Ohio
Naples Ill
Niantic Ill
Nilwood Ill
Normal Ill
New Boston Ill
New Carlisle ..... Ind
New Haven ..... Ind
Noblesville ..... Ind
New Paris ..... Ind
New Elizabeth ..... Ind
Napoleon ..... Mich
Norvell ..... Mich
Nebraska City ..... Neb
New Florence ..... Mo
New Sharon ..... Iowa
Newton ..... Iowa
New York City ..... N Y
Northfield ..... Minn
Oakland ..... Ohio
Oak Harber ..... Ohio
Oberlin ..... Ohio
Orangeville ..... Ohio
Osborn ..... Ohio
Ottawa ..... Ohio
Oxford ..... Ohio
Oskaloosa ..... Iowa
Ossian ..... Iowa
Ottumwa ..... Iowa
Odell ..... wl
Ottawa Ill
Oakford Ill
Ogden Ill
Osage ..... Mo
Otterville ..... Mo
Oxford ..... Ind
Oil City ..... Pa
Omaha ..... Neb
Osseo ..... Mich
Owatonna ..... Minn
Olathe ..... Kan
Palmer Ill
Paris Ill
Pekin Ill
Peoria Ill
Peru Ill
Petersburg Ill
Philo Ill
Piper City Ill

Pittsfield Ill
Plainview Ill
Pontiac Ill
Princeville Ill
Putnam Ill
Pleasant Hill Ill
Paxton Ill
Perrysburg .... Ohio
Pettisville .... Ohio
Phalanx .... Ohio
Piqua .... Ohio
Plain City .... Ohio
Plymouth .... Ohio
Poast Town .... Ohio
Polk, Ashland Co .... Ohio
Port Clinton .... Ohio
Pendleton .... Ind
Peru .... Ind
Plymouth .... Ind
Pittsboro .... Ind
Pella .... Iowa
Perry .... Iowa
Postville .... Iowa
Prairie City .... Iowa
Paris .... Mo
Parkville .... Mo
Pattonsburg .... Mo
Phelps .... Mo
Pleasant Hill .... Mo
Platte City .... Mo
Plattsburg .... Mo
Princeton .... Mo
Palmyra .... Wis
Prairie du Chien .... Wis
Paris .... Mich
Petersburg .... Mich
Pittsford .... Mich
Plainwell .... Mich
Pierson .... Mich
Panama .... N Y
Paola .... Kan
Quincy .... Ohio
Quincy Ill
Quincy .... Mich
Red Key .... Ind
Remington .... Ind
Richmond .... Ind
Ridgeville .... Ind
Ridge Farm .... Ind
Roanoke .... Ind
Rockfield .... Ind
Rochester .... Ind
Rolling Prairie .... Ind
Rome City .... Ind
Rushville .... Ind
Reynolds .... Ind
Raymond Ill
Rock Island Ill
Roodhouse Ill
Randolph .... N Y
Ravenna .... Ohio
Richmond .... Ohio
Rushsylvania .... Ohio
Ridgeway .... Ohio
Reno .... Pa
Riceville .... Pa
Reed City .... Mich
Rockwood .... Mich
Rockford .... Mich
Richmond .... Mo
Renick .... Mo
R. and Lex. Junction .... Mo
Racine .... Wis
Salisbury .... Mo
Savannah .... Mo
Sedalia .... Mo
Smithton .... Mo

South Point .... Mo
St. Auberts .... Mo
St. Charles .... Mo
St. Joseph .... Mo
St. Louis .... Mo
Sturgeon .... Mo
Syracuse .... Mo
Sadorus Ill
San Jose Ill
Sciota Ill
Secor Ill
Seneca Ill
Sheffield Ill
Sheldon Ill
Shipman Ill
Sidney Ill
Sparland Ill
Springfield Ill
Stanford Ill
State Line .... Ind and Ill
Staunton Ill
Stonington Ill
Streator Ill
St. Joseph Ill
Saybrook Ill
Sandusky .... Ohio
Seville .... Ohio
Shelby .... Ohio
Sidney .... Ohio
Solon .... Ohio
Springfield .... Ohio
St. Louisville .... Ohio
St. Paris .... Ohio
Stryker .... Ohio
Sylvania .... Ohio
Seda .... Ind
Selma .... Ind
Sparksville .... Ind
South Bend .... Ind
Silver Lake .... Inp
Spring Green .... Wis
Stoughton .... Wis
Schoolcraft .... Mich
Sturgis .... Mich
Sand Lake .... Mich
Saegertown .... Pa
Sharon .... Pa
Salamanca .... N Y
Steamburg .... N Y
State Line .... Kansas and Mo
St. Paul .... Minn
Stillwater .... Minn
Shakopee .... Minn
Sigourney .... Iowa
Steamboat Rock .... Iowa
Stuart .... Iowa
Summit .... Iowa
Talmadge .... Ohio
Tiffin .... Ohio
Tippecanoe .... Ohio
Toledo .... Ohio
Tontogany .... Ohio
Trenton .... Ohio
Troy, Miami Co .... Ohio
Tallula Ill
Taylorville Ill
Tiskilwa Ill
Tolono Ill
Toulon Ill
Towanda Ill
Tremont Ill
Tecumseh .... Mich
Three Rivers .... Mich
Trenton .... Mich
Tipton .... Mo
Trenton, Butler Co .... Mo
Tipton .... Ind

Titusville .... Pa
Urbana .... Ohio
Utica .... Ohio
Union City .... Ohio and Ind
Union, Erie Co .... Pa
Utica, Venango Co .... Pa
Urbana Ill
Utica Ill
Upper Alton Ill
Vanlue .... Ohio
Vermillion .... Ohio
Versailles .... Ohio
Varna Ill
Versailles Ill
Virden Ill
Virginia Ill
Venango, Crawford Co .... Pa
Victor .... Iowa
Valley City .... Ind
Wadsworth .... Ohio
Wakeman .... Ohio
Wapakoneta .... Ohio
Warren .... Ohio
Washington, Henry Co .... Ohio
Wauseon .... Ohio
West Liberty .... Ohio
Weston .... Ohio
West Salem .... Ohio
White House .... Ohio
Woodstock .... Ohio
Wabash .... Ind
Walkerton .... Ind
Waterloo City .... Ind
Waverly, Cass Co .... Ind
Waynetown .... Ind
Wawaka .... Ind
West Lebanon .... Ind
West Point .... Ind
Williamsport .... Ind
Winchester .... Ind
Wolcott, White Co .... Ind
Wolcottville .... Ind
Warsaw .... Ind
Warsaw Ill
Watseka Ill
Washburn Ill
Washington Ill
Waukegan Ill
Wenona Ill
Whitehall Ill
Williamsville Ill
Wilmington Ill
Wyoming Ill
Waverly Ill
Warrenton .... Mo
Warrensburg .... Mo
Washington .... Mo
Wellsville .... Mo
Wentzville .... Mo
Weston .... Mo
Wright's City .... Mo
Wheatland .... Iowa
Wyoming .... Iowa
Washington .... Iowa
Waukee .... Iowa
West Liberty .... Iowa
Wilton .... Iowa
Winterset .... Iowa
Waukesha .... Wis
Whitewater .... Wis
Wayland .... Mich
White Pigeon .... Mich
Wyandotte .... Mich
Wyandotte .... Kan
Xenia .... Ind
Yorktown .... Ind
Youngstown .... Ohio

Classified Index to Advertisements.

Teas—Wholesale.

Huestis & Hamilton.

Trunks, Valises &c.

Lingenfelser H. 52

Tobacco Factory.

Ford Charles. 44

Walnut Lumber.

Hoffman J. R. & Bro. 34

Watches, Clocks, &c.

Mayer George J. E. & F. Voirol 43
Mayer & Graffe 56
Pietz, J. Ferdinand

Wines and Liquors.

Leutz, Bourie & Co. 64
Laurent J. & Son

Woolen Mills.

French, Hanna & Co. 34

Constitution of the United States.

WE, the People of the United States, in order to form a more perfect union, establish justice, insure domestic tranquility, provide for the common defence, promote the general welfare and secure the blessings of liberty to ourselves and our prosperity, do ordain and establish this Constitution for the United States of America:

ARTICLE I.

§ I.—All legislative powers herein granted shall be vested in a Congress of the United States, which shall consist of a Senate and House of Representatives.

§ II.—1. The House of Representatives shall be composed of members chosen every second year by the people of the United States; and the electors in each State shall have the qualifications requisite for electors of the most numerous branch of the State Legislature.

2. No person shall be a representative who shall not have attained the age of twenty-five years, and been seven years a citizen of the United States, and who shall not, when elected, be an inhabitant of the State in which he is chosen.

3. Representatives and direct taxes shall be apportioned among the several States which may be included in this Union, according to their respective numbers, which shall be determined by adding to the whole number of free persons, including those bound to service for a term of years, and excluding Indians not taxed, three-fifths of all other persons. The actual enumeration shall be made within three years after the first meeting of the Congress of the United States, and within every subsequent term of ten years, in such manner as they shall by law direct. The number of representatives shall not exceed one from every thirty thousand, but each State shall have at least one representative; and until such enumeration shall be made, the State of New Hampshire shall be entitled

to choose three; Massachusetts, eight; Rhode Island and Providence Plantations, one; Connecticut, five; New York, six; New Jersey, four; Pennsylvania, eight; Delaware, one; Maryland, six; Virginia, ten; North Carolina, five; South Carolina, five; Georgia, three.

4. When vacancies happen in the representation of any State, the executive authority thereof shall issue writs of election to fill such vacancies.

5. The House of Representatives shall choose their speaker and other officers, and shall have the sole power of impeachment.

§ III.—1. The Senate of the United States shall be composed of two Senators from each State, chosen by the legislature thereof, for six years; and each Senator shall have one vote.

2. Immediately after they shall be assembled in consequence of the first election, they shall be divided as equally as may be, into three classes. The seats of the Senators of the first class shall be vacated at the expiration of the second year, of the second class at the expiration of the fourth year, and the third class at the expiration of the sixth year, so that one third may be chosen every second year; and if vacancies happen, by resignation or otherwise, during the recess of the legislature of any State, the executive thereof may make temporary appointments until the next meeting of the legislature, which shall then fill such vacancies.

3. No person shall be a Senator who shall not have attained the age of thirty years, and been nine years a citizen of the United States, and who shall not, when elected, be an inhabitant of that State for which he shall be chosen.

4. The Vice-President of the United States shall be President of the Senate, but shall have no vote, unless they be equally divided.

5. The Senate shall choose their other officers, and also a president pro tempore in the absence of the Vice-President, or when he shall exercise the office of President of the United States.

6. The Senate shall have the sole power to try all impeachments. When sitting for that purpose, they shall be on oath or affirmation. When the President of the United States is tried, the Chief Justice shall preside; and no person shall be convicted without the concurrence of two-thirds of the members present.

7. Judgment, in cases of impeachment, shall not extend further than to removal from office, and disqualification to hold and enjoy any office of honor, trust or profit under the United States; but the party convicted shall, nevertheless, be liable and subject to indictment, trial, judgment, and punishment, according to law.

§ IV.—1. The times, places, and manner of holding elections for senators and representatives shall be prescribed in each State by the legislature thereof; but the Congress may, at any time, by law, make or alter such regulations, except as to the places of choosing senators.

2. The Congress shall assemble at least once in every year; and such meeting shall be on the first Monday in December, unless they shall by law appoint a different day.

§ V. Each house shall be judge of the elections, returns, and qualifications of its own members; and a majority of each shall constitute a quorum to do business; but a smaller number may adjourn from day to day, and may be authorized to compel the attendance of absent members, in such manner and under such penalties as each house may provide.

2. Each house may determine the rules of its proceedings, punish its members for disorderly behavior, and, with the concurrence of two-thirds, expel a member.

3. Each house shall keep a journal of its proceedings, and from time to time publish the same, excepting such parts as may, in their judgment, require secrecy; and the yeas and nays of the members of either house on any question shall, at the desire of one-fifth of those present, be entered on the journal.

4. Neither house, during the session of Congress, shall, without the consent of the other, adjourn for more than three days, nor to any other place than that in which the two houses shall be sitting.

§ VI.—1. The senators and representatives shall receive a compensation for their services, to be ascertained by law, and paid out of the treasury of the United States. They shall, in all cases except treason, felony, and breach of the peace, be privileged from arrest during their attendance at the session of their respective houses, and in going to or returning from the same; and for any speech or debate in either house they shall not be questioned in any other place.

2. No senator or representative shall, during the time he was elected, be appointed to any civil office under the authority of the United States which shall have been created, or the emoluments whereof shall have been increased, during such time; and no person holding any office under the United States shall be a member of either house during his continuance in office.

§ VII.—1. All bills for raising revenue shall originate in the House of Representatives; but the Senate may propose or concur with amendments, as on other bills.

2. Every bill which shall have passed the House of Representatives and the Senate shall, before it becomes a law, be presented to the President of the United States; if he approve, he shall sign it; but if not, he shall return it with his objections, to that house in which it shall have originated, who' shall enter the objection at large on their journal, and proceed to reconsider it. If, after such reconsideration, two-thirds of that house shall agree to pass the bill, it shall be sent, together with the objections, to the other house; and, if approved by two-thirds of that house, it shall become a law. But in all such cases the votes of both houses shall be determined by yeas and nays; and the names of the persons voting for and against the bill shall be entered on the journals of each house respectively. If any bill shall not be returned by the President within ten days (Sundays excepted) after it shall have been presented to him, the same shall be a law, in like manner as if he had signed it, unless Congress, by their adjournment, prevent its return; in which case it shall not be a law.

3. Every order, resolution, or vote to which the concurrence of the House of Representatives may be necessary (except on a question of adjournment) shall be presented to the President of the United States, and before the same shall take effect shall be approved by him, or, being disapproved by him, shall be repassed by two-thirds of the Senate and House of Representatives, according to the rules and limitations prescribed in the case of a bill.

§ VIII.—The Congress shall have power—

1. To lay and collect taxes, duties, imposts, and excises; to pay the debts and provide for the common defense and general welfare of the United States; but all duties, imposts and excises shall be uniform throughout the United States:

2. To borrow money on the credit of the United States:

3. To regulate commerce with foreign nations, and among the several States, and with the Indian tribes:

4. To establish a uniform rule of naturalization, and uniform laws on the subject of bankruptcies, throughout the United States:

5. To coin money, regulate the value thereof, and of foreign coin, and fix the standard of weights and measures:

6. To provide for the punishment of counterfeiting the securities and current coin of the United States:

7. To establish post offices and post roads:

8. To promote the progress of science and useful arts, by securing, for limited times, to authors and inventors the exclusive right to their respective writings and discoveries:

9. To constitute tribunals inferior to the Supreme Court:

10. To define and punish piracies and felonies committed on the high seas, and offences against the law of nations:

11. To declare war, grant letters of marque and reprisal, and make rules concerning captures on land and water:

12. To raise and support armies; but no appropriation of money to that use shall be for a longer term than two years:

13. To provide and maintain a navy:

14. To make rules for the government and regulation of the land and naval forces:

15. To provide for calling forth the militia to execute the laws of the Union, suppress insurrections, and repel invasions:

16. To provide for organizing, arming, and disciplining the militia, and for governing such part of them as may be employed in the service of the United States, reserving to the States respectively the appointment of the officers, and the authority of training the militia, according to the discipline prescribed by Congress:

17. To exercise exclusive legislation, in all cases whatsoever, over such district (not exceeding ten miles square) as may, by cession of particular States, and the acceptance of Congress, become the seat of government of the United States, and to exercise like authority over all places purchased by the consent of the legislature of the State in which the same shall be, for the erection of forts, magazines, arsenals, dock yards, and other needful building: And,

18. To make all laws which shall be necessary and proper for carryrying into execution the foregoing powers, and all other powers vested by this Constitution in the government of the United States, or in any department or officer thereof.

§ IX.—1. The migration or importation of such persons as any of the States, now existing, shall think proper to admit, shall not be prohibited by the Congress prior to the year one thousand eight hundred and eight; but a tax or duty may be imposed on such importation, not exceeding ten dollars for each person.

2. The privilege of the writ of habeas corpus shall not be suspended, unless when, in cases of rebellion or invasion, the public safety may require it.

3. No bill of attainder, or ex post facto law, shall be passed.

4. No capitation or other direct tax shall be laid, unless in proportion to the census or enumeration herein before directed to be taken.

5. No tax or duty shall be laid on articles exported from any States. No preference shall be given, by any regulation of commerce or revenue, to the ports of one State over those of another; nor shall vessels bound to or from one State be obliged to enter, clear or pay duties in another.

6. No money shall be drawn from the treasury but in consequence of appropriation made by law; and a regular statement and account of the receipts and expenditure of all public money shall be published from time to time.

7. No title of nobility shall be granted by the United States; and no person holding any office of profit or trust under them shall, without the consent of the Congress, accept of any present, emolument, office, or title of any kind whatever, from any king, prince, or foreign State.

§ X.—1. No State shall enter into any treaty, alliance or confederation; grant letters of marque and reprisal; coin money; emit bills of credit; make anything but gold and silver a tender in payment of debts; pass any bill of attainder, ex post facto law, or impairing the obligation of contracts; or grant any title of nobility.

2. No State shall, without the consent of Congress, lay any imposts or duties on imports or exports, except what may be absolutely necessary for executing its inspection laws; and the net produce of all duties and imposts laid by any State on imports or exports shall be for the use of the treasury of the United States; and all such laws shall be subject to the revision and control of the Congress. No State shall, without the consent of Congress, lay any duty on tonnage, keep troops or ships of war in time of peace, enter into any agreement or compact with another State or with a foreign power, or engage in war, unless actually invaded, or in such imminent danger as will not admit of delay.

ARTICLE II.

§ I.—1. The executive power shall be vested in a President of the United States of America. He shall hold his office during the term of four years, and, together with the Vice-President, chosen for the same term, be elected as follows:

2. Each State shall appoint, in such manner as the legislature thereof may direct, a number of electors, equal to the whole number of Senators

and representatives to which the State may be entitled in the Congress; but no senator or representative, or person holding an office of trust or profit under the United States, shall be appointed an elector.

3. [Annulled. See Amendments, Art. 12.]

4. The Congress may determine the time of choosing the electors, and the day on which they shall give their votes, which day shall be the same throughout the United States.

5. No person except a natural-born citizen, or a citizen of the United States at the time of the adoption of this Constitution, shall be eligible to the office of President; neither shall any person be eligible to the office who shall not have attained the age of thirty-five years, and been fourteen years a resident within the United States.

6. In case of the removal of the President from office, or of his death, resignation, or inability to discharge the powers and duties of said office, the same shall devolve on the Vice-President; and the Congress may by law provide for the case of removal, death, resignation, or inability both of the President and Vice-President, declaring what officer shall then act accordingly, until the disability be removed, or a President shall be elected.

7. The President shall, at stated times, receive for his services a compensation which shall neither be increased nor diminished during the period for which he shall have been elected; and he shall not receive, within that period, any other emolument from the United States, or any of them.

8. Before he enter on the execution of his office, he shall take the following oath or affirmation:

"I do solemnly swear (or affirm) that I will faithfully execute the office of President of the United States, and will, to the best of my ability, preserve, protect, and defend the Constitution of the United States."

§ II.—1. The President shall be commander-in-chief of the army and navy of the United States, and of the militia of the several States, when called into the actual service of the United States: he may require the opinion, in writing, of the principal officer in each of the executive departments upon any subject relating to the duties of their respective offices; and he shall have power to grant reprieves and pardons for offences against the United States, except in cases of impeachment.

2. He shall have power, by and with the advice and consent of the Senate, to make treaties, provided two-thirds of the Senators present con-

cur; and he shall nominate, by and with the advice and consent of the Senate shall appoint, ambassadors, other public ministers, and consuls, judges of the Supreme Court, and all other officers of the United States whose appointments are not herein otherwise provided for, and which shall be established by law. But the Congress may, by law, vest the appointment of such inferior officers as they think proper in the President alone, in the courts of law, or the heads of departments.

3. The President shall have power to fill up all vacancies that may happen during the recess of the Senate, by granting commissions, which shall expire at the end of the next session.

§ III.—He shall, from time to time, give to the Congress information of the state of the Union, and recommend to their consideration such measures as he shall judge necessary and expedient; he may on extraordinary occasions, convene both houses, or either of them, and in case of disagreement between them with respect to the time of adjournment, he may adjourn them to such time as he shall think proper; he shall receive ambassadors and other public ministers; he shall take care that the laws are faithfully executed; and shall commission all the officers of the United States.

§ IV.—The President, Vice-President, and all the civil officers of the United States, shall be removed from office on impeachment for, and conviction of, treason, bribery, or other high crimes and misdemeanors.

ARTICLE III.

§ I.—The judicial power of the United States shall be vested in the Supreme Court, and in such inferior courts as the Congress may, from time to time, ordain and establish. The judges, both of the supreme and inferior courts, shall hold their offices during good behavior, and shall, at stated times, receive for their services a compensation which shall not be diminished during their continuance in office.

§ II.—1. The judicial power shall extend to all cases in law and equity arising under this Constitution, the laws of the United States, and treaties made, or which shall be made under their authority; to all cases affecting ambassadors, and other public ministers and consuls; to all cases of admiralty and maritime jurisdiction; to controversies to which the United States shall be a party; to controversies between two or more States; between a State and citizens of another State; between citizens of different States; between citizens of the same State, claiming lands under grants of different States, and between a State, or the citizens thereof, and foreign States, citizens or subjects.

2. In all cases affecting ambassadors, other public ministers, and consuls, and those in which a State shall be a party, the supreme court shall have original jurisdiction. In all other cases before mentioned, the supreme court shall have appellate jurisdiction, both as to law and fact, with such exceptions, and under such regulations, as the Congress shall make.

3. The trial of all crimes, except in cases of impeachment, shall be by jury; and such trial shall be held in the State where such crime shall have been committed; but when not committed within any State, the trial shall be at such place or places as the Congress may by law have directed.

§ III.—1. Treason against the United States shall consist only in levying war against them, or in adhering to their enemies, giving them aid and comfort. No person shall be convicted of treason, unless on the testimony of two witnesses to the same overt act, or confession in open court.

2. The Congress shall have power to declare the punishment of treason; but no attainder of treason shall work corruption of blood, or forfeiture, except during the life of the person attainted.

ARTICLE IV.

§ I.—Full faith and credit shall be given in each State to the public acts, records, and judicial proceedings of every other State. And the Congress may, by general laws, prescribe the manner in which such acts, records, and proceedings shall be proved, and the effect thereof.

§ II.—1. The citizens of each State shall be entitled to all privileges and immunities of citizens in the several States.

2. A person charged in any State with treason, felony, or other crime, who shall flee from justice, and be found in another State, shall, on demand of the executive authority of the State from which he fled, be delivered up to be removed to the State having jurisdiction of the crime.

3. No person held to service or labor in one State, under the laws thereof, escaping into another, shall, in consequence of any law or regulation therein, be discharged from such service or labor, but shall be

delivered up on claim of the party to whom such service or labor may be due.

§ III.—1. New States may be admitted by the Congress into this Union; but no new State shall be formed or erected within the jurisdiction of any other State; nor any State be formed by the junction of two or more States, or parts of States, without the consent of the legislature of the States concerned, as well as of the Congress.

2. The Congress shall have power to dispose of and make all needful rules and regulations respecting the territory or other property belonging to the United States; and nothing in this Constitution shall be so construed as to prejudice any claims of the United States, or of any particular State.

§ IV.—The United States shall guaranty to every State of this Union a republican form of government, and shall protect each of them against invasion, and, on application of the legislature, or of the executive, (when the legislature cannot be convened,) against domestic violence.

ARTICLE V.

The Congress, whenever two-thirds of both houses shall deem it necessary, shall propose amendments to this Constitution, or, on the application of the legislatures of two-thirds of the several States, shall call a convention for proposing amendments, which, in either case, shall be valid to all interests and purposes, as part of this Constitution when ratified by the legislatures of three-fourths of the several States, or by conventions in three-fourths thereof, as the one or the other mode of ratification may be proposed by the Congress; provided that no amendment which may be made prior to the year one thousand eight hundred and eight shall in any manner affect the first and fourth clauses in the ninth section of the first article; and that no State, without its consent, shall be deprived of its equal suffrage in the Senate.

ARTICLE VI.

1. All debts contracted, and engagements entered into, before the adoption of this Constitution, shall be as valid against the United States under this Constitution as under the confederation.

2. This Constitution, and the laws of the United States which shall be made in pursuance thereof, and all treaties made, or which shall be made, under the authority of the United States, shall be the supreme law

of the land; and the judges in every State shall be bound thereby; any thing in the Constitution or laws of any State to the contrary notwithstanding.

3. The senators and representatives before mentioned, and the members of the several State legislatures, and all executive and all judicial officers, both of the United States and of the several States, shall be bound by oath or affirmation to support this Constitution; but no religious test shall ever be required as a qualification to any office or public trust under the United States.

RRTICLE VII.

The ratification of the conventions of nine States shall be sufficient for the establishment of this Constitution between the States so ratifying the same.

Done in Convention, by the unanimous consent of the States present, the seventeenth day of September, in the year of our Lord one thousand seven hundred and eighty-seven, and of the Independence of the United States of America the twelfth. In witness whereof we have hereunto subscribed our names.

GEORGE WASHINGTON,
President, and Deputy from Virginia.

NEW HAMPSHIRE.
John Langdon,
Nicholas Gilman.

MASSACHUSETTS.
Nathaniel Gorham,
Rufus King.

CONNECTICUT.
Wm. S. Johnson,
Roger Sherman.

NEW YORK.
Alexander Hamilton,

NEW JERSEY.
William Livingston,
David Brearley,
William Patterson,
Jonathan Dayton.

PENNSYLVANIA.
Benjamin Franklin,
Thomas Mifflin,
Robert Morris,
George Clymer,
Thomas Fitzsimmons,
Jared Ingersoll,
James Wilson,
Gouverneur Morris.

DELAWARE.
George Read,
Gunning Bedford, jr.,
John Dickinson,
Richard Bassett,
Jacob Broom.

MARYLAND.
James McHenry,
Daniel of St. Tho. Jenifer,
Daniel Carroll.

VIRGINIA.
John Blair,
James Madison, jr.,

NORTH CAROLINA.
William Blount,
Rich. Dobbs Spaight,
Hugh Williamson.

SOUTH CAROLINA.
John Ruthledge,
Charles C. Pinckney,
Charles Pinckney,
Pierce Butler.

GEORGIA.
William Few,
Abraham Baldwin.

Attest: WILLIAM JACKSON, *Secretary.*

Amendments to the Constitution.

ART. I.—Congress shall make no law respecting an establishment of religion, or prohibiting the free exercise thereof; or abridging the freedom of speech, or of the press; or the right of the people peaceably to assemble and petition the government for a redress of grievances.

ART. II.—A well-regulated militia being necessary to the security of a free State, the right of the people to keep and bear arms shall not be infringed.

ART. III.—No soldier shall in time of peace, be quartered in any house without the consent of the owner, nor in time of war but in a manner to be prescribed by law.

ART. IV.—The right of the people to secure in their persons, houses, papers, and effects, against unreasonable searches and seizures, shall not be violated; and no warrants shall issue but upon probable cause, supported by oath or affirmation, and particularly prescribing the place to be searched, and the persons or things to be seized.

ART. V.—No person shall be held to answer for a capital or otherwise infamous crime, unless on a presentment or indictment of a grand jury, except in cases arising in the land or naval forces, or in the militia when in actual service, in time of war or public danger; nor shall any person be subject for the same offence to be twice put in jeopardy of life or limb; nor shall be compelled, in any criminal case, to be witness against himself, nor be deprived of life, liberty, or property, without due process of law; nor ahall private property be taken for public use without just compensation.

VI.—In all criminal prosecutions, the accused shall enjoy the right of a speedy and public trial by an impartial jury of the State and district wherein the crime shall have been committed, which district shall have been previously ascertained by law, and to be informed of the nature and cause of the accusation; to be confronted with the witnesses against him; to have compulsory process for obtaining witnesses in his favor; and to have the assistance of counsel for his offence.

ART. VII.—In suits of common law, where the value in controversy shall exceed twenty dollars, the right of trial by jury shall be preserved; and no fact, tried by a jury, shall be otherwise re-examined in any court of the United States than according to the rules of the cammon law.

ART. VIII.—Excessive bail shall not be required, nor excessive fines imposed, nor cruel and unusual punishment inflicted.

ART. IX.—The enumeration in the Constitution of certain rights shall not be construed to deny or disparage others retained by the people.

ART. X.—The powers not delegated to the United States by the Constitution, nor prohibited by it to the States, are reserved to the States respectively, or to the people.

ART. XI.—The judicial power of the United States shall not be construed to extend to any suit in law or equity commenced or prosecuted against one of the United States by citizens of another State, or by citizens for subjects of any foreign State.

ART. XII.—The electors shall meet in their respective States, and vote by ballot for President and Vice-President, one of whom, at least, shall not be an inhabitant of the same State with themselves; they shall name in their ballots the person voted for as President, and in distinct ballots the person voted for as Vice-President; and they shall make distinct lists of all persons voted for as President, and of all persons voted for as Vice-President, and of the number of votes for each; which lists they shall sign and certify, and transmit, sealed, to the seat of government of the United States, directed to the president of the Senate. The president of the Senate shall, in the presence of the Senate and House of Representatives, open all the certificates, and the votes shall then be counted; the person having the greatest number of votes for President shall be President, if such number shall be a majority of the whole number of electors appointed; and if no person have such a mojority, then from the persons having the highest number, not exceeding three, on the list of those voted for as President, the House of Representatives shall choose immediately, by ballot, the President. But, in choosing the President, the votes shall be taken by States, the representation from each State having one vote; a quorum for this purpose shall consist of a member or members from two-thirds of the States, and a majority of all the States shall be necessary to a choice. And if the House of Representatives shall not choose a President, whenever the right of choice shall devolve upon them, before the fourth day of March next following, then the Vice-President shall act as President, as in the case of the death or other constitutional disability of the President.

2. The person having the greatest number of votes for Vice-President shall be the Vice-Presidert, if such number be a majority of the whole number of electors appointed; and if no person have a majority, then from the two highest numbers on the list the Senate shall choose the Vice-President; a quorum for the purpose shall consist of two.thirds of the whole number of senators, and a majority of the whole number shall be necessary to a choice.

3. But no person constitutionally ineligible to the office of President shall be eligible to the office of Vice President of the United States.

The Constitutional Amendment.

ABOLISHING SLAVERY.

ARTICLE V. of the Constitution of the United States clearly and distinctly sets forth the mode and manner in which said instrument may be amended, as follows:

"The Congress, whenever two-thirds of both houses shall deem it necessary, shall propose amendments to this Constitution, or, on the application of the Legislatures of two-thirds of the several States, shall call a convention for proposing amendments, which in either case shall be valid to all intents and purposes, as part of this Constitution, when ratified by the Legislatures of three-fourths of the several States, or conventions in three-fourths thereof, as the one or the other mode of ratification may be proposed by the Congress."

In accordance with this article of the Constitution, the following resolution was proposed in the Senate, on February 1, 1864, adopted April 8, 1864, by a vote of thirty-eight to six, and was proposed in the House June 15, 1864, adopted January 31, 1865, by a vote of 119 to 56:

Resolved, By the Senate and House of Representatives of the United States of America, in Congress assembled, two-thirds of both Houses concurring, that the following article be proposed to the Legislatures of the several States, as an amendment to the Constitution of the United States, which, when ratified by three-fourths of said Legislatures, shall be valid to all intents and purposes, as part of said Constitution, namely:

Article XIII.—1st. Neither slavery or involuntary servitude, except as a punishment of crime, whereof the party shall have been duly convicted, shall exist within the United States, or any place subject to their jurisdiction.

The amendment was now sent by the Secretary of State to the Governors of the several States for ratification by the Legislatures; a majority vote in three-fourths being required to make it a law of the land.

On December 18, 1865, Secretary Seward officially announced to the country the ratification of the amendment, as follows:

To all to whom these presents may come, Greeting:

KNOW YE, That, whereas the Congress of the United States, on the 1st of February last, passad a resolution, which is in the words following, namely:

"A resolution submitting to the Legislatures of the several States a proposition to amend the Constitution of the United States."

"*Resolved*, By the Senate and House of Representatives of the United States of America in Congress assembled, two-thirds of both Houses concurring, that the following article be proposed to the Legislatures of the the several States as an amendment to the Constitution of the United States, which, when ratified by three-fourths of said Legislatures, shall be valid to all intents and purposes as a part of said Constitution, namely:

"'ARTICLE VIII.

"'SECTION 1. Neither slavery nor involuntary servitude, except as a punishment for crime, whereof the party shall have been duly convicted, shall exist within the United States, or any place subject to their jurisdiction.

"'SECTION 2. Congress shall have power to enforce this article by appropriate legislation.'"

And whereas, It appears from official documents on file in this department, that the amendment to the Constitution of the United States proposed as aforesaid, has been ratified by the Legislatures of the States of Illinois, Rhode Island, Michigan, Maryland, New York, West Virginia, Maine, Kansas, Massachusetts, Pennsylvania, Virginia, Ohio, Missouri, Nevada, Indiana, Louisiana, Minnesota, Wisconsin, Vermont, Tennessee, Arkansas, Connecticut, New Hampshire, South Carolina, Alabama, North Carolina, and Georgia, in all twenty-seven States.

And whereas, The whole number of States in the United States is thirty-six.

And whereas, The before specially named States, whose Legislatures have ratified the said proposed amendment, constitute three-fourths of the whole number of States in the United States:

Now, therefore, be it known that I, William H. Seward, Secretary of State of the United States, by virtue and in pursuance of the second section of the act of Congrees approved the 20th of April, 1818, entitled "An act to provide for the publication of the laws of the United States, and for other purposes," do hereby certify that the amendment aforesaid has become valid to all intents and purposes as a part of the Constitution of the United States.

In testimony whereof, I have hereunto set my hand and caused the seal of the Department of State to be affixed.

Done at the City of Washington, this 18th day of December, in the year of our Lord 1865, and of the Independence of the United States of America the ninetieth.

WILLIAM H. SEWARD,

Secretary of State.

Townships in Allen County,

WITH SHORT SKETCHES OF THEIR

LOCATION, SOIL, PRODUCTIONS, MANUFACTURES, RELIGIOUS AND SOCIAL ORGANIZATIONS, &c.

ABOITE

Township, situated in the western part of the county, and bounded on the north by Lake, on the east by Wayne, on the south by Lafayette, and on the west by Whitley County, was first settled in 1833 by Jesse Vermilyea, Richard Andrews, Richard Clark, Enoch Turner, William A. Gouty and Lot S. Bayless. Enoch Turner is the only one of these first settlers now residing in the Township. The surface of the Township is rolling, the soil fertile and well timbered. The Aboit river, from which the township derives its name, flows through is in a southerly direction. The most direct means of communication with the township are by the Huntington and Illinois State Roads. The former striking the township about five miles from Fort Wayne, the latter branching off from the Huntington road about four miles from the city and running in a westerly direction through the northern portion of the township. The Toledo, Wabash and Western Railroad passes through the southern portion of the township, but has no station. There is no post-master or post office, Fort Wayne being the post office address of nearly all the inhabitants. There is a Township Library of 201 volumes, Wm. A. Hamilton, Librarian. The Township contains eight School Houses, and one Church. The population of the township is, males, 361; females,, 363; total, 724.

ADAMS

Township, bounded on the north by St. Joseph, on the east by Jefferson on the south by Marion and on the west by Wayne townships, was first settled about the year of 1823, by Jesse Adams, L. Edmonds, Charles Weeks and Israel Taylor, who were soon followed by others. The first birth in the township was that of John S. Rogers, October, 1825. The first death that of a daughter of Mrs. L. Adams, in the same month of the same year. The surface of the country is level and very heavily timbered, the soil fertile, a rich clayey loam, and well adapted to the raising of wheat, rye, oats and root crops.

The Maumee river flows through the township from east to west. The Six Mile creek also insures fertility in its immediate vicinity, and affords an excellent milling power. This township contains the village of New Haven, the largest and most enterprising village out side of Fort Wayne in Allen County. The means of transportation through and communication with this township are most ample. The Toledo, Wabash and Western Railway passes through the northern part, the Pittsburgh, Fort Wayne and Chicago Railway through the central part, and the Wabash and Erie canal through the northern part.

The old Piqua road and New Haven Pike, the latter deserving especial mention as the best road in the county, are the principal ones in the township. John Rogers is probably the oldest of the first settlers now residing in the township. The population of Adams township, exclusive of the village of New Haven, is as follows: males, 796; females, 640; total, 1,436.

New Haven, the only town of any note in the township, and the largest and most enterprising village in the county, is situated on the Wabash and Erie Canal and Toledo, Wabash and Western Railway, six miles east of Fort Wayne. This is a finely located and rapidly growing town, was laid out about the year 1846, by Henry Burgess, a native of the State of Connecticut, who gave it the name of New Haven in Honor of that "City of Elms" in his native State.

As a place of buisness, a location for a fine residence, or a manufacturing point, New Haven has many advantages--a good soil, good water power, facilities for transportation and travel by canal and railroad, and situated in an almost inexhaustable tract of the best timber country, which supplies the material for several large manufactorties of lumber, staves, heading, barrels, lath, shingles, etc., and gives constant employment to a great number of hands. The population of the place is, males, 510; females, 456. Making a total in Adams Township, including New Haven, of 2,057 souls.

CEDAR CREEK

Township, is bounded on the north by DeKalb County, east by Springfield Township, south by Milan and St. Joe, west by Perry. It was settled by Joseph Shields, William Shields, John Manning, Moses Siwitz, sr., P. Notestine and others. Cedar Creek, from which the Township derives its name, flows through the central part, from north-east, furnishing good water power which is being employed by Mr. John Vanzile, at the Pin Oak Mills, near the west line of the township, and by Miller, Stoner & Bro., at Cedarville, in running a first-class flouring mill, circular saw mill and plaining mill. The St. Joseph river flows through the eastern part of the township, from north-east to south-wast. The bottom lands along this river are among the most fertile in the county. The soil in the Cedar Creek bottoms is mostly sand, that near the river loam, and on the uplands a mixture of sand, clay and loam. The timber is hickory, oak, beach, ash, elm, butternut, walnut, willow, and some cottenwood. Grain, hay, fruit, stock, etc., are raised in abundance in all parts of the township. Farms and roads are generally well kept. The township contains ten school houses, valued at $6,000; four churches valued at about $6,000; four flouring mills valued at $33,000; five saw mills valued at $10,-500; a woolen factory worth $4,000; a stavé factory worth $5,000, and a shingle mill worth $4,000. There are two post offices, Leo, J. W. Baird, P. M., and Cedarville, John W. Smith, P. M. Population, 1613; males 775, females, 838.

HAMILTON, Leo Post Office, is situated on the west bank of the St. Joe river, about fourteen miles north-east of Fort Wayne. It contains three churches, one Methodist Episcopal, one United Brethren, one Catholic; a two story brick school house, one flouring mill, one steam saw mill, one tannery, a stave factory, a shingle factory, a woolen factory, three stores, one saloon, two blacksmith shops, a manufactory of horse rakes, three boot and shoe shops, one tin shop and two wagon shops. There is one physician in that place, and a pastor to each of the churches. A lodge of F. & A. M. meets monthly. There is also a flourishing lodge of Good Templars. Population about 240.

CEDARVILLE is pleasantly situated between the St. Joe river and Cedar Creek, near the mouth of the latter. It contains one church, (Methodist Episcopal,) one saw mill, one grist mill, a planing machine, a shingle factory, one store, one grocery, in which the post office is kept, a blacksmith shop, and one wagon shop. Cedarville, though its name has long been on the connty map, is in fact, now only in the third year of its existence, is rapidly growing, and its inhabitants feel sanguine that it will become one of the first villages of the county. They are encouraged in this belief by the fact that it is accessible by steamboats on the St. Joe river, even at the lowest water mark.

EEL RIVER

Township, situated in the north-western part of the county, is bounded on the north and west by Noble County, on the east by Perry, and on the south by Lake and Washington townships. It was first settled in the year 1823 by F. S. Shoaff, Wm Mooney, Oliver Potter, Geo. Hand, and others. The surface of the township is generally level. The southern and eastern part being almost entirely prairie. The soil is a rich loam, well adapted to the raising of corn and grass. The principal streams are Eel River and Willow Creek. The township contains nine school houses, and one in the course of construction, two of which are brick, and the remaining seven are wooden structures; three churches, one Methodist, one Baptist and one United Brethren; two post offices, one Heller's Corners, west of the centre of the township, Thomas R. Morrison, post master, another in the western part of the township, on the Goshen road, Norris Heller, post master; one steam saw mill, one dry goods store, one boot and shoe establishment, two gunsmith shops, and one lodge of Good Templars. There are two ministers, two physicians, and one lawyer residing in the township, from which any inference may be drawn that will suit the taste of the reader. The number of scholars enrolled the last enumeration was 526. The oldest citizens residing in the township are William Bennett, 88 years old; Samuel Harrison, 72; Nathan Bennett, 72. The population of the township is as follows: Males, 570; females, 521; total, 1,091.

JACKSON

Township, situated in the eastern (or south-eastern) part of Allen county, is bounded on the north by Maumee, on the south by Monroe, on the west by Jefferson and on the east by Paulding county.

The surface of the county is flat and very heavily timbered, the lumber which it affords finding a very ready and convenient market at Monroeville. Flat Rock Creek and an unnamed tributary are the only streams in the county. The soil is strong and well adapted to the growing of grains and grasses, and fruit and root crops. Some of the land, however, would be greatly improved by a thorough system of drainage. The first settlement was made in the year 1840 by George Bale, George Hollinger and Robert Mooney. The oldest settler now living in the township is George Hollinger.

The township contains three school houses, the last one being erected in 1868; no church, and one township library, in care of the Trustee, Samuel Balyard. The principal roads traversing the township are the Sugar Ridge Road, from Fort Wayne to Van Wert, Ohio, the Paulding and Van Wert and the Paulding and Monroeville roads.

Monroeville and New Haven are the principal shipping points and post office address for citizens of this township.

The township is very sparsely settled as yet, most of the land being owned by capitalists in Fort Wayne and other points abroad. The number of males in the township is 102; females, 85; total population, 187.

JEFFERSON

Township is bounded on the north by Milan, on the east by Jackson, on the south by Madison, and on the west by Adams townships. The surface is generally level, with a few good ridges of excellent land. The level land lying on the eastern part of the township is well timbered and only requires drainage to make it the most productive in the county, for grasses especially. The first settlement was made by Messrs. Whitney and Blackmore, in the year 1833. This was once a favorite Indian hunting ground, the streams abounding in fish, and to this day traces of the beaver are plain in many of the creeks, and arrows and tomahawks of rude manufacture are frequently upturned by the plowshare. Wolves are said to have been a great pest to the early settlers, frequently committing serious depredations on their smaller stock. The oldest inhabitants in the townshtp are Joseph Gronauer, A. Whitney, A. Wolf, Aretas Powers and William Harper. The first birth was that of Reuben Powers, in the year 1837. The first marriage was that of Reuben Powers, sr., to Miss Eveline Whitney, in 1838, by William Brown, Esq.; first death was that of a child (drowned), in the year 1836. The Maumee river flows through the northwestern part of the township. The Wabash & Erie canal and the Toledo, Wabash & Western railway pass through the northern and the Pittsburgh, Fort Wayne & Chicago railway through the southeastern corner of the township.

MAPLES, a small post office village of about 200 inhabitants, situated on the Pittsburgh, Fort Wayne & Chicago railway, about ten miles from Fort Wayne, boasts one dry goods store, one grocery and saloon, one stave factory, Fitch & Maples, proprietors, which is doing a very prosperous business. It has also a prosperous I. O. G. T. lodge. Two doctors reside in the village. The township contains one church (Catholic) comprising a charge of 103 families, eleven schools and a township library in good condition. The population of the township is rated as follows: Males, 615; females, 512; total, 1,127.

LAFAYETTE

Township, which receives its name from the Marquis de Lafayette, so celebrated for the part he bore in our Revolutionary history, the southwest corner township of Allen county, is bounded on the north by Aboite and on the east by Pleasant townships, on the south by Wells and on the west by Huntington counties. It was laid out by sections in 1840 and was first settled in the following year by James Wilson, William Jobs and Samuel Fogwell. Rebecca Fogwell was the first white child born. The first death was that of Samuel Fogwell. The township is well watered —in the southern part by Eight Mile creek, in the northern part by Little river and in other parts by smaller streams. The Indianapolis and Huntington roads cross the township in a southwesterly direction and are the principal means of transportation. In the northwestern part the surface is very rolling, but becomes more level toward the opposite corner. The soil is very fertile and is well timbered, principally with maple, hickory, oak and walnut, but in some parts of the township considerable quantities of poplar is found. As a proof of the quality of the soil and the industry of the inhabitants, one need only to look at the finely improved farms whose bountiful harvests of grains and fruits, and substantial buildings and surroundings that now gladden the eye of the old pioneer as well as the passer-by, where thirty years ago the silence of an almost impenetrable forest reigned supreme. The principal products are wheat, corn, oats and flax. The township contains eleven school houses, two churches (one German Methodist and one Evangelical Association), three saw mills and three post offices—Aboite, in the northwestern part of the township, nine miles from Fort Wayne; the Nine Mile post office, which, as its name implies, is nine miles from Fort Wayne, is in the eastern part, and

ZANESVILLE, a small postal village of about 250 inhabitants, in the southern part, on the line of division between Wells and Allen counties, fifteen miles from Fort Wayne. It contains one church, one general store, one shoe shop, one blacksmith shop, one wagon shop, and one saw mill.

The Toledo, Wabash & Western railway passes through the northwestern part of the township, along the northern bank of Little river, but has no station. The population of the township ranks: Males, 657; females, 622; total, 1,279.

LAKE

Township, in the western part of the county, is bounded on the north by Whitley county and Eel River township, on the east by Washington and on the south by Aboite townships, and on the west by Whitley county. It was first settled in 1835 by Andrew Forsythe, who was followed in the fall of the same year by William Luckey, Samuel Caffrey and James Pringle. John McClure, Francis Sweet and Samuel Pierson settled here in 1837, and the first election was held in April of the same year. There are three churches (one Methodist Episcopal, one Free Will Baptist and one United Brethren), one church organization of the Catholic faith, with a membership of seventy families, mostly of foreign birth; a Good Templar's lodge and a township library. The soil is fertile, but in some parts rather low, all of this, however, is capable of being improved under a system of thorough drainage. Wheat and corn are the principal products. Sorghum is also raised in considerable quantities in some parts of the township. The Pittsburgh, Fort Wayne & Chicago railway traverses the southern portion of the township. It is well watered by Aboite creek in the southern part and a fine lake and its tributary in the northern part. There are eleven school districts, with an attendance of 473 scholars. The township (Arcola included) has a population of 629 males and 537 females; total 1,166.

ARCOLA is a post office village in the southwestern part of the township, and a station on the Pittsburgh, Fort Wayne & Chicago railway, eight miles from Fort Wayne. It contains one grocery and dry goods store, one saw mill, one shingle and lath factory, one wagon shop, one blacksmith shop, one boot and shoe shop, one saloon and two physicians. Population: Males, 66; females, 35; total, 101.

MADISON

Township is located in the southeastern part of Allen county, and is bounded on the north by Jefferson township, on the south by Wells county, on the east by Monroe and on the west by Marion township. The Pittsburgh, Fort Wayne & Chicago railway passes through the northeast corner of the township and is the only means of transportation. Monroeville, in Monroe township, is the nearest shipping point, being about five miles from the center of this township. The first settlement was made in 1838 by Messrs. ——— Browning, William Hill, George Eagy, Andrew Meek, John Edwards and Milton Holmes. The oldest man in the township is Adam Emencheiser, age 92. The township contains several saw mills, carpenters, two blacksmith shops, three churches (one Presbyterian, erected in 1848; one Evangelical Lutheran, erected in 1866; one Lutheran, erected in 1846), ten district schools, with an average attendance of thirty-five scholars each, one Vigilant Committee, or society, organized ten or fifteen years ago, owing to the depredations of horse-thieves. The surface is flat and heavily timbered with oak, ash, walnut, poplar, etc. The soil good and well adapted to the raising of all kinds of grain, fruit and grass —grazing being especially good.

This township was traversed by old General Wayne in his route to Fort Wayne from Piqua. There is no post office in the township, the mails being received at Monroeville. There are no running streams in the township, but it is well watered by springs, &c. Population: Males, 483; females, 425; total, 908.

MARION

Township, the keystone in the southern tier of Allen county townships, is bounded on the north by Adams, on the east by Madison, on the west by Pleasant townships and on the south by Adams county. The surface is slightly rolling, heavily timbered and well watered. The soil is rich, sandy loam and universally good, there being no waste land in the township. Wheat, oats and corn are the principal product. The township was first settled in 1835 by Jesse Heaton, sen., David Spitler, C. Lipes, Garret Norton, Thomas Thompson and —— Marion, from whom the township derived its name at its organization in 1836. These were soon followed by Judge McLain, David McLain, John M. Sorg and others, who settled on the east bank of the St. Mary's river, along the present location of the Piqua road.

The oldest inhabitant now living in the township is Jesse Heaton, 80 years of age. Himself and wife still live on the farm located by him 34 years ago.

The principal roads traversing the township are the Piqua road, or old plank road from Fort Wayne to Decatur, the Winchester road, running along the western ridge, the Flat Rock road from Williamsport to Van

Wert, Ohio, and the old Piqua road, or what is generally known as the Wayne trace, the route Gen. Wayne and his army traversed on their way to Fort Wayne.

WILLIAMSPORT, a small post office town, is situated in the southwestern part of the township, on the west bank of the St. Mary's river. It contains one store, one saw mill, one flouring mill, M. Cody, of Fort Wayne, proprietor, one shoe shop, one wagon shop, two blacksmith shops, two churches (one Presbyterian and one Methodist Episcopal), one school house and a post office.

MIDDLETOWN, another modest hamlet, is situated about a mile and a half from the center of the township, on the Piqua road, eleven miles from Fort Wayne. It contains one store, one blacksmith shop, one saw mill, Messrs. Moneysmith and Morton, proprietors, one post office, two cooper shops, one hotel, one church (Methodist Episcopal, erected in 1854), one school house and a Masonic lodge, organized in 1854, and now in a very flourishing condition.

The township is well supplied with religious and educational advantages. There are seven church organizations—one Roman Catholic, one Baptist, one Presbyterian, two Methodist Episcopal and two German Lutheran. There are fourteen schools in the township—two Roman Catholic (one a Sisters' school, situated near the church, on the Piqua road, eight miles from Fort Wayne), two German Lutheran, and ten district schools, with a population of 656 males and 607 females; total, 1,263.

MAUMEE

Township, located in the eastern part of the county, is bounded on the north by Springfield and Scipio, on the south by Jackson, on the west by Milan townships and on the east by Paulding county, Ohio. It was first settled by Ulrich Saylor, sr., Ulrich Saylor, jr., and Solomon Swisher, in 1837. The township was organized in 1843. The first marriage was that of Betsey E. Saylor and Charles Harding, in 1841. The oldest settlers now living are Ulrich Saylor, sr., Ulrich Saylor jr., and William Johnson. The township is traversed by the Maumee river, the Wabash & Erie canal and the Toledo, Wabash & Western railway. The surface is flat and in many places swampy. There are three school houses, a township library, a grocery at Bull Rapids and a station and post office called Woodburn, on the Toledo, Wabash & Western railway, sixteen miles from Fort Wayne. Population: Males, 179; females, 150; total, 329.

MILAN

Township, lying on the eastern part of the county, is bounded on the north by Cedar Creek and Springfield, on the east by Maumee, on the south by Jefferson and on the west by St. Joseph townships. The first settlements were made from 1838 to 1840 inclusive, near the Maumee river, by Alvin Hall, George Forstater, Charles Schreiner, Nathan Lake, John Nuttle, Wilkes Gillet, Andrew Wakefield, Richard Barrow and others. The oldest inhabitants now living are R. D. Nuttle, Charles Schreiner and Alvin Hall, who came respectively in the years 1835, 1837 and 1838. The township contains eight school houses, valued at $3,500, a Lutheran society, holding its services in a school house, a township library and a post office on the Ridge road. The principal streams are Maumee river, Six Mile, Nine Mile and Ten Mile creeks. The Wabash & Erie canal and the Toledo, Wabash & Western railway pass through the township. The northwest part (about one-third of the township), contains some of the finest farming lands in the county. The balance, however, is rather low and swampy, but, if properly drained, would make a good grazing country. Population: Males, 604; females, 596; total, 1,100.

MONROE

Township is located in the southeast corner of Allen county, midway between the St. Mary's and Maumee river, a distance of sixteen miles from Fort Wayne and bordering on the Ohio State line fourteen miles from Van Wert. This township has the facilities afforded by the Pittsburgh, Fort Wayne and Chicago railroad running direct through its center, thus rendering an easy access to the city of Fort Wayne, or the village of Van Wert, by rail, and affording a good market for the immense amount of choice timber for which it is noted. The land is of an undulating surface, composed of rich, black sandy loam well adapted to the raising of corn, wheat, oats, rye, barley, potatoes and grass, with all the cereals requisite for table use. The principal commerce consists of the large quantity of staves, spokes, lumber and hub timber, together with the hoop poles and live stock which are being constantly shipped from Monroeville, the principal market place, situated in the center of the township. It was first settled in 1838 or 1839 by a few hardy pioneers who had the courage and fortitude so essential to the early settlers to induce them to forego the comforts and societies of older States for the new and most bitter trials of manhood which have to be endured in settling up a new country, in the midst of a dense wilderness, far from markets of any kind, with nothing to cheer them but the prospects of the future. Among them there are none more worthy of note than Peter Slemmer and Hugh Anderson, the two first settlers of this township, or of those who immediately followed them, Noah Clem, Samuel Clem, William Rabbit, Moses Ratledge, William Ratledge, Elijah Redenhouse, John Fredline, John Stephenson, Thomas Meeks and Asa Dillon, many of whom are still living upon their now old and improved farms, and are capable yet of telling of the self-trying times they have endured that they might reap the benefits in their old days.

The first white male child born in the township was John Ratlege. The oldest man now living in the township is Hugh Anderson, who, though very old, is still able to look to the interests of his farm and household. This, unlike most other townships, can boast of a smart, thriving village situated about the center of it, wherein are constantly in operation a number of factories, steam saw and grist mills, together with all the other branches of mechanism usually carried on in inland towns or villages, while as for churches, schools and societies in general it is unsurpassed by any township in the county except Wayne. It can boast of every convenience calculated to make life pleasant in a society where benevolence and energy are necessary for public improvements as will be seen readily by observing the various churches, schools and benevolent societies, such as Masonic, Odd Fellows, Good Templars, together with the Ladies' Sociable, wherein the mite is given freely for such charitable purposes as the society think most needy. For a more full description of the township, we would refer the reader to the history of Monroeville, herewith connected.

MONROEVILLE, the center of Monroe township, was first laid out as a town by John Barnhart, Esq., in 1854, and is located sixteen miles eastward from Fort Wayne, on the Pittsburgh, Fort Wayne & Chicago railway, and is sixteen miles from Van Wert, Ohio, and twelve miles from Decatur, the county seat of Adams county, Indiana; thus rendering it a thriving inland business point with a population of about 1,300 inhabitants, has four extensive stave manufactories, two steam saw mills, one large flouring mill, five dry goods stores, three grocery and provision stores, two blacksmith shops, two wagon shops, with various others, such as carpenter, cabinet, boot, shoe and harness shops. This town, for many years after it was laid out, was nothing but a mail station upon the railroad, and its entire growth as seen at present, has been accomplished in the past five or six years, and so rapid has been its prosperity that within one year's time it has surpassed every village in the county for business facilities derived from manufactories and merchandise.

The citizens of Monroeville are, in general, enterprising and industrious, and seem to possess a public pride worthy of commendation, as will be readily observed from their fine churches that have been lately erected, with other fine buildings already completed and in progress of erection, such as school houses, town halls, &c. The streets are kept in good repair, and few towns having double the age of Monroeville, can boast of better sidewalks. The inhabitants take a high stand in favor of education, and contributed largely for the erection of a graded school suitable for the town and surrounding country. Churches are well attended, and all seem to vie with each other in helping to preserve order and friendly feeling throughout the town. Of religious denominations there are three (Catholic, Methodist Episcopal and Lutheran), each denomination having a fine church and a large congregation. The benevolent institutions of Monroeville are as follows: The Monroeville Masonic Lodge, No. 293, the Independent Order of Good Templars and the Brotherhood of Odd Fellows, each order having a large number of members, and are in a thriving condition, possessing good halls and meet regularly.

The principal business of the town is derived from the timber that surrounds it and from the immense amount of staves, lumber, spokes and hubs that are bought at this place, giving employment to numerous hands in the manufacture of the same, and distributing weekly from ten to fifteen thousand dollars for those articles of trade. While at the same time Monroeville is the principal market place for Decatur, the county seat of Adams county, thus helping to contribute occupation for teaming to and fro between the two towns and affording plenty of business for livery and horse dealers, together with the advantages derived therefrom for two hotels of the place, where accommodations can be obtained well worthy of the landlords, who endeavor to render the comfort and happinesss of their guests their chief satisfaction.

Population of Monroeville; Males, 463; females, 412; total, 875. Population of Monroe township (including Monroeville): Males, 784; females, 730; total, 1,514.

PERRY

Township is bounded on the north by DeKalb county, on the south by Washington and St. Soseph, on the east by Cedar Creek and on the west by Eel River townships. The surface of the country is rolling and heavily timbered. The soil is well adapted to raising all kinds of grain and fruits, the principal products being wheat and corn.

The first settlement was made in 1830 by Mr. Weeks (who felled the first tree), W. S. Hunter, Joseph Hunter and Mr. Hatch. The country, previous to this time, had been an umbroken wilderness, and the sleep of the little settlement was only disturbed by the fierce howl of the wolf and other animals. The incidents following the first settlement for a great many years were not unlike other new settlements. This being a heavily timbered country, with a rich soil, the production of corn, wheat, oats, &c., were the first things thought of, and, to accomplish this end, the timber was soon hewn away, and where the giant forest then stood we now see extensive fields of the common products of Northern Indiana. The first white child born was Harriet Weeks and the first death was Mr. Jason Hatch. This township contains one hotel, three groceries, two boot and shoe stores, three blacksmith shop, one steam and two water power saw mills, five churches (one Presbyterian, two Methodist, one United Brethren, one Lutheran and one Universalist); one cemetery, situated in the center of the township, and eight district schools, with an average attendance of 495 scholars; one township library, one Masonic lodge, which meets once a month, and one lodge of Good Templars who meet weekly.

HUNTERTOWN (Perry Post Office), is an incorporated town, situated in the northwestern part of the township, about ten miles from Fort Wayne, on the Lima plank road. The Fort Wayne, Jackson & Saginaw and the Grand Rapids & Indiana railroads run on the same grade to this place, where they form a junction—one taking an easterly and the other a westerly course. The village contains 110 inhabitants (60 males and 50 females), one dry goods and grocery store, with post office, two grocery stores, three blacksmith shops, two boot and shoe stores, one fur glove factory, one hotel and one physician. Thus it may be seen that with the rich fertile soil, adapted to all kinds of fruit raising and agriculture, together with the easy mode of transportation, to say nothing of the mineral resources, this is destined to be one of the leading places of the county, if not of northern Indiana. Population of the township, 1,091 (611 males and 480 females).

PLEASANT

Township, situated in the southern or southwestern part of the county, is bounded on the north by Wayne, on the east by Marion and on the west by Lafayette townships, and on the south by Wells county. The surface of the township is level, the soil fertile, well watered and timbered, and particularly adapted to the growth of corn and wheat, which are its principal products.

The St. Mary's river runs through the northeast corner and the Little river, in a very winding course, traverses the whole length of the township. The most direct route to and through the township is the Bluffton road, which runs north and south along the center of it. There are two other roads, running parallel with the Bluffton road—the Murray road, two miles to the west, and the County road, one and a half miles east—which also afford ample means of communication with all parts of the township.

There are four churches, nine school houses, one township library of 333 volumes, kept at the house of the librarian, A. F. Unger, and one post office (called Nine Mile post office), but Fort Wayne is the post office address of a majority of the inhabitants. Population: Males, 638; females, 668; total, 1, 306.

SCIPIO

Township is situated in the northeastern part of the county, twenty miles from Fort Wayne. The southern part is somewhat low, but well adapted to the raising of corn, hay and stock. The northern part contains some of the most fertile soil in the State. Finer farms than are seen here can scarcely be found in any country. In passing up the Ridge road, the eye of the traveler will be delighted in a high degree with the well-tilled fields, the carefully-tended flocks, the substantial barns and out-houses, the neat and tasteful dwellings, surrounded by trees and shrubbery, and well-kept lawns, all showing, in addition to a high state of thrift and industry, a degree of intelligence and refinement too seldom found in farming communities. Too much can scarcely be sasd of the beauty of this locality.

The township was first settled by Platt Squire, Benjamin Borden, Jehiel and Marvin Parks, Lucius, Nathan and William Parmer, George and Robert Dorsey, Philip J. Schell and John Wentworth. The first birth was that of Lafayette Squire and Laura Squire was the first death, caused by burning.

The early settlers, like all other pioneers, had to endure severe hardships during the first years of their settlement. At Fort Wayne—then only a trading post—they were compelled to buy their provisions and clothing and float them down the Maumee river in pirogues to the State line, and from there carry them on their backs six miles through an unbroken wilderness, infested with wolves, bears, wildcats, and the no less savage Indians, to whose mercy their wives and children were exposed in their absence.

This township (which is a small one, being only about one-third the size of a full township) has three school houses, valued at $1,000, and a Methodist church, valued at $1,200. It has a population of 414 (249 males and 165 females).

SPRINGFIELD

Township, lying in the northeastern part of the county, is bounded on the north by DeKalb county, on the east by Scipio, on the south by Milan and Maumee and on the west by Cedar Creek townships.

It was first settled in 1836 by Henry Gruber, William Ringwalt, Mr. King, Isaac Hall, Ezra May, William Sweet and William Glaze, who built the first house in the township west of the present site of the village of Maysville. The township was organized in 1837. It was named by Isaac Hall after a township of the same name in Summit county, Ohio, Mr. Hall's former home. The first marriage was celebrated between Isaac Hall and Jane S. Burdee. Ezra May was the first Justice of the Peace. The first school house was built near where Maysville now stands, and Miss Anna S. Bracy was the first to wield the birch and give direction to the shooting of the young idea in the new township. The oldest settler now living is Samuel Orno, aged about 85 years, who served as a soldier in the campaigns of the First Napoleon.

There are two post offices (Hall's Corners, in the northeast part of the township, and Harlan, in the village of Maysville). It contains twelve school houses, valued at $6,000, and eight churches, worth about $5,000. They are of the following denominations: Two Methodist Episcopal, two Methodist Protestant, two Lutheran, one Dutch Reform and one United Brethren.

MAYSVILLE (Harlan Post Office), a village of 260 inhabitants, lies one mile west and two miles south from the center of the township and is fourteen miles northeast of Fort Wayne, on the Ridge road. It contains one steam flouring mill, two steam saw mills, a shingle mill, four stores, one grocery, one cabinet shop, a butcher shop, two blacksmith shops, a boot and shoe shop, two wagon shops, a harness shop, a manufactory of window shades, a post office, an Ætna insurance agency, a Masonic and a good Templars lodge, a two-story school house, containing three rooms, three churches, a photograph gallery, a veterinary surgeon and three physicians.

CUBA, a hamlet containing about fifty souls, is situated on the Ridge road, near the south line of the township. It has a steam saw mill, a school house, a boot and shoe maker and a physician.

The soil is generally very good, the farms are mostly well cultivated and neatly kept, churches and school houses are numerous and very well attended, newspapers are liberally patronized, and it is perhaps safe to say that the people of Springfield township are excelled by none in the county in enterprise, industry, morality and general intelligence. Population: Males, 856; females, 864; total, 1,722.

ST. JOSEPH

Township, one of the center townships of Allen county, is bounded on the north by Perry and Cedar Creek, on the east by Milan, on the south by Adams and on the west by Washington townships. It was first settled in the spring of 1835, by Uriah Notestine, John Tilbury, Jacob Sturm, Philip Lee, Christian Parker and John Herbert. The surface is flat and the soil fertile, a clayey loam, well watered by the St. Joseph river, from which it derives its name, and some smaller tributaries, and is very well adapted to the raising of root and cereal crops. The timber with which the township is well supplied, is mainly white oak, beach and maple. It contains ten district schools, four churches (one of all denominations, built in the year 1848, one German Lutheran, built the same year, one Methodist, built in 1864, and one Catholic, built in 1866), and one township library, Daniel Eby, Librarian. The Fort Wayne paper mills, an extensive manufactory, of which Freeman, & Barnett are proprietors, besides several saw mills, have their situations in this township.

The Academy of the Sacred Heart, an offshoot of the church of St. Vincent de Paul, built in the year 1866, has a beautiful location and extensive grounds on the Auburn road, six miles from the city of Fort Wayne. The main building is of brick, four stories high, eighty by forty-five feet. The attendance has rapidly increased since its opening. The pupils are under the charge of eight Sisters of Charity. The principal means of communication with the township is by the St. Joseph river road, following the course of that river through the township. The number of males in the township is 652; females, 719; total, 1,371.

WASHINGTON

Township, one of the center townships of Allen county, borders on the northern line of Wayne township and by the annexation of the village of Bloomingdale, embraces a small portion of the city of Fort Wayne within its borders. Its remaining borders are, on the east by St. Joseph, on the west by Lake and on the north by Eel River and Perry townships. The first settlements in the township were made by Isaac and Nicholas Klinger, and Rheinhart Gripe in the year 1824, by Andrew Moore in 1825, and by John S. Archer, David Archer, Adam Pettit, Thos. Hatfield, Asahel Savery and John Cook in 1826. The township was organized in March, 1832, at the March session of the County Commissioners. John S. Archer was appointed, during the same year, inspector of elections until the following April. The election was held at the residence of Thomas Hatfield. Moses Sivets was elected Justice of the Peace. The first white child born was David L. Archer, Jan. 1, 1827, and the first death was that of Catharine Ihler, July 2, 1825. The surface is rolling, sloping gradually to the south and east. The soil is a good sandy loam, well adapted to the raising of wheat, corn, oats and grasses. The St.

Joseph river, which floats through the southeastern part of the township in a winding, mainly southwesterly direction, together with Spy run, Beckett's branch, and the Feeder Canal, afford ample facilities for all necessary water privileges. The Lima, Goshen and Leesburg plank roads traverse the township in northeasterly directions. The Fort Wayne, Jackson & Saginaw and the Grand Rapids and Indiana railroads traverse the township in a northerly direction. It contains two churches—one Catholic, St. Vincent de Paul, situated in the northeastern part, on the line between St. Joseph and Washington, Rev. Auguste Adams in charge. This church was built in 1861 and its parsonage in 1862. The number of families attending it is about 125. One Methodist (Bethel Chapel), built in 1842, situated in the northwestern part. There are three libraries, —one township of six or seven hundred volumes and two Sunday School of about 125 volumes each.

The first school held in the township had an attendance of ten scholars and was taught by Alexander Waldron, in a log cabin, in 1829. It now contains eight free schools, with an average attendance of about 800 scholars, and two German Lutheran, one of which is situated in the eastern and the other in the southwestern part, with an average attendance of about thirty scholars each. The oldest inhabitants now residing in the township are Babel Wainwright, 95 years of age, and Victor Beurre, 75. The township boasts two saw mills, one tannery, two grist mills, one spoke factory, two breweries (Bloomingdale and French), two sorgho mills, two lawyers and two ministers. Population: Males, 780; females, 844; total, 1,624.

WAYNE

Township. Of the twenty townships comprising Allen county, Wayne is by far of the most importance, being situated on an elevated plain, at the junction of the St. Mary's and St. Joseph rivers, and containing the city of Fort Wayne, the county seat and one of the most important commercial centers in the State. The township is bounded on the north by Washington, on the south by Pleasant, on the east by Adams and on the west by Aboite townships. The surface is rolling, with a gradual slope in every direction from the city of Fort Wayne. The soil is well adapted to raising wheat, corn, oats, buckwheat, timothy and clover, and is well watered by the St. Mary's, St. Joseph and Maumee rivers. There are some fine belts of timber in this township, principally walnut, hickory, oak, maple and poplar. Generally, however, the supply for building purposes has become quite limited, especially in the neighborhood of Fort Wayne. As early as 1700, this point at the junction was visited by the French for the purpose of trading with the Indians and before 1800 a regular trading post was established in the township, thus making it a grand commercial center, destined to become the most important township in Northern Indiana. It is now traversed in every direction from Fort Wayne by roads, generally good, affording easy communication with every part of the county. The schools are excellent and so situated that they are within the reach of all, several of them being graded schools. The township library is situated in the city, comprising about 2,000 volumes, and is open to all every Saturday. The librarian and township trustee is John E. Hill.

Notwithstanding the churches in the city are convenient to all the inhabitants in the township, there are several well-built churches in the country, well attended by interested congregations and having good Sunday school libraries. The farms are all well improved, having good buildings, with many orchards of choice fruit.

The township is thickly settled, having (exclusive of Fort Wayne) the largest population of any township in the county. Males, 1,186; females, 1,014; total, 2,200.

General Index.

www.ingramcontent.com/pod-product-compliance
Lightning Source LLC
Chambersburg PA
CBHW032109230426
43672CB00009B/1685
9783337307882